The United States and Germany during the Twentieth Century presents a wide-ranging comparison of the development of two societies over an extended period of time. The two countries – the world's leading "rising powers" at the opening of the twentieth century – were both more similar and more different than is widely understood. Above all, their dual encounter with modernity brings out the richness of both societies as they faced unprecedented internal and external challenges, sometimes in isolation, but more often in combination or in parallel with one another.

Christof Mauch is Director of the Rachel Carson Center for Environment and Society and of the Lasky Center for Transatlantic Studies at Ludwig Maximilian University, Munich. Before joining Munich University, he was the director of the German Historical Institute in Washington, D.C. Dr. Mauch is the author or editor of more than thirty books, some of them award winning, including *Natural Disasters, Cultural Responses: Case Studies toward a Global Environmental History* (2009, edited with Christian Pfister); *The World beyond the Windshield: Landscapes and Roads in Europe and North America* (2008, edited with Thomas Zeller); *Rivers in History: Perspectives on Waterways in Europe and North America* (2008, edited with Thomas Zeller); *Shadow War against Hitler* (2003); and *Berlin–Washington, 1800–2000* (2005, edited with Andreas Daum).

Kiran Klaus Patel is Professor of European History and Transatlantic Relations at the European University Institute, Florence. He is the author of multiple publications, including *Soldiers of Labor: Labor Service in Nazi Germany and New Deal America, 1933–1945* (2005) and *Fertile Ground for Europe? The History of European Integration and the Common Agricultural Policy since 1945* (2009). Professor Patel has directed and co-directed several large projects, particularly "Imagined Europeans: The Scientific Construction of Homo Europaeus" and "Europeanization and History: Concepts, Conflicts, Cohesion."

PUBLICATIONS OF THE GERMAN HISTORICAL INSTITUTE

Edited by Hartmut Berghoff
with the assistance of David Lazar

The German Historical Institute is a center for advanced study and research whose purpose is to provide a permanent basis for scholarly cooperation among historians from the Federal Republic of Germany and the United States. The Institute conducts, promotes, and supports research into both American and German political, social, economic, and cultural history; into transatlantic migration, especially in the nineteenth and twentieth centuries; and into the history of international relations, with special emphasis on the roles played by the United States and Germany.

Recent books in the series

Monica Black, *Death in Berlin: From Weimar to Divided Germany*

J. R. McNeill and Corinna R. Unger, editors, *Environmental Histories of the Cold War*

Roger Chickering and Stig Förster, editors, *War in an Age of Revolution, 1775–1815*

Cathryn Carson, *Heisenberg in the Atomic Age: Science and the Public Sphere*

Michaela Hoenicke Moore, *Know Your Enemy: The American Debate on Nazism, 1933–1945*

Matthias Schulz and Thomas A. Schwartz, editors, *The Strained Alliance: U.S.–European Relations from Nixon to Carter*

Suzanne L. Marchand, *German Orientalism in the Age of Empire: Religion, Race, and Scholarship*

Manfred Berg and Bernd Schaefer, editors, *Historical Justice in International Perspective: How Societies Are Trying to Right the Wrongs of the Past*

Carole Fink and Bernd Schaefer, editors, *Ostpolitik, 1969–1974: European and Global Responses*

Nathan Stoltzfus and Henry Friedlander, editors, *Nazi Crimes and the Law*

The United States and Germany during the Twentieth Century

COMPETITION AND CONVERGENCE

Edited by

CHRISTOF MAUCH

Ludwig Maximilian University, Munich

KIRAN KLAUS PATEL

European University Institute, Florence

GERMAN HISTORICAL INSTITUTE
Washington, D.C.

and

CAMBRIDGE
UNIVERSITY PRESS

CAMBRIDGE UNIVERSITY PRESS
Cambridge, New York, Melbourne, Madrid, Cape Town, Singapore,
São Paulo, Delhi, Dubai, Tokyo, Mexico City

Cambridge University Press
32 Avenue of the Americas, New York, NY 10013-2473, USA

www.cambridge.org
Information on this title: www.cambridge.org/9780521145619

First published 2010

Printed in the United States of America

A catalog record for this publication is available from the British Library.

Library of Congress Cataloging in Publication data

The United States and Germany during the twentieth century : competition and convergence /
edited by Christof Mauch, Kiran Klaus Patel.
p.   cm. – (Publications of the German Historical Institute)
Includes bibliographical references and index.
ISBN 978-0-521-19781-6 (hardback) – ISBN 978-0-521-14561-9 (pbk.)
1. United States – Relations – Germany.   2. Germany – Relations – United States.
3. United States – Social conditions – 20th century.   4. Germany – Social conditions – 20th
century.   5. National characteristics, American.   6. National characteristics, German.
I. Mauch, Christof.   II. Patel, Kiran Klaus.   III. Title.   IV. Series.
E183.8.G3U57   2010
327.7304309'034–dc22   2010005232

ISBN 978-0-521-19781-6 Hardback
ISBN 978-0-521-14561-9 Paperback

Contents

Contents

Contributors

Thomas Bender is University Professor of the Humanities and Professor of History at New York University.

Manfred Berg is Curt Engelhorn Professor of American History at the University of Heidelberg.

Eileen Boris is Hull Professor and Chair, Department of Feminist Studies, and Professor of History and Black Studies, University of California, Santa Barbara.

Tobias Brinkmann is Malvin and Lea Bank Associate Professor of Jewish Studies and History at Pennsylvania State University.

W. Fitzhugh Brundage is William B. Umstead Professor of History at the University of North Carolina at Chapel Hill.

Edward Dimendberg is Professor of Film and Media Studies, Visual Studies, and German at the University of California, Irvine.

Christiane Eifert is Lecturer in History at the Free University, Berlin.

Philipp Gassert is Professor of Transatlantic Cultural History at the University of Augsburg.

Michael Geyer is Samuel N. Harper Professor of German and European History at the University of Chicago.

Dieter Gosewinkel is Lecturer in History at the Free University of Berlin.

Heinz-Gerhard Haupt is Professor of History and Civilization at the European University Institute, Florence.

Christina von Hodenberg is Reader in European History at Queen Mary, University of London.

Konrad H. Jarausch is Lurcy Professor of European Civilization at the University of North Carolina at Chapel Hill.

Anton Kaes is Class of 1939 Professor of German and Film Studies at the University of California, Berkeley.

Simone Lässig is Professor of Modern History at the Technische Universität Braunschwieg and Director of the Georg Eckert Institute for International Textbook Research, Braunschwieg.

Daniel Letwin is Associate Professor of History at Pennsylvania State University.

Christof Mauch is Director of the Rachel Carson Center for Environment and Society and of the Lasky Center for Transatlantic Studies at Ludwig Maximilian University, Munich.

Gabriele Metzler is Professor of History at Humboldt University, Berlin.

Paul Nolte is Professor of History at the Free University of Berlin.

Kathryn M. Olesko is Associate Professor of History at Georgetown University, Washington, D.C.

Kiran Klaus Patel is Professor of European History and Transatlantic Relations at the European University Institute, Florence.

Rainer Prätorius is Professor of Public Administration at Helmut Schmidt University, Hamburg.

Annemarie Sammartino is Assistant Professor of History at Oberlin College, Ohio.

Dirk Schumann is Professor of Modern and Contemporary History at Georg August University, Göttingen.

Judith Sealander is Professor of History at Bowling Green State University, Ohio.

Christoph Strupp is Research Fellow at the Forschungsstelle für Zeitgeschichte, Hamburg.

Acknowledgments

The editors would like to voice their gratitude first and foremost to the contributors to this volume and the Robert Bosch Stiftung. Without the generous support the Robert Bosch Stiftung provided, this project would not have been possible. We give special thanks to Dieter Berg, the chairman of the Robert Bosch Stiftung's Management Board, and Peter Theiner, the head of its Department for International Relations. We would also like to thank the German Historical Institute, Washington, D.C., and the Humboldt-Universität zu Berlin for their financial and organization support. We owe a special debt of gratitude to those who helped prepare the manuscript for submission: Michael Kimmage at the Amerika-Institut, Munich; Ken Weisbrode at the European University Institute, Florence; and Bryan Hart and David Lazar at the German Historical Institute, Washington. Finally, we would like to thank Eric Crahan and Frank Smith of Cambridge University Press for the encouragement and support they offered this project from the very outset.

Christof Mauch and Kiran Klaus Patel

Modernities: Competition versus Convergence

CHRISTOF MAUCH AND KIRAN KLAUS PATEL

President Barack Obama's summer 2009 visits to Omaha Beach and the Buchenwald concentration camp evoked events that have profoundly shaped the relationship between the United States and Germany. Nazi crimes against humanity, World War II, and postwar occupation dominate our collective memory to this day. They also mark the moment in the history of both societies when American military and cultural hegemony achieved its absolute zenith, as exemplified by GIs, jeans, rock n' roll, and the Cold War. Given the enormous differences and power imbalances of 1944–5 and the early postwar years, does it make much sense to compare Germany and America?

From this perspective, it is easy to forget that Germany and the United States had very similar starting points when they entered modernity at the end of the nineteenth century. To understand the paths subsequently taken by the two countries, their differences and similarities, the rivalries and alliances that shaped German and American history in the twentieth century, we would do well to revisit the late nineteenth century.

ON THE THRESHOLD OF THE TWENTIETH CENTURY

The surprising closeness of the two societies is reflected in the matter-of-fact way Germans and Americans compared, looked at, listened to, and took stock of each other at the turn of the last century. "North America appears as a typical Low German settlement in the West, while Prussia seems to be the same thing in the East," remarked the German American writer, August Julius Langbehn, in 1890. In both Germany and America, he continued, we see "a mad dash towards all kinds of cultural accomplishments," and even the German capital city seems "North American" because "a significant portion of the population is made up of immigrants." Similarly, the German American psychologist, Hugo Münsterberg, magnified the irony in each country's perception of the other and had a good laugh in the process when he wrote at the beginning of the new century:

In the eyes of Americans the German is a poorly dressed, scruffy, uncouth Philistine, a clumsy, narrow-minded pedant, who takes pleasure only in his pipe, beer, and skat [a card game], who marches in parades and is paralyzed by bureaucracy, marries only for money and treats women like servants or toys, who bows to authority and brutalizes those beneath him, who fears the policeman, quarrels with his neighbor, and hates anything progressive. Germans, on the other hand, consider the Yankee to be an ill-bred fellow who is corrupt in public life and cheats in business, who chases after every dollar and any sensation, a barbarian in scientific and artistic matters, a bigoted hypocrite, who chews tobacco and takes great pleasure in a public lynching.

Despite their cultural differences, Germans and Americans at the beginning of the twentieth century both believed in a common and shared future – in science, in business, and also in politics. In 1905, the German chancellor, Prince Bernhard von Bülow, praised his American colleague, President Theodore Roosevelt, for having recognized "how useful Germany and America will be for each other in the future." That it could ever come to a "transatlantic war with America" seemed to the German chancellor absolutely "absurd."

Indeed, the German Empire and the United States were entering into the new century under similar circumstances and with important features and viewpoints in common. Both were prominent political and economic powers. A spirit of adventure and optimism reigned on both sides of the Atlantic. Both Germany and America were profiting from an enormous economic upswing and were rapidly evolving into wealthy industrial nations. In both countries, the second wave of industrialization was driving economic and social change. It was not the textile industry, as in the case of the industrial pioneer, England, but rather heavy industry and an array of newer industrial activities that catapulted Germany and America into global leadership positions around 1900. The German Empire dominated the new industries, in particular the chemical and electrical sectors, whereas the United States became the world's greatest steel producer at the turn of the century, after tripling its production in just fifteen years, between 1877 and 1892.

German engineers invented the internal combustion engine, the bicycle, and the automobile. Their American counterparts prided themselves on the invention of the sewing machine, the electric light bulb, and the typewriter. Nowhere else in the world were so many patents and inventions registered as in Germany and the United States, and in no other country was the economy growing as fast as it was in these two nation-state latecomers. Great Britain was still the undisputed global leader in the production of industrial goods in the 1860s, but by 1900 the German Empire was producing one-quarter of all European industrial goods. By 1913, the United States and Germany occupied the top two positions in this global industrial competition, noticeably ahead of Britain.

Even in the realm of international trade, which the British Empire, with its global reach, had clearly dominated throughout the nineteenth century, Germany and the United States were rapidly closing the gap in the years before World War I. In the economic sphere, modernity was increasingly equated with industrial growth and the development of global markets, and the United States and Germany were the pacesetters in both.

This economic upsurge was also reflected in the brisk growth rates of their respective populations. The population of the United States more than doubled in only thirty years (1860–90), from thirty-one million to sixty-three million. By 1890, the population of the German Empire had already reached fifty million, which was significantly larger than any of the other nation-states in Western Europe. France had roughly thirty-eight million inhabitants, England and Italy had about thirty million each, and Spain had only eighteen million. Another important demographic development was that the flow of immigrants from Europe to the United States – between 1820 and 1890, 7.1 million Germans had emigrated to the United States – had leveled off noticeably by 1900. This stream of European immigrants across the Atlantic would soon shrink to only several tens of thousands per year, and this more balanced population growth in the United States and Germany tended to add to the similarities between the two countries.

Linked closely to these demographic developments was the pace of urbanization in both countries. Their cities grew at rates unequaled elsewhere. Between 1880 and 1900, America's large cities gained fifteen million residents; Chicago's population alone tripled to more than 1.5 million. At the time of the German Empire's founding in 1871, there were only three cities with populations of more than 200,000: Berlin, Hamburg, and Breslau (Wrocław). By 1913, there were twenty-three cities of that size. Industrial cities in Germany, like Gelsenkirchen, saw a tenfold increase in population between 1871 and 1910.

The two capital cities, Berlin and Washington, which had in the past appeared to be quite different from one another, were becoming more similar. In the latter part of the nineteenth century, Berlin was already a pulsating metropolis, whereas Washington, the seat of America's federal government, had for generations retained the character of an underdeveloped small town. Visiting the American capital in 1842, Charles Dickens remarked ironically that Washington was a "city of grand intentions" with "broad avenues that had no beginning and did not seem to lead anywhere." But by 1910, Washington had transformed itself into a proud city of marble, a kind of "Rome on the Potomac" with enormous neoclassical buildings, modern museums and government buildings, luxurious residences, and an expansive mall that lent a cosmopolitan air to the center of the city.

The dynamic growth of the economies and populations of these two nations was also reflected in the expansion of their naval fleets, which by 1900 were seriously challenging the hitherto undisputed global dominance of the British Royal Navy. After the United States triumphed over Spain in the Spanish-American War of 1898, Great Britain tacitly relinquished to the United States its commanding position in the Caribbean. The German naval and merchant marine fleets were expanding steadily and soon ranked right behind the British in terms of worldwide sea power. In overall military strength, it seemed to be only a matter of time before Germany and America would overtake the United Kingdom as the dominant world powers, and in this competition Germany had a decided edge over the United States. In 1890, the United States maintained a standing army of 126,000 troops; in contrast, the army of the German Empire numbered 490,000.

Even in the area of culture, these two societies on either side of the Atlantic displayed some significant similarities. In contrast to France and England, the Ottoman Empire, and the Hapsburg monarchy, neither the United States nor the German Empire had much national or imperial history on which to look back. Both countries had reestablished themselves through armed conflicts in the latter third of the nineteenth century – the Americans through their Civil War and the Germans through their wars of unification. Yet both "young" nations fit their times perfectly. Faith in progress and a hope that all would be possible motivated the upsurge in both societies. These attitudes were, however, coupled in both countries with aggressive gestures of power, ostentatious displays of nouveau-riche magnificence, and missionary zeal.

At the same time, many in both countries, particularly among the social elite, questioned whether the meteoric rise of their respective societies could be sustained. As of 1890, the United States was deemed to have lost its frontier – that diffuse boundary between "civilization" and "wilderness" that had served as the driving force for much of the country's expansion and development. The leaders of Germany felt even more hemmed in by its geographic location in the middle of Europe.

The mixture of economic, demographic, and political power, on the one hand, and anxiety induced by rapid change, on the other, fueled imperialistic ambitions and nationalistic delusions of grandeur in Germany and the United States alike. Each saw itself as engaged in a struggle to win a "place in the sun." Not only in their accomplishments but also in their imagined and experienced deficits, the United States and the German Empire were strikingly similar.

There were, of course, also unmistakable differences and dissimilarities between the two countries. Perhaps the most conspicuous disparity was the difference in size. The territory of the United States encompassed more than nine million square kilometers at the opening of the twentieth century. Germany, measuring roughly a half-million square kilometers in area, seemed tiny in comparison. With overseas possession taken into account, however, Germany was only one-third, rather than one-twentieth, the size of the United States and its territories. Likewise, the ethnic diversity of the United States should not obscure the fact that the German Empire included sizeable Polish, Jewish, and other minorities and, even more important, encompassed roughly fifteen million colonial subjects in Africa, Asia, and the South Seas.

Perhaps because of the similarities between the United States and the German Empire, many observers and commentators at the opening of the twentieth century thought the two countries were engaged in a kind of friendly competition. The Americans were ahead in some areas, the Germans in others. Pittsburgh, for instance, boasted the largest steel factory in the world. With the discovery of oil in five states, the U.S. energy reserves appeared to be unlimited. America's skyscrapers signaled the beginning of a new architectural era, and its national parks – the "green discovery" of the nineteenth century – were the envy of the world. In other respects, the Germans seemed to be setting the pace for this race into modernity. The German university, for example, served as a model for the modern American research university, furnishing American academics with the blueprint for the scientific laboratory, seminar, lecture, dissertation, and even the footnote. In the realm of high culture, the United States was on the whole not able to keep up with the "land of poets and thinkers" (*Land der Dichter und Denker*). And Germany was clearly ahead of the United States in the size of its armed forces and of its military budget.

In a discussion with Fritz Stern, the prominent American historian of Germany, the famous French philosopher and sociologist Raymond Aron once commented that the twentieth century could have been Germany's century. That did not come to pass, however one may care to interpret events. Jumping ahead to the beginning of the twenty-first century, it is obvious how much has changed: in some areas in which the Germans led around 1900, the United States has surged ahead, and vice versa. Today, the United States has at its disposal the most modern armaments and is the undisputed military superpower, whereas Germany ranks relatively low in military might. In the realm of scientific research, the Americans are also clearly in the lead. In terms of the environment, in contrast, the United States, despite its national parks, is clearly way behind in the race to be "green." Problems and political controversies notwithstanding, Germans continue to be proud of their state-regulated social welfare and health care systems, which have served repeatedly as points of reference in American debates on social policy over the past century. All in all, the yardstick for measuring the success of any homegrown accomplishment often seems to lie on the other side of the Atlantic.

COMPETING MODERNITIES

The phrase *competing modernities* ties together the essays in this collection. It should be understood metaphorically, not literally. The image of a "race" is meant to convey the notion that, very often, modern societies find themselves in a competition with each other − a competition that, going beyond traditional rivalries for wealth and power, encompasses the struggle to define the norms and standards of what it means to be modern. With the rise of modern scientific expertise in the twentieth century, statistics, graphs, and narrative descriptions have been brought to bear on nearly every aspect of these modern societies, resulting in some assuming the status of pacesetters in the race to be modern and others appearing to be rather backward, the caboose of the train chugging into modernity. In this race, Germany and the United States at times have moved closer to one another. For example, today both belong to the group of postindustrial, Western democracies. At other times, however, this competition has produced extremely aggressive confrontations, such as the two world wars and the conflicting systems of the Cold War, during which Germany was split between the two rival ideological camps.

The intensive phase of the competition between these two nations began in the 1890s. Of course, the United States was already a more important role model for Germany than vice versa, and that tendency was to grow over time. All the same, it was during these years that events in both countries shaped a number of crucial developments that would significantly determine their respective paths into modernity. These developments were in the areas of heavy industrialization, urbanization, the advent of a mass-market consumer economy, imperialism, modern art, and communications as well as the first waves of economic globalization.

The meaning of the word "modern" has never been as subject to debate as it is today. In 1970, for instance, most scholars in a variety of disciplines would have equated "modern" with "progressive." The term "modern" was applied to phenomena such as economic growth, Western science, democratization, industrialization, secularization, and increasing individualism as well as to new trends in music, art, and literature. Postmodern and postcolonial criticism has increasingly challenged this perspective. The modern era had both bright and dark sides. Without modern technology, Auschwitz would not have been possible. Industrialization and Western consumption have produced not only progress but also serious problems, ranging from the alienation of workers and a decline in the quality of life to the degradation and destruction of the environment. Furthermore, the criteria for defining modernity have been derived almost exclusively from the European and American experiences and thus cannot claim any global validity. For this reason, we hear today about the "paradox of modernity," about "reflexive modernity," and about "multiple modernities." These concepts indicate that there is no longer any consensus as to how modernity should be defined.

Building on these discussions, we view modernity as characterized by two features. First, modernity can be seen as a specific period – as an era in which societies cast off their attachments to the past, to concepts and values that had shaped their development. What counted as "new" and as "modern" had to be fundamentally new, not just a return to the "good old days." Belief in progress and the future went hand in hand with dynamism and the acceleration of social change and, maybe even more importantly, with a "surplus of possibilities" (Niklas Luhmann). Furthermore, the modern age ushered in the era of both the masses and the individual. Through demographic shifts, economic growth, new modes of participation, and more rapid flows of various forms of exchange during the twentieth century, many more people than in earlier times took part in social, cultural, and political life. Leisure and consumption in the twentieth century were no longer the privilege of a small minority. Politics took on new, hitherto unknown forms in the public arena and evolved into the "political mass market" (Hans Rosenberg). Societies mobilized mass armies that became brutal killing machines, waging of mass destruction that annihilated not just tens of thousands but millions at a time. And women suddenly took on a multitude of roles that had been denied to them for centuries. To be sure, these processes had been underway since the late eighteenth century. They intensified markedly around 1890, however, and that is when modernity began in the sense of a defined epoch.

Second, we see modernity as a discourse, as a concept about which contemporary observers argued heatedly and, through their debates and actions, gave meaning and form. Over the course of the nineteenth and twentieth centuries, the concept has evolved to serve increasingly as a point of self-reflection and self-assurance for societies. Contemporary observers have negotiated linguistically and philosophically to arrive at what we understand as modernity today: civilization and culture, freedom and equality, expansion and conservation. Modernity became a goal to be pursued, to be rejected, to be confronted and struggled over. Modern societies were thus motivated to detach themselves from tradition and convention, to view themselves not just as distinct from their own past but also from other countries. It follows that the concept of modernity was not only interpreted differently within different societies but has also been subject to change over time.

NEW PATHS OF EXCEPTIONALISM?

The war that the United States waged against Iraq in 2003 revealed abruptly that the gap that had opened up between Germany and America since the end of the Cold War was much wider than most observers had thought possible. The

Germans and the Americans were worlds apart in their estimates of the threat to world stability posed by Saddam Hussein and his regime. Robert Kagan's claim that Americans were "from Mars" and Europeans "from Venus" acknowledged these differences in a very pointed and polemical fashion. He was suggesting that Americans viewed the world order as a struggle of all against all. In contrast, Germans, along with some of their European neighbors, appeared to be self-obsessed and to have forgotten the meaning of power, because they seemed to be dreaming of achieving universal peace through reasonable means, à la Immanuel Kant. Self-assertion or downfall, a sense of reality or a utopian striving for peace, power or powerlessness: these were the two extremes to which conservative (or neoconservative) commentators like Kagan attempted to reduce the American and German positions.

The election of Barack Obama to the presidency has been accompanied in Germany – as in many other European countries – by a new wave of enthusiasm for America (although we could ask whether this is not merely obscuring long-term shifts of the kind that Kagan identifies). Conversely, American interest in Germany has dwindled noticeably. Other societies have replaced Germany as a major strategic partner, economic rival, and inspiration in the field of scientific and technological innovation.

The marked differences between Germany and the United States at the beginning of the twenty-first century have found expression not only in attitudes to the Iraq War and in the intensity of their interest in each other but also in other social spheres, such as religion, demographics, and ethnicity. In Germany, church attendance has dropped dramatically. In many traditionally Protestant regions, fewer than 10 percent of Germans are churchgoers even on major religious holidays, whereas more than 40 percent of all Americans regularly attend religious services. Consequently, the United States has become the most religious of the Western industrialized countries. At the same time, the U.S. population has experienced a remarkable demographic upswing. Whereas the birthrate in the Old World has declined steadily since the 1980s, the fertility rate in the United States has risen during the same period and today has reached an average of more than 2.1. Alone among the industrialized nations, the United States is not facing a rapid aging of its population.

Linked closely to this demographic upsurge is the striking growth of ethnic minorities in the United States. As the numbers of immigrants from Central and South America and Asia have grown, Caucasians have come to represent a shrinking portion of the American population. According to current demographic projections, Caucasians will make up less than half the population by the middle of the twenty-first century. The ethnic composition of Europe and the United States is thus drifting increasingly apart. At present, more Americans claim German ancestry – 14.3 percent of the population – than any other national or ethnic background. That figure has been decreasing, however, as have the figures for all other European immigrant groups.

The Federal Republic of Germany is also experiencing significant changes. In fact, because the effects of the European unification process have been so strong during the past two decades, it seems almost obsolete today to even speak of *a* German position or approach. In terms of political, social, and cultural developments, the societies of Europe have for some time been moving closer and closer together. In contrast to the United States, which since the end of the Cold War and even more so since September 11, 2001, has been pressing its claim to national sovereignty and unrestrained modes of action, the Europeans seem to be willing to transfer important political and societal functions to a level beyond their national borders.

At the same time, however, transatlantic relations continue to flourish. The economic ties between Germany and the United States have never been so close or extensive as they are today. The possibilities for exchange between the two societies are as diverse and strong in the area of popular culture as they are in the realm of science and technology. Owning a Mercedes, a Porsche, or a BMW is still a potent status symbol in the United States, and even the foreign policy of the George W. Bush administration had little effect on the enduring popularity of jeans, Coca-Cola, and American music in Germany. The possibility that Germany and the United States might find themselves at war in the foreseeable future is inconceivable.

This collection of essays explores the volatility and the ambivalence in the relationship between the United States and Germany during the twentieth century. What insights can we gain from history? Is American society today closer to or more distant from Germany than it was twenty, fifty, or one hundred years ago?

Hundreds of monographs in the fields of history and political science and thousands of scholarly articles have grappled with the relations between Germany and the United States and their international ramifications. The most comprehensive survey of relations between the two countries – social and cultural as well as political and economic – is *The United States and Germany in the Era of the Cold War* edited by Detlef Junker and his colleagues at the German Historical Institute in Washington. More than 150 scholars contributed to this monumental examination of a crucial half-century in transatlantic history.

However, until now, no attempt has been made to compare the history of these two societies over a long period of time, despite the fact that historical scholarship has ascribed to the development of both nations' special historical circumstances – a *Sonderweg* (separate path) for Germany and the concept of "exceptionalism" for the United States. Compared to the rest of Western Europe, according to the *Sonderweg* narrative, Germany developed anachronistically, with trust in authority and antidemocratic tendencies gaining the upper hand. America's path through history, proponents of American exceptionalism argue, has been characterized by a special mission in the world, a lack of authoritarian movements, the dominance of ethnic groups, and the abundance of opportunities symbolized by the idea of the "American dream." Only by means of a thorough, broad-based comparison like the one undertaken in this volume can such assumptions be either confirmed or refuted.

COMPARISON AND TRANSFER

When a particular piece of historical scholarship is found to be too narrow or too provincial in its orientation, the standard corrective is to introduce more comparisons. Why is it then that the call for more comparative research is so rarely followed? The main reason may be that effective comparisons require a great deal of methodological and historical expertise. Whoever sets out to compare two individuals or two movements with one another must be highly informed not only about the two subjects in question. The construction of a valid comparison also requires considerable imagination and critical thought. If the differences involved in the comparison are too great, then the historian must decide whether the comparison will yield any significant findings at all. If, however, individual phenomena are pulled from their original context and viewed in parallel with another seemingly comparable phenomenon, one runs the risk of overlooking or relegating to the sidelines the genuinely characteristic features to be derived from the comparison. In practice, thus, every comparison is a difficult balancing act.

Dozens of scholars and commentators have approached German and American history from a comparative perspective in recent decades. They have produced a multitude of excellent books on specialized topics ranging from the history of employees in both countries, the role of women in the armaments industry, to the history of railroads. All of these monographs and essays have a narrow chronological focus, and none has attempted to present and analyze the social developments in both countries in their broadest context. And none, moreover, has sought to address general readers interested in German and American history as well as professional scholars. In this respect, the present collection represents a completely new approach to comparative history.

Because, as noted earlier, modern societies are always observing each other and engaging in all manner of exchanges with one another, it would be shortsighted to limit this study to a strict comparison. If we search exclusively for similarities and differences, we tend to overlook important connections between societies. We may be tempted to explain certain similarities as the result of seemingly local factors, whereas they are caused de facto by exchange relationships or foreign influences. For this reason, we have also included in our investigation reciprocal perceptions, transfers, and modes of exchange.

More precisely, we make this attempt because Germany and America were part of each other from the very beginnings of the European settlement of the New World. The mass immigration of Germans to North America – the first German immigrants arrived in the British colonies nearly a century before the American Revolution – has left its mark in many areas of American society, from preferred foodstuffs and names of streets to certain agricultural practices. Similarly, American influence in shaping the Old World – from fast food to the formation of democracy and capitalism – is beyond dispute. Alongside the Americanization of German society – the topic of a burgeoning literature – the contributors to this volume also consider forms of exchange and influence that have crossed the Atlantic in the opposite direction. Through incorporating such developments into its analysis, the present collection attempts to contribute to a transnational approach to American and German history. At the same time, we would like to emphasize the potential of transnational history, which is much discussed but rarely implemented in practice. Its combination of comparative and transnational approaches thus makes this volume conceptually innovative.

In light of the aforementioned challenges and difficulties, it is not surprising that this collection is the only attempt so far to investigate systematically the development of two countries over a long period of time. This adds an experimental aspect to the present collection of essays. It was inspired by the conviction that a transnationally enriched comparison of Germany and the United States over an extended period of time would illuminate historical circumstances, collective attitudes, and societal characteristics more than would a focus on just *one* national history. Ideally, a comparative history of this sort will explain why a particular development takes very different courses in the two countries. To understand, for example, how a religious movement like Scientology could be so broadly accepted in the United States but arouse so much concern and suspicion in Germany, it will be more fruitful to examine the past than the present. One would see, for instance, how the National Socialist past has sharpened Germans' sensitivity to perceived totalitarian tendencies in Scientology and how Americans' high regard for religious freedom has shaped their reaction to Scientology.

TRANSATLANTIC TANDEMS

This book draws on the work of researchers from both Europe and North America and is the product of a type of teamwork that is extremely rare in the world of historical scholarship. To carry out the broad comparison described herein, scholarly "tandems" were formed, each consisting of one expert on the United States and one on Germany, to address broad topics such as the role of law, gender relations, and consumer society. We are pleased that so many prominent – and very busy – scholars agreed to participation in this project. Without their wide-ranging expertise and willingness to stretch the limits of their knowledge and abilities, this project would never have succeeded.

Two planning workshops took place in Berlin and Washington, during which the scope and collaborative nature of the project were determined. At the time, no one could foresee that during the course of the project a number of the participants would change their academic bases, in some cases several times. The editors themselves were by no means spared this fate of the mobile scholar: they started off in Washington and Berlin, one moved later to Cambridge, Massachusetts, and they now live and work in Munich and Florence, respectively. Other tandem pairs experienced moves on the order of Berkeley to London, and from Heidelberg to Philadelphia and then Washington, and from there to Augsburg. Despite all this movement and dislocation, collaboration within and between the tandems and across the Atlantic functioned extremely well. At the same time, the project would have been impossible before the age of electronic communication.

Unlike most scholarly projects, this book is more concerned with synthesis than basic research. The tandems were not commissioned to write encyclopedic articles, however. Rather, they were encouraged to produce sweeping, thought-provoking, and very readable essays that rested on solid research and reflection. Each tandem was asked to blaze a trail for comparison through the material at hand. It was the development of commonalities and differences, continuities and ruptures, reciprocal perceptions and transfers in the history of Germany and the United States that drew our attention. In this process, the histories of two countries and several German states – including the German Democratic Republic (GDR), which is considered at least partially in each essay – are examined for the first time not just selectively or in relation to a single issue but rather over a long period of time and with respect to a wide range of issues. We have not shied away in this undertaking from relating the history of National Socialism to certain aspects of American history – knowing full well that comparing and equating are not to be confused with one another.

This collection offers even the expert reader many new insights. Each essay develops a set of innovative and overarching comparative hypotheses; the collaborative efforts of each tandem cast new light on subjects familiar even to specialists. On the one hand, these interpretations themselves are products of a transatlantic exchange of ideas; on the other, they represent a particular moment in the historiography of both countries. After decades of specialized research, it is now time to consider the broad movements and the larger contexts of transatlantic history. Historians have long left this task to scholars in other disciplines, above all sociologists and political scientists, while bemoaning the lack of empirical intensity in such work. In today's increasingly globalized world, there is an obvious need for comprehensive analysis that can provide a frame of reference for further specialized research.

It is equally important in this endeavor that our approach has the capacity to generate points of reference for the historical analysis of additional societies. In this spirit, we hope that our volume will have something to say to experts on the welfare state in Great Britain as well as to scholars focusing on the educational system in Japan – to give just two examples. Obviously, the United States and Germany have never been alone in this world, and the logical next phase of this investigation would be to consider their respective paths into modernity in relation to those of other societies. Ultimately, this study is striving to make a contribution beyond the context of German–American history and to overcome the dominant national fixation of historical research to date.

To what extent have Germany and the United States moved away from each other in the course of the twentieth century? How different from one another are the consumer societies, the legal cultures, or the academic landscapes in these two countries? Why are Americans more religious than Germans, and why are Germans more environmentally conscious than Americans? To these and many other questions, this collection of essays provides authoritative and, in many cases, surprising answers.

We find, for instance, in Chapter 6 on immigration that when the histories of these two countries are carefully compared from a transatlantic perspective, the United States does not always appear to be *the* classic land of immigration that it is usually taken to be. Chapter 14 about media raises the question of whether the American mass media were always more commercially oriented than their German counterparts. Chapter 4, which discusses law, posits the thesis that the German tradition of constitutional law is better equipped to secure social peace and justice than the American one. The authors of Chapter 7 about mass politics take a critical look at the thesis that the American political tradition has always been interpreted as basically revolutionary, whereas the German tradition is viewed as authoritarian. In Chapter 3, we learn that the decline of traditional religious values should not necessarily be viewed as characteristic of the modern era and that perhaps pious America is less exceptional than secular Germany. Needless to say, this list could be extended.

The common thread running through all of these essays is the attempt to critically reexamine the accepted clichés about Germany and America. Neither the assumption that Germany's advance into the modern era followed, with delay, America's nor the argument that the two nations in the course of their histories have been moving closer or farther apart can simply be taken at face value. Instead, we see an interplay of diverging and converging trends. The drifting apart in the spheres of "empire," "environment," and "religion" coincides chronologically with a convergence in other realms, such as "markets" or "popular culture." Thus, neither the burgeoning discussion of transatlantic rifts nor evocations of unity are subtle enough. This book demonstrates, rather, that in comparing the United States and Germany over the course of the twentieth century, one finds convergence, competition, conflict, copying, and cooperation, all occurring at the same time. The essays gathered here, in short, demonstrate that the paths Germany and the United States followed in their pursuits of modernity were not as straightforward or as easy to map as often assumed.

Further Reading

Bender, Thomas, *A Nation among Nations: America's Place in World History* (New York, 2006).

Daum, Andreas, and Christof Mauch, eds., *Berlin, Washington, 1800–2000: Capital Cities, Cultural Representation, and National Identities* (Cambridge, 2005).

Glaser, Elisabeth, and Hermann Wellenreuther, eds., *Bridging the Atlantic: The Question of American Exceptionalism in Perspective* (Cambridge, 2002).

Jarausch, Konrad H., and Michael Geyer, *Shattered Past: Reconstructing German Histories* (Princeton, NJ, 2003).

Junker, Detlef, in association with Philipp Gassert, Wilfried Mausbach, and David B. Morris, eds., *The United States and Germany in the Era of the Cold War, 1945–1990: A Handbook.* 2 vols. (Cambridge, 2004).

Keylor, William R., *The Twentieth-Century World and Beyond: An International History since 1900* (New York, 2006).

Maier, Charles S., *Among Empires: American Ascendancy and its Predecessors* (Cambridge, MA, 2006).

Trommler, Frank, and Elliott Shore, eds., *The German–American Encounter: Conflict and Cooperation between Two Cultures, 1800–2000* (New York, 2001).

Tyrrell, Ian, *Transnational Nation: United States History in Global Perspective since 1789* (New York, 2007).

Winkler, Heinrich August, *Germany, the Long Road West.* 2 vols. (Oxford, 2006–7).

2

Empires: Might and Myopia

THOMAS BENDER AND MICHAEL GEYER

After the tragic events of September 11, 2001, and the disordered world they seemed to imply, the United States sought to secure itself by turning to empire. For the first time since 1898, arguments for empire and its benefits were being made in the United States. The embrace of empire concerned both "homeland" security, as it was called, and foreign adventures. Yet, after a few years, the public turned against the worst of the imperial moment, and Barack Obama was elected president in 2008, not least on the basis of his offer of a revived republic at home and an alternative to empire abroad – of a world of global connection, cosmopolitanism, and constitutionalism. This moment invites a reconsideration of empire in the twentieth century, and the central roles Germany and the United States have played in the history of nations extending themselves as empires.

At the beginning of the twentieth century, the United States and Germany were the quintessential modern nations of the transatlantic world. Both had been re-founded in mid-nineteenth-century wars: the American Civil War and the Prussian wars of unification, respectively. What is more, they had been originally founded and then re-founded as nation-states, as self-conscious alternatives to empires as normality. With their significant transnational interconnections, both nations might have become paragons of internationalism. Yet, at crucial moments in their history, they turned global interconnections in the direction of embracing empire.

Empire is, of course, a rather elastic concept. Commonplace templates of empire fit the history of neither country. Some reject altogether the moniker "empire" or "imperial nation" for the United States because Americans have repeatedly denied their imperial ambitions. By contrast, extraordinary attention has been focused on the diminutive, late-nineteenth-century German Empire, and far-reaching conclusions have been drawn from Germany's imperial ventures because of the literally fantastic, popular ambitions associated with its *Weltpolitik*. By the same token, Nazi rule – the assertion of imperial and racial primacy – has been recognized only slowly as Nazi empire. Many historians are still more comfortable seeing the National Socialist empire as a type of regime all its own or as manifestation of "totalitarianism." They see it more as an abomination than as a political formation that could and should be compared to others, lest it taints them by the act of comparison.

We consider twentieth-century empire to be a polity different from both a republic and the old territorial empires, whether British or Hapsburg, which represented earlier political formations. Twentieth-century empire had two defining aspects: a presumption of being a model of modernity for the world and an aspiration to be the manager of the world to its own advantage, using the resources of culture, economy, and ultimately war toward that end. It is obvious that Germany and the United States pursued different paths toward empire. But as distinct from each other as they were, the two also departed from the model of older territorial regimes. The result, at its most extreme, was two wars for global dominion. During World War II, Hitler and Roosevelt each thought that his county would be the last one standing. Each saw the other nation as an enemy that threatened the values and even the existence of his own country.

This existential competition shapes any comparison of the two countries, whether as empire or not. It also raises the more basic question: Why do nations – why did the United States and Germany at crucial moments in their history – aim to dominate rather than cooperate?

The nineteenth-century American republic understood itself and its heritage to be aligned against empire, to be a standing rebuke to European monarchies and empires. Ostentatiously refusing the category of empire, the United States celebrated itself as a republican guardian of universal values. It would be exemplary. Abraham Lincoln, who condemned empire by conquest in opposing the war with Mexico, envisioned America as an exemplar of republican values, most famously in his Gettysburg Address. In that and other speeches and writings, he defined the United States as a nation for the world but not as a nation to rule over the world. As it turned out, however, many Americans had dreams of commercial, if not territorial, dominion, even as their tradition of anticolonialism and universalism made it difficult for them to understand their own imperial quest.

Born into a world dominated by global war between France and Great Britain and constrained by that conflict, Americans of the early nineteenth century, following the advice of George Washington, avoided international political entanglements. But they did eagerly seek international markets, using force when necessary to secure them. Farmers no less than urban merchants advocated free trade as being both in their interest and a universal good, and Thomas Jefferson, believing the same, brought the United States into its first foreign war to protect American shipping in the eastern Mediterranean. A decade later, James Madison, Jefferson's great collaborator, went to war, again in large part to protect American rights on the seas. Jefferson's vision of open seas and free trade is more in line with that of our own time than Alexander Hamilton's advocacy of "domestic manufactures," which he hoped would reduce America's vulnerability by making the nation more self-sufficient.

The most ardent champion of American empire during the nineteenth century was Senator William H. Seward, who later served as Lincoln's secretary of state. Rejecting old-style empires, he imagined an American empire based on advanced technologies of transportation and communication, internal industrial development, and global commerce. It would be an empire based on enrollment, not conquest or coercion. Henry J. Raymond, founding editor of the *New York Times*, wrote his friend Seward, "*Empire* is a grand ambition, but *Freedom* is loftier . . . and I fear we shall sacrifice our liberties to our imperial dream."

The first phase of American empire, sanitized in the history books as the "westward movement," was decidedly territorial and founded upon claims of Anglo-Saxon racial superiority. This expansion was made possible by levels of violence that approached genocide. In American memory, however, the concept of "Manifest Destiny" was not racist but universalist. Put more crudely, Americans imagined themselves commissioned by God to spread the universal blessings of freedom to benighted peoples. Often that racialized universalism served as a cover for American self-interest. Lincoln's liberal nationalist opposition to the Mexican War and to Manifest Destiny was marginalized, and that position remained so after the Civil War in the run-up to the Spanish–American War of 1898 and during most of the twentieth century.

The logic of American empire fused ideas of racial hierarchy and economic modernization. Proponents of Anglo-Saxonism, like President Warren G. Harding, who observed that "the Negro problem in America is but a local phase of a world problem," would not dispute W. E. B. DuBois's insistence that "the problem of the twentieth century is the problem of the color line – the relation of the darker to the lighter races of men in Asia and Africa, in America and the islands of the sea." The words were the same on both sides of the color line, but the meanings were not. For DuBois, the issue was freedom, justice, and dignity for all peoples. Those shouldering the "white man's burden" saw their task as efficiently managing people of color as a labor force. Writing in the midst of the debate over annexation of the Philippines in the wake of the Spanish–American War, Franklin H. Giddings of Columbia University argued in *Democracy and Empire* that the "governing . . . of the inferior races of mankind will be [a task] of great difficulty," but it must done so that the "civilized world" can continue the "conquest of the natural resources of the globe." The Philippines became a formal colony of the United States. However, the Filipino insurgency that lasted for a decade soured American imperialists on the idea of territorial empire.

Americans turned to empire without territorial colonization. As mentioned earlier, the United States had always demanded open seas and free trade. Initially, Americans traded agricultural products but, by the end of the nineteenth century, American industrial production had surpassed that of both England and Germany, and its manufactured products were reaching world markets. Before World War I, the United States had been a debtor nation but, after the war, it became the leading creditor nation, and the American empire was increasingly based on finance, a consequential change for the practice of empire. The nineteenth-century free-trade empire required little attention to the internal affairs of trading partners; open seas, most-favored-nation tariff policies, safe harbors, and extraterritorial status for its merchants and mariners (in the nonwestern world) were sufficient. Overseas investors, however, had additional security needs: they had a considerable stake in their foreign nations' internal affairs – their laws of contracts and property, labor legislation, taxation policies, police procedures, and judicial rulings on negligence. Informal empire became more intrusive and interventionist, and the United States was drawn into semi-imperial relationships.

Drawing a clear distinction between colonialism and empire helps clarify the particular nature of American imperialism. Colonialism implies control of territory, property, and people abroad. Empire, in contrast, needs no permanent governance, though it could require episodic military or fiscal interventions and, above all, ad hoc jurisdiction. This approach to empire was formalized under Theodore Roosevelt and William Howard Taft, and it underlay Woodrow Wilson's ambitions at Versailles and in the Caribbean. A critic of old empires no less than Lenin, Wilson sought to make the world safe not only for democracy but also for global capitalism and free trade.

Germany, the other "new" nation of the mid-nineteenth century, was a quintessential part of traditional Europe, the Europe of empires and monarchies that Americans loathed – and, hence, was and is commonly understood as self-evidently imperialist and aggressive. For Americans at the time of World War I, Germany came to exemplify the European vices of tyranny and imperialism. This image never quite squared with the other, more fraternal image of Germany as the miracle nation of industry, technology, knowledge, and education. Neither of the two images prepared Americans for the very real barbarism of the Nazi empire. Neither do they help explain the contorted relations of the Germans to empire. There is a strong anti-imperial streak in German history, which may be surprising. At the same time, however, the insistence on expansion and control beyond the nation as a prerequisite for national survival in a world of enemies is also a recurring feature of the German past. This haunted, existential quality of German thought on empire distinguishes it most clearly from that of the United States.

History and memory play an important role in both societies' ideas of empire. We should recall that the German process of nation-building, although slower than the American one, began at the time of the Franco-British war of empires that set free the American colonies. The German nation emerged not, however, from revolution and victory but from utter defeat. When Napoleon Bonaparte's revolutionary armies smashed through Europe, defeating and dissolving the Holy Roman Empire that had held the German lands together, they jolted a nationalist movement into existence. French soldiers and the design for a new Europe, drawn up in Paris, stimulated modern German nationalism. When Napoleon was defeated, the old imperial metropoles of Vienna, London, and St. Petersburg shaped Europe's future and the future of the German lands at Europe's center.

Prussia actually had an imperial hinterland – or so historians have come to argue, with its newly gained Polish territories and its Catholic (German) provinces in the west – but it was nonetheless the minor power among the Great Powers. State officials and, even more so, the emergent bourgeois public were keenly aware of Prussia's minor place. It was neither a Piedmont nor a Serbia but, as an upstart monarchy, it was not a Russia or Great Britain either. It took another half-century for the actual nation to emerge. German unity was achieved in duel-like wars of unification – in 1864, 1866, and 1870 – against its neighbors: the nationalizing Danish, a defensive Hapsburg Empire, and a reenergized French imperial nation. Although the German nation of 1871 was not anticolonial in the American sense, it was created in an act of self-assertion against empire.

German imperial ambitions, like American, were conditioned by early nineteenth-century developments. Important differences existed, however, between the German and American experiences. In Germany, there were worries about security in the face of France's military superiority and a grudging admiration of Russia and Great Britain. Germany also made efforts to imitate the more powerful metropoles and debated whom to imitate. These mixed emotions were countered by a Germanic nativism and chauvinism and a hypermasculine assertiveness that had their most evident parallel in Japan. Germans – and especially German nationalists – expressed a deep sense of weakness and vulnerability and, not least, of sheer envy. Eventually, this sense of weakness encouraged even liberal nationalists to favor an autocratic military. It also gave a negative emotional tenor to mass emigration and spurred the desire for colonial expansion, or *Lebensraum*. Above all, it generated a compulsive desire for unity within – a mythopoetic politics of memory that set the nation over and against the real differences in the history of its parts. After all, some of the German states had fought with but embraced Napoleon; Bavaria had fought on the side of the Hapsburgs in 1866; and Baden had risen up in a liberal-democratic revolution (1848) that was put down by the Prussians. Add to these incoherencies of the past the fact that the emergent German industrial sector, especially in western Germany, lived off technology and capital accumulated in Great Britain – and the sway of empires over the past and future of an emergent nation becomes patently apparent. That sway certainly explains the twisted shape of German nationalism and its peculiar drive to empire.

In contrast, standard historiographic explanations point to old elites – the monarch, the royal houses, the Junkers, and feudalized steel barons – and assume that they set the course for German imperialism, aided eventually, in the 1890s, by an emergent right-wing populism, a populism that was "antimodern" in its fear that the nation had been taken over by evil forces such as capitalism, feminism, socialism, Judaism, hedonism, and materialism. However, these explanations confuse nostalgic memory, the imaginary pursuit of a world that never quite was, with actual history. The dream of restoring the glory of old empire – which, in any case, was Catholic, whereas the new nation was to be Protestant – was at odds with the dynamic modernity of German nation-building. "Railways and rifles" were what won the wars. Colonial empire, for all its fantastic schemes to overcome modernity, was also a "laboratory of modernity." The new state fostered a distinctly national sphere that sustained a sense of mission and a strong sentiment that the German "spirit" and commodities "made in Germany" were good for the world. It was the nation that developed this nostalgia in the context of accelerated industrialization and urbanization and a rather more slowly developing nationalization. State's rights, after all, were paramount until 1918. Persistent provincialism and localism gave chauvinism its hard edge.

For all these expressions of hide-bound provincialism and rampant chauvinism, Germany as a nation became deeply enmeshed in international markets, far more so than the United States with its huge domestic hinterland. Moreover, many members of German society, far from sprouting Teutonic horns, revived an older cosmopolitanism and became defenders of a new internationalism. *Kultur*, scientific knowledge, and higher education were there to be shared as European goods, and the same was true for socialism, feminism, and the many reform movements at the turn of the twentieth century. Even Wagner's music became a global commodity, its embrace of an anti-Semitic nationalism notwithstanding. Germany became a nation in an interconnected world, and even its nationalism was deeply entangled in that world. It was this entanglement that led Germany to its pursuit of empire. The nation's future lay not in international cooperation but in unilateral domination and war.

If Germany was so much more a part of the (European) world than commonly assumed, where did Germany's path to domination and war begin? Why did domination win out over cooperation? The Prussian legacy of military extra-constitutionalism and the German nationalists' fear of foreign (and domestic) contamination played a role. Resentment was another powerful force, as the belated German turn to acquiring colonies suggests. German colonialism brought into the open and into politics an elaborate fantasy world of colonial dominion, in which men were still men, Germans ruled supreme, and degeneration was undone in the struggle with nature and natives. America was not free from such fantasies in the run-up to the Spanish-American War of 1898, but the American variants were less nativist and less primitivist than the German. Moreover, they were subsumed in the practical requirements of westward expansion, for which the colonies that Germany eventually acquired provided no equivalent outlet. In Germany, a still-emergent national public coalesced around colonialism as a resonant new focus. The colonial debate was amplified by media attention, which also occurred in the United States, where the "yellow press" stirred up nationalist feelings in 1898. Yet this fantastical world of colonial empire, although evocative of German desires, is also easily overrated as a driving force toward German empire.

Far more important in fomenting a specifically German imperialism was the rapidly growing perception of Germany's inadequate global competitiveness. Germany had become a nation, to be sure, but in the meantime the United States had unified a continent. Germany had become an industrial power, but its resource base and its markets were controlled by others. Max Weber formulated the classic version of this lament in his inaugural lecture at the University of Freiburg in 1895, "The National State and Economic Policy": with or without power alliances, with or without world trade, the nation as it was would just not be enough – not strong enough, not large enough, not self-sufficient enough – to prevail on its own in the future. Although newly unified and uniquely dynamic among "new nations," Germany was too small and too deeply entangled in the world to be truly sovereign. Therefore, the future demanded a Greater Germany to compete in a world that would be defined by empire (Great Britain), vast territorial states (United States and Russia), or a combination of both. In short, the newly created Kaiserreich was too much of a nation-state and needed to become more of a nation-empire.

The German word for this politics of competitive expansion was *Weltpolitik*, a politics that was ill defined beyond insisting on the necessity of empire and the compulsive pursuit of unilateral politics in a world that depended on the workings of multilateral exchanges. Typically, the rhetoric of *Weltpolitik* far exceeded the practice of it, and unilateralism tended to undermine the achievement of its goals. Much of the energy of *Weltpolitik* was consumed in a scramble for more and better colonies. A wholesale redivision of Africa and the establishment of German settlement clusters in Brazil were as much pursued as claims on China and the Ottoman Empire. Much effort has been spent on decoding the political adventurism of the Wilhelmine Empire and the fury with which it was pursued to the detriment not only of the actual involvement of Germany in Europe and the world but also of its own goals. Whatever else may be said about German naval policy and the arms race with Great Britain, they were not clever politically and turned out to be disastrous military strategies.

The truly striking feature of these adventures in global politics is that the more Germany grew into an interconnected world, the more the sense developed and spread that these ties spelled doom for a sovereign Germany. The language of a new bondage dated back to the Napoleonic Wars. At the turn of the century these concerns were expressed in the rhetoric of the age, the Social Darwinist language of empire and race. This language was commonplace in the United States as well as in Germany, although it may have carried more frightening connotations, an altogether darker hue, in Germany. But much of this is hindsight. What we do know is that Germany and the United States both turned to the pursuit of global empire but with radically different outcomes.

No simple dichotomy between a democratic nation and an autocratic empire can be applied to the comparison of America and Germany. In both the United States and Germany, the idea and the pursuit of empire were espoused by many diverse participants in civil society. The main difference is that in the nineteenth century, American civil society increasingly felt secure and found a solid foundation for self-government in an assertive nation, whereas the opposite was the case across the Atlantic. The nationalization of German civil society was accompanied by a spreading distrust in government and governance. In both countries, the shock of modernity generated a "paranoid style" of politics. But whereas suspicion of the government in the United States was found mostly on the margins of public culture, in Germany it was nearer the center. Surprisingly and, in view of prevailing stereotypes, paradoxically, trust in the government to do right was more highly developed in the United States than in Germany.

It is possible to argue that the pressure on the German government was so much greater than it was on the U.S. government because of the deeper entanglement of the former and the relative autonomy of the latter. In the end, though, the weakness of autocratic rule and a military-based executive and its inability to cope with an interconnected world catapulted the German Reich into an aggressively unilateralist and imperialist stance. In Germany, the rising clamor for empire was inseparable from panics over sovereignty, generated by the fear of losing autonomy in an ever more mobile, urban, and industrial society and interdependent world. In general, such panics turn violent and do not die down after an initial period of high excitement when government is perceived as inactive or incompetent.

However, it would be inaccurate to argue that the German Reich embraced empire and the United States rejected it. Rather, for Germany and America, empire came to mean different things. Simply put, American empire turned benevolent and "inviting," whereas German designs on empire became ever more malevolent. Indeed, the rise of imperial benevolence was predicated on and con-ditioned by the malevolence of Nazi rule. Of course, it has been argued, and is argued with increasing frequency today, that this contrast is but American propa-ganda in that the image of benevolence was fed more by the negative portrayal of the Germans than by facts on the ground – that the contrast between American and German empire is but a play with mirrors. The United States was not the city on the hill, the beacon and arsenal of democracy, the nation that universalized the values of self-government but rather was vindicated by its German opposite, whose pride in *Kultur* was incapable of hiding a streak of barbarism, expressed in total war and a politics of extermination. Carl Schmitt in the 1940s presented this mirror-imaging theory: he insisted that the American dream of spreading democracy and human rights is but ugly global dominion with a sunny face. We think his theory is wrong. However, the German and the American turn to twentieth-century empire is inextricably linked in that the "benevolent" moment of American empire is less a matter of good intentions and more a result of the competition and comparison with Nazi Germany (and, subsequently, the Soviet Union).

This formulation will not satisfy all those who would distinguish between empire proper and the many forms of hegemony (political, military, economic, cultural) and, in turn, to separate both from the mere muscle flexing of Great Powers. To be sure, there are advantages to such distinctions, although it would be better to focus on processes of territorialization and racialization of empire and the countervailing tendencies of de-territorialization and de-racialization of empire, for which the United States came to stand after a great deal of internal struggle. But even this focus misses the salient point: what empire became in the twentieth century was crucially worked out in the confrontation between Germany and the United States.

Germany's development after World War I from a neurotically competitive nation with colonial ambitions to imperial *genocidaire* was not predestined. Even in the aftermath of defeat and the widely condemned Versailles Treaty, the radical right did not have that much going for it. Germans wanted peace, not war. The outlook of the right-of-center spectrum of political parties was tied more to a restoration of the old order than to the outlandish ideas of the extremist fringe demanding an apocalyptic remaking of the German nation. But the right in Germany, and especially its crazy fringe, had two advantages – and that proved to be decisive. It had always argued that the German state was incapable of reining in the licentious desires of the masses and of securing Germany in a world of global empires. It also continually predicted the disastrous failure of the German state and the inevitable collapse of German society if Germany did not follow its advice. If the prediction of the right was "right" about the failure of the state and the collapse of society in war and hyperinflation and depression, how could it be totally wrong about the remedy? In 1918, the radical right never made any bones about German defeat and weakness, but it did insist that defeat could have been prevented and could yet be undone if drastic measures were taken. One of these measures was the pursuit of *Lebensraum*; the other was the radical cleansing of the body politic as prerequisite for a new German dominion.

Such right-wing beliefs were virulent, but their success crucially depended on the failure of the state and of politics. Trust in government and governance and in the ability of the state to set things right collapsed in spectacular fashion as a result of war, hyperinflation, and depression. Worse, this collapse seemed to vindicate much older disgruntlements. The Kaiserreich, we recall, had an autocratic but altogether weak central government, and in this respect, as well as in the limited expansion of central-state capabilities, it was not so different from the United States. The imperial government's mixture of self-righteousness and incompetence was egregious, and the consequences were disastrous. It is one thing if nations and their autocratic leaders flex their muscles and dream publicly of "a place in the sun." It is yet another thing if they pursue fantasies of global empire (*Weltpolitik*) and fail to deliver. What made the situation worse was that the German people – in contrast to Americans – most definitely expected their state to be strong and decisive.

Recent scholarship has come to emphasize that the peculiar German politics of staging "Final Solutions" – pursuing absolutes in the face of policy failure – emerges from this mixture of grandstanding and underperforming. After pushing ever further and ever upping the ante, there was, finally, nothing left but unequivocal victory or abject defeat. This quest for unequivocal solutions facilitated the politics of genocide in Southwest Africa. It informed the last German offensive in the spring of 1918, the politics of hyperinflation in 1923, and the austerity politics of the world economic depression. Last, and most decisively, it drove the acceleration of conquest and of racialization in the Third Reich after 1936–7. Rather than cut their losses (or take modest revisionist gains), the German ruling elites decided again and again to risk total defeat in pursuit of total victory.

Much as politics mattered, it does not explain the shifts in imperial policies – away not only from cooperation but also from *Weltpolitik* to *Lebensraum*. Radical nationalism proved to be the decisive agent of this shift. The idea was born from a particular German Gothic, a celebration of medieval colonization – of Teutonic Knights, free peasants, and civilizing burghers in Europe's East. These figments of historical fantasy became common currency during World War I. Never were German ideas about empire more expansive than in 1917–18. Never were these fantasies more violent than in the pulp-fiction world of the early 1930s, in which Germanic tribes, overcoming impossible odds, slaughtered and pillaged their way into the centers of power, while staying clean in spirit. The idea of a purified *Lebensraum* for a German master race was never more evocative and tempting than it was in Nazi propaganda of 1942–3 at the cusp of defeat. Nazi propaganda's core ideas about empire and *Lebensraum* proved to be remarkably popular. This was German empire, born from a sense of panic over the loss of self-control and self-government, exacerbated by the humiliation of defeat, and growing into political fantasy worlds of conquest and supremacy. Empire promised a sovereign future beyond interdependence.

The solutions of the right had always been extreme – sterilize bastards, extirpate racial minorities, exterminate enemies, conquer space for global action, ascertain racial supremacy – and these solutions caught on. The notion of *Lebensraum*, which Nazi propaganda disseminated, lived off the promise of a German society that was freed from global entanglement and in control of its own destiny. This idea thus came to fasten on eastward expansion and colonization. Older Wilhelmine fantasies, such as the image of a unified *Mitteleuropa* under German leadership, yielded to a more radical politics of space, which combined ever more expansive and violent projects of homesteading with a German-led politics of colonial exploitation imposed on the "native" populations judged unfit to rule. Violent conquest, national homogenization, and Germanic supremacy all came together to turn *Lebensraum* imperialism from fantasy to reality, into a uniquely vicious and inhuman enterprise. Although empires come in many shapes and forms, the fusion of nationalism and empire, as exemplified by the Nazis, proved to be genocidal.

The violent assertion of imperial sovereignty was the prescription of Nazi policies. A plan for Nazi conquest and world empire was unnecessary because it was widely accepted that for Germany to survive, the German nation would have to expand further and faster than any other country – as the Americans had done in the nineteenth century. In a more profound sense, this quest for sovereignty and thus a protected market reflected a desire for self-control and self-government in a world in which the nation-state, although just coming into its own, neither guaranteed security nor welfare nor a sense of moral well-being. The needs and desires that impelled national imperialism, the quest for sovereignty in an interdependent world, were not particularly German. The uniquely German and Nazi dimensions of this quest were, rather, the uncompromising radicalism and the genocidal ferocity characterizing the pursuit of a world in which Germans, and Germans alone, were in control of their own destiny. It is grating, but liberty from foreign bondage was one of the favorite Nazi propaganda slogans.

German history was not inescapably pointed in the direction of *Lebensraum* and an "end of history" in 1945. Germany's postwar recovery, in the West and the East, was not dictated entirely by the American and Soviet occupations and regime changes. The uprooting of the Nazi heritage worked only because Germany could fall back on its own democratic traditions. The Allies liberated these traditions – of liberal and social democracy – from captivity. The emerging German Democratic Republic wrecked what had been a very powerful German tradition of social democracy by "sovietizing" it. In the Federal Republic, the recovery of liberal traditions and trust in democratic government developed slowly. In the end, though, it was a new engagement with the world, a growing trust in interdependence, initially grounded in dependence, that secured the democratic revival. In the East, the suppression of this engagement – reflected, for example, in the limitation of the freedom to travel – became a source of opposition.

East Germans invented for themselves the role of socialist Über-teachers, traveling the world from Yemen to Mozambique, Namibia, and Nicaragua as indefatigable missionaries of "modern" technology, organization, and progress. There is no reason to believe that the many East Germans involved in cultural exchanges saw them as just a propaganda facade. West Germans also began to flourish in the wider world and rediscovered what had been the source of German wealth and well-being. Within three decades after the war, West Germany was leading the world in industrial exports, and in the last quarter of the century, its citizens proved unsurpassed in their desire for global travel. West Germany became what Germany always could have been: a cosmopolitan nation. Of course, pundits, mostly on the left, argued that this was an imperialism all its own. Others, mostly on the right, worried that this novel bonanza of openness would entail a loss of sovereignty and, even more, that in-migration would undercut the moral integrity of the nation. But overall, Germans came to embrace interdependence and increasingly thought of themselves as a postnationalist nation.

It was the United States that provided the geopolitical condition for West Germany's pursuit of happiness, and as long as this trade-off worked, nothing –

not the Vietnam War, not currency crises, not Pershing missiles – could imperil the trust in the United States as a benevolent, global, and imperial custodian. The acceptance and, indeed, the invitation to the United States to serve not simply as a hegemon (as leader among equals) but also as a guarantor and ultimate provider of security and well-being and, hence, as imperial protector formed a seminal reversal for both Germany and the United States. The American empire was benevolent empire in Europe, but it was empire all the same.

American global dominance dated from World War I, not World War II. At the beginning of the century, Germany and the United States offered competing visions of modernity, with Great Britain as their common competitor. In the wake of 1917, the Soviet Union joined the competition, and in the 1920s, Japan's ambitious plans for a pan-Asian empire offered yet another version of modernity. Woodrow Wilson and V. I. Lenin stood out, however, in their challenges to the old European empires, including Germany's. Wilson and Lenin spoke of the right to self-rule of the restive colonial subjects and national minority populations in Europe, with Wilson offering a liberal alternative to the communist route to nationhood and modernity. According to Wilson, the world needed fixing so it could match the pattern of American democracy and meet American economic interests. Much to the distress of both the Soviet Union and the United States, German fascism developed its own appeal in Europe and beyond in the 1930s. This appeal was temporary, however, and was defeated unequivocally. A more significant challenge derived from the will to self-determination, which both the Soviet Union and the United States had endorsed. A seemingly endless series of "little wars" of liberation and nationalist revolutions had already began with the Balkan crisis that triggered World War I; these wars and revolutions would reach their apogee during the Cold War. For both Wilson and Lenin – and their successors – building a world of cooperating nations was a daunting challenge.

When the twentieth century opened, Germany and the United States were the most rapidly industrializing and modernizing nations in the world. By 1918, the United States was clearly on top. Between 1897 and 1914, its international invest-ment increased by a multiple of five, and at the end of the war the United States was the world's largest producer of goods and services, exceeding the combined production of the United Kingdom, Germany, and France. After World War II, the economic dominance of the United States held; 50 percent of the world's manufacturing was American. During the long half-century from 1918 to 1981, the United States was the world's largest capital exporter. After World War II, it took "systemic" responsibility for the world economy. It could do so in part on account of the size of its economy but also as a result of the creation of the American-dominated global financial institutions associated with Bretton Woods – most importantly the World Bank and the International Monetary Fund (IMF).

It might be assumed that economic dominance would have stifled the rise of hypernationalist movements in the United States, but Americans did indeed participate in the extremist politics of the right. The 1920s were a complicated decade. In political history, it saw the rise of right-wing nationalist movements; in cultural history, it was a time of artistic and scientific modernism. The prewar association of modernism in the arts with radical politics weakened significantly in the 1920s. Urban culture moved toward cosmopolitanism and a new openness in urban lifestyles, pushing the limits of aesthetic traditions and even propriety. In the United States no less than in Germany, modern art, the night club, the "dance craze," short-haired women smoking in public, and the movies shared the public stage with worrisome political movements during this decade: a revived Ku Klux Klan, the American Legion, intolerant Prohibition crusaders, and, a bit later, Father Coughlin's right-wing populism and Huey Long's Silver Shirts. When Upton Sinclair titled a novel *It Can't Happen Here* (1935), he was suggesting that fascism could appear in America. If the United States was not entirely immune to the allure of the extreme right, Germany was not predestined to turn to Nazism in 1929 or even 1933. Still, the feel of the two political systems was quite different. Whereas the United States seemed rich, awash in an abundance of consumer goods, Germans knew that their economy could not deliver a consumer society on the American scale.

The legacy of World War I explains a great deal. The Versailles Treaty was not what the United States hoped it would be – a "peace without victory" – but it was the Germans, not the Americans, who suffered from that failure. The politics of resentment that emerged in Germany was largely absent in the United States, though of disillusion with war there was plenty, which would slow the American response to the danger of the increasing militarism of Germany in the 1930s.

Culture was as important as politics and production statistics to the competition between the two nations. The crass materialism that Europeans saw in the United States and the ever more visible spectacle of "the world's first regime of mass consumption" were symbolic challenges to the cultural commitments of Europeans in general and of Germans in particular. In the view of Victoria de Grazia, the Third Reich understood itself and offered itself "as the one European power capable of offering a winning alternative to American dominion."

With the global financial collapse in 1929, the American government, like the German, faced a challenge of legitimacy. The Great Depression's impact on the two nations was similar: both experienced a decline of about one-third in their gross national product and similar levels of unemployment (30 percent in Germany, 25 percent in the United States). Hitler and Roosevelt, who seem to have been highly aware and contemptuous of each other, each had to win over a confused and in many ways disaffected population. To overcome the crisis of confidence in their respective nations, the new leaders had to communicate a sense of direction and motion. In the United States no less than in Germany, Japan, or the Soviet Union, nationalism was mobilized to build allegiance to the nation, and the state extended its powers. The early New Deal relied on tactics not much different from those being used in Germany, including nationalist parades and rallies and the proliferation of nationalist symbols, particularly the Blue Eagle of the National Recovery Administration (NRA). The short-lived NRA used techniques not unfamiliar in Germany to stabilize the economy: notably, government-mandated negotiated agreements between management and labor. Facile comparisons with fascism are not useful, but this phase of the New Deal has been fairly characterized as an American-style "corporative state."

After the Supreme Court declared key elements of the so-called first New Deal unconstitutional in 1935, Roosevelt's efforts to expand and centralize state capacity incorporated a greater degree of local authority. The states administered many of the most important programs, including housing, welfare, and employment, thus accommodating both legal rulings and local traditions, which often included blatant racial discrimination. That said, such political accommodations were more than matched by progressive and cosmopolitan policies. The Democratic Party, which had accommodated the Ku Klux Klan in southern and some Midwestern states before 1928, was transformed into a party committed to positive social policy and ethnic pluralism, though it remained hesitant about championing civil rights for African Americans in the South and open housing in northern cities. The expanded state established the Social Security insurance programs and thereby wedded diverse Americans to the state, thus helping sustain the New Deal's ethnic pluralism. Although the New Deal modernized and centralized the national state, localism, individualism, and a fear of statism put limits to this expansion. Yet perhaps the traditional American suspicion of state power had its virtue: it may have limited the temptation of fascism.

The positive experience with social policy and Keynesian economics during the New Deal was furthered by the American mobilization and management of human and material resources in World War II. The ideology and practice of the American empire that emerged after the war, with West Germany and Japan now favored clients, built on the premises of the Keynesian domestic policies associated with New Deal liberalism. West Germany and Japan were built up as anticommunist anchors in Europe and East Asia. In the longer run, however, the Atlantic Charter and the Nuremberg Trials (or the idea behind them) provided the foundation for the international human rights regime that transformed global history over the course of the second half of the twentieth century and into the twenty-first.

The Charter, crafted by Roosevelt and Winston Churchill in 1941, echoed Roosevelt's earlier enunciation of four essential freedoms (freedom of speech and worship, freedom from want and fear). It was intended to establish a "moral contrast" to the values associated with Nazi Germany. Put differently, the Charter universalized a set of traditional Anglo-American constitutional rights. The international implications were obvious, and the Charter established the foundation for the global human rights talk that developed over the remainder of the century. But it had domestic implications as well in calling into question American race policies. Both domestically and internationally, the United States talked the language of rights and was then pressed to make them real at home and abroad – often in self-contradictory ways, depending on the time, place, and the rights at issue. The language of anti-imperialism and antiracism set the stage for the UN Declaration of Human Rights and the modern American civil rights movement, which gained its first victories in the 1940s, among them the desegregation of the Armed Forces. Domestically, a combination of pressure from the civil rights movement, presidential leadership, and the courts, particularly the Supreme Court under Chief Justice Earl Warren, nationalized the rights revolution, making the federal government the ultimate protector of them. It also separated a constitutional domain of "civil rights" from an international domain of "human rights," with long-lasting effects.

The war against fascism and the impact of the Holocaust forced Americans to consider their own racial and ethnic exclusions as well as the nation's racist immigration laws. By this unhappy route, Germany greatly advanced cosmopolitanism and the expansion of rights in the United States. During the Cold War, America competed with the Soviet Union for ideological dominance of the Third World as well as for access to its resources, and it worried about the impact of its racial policies and practices in Africa and elsewhere. U.S. State Department policymakers pressed for the end of regional segregation. Racism and intolerance were defined as antimodern, and cosmopolitanism and equal rights were advanced as modern and deserving of state advocacy. America represented itself as modern. The circulation of American technology and culture, popular and elite, won adherents everywhere. Yet even in this moment of triumph, the American scene was tarnished by the ugly presence of McCarthyism, which wrought damage that reverberates yet.

Internationally, the United States promoted a version of nation-building underwritten by modernization theory, which carried a promise of global convergence on the American model. Part of that agenda was the spread of fundamental principles of law, which included not only the security of contracts and investments but also the inviolability of rights that would later become a global human rights movement. This nation-building project depended on American capital outlays – either foreign direct investment for development or, more commonly, military aid. This development and the American hegemony it sustained were mostly achieved through international treaties and multilateral institutions rather than unilaterally between metropole and client. In his final inaugural address a few months before his death, Roosevelt had endorsed this approach, which was already being institutionalized with the United Nations and other American-sponsored international institutions: "We have learned that we cannot live alone, at peace; that our own well-being is dependent on the well-being of other nations, far away." Multilateralism had always been embattled in the United States and the earlier international ambitions of Woodrow Wilson and others had been sidelined. Nonetheless, the liberal internationalist commitment to multilateralism won bipartisan support in the early Cold War era. Only at the beginning of the next century did the nation reassert a unilateral approach to foreign affairs. However, with the 2008 election of Barak Obama and its repudiation of the Bush–Cheney foreign affairs regime, that shift was short-lived. Still, U.S. internationalism and multilateralism remain limited; for example, the United States has not joined the International Criminal Court, and its support for global environmental policies remains uncertain.

The United States invested heavily in reconstructing the Federal Republic of Germany and Japan as modern, demilitarized liberal democracies, while the GDR embraced modernity within the orbit and definitions established by the Soviet Union. As a result, a divided Germany and, more particularly, Berlin became ground zero for the Cold War in Europe. Central to modern history but no longer an independent actor, Germany remained the European focus for the elaboration of American dominion. In fact, the Americans' commitment to the reconstruction of Germany and Japan was intended to create regional icons of an Americanized modernity, as part of America's effort to present to new and recovering nations an appealing alternative to the Soviet Union, whose accelerated industrialization was seen by many as a model for the Third World. This strategy was undercut in the 1960s and 1970s, however, by military failure in Vietnam.

Is it useful to think of the U.S. dominion over Europe and the Far East as empire? Inasmuch as it was an unequal relationship in which the United States asserted its dominion, it resembled empire. American aid came with agendas representing American national interests. Moreover, American-dominated financial institutions strongly shaped the economic policy formulations of their client states. Inasmuch as the United States controlled key aspects of other nations' sovereignty, such as their security, it was empire. Then again, security was organized in a multilateral (but not quite egalitarian) alliance of nations, in which these nations had a voice. More important, American society grew more receptive not just to the import of foreign goods but also to the incorporation of "foreign" – or "transnational" – elites and migrants, many of whom found opportunities for achievement and advancement in postwar America, as did multinational corporations. By the 1970s, Germans, Japanese, and other non-Americans had begun to run their own economies with skill and success and to manage American subsidiaries as well, which made many Americans nervous. That's empire, too, but unlike anything that has been seen since Roman times.

It was the nationalizing Third World, however, not Europe or East Asia, that suffered the costs of Cold War competition. The United States and the Soviet Union were ideologically committed to their own versions of modernity as universal, and they competed for the allegiance of emerging nations. These new nations identified themselves as the "Third World" at the Bandung Conference in 1955, seeking to gain support while avoiding capture by either of the superpowers. There was no such safe space. The various nationalist movements and ambitious modernizers in Africa, Asia, and Latin America found themselves drawn into the global conflict, just as the superpowers were drawn into the nationalist politics of the new nations.

As early as 1956, the United States had shown the limits of its interest in changing the European status quo when it did not intervene in the Hungarian uprising, which was crushed by the Red Army. By 1963, the European theater of the Cold War was stabilized, and the former European colonies, now emerging as new nations, had become the main playing field for the Cold War. Both superpowers intervened repeatedly on behalf of competing claimants to power and legitimacy in Africa, Asia, and Latin America. In its global dimension, the Cold War, deeply entwined with nationalist movements and nation-building, was hot, claiming the lives of millions, mostly people of color.

The United States, driven by its universalist ideology, was determined to undermine and destroy any emerging regime that might turn to the false god of communism, the rival universalism. It relied on both formal military action and covert operations in this project. Outside of Europe, however, positive results were rare. The thirty U.S. interventions in the Third World after 1945 produced successes only in South Korea and Taiwan, and Vietnam was a human and policy disaster. Seen from a world perspective, Odd Arne Westad points out, "the results of America's interventions are truly dismal." Instead of being beneficial, a force for good, as Americans understood their actions to be, the interventions "devastated many societies and left them more vulnerable to further disasters of their own making."

The sudden dissolution of the Soviet bloc in Eastern Europe in 1989, which was followed by the collapse of the Soviet Union in 1991, left the United States as the world's lone superpower. The popular reading of those events was as a triumph of American power, particularly its economy, which could support an arms race that the Soviets could not match. Of course, this collapse also owed something to social movements and other changes within the Soviet Union and the Soviet bloc. There were also larger global developments that enabled this American success. Other players on the periphery of the historic North Atlantic centers of power began to count in new and consequential ways in global affairs. A militant Islamic movement in its Central Asian iteration resisted and turned back Soviet forces in Afghanistan, revealing Soviet military weakness and wreaking a large psychological toll. The historic split between the Soviet Union and China played to the advantage of the Americans. China's emergence was an opportunity that was grasped by Richard Nixon and Ronald Reagan, both of whom traveled to China. Having the assurance that China, an independent nuclear power, would remain neutral in respect to U.S. dealings with the Soviet Union enabled the Americans to stare down the Soviets by embarking on an arms race that the smaller Soviet economy could not match.

Yet, the same new global actors that helped the United States become the sole superpower soon became counterforces to American global ambitions. China became an essential economic partner and potential competitor, with the possibility of sharing global economic power and political influence to a greater degree than the United States had accepted in the course of the twentieth century. At the same time, an increasingly militant Islam created new security challenges, particularly in respect to access to the oil resources of the Middle East, a point made violently clear on September 11, 2001. Militant Islam represented a wholly new kind of threat to existing notions of hegemony or empire: it was a nonstate actor that could operate globally in a world of nation-states. The ways and means and possibilities of American leadership of global "management" of economic and security affairs, to say nothing of environmental issues, seem to demand a far stronger global sensibility, cosmopolitanism, and international institutions than have so far been imagined.

By the end of the twentieth century, the American faith in state-managed development strategies posited by modernization theory was discredited, the result of both economic developments and ideological shifts within the United States and failures abroad. The Vietnam War – and, more particularly, Lyndon Johnson's commitment to "guns and butter" – produced an inflationary spiral. The failed war divided America and discredited the United States around the world. Along with the war, urban riots, Watergate, and a weakened economy sapped the confidence of Americans in their government. At the same time, Americans felt threatened by the seemingly more dynamic economies of West Germany and Japan. Although neither the German nor the Japanese economy could be described as a beneficiary of laissez-faire governance, American business leaders, University of Chicago economists, and, increasingly, the public blamed the nation's declining capacity to compete with them on too much government and too many regulations. If from the 1940s through the 1960s the state was seen as the vehicle of modernization, by the 1980s it was seen as an obstacle to development and growth. "Deregulation" commenced during the administration of Jimmy Carter, beginning with the airlines and communications.

The antigovernment mood paved the way for "deregulation" at home and "restructuring" abroad. Committed to the workings of the market, economists dismissed policy solutions, citing the "policy ineffectiveness proposition." Put simply, this meant that any government policy devised to solve a particular economic problem would at best have no impact; more likely, it would produce adverse effects. More importantly, global economic integration limited the capacity of nation-states to manage their economies. The route to modernity, it was thus proposed, was by way of the market; the entire world was a market. With practical and rhetorical assistance from Britain's Margaret Thatcher, who was adamant about the need for market-oriented policies, the Reagan administration began exporting policies of deregulation and smaller government. The emerging "Washington Consensus," enforced by international institutions dominated by the United States, called for austerity regarding social investments, privatization of public assets and services, and the liberalization of trade. Such was the price demanded by the American universal empire for much-needed foreign direct investment, debt relief, and access to American markets.

This push for "deregulation" was justified by the suddenly omnipresent word "globalization," said by some to have been coined at the Harvard Business School in 1983. The term claimed to describe an empirical condition but was in fact an ideology that normalized the global market – itself an updated version of Jefferson's open seas and free trade, John Hay's Open Door notes of 1899, and Wilson's appeals to a world made safe for democracy and capitalism. However, in contrast with a free-trade liberal imperialism, neoliberalism came heavily armed, ready to pounce anywhere. Central America and several parts of Latin America became the proving ground of a new international political economy that abandoned state-led development for free-market strategies while ratcheting up covert action. The state was seemingly reduced to policing and its military capacities.

The global financial and banking crisis that began in 2008, which was partly caused by American-style unregulated financial operations, may have taken the luster off the market model. In any event, regulation and perhaps a new commitment to social spending seem to be finding a place in discussions of both national governments and those of the international organizations (IMF and World Bank) that had pushed the neoliberal agenda over the past thirty years.

When the Soviet Union fell, President George H. W. Bush announced the prospect of a "New World Order," a world no longer divided that would be managed by multilateral institutions. The subsequent administration of Bill Clinton continued the multilateral diplomacy and neoliberal economics. The younger Bush, George W. Bush, and especially his vice president, Dick Cheney, had different ideas. The attack on the World Trade Center on September 11, 2001, gave them an opportunity to make of the United States a different kind of empire at home and abroad. They limited constitutional rights and claimed novel executive powers. Their announced "War on Terror" resulted in a national security state at home, unilateralism in international relations, and wars in Afghanistan and Iraq.

The United States, not the demilitarized and newly unified Germany, seemed more and more to represent the dangers of empire, of military rule abroad, and of security pursued at home beyond the law. If in the early postwar period the United States looked good because of the Nazi regime in Germany, in the first decade of the twenty-first century, Germany, called "old Europe" by the Bush administration, looked good in relation to the hypernationalistic and militaristic United States.

Growing revelations about abuses of constitutional rights and claims of "inherent" powers of the presidency at home, combined with the catastrophic course of the wars – including disturbing reports of inhumane treatment of prisoners in the war zones, the secret "black sites" used for torture, and the use of the prison at Guantanamo in American-occupied Cuba – turned public opinion against the administration and the adventure in empire. Barack Obama was elected president in 2008 primarily on the basis of his opposition to the war and to violations of constitutional and human rights. He also promised a multinational approach to international affairs and so far has more or less made good on that commitment.

Germany does not play a prominent role in this new world order. To be sure, some thought that the end of the Cold War allowed for a turn to a more self-assertive national presence. In public debates during the 1990s, the entire history of German empire was revisited. How about a new *Mitteleuropa*, a continental alliance with Russia, a stronger presence in the Near East (Turkey and its accession to the European Union being the touchstone for these debates), a permanent place in the Security Council, a cohesive Franco-German-driven European Union, and, perhaps, more self-assertion in relation to the United States? For a while, Europe seemed to be poised to take over the "soft-power" role that the United States had abandoned. In practice, German foreign policy aggravated the tenuous situation in Yugoslavia by siding with its client from a previous world, Croatia. For the most part, though, old recipes proved useless. The new Europe did not tolerate national empire and had no desire to turn the European Union into an imperial supra-state, least of all a Franco-German one, even though it might well turn out to be the vehicle for a European civil society.

The question really is whether the way forward is to go back to the old empire by invitation. In some ways, the chances that might happen are not bad, but not because of European-style cosmopolitan dreams. The world needs governance, and the United States is well equipped to develop a global politics in cooperation with others, as even America's likely competitors such as China and its most hot-headed challengers like Iran are keenly aware. There is no one-way street to American unilateralism. As the events of the opening decade of the twenty-first century have indicated, that approach endangers the struggle against transnational terrorism. This said, the nearly hundred-year experiment of managing global governance through empire is coming to an end. The last one standing, the United States, was also the last one to try – and it was or will be the last one to fail. The lesson of global turbulence is not a return to empire but rather global governance beyond empire.

With its presumption of a unilateral freedom of action, the United States has come to act like a nationalist empire. The United States – not demilitarized and newly unified Germany – seems more and more to represent the dangers of military rule beyond the law, not only in the way it used force but also in the effects of a national security state on a 200-year history of constitutionalism and rights. The transformation of American universalism into a hypernationalism – an uncanny parallel to the German exceptionalism of a century ago – threatened to cut the United States off from the principles it promoted a half-century ago. The failures associated with this orientation to the rest of the world and to strategic policy have produced a painful reexamination by Americans, most evident in the 2008 presidential campaign. Americans are looking with more sympathy on German and European hopes for a future that is cosmopolitan, to a world of nations that cooperate. The resilience of American politics and the trust in the bedrock of the Constitution have proven a vital source for renewal. But will that be enough to withstand the turbulences of global politics, from which many Americans would wish to escape?

Further Reading

Ames, Eric, Marcia Klotz, and Lora Wildenthal, eds. *Germany's Colonial Pasts* (Lincoln, 2005).

Bender, Thomas. *A Nation among Nations: America's Place in World History* (New York, 2006).

Borgwaldt, Elizabeth. *A New Deal for the World: America's Vision for Human Rights* (Cambridge, 2005).

Cooper, Frederick. *Colonialism in Question: Theory, Knowledge, History* (Berkeley, 2005).

De Grazia, Victoria. *Irresistible Empire: America's Advance through Twentieth-Century Europe* (Cambridge, 2005).

Friedrichsmeyer, Sara, Sara Lennox, and Susanne Zantop, eds. *The Imperialist Imagination: German Colonialism and Its Legacy* (Ann Arbor, 1998).

Hofstadter, Richard. *The Paranoid Style in American Politics* (New York, 1965).

Hull, Isabel V. *Absolute Destruction: Military Culture and the Practice of War in Imperial Germany* (Ithaca, 2005).

Knock, Thomas J. *To End All Wars: Woodrow Wilson and the Quest for a New World Order* (New York, 1992).

Kundrus, Birthe. *Moderne Imperialisten: das Kaiserreich im Spiegel seiner Kolonien* (Cologne, 2003).

Lundestad, Geir. *The United States and Western Europe since 1945: From "Empire" by Invitation to Transatlantic Drift* (Oxford, 2003).

Maier, Charles S. *Among Empires: American Ascendancy and Its Predecessors* (Cambridge, 2006).

Manela, Erez. *The Wilsonian Moment: Self-Determination and the International Origins of Anticolonial Nationalism* (Oxford, 2007).

Mazower, Mark. *Hitler's Empire: How the Nazis Ruled Europe* (New York, 2008).

Moses, Dirk A., ed. *Empire, Colony, Genocide: Conquest, Occupation, and Subaltern Resistance in World History* (New York, 2008).

Rosenberg, Emily. *Financial Missionaries to the World: The Politics and Culture of Dollar Diplomacy, 1900–1930* (Cambridge, 1999).

Schmitt, Carl. *The Nomos of the Earth in the International Law of the Jus Publicum Europaeum*, transl. by G. L. Ulmen (New York, 2003).

Smith, Woodruff D. *The Ideological Origins of Nazi Imperialism* (New York, 1986).

Weber, Max. "The National State and Economic Policy [Inaugural Lecture, Freiburg, 1895]." *Economy and Society* 9, no. 4 (1988): 420–49.

Westad, Odd Arne. *The Global Cold War: Third World Interventions and the Making of the Contemporary World* (Cambridge, 2006).

Zielonka, Jan. *Europe as Empire: The Nature of the Enlarged European Union* (Oxford, 2006).

3

Religion: Belief and Power

SIMONE LÄSSIG AND RAINER PRÄTORIUS

For quite some time, the modern era has been viewed as a period in which faith, religion, and the church have been in decline. Movements such as industrialization and urbanization and the rise of science and technology were considered to be much more characteristic of this era. The "demystification of the world" that accompanied these movements seemed to rupture irrevocably the fragile unity of the religious and social spheres of life. Our modern, increasingly more mobile society – oriented toward market forces, performance, and competition – has established new ways of life. Religion, so it seemed, was a dinosaur headed toward extinction.

The German past and present seem to confirm this prognosis. One-third of the German population is now without any religious affiliation. In the eastern states, (the former GDR), this category covers nearly three-quarters of the population. Although more than 80 percent of those living in the GDR still belonged to a church (primarily Protestant) in 1950, this figure had slipped to only 24 percent by 1989, and there is nothing to suggest now that this trend will reverse itself. Despite the fact that the churches and clergy played a crucial role in the peaceful revolution of 1989, churches in eastern Germany remain empty today, and the secular coming-of-age celebration initiated during GDR times is still more popular than the Christian confirmation ceremony. In the "old" states in western Germany, especially in the large cities, the importance of the church is also waning. The number of weddings and baptisms performed in western Germany has been in steady decline since the 1960s, and even among those who balk at leaving the church, only a minority (16 percent of all Catholics and 4.6 percent of all Protestants) still regularly attend Sunday services. In 2002, only 7 percent of Catholics under thirty years old declared themselves to be close to the church. Even in questions of personal morality, only a small minority of Germans recognize their churches as a source of social authority. Religiously affiliated schools in Germany are also a marginal phenomenon; they enroll scarcely more than 4 percent of all pupils.

In the United States, we encounter a very different situation. A rich and diverse religious culture continues to exist. A large number of Americans consider faith in God to be an indispensable prerequisite for a modern, well-functioning community. The importance of religion in American life was made glaringly clear in recent presidential elections. Electoral researchers determined that in 2004, the deciding factor was no longer the gender gap (liberal candidates were

32

more popular with women than with men) but rather the gap in religious faith. Specifically, confessional affiliation was less important than intensity of religious practice in influencing voters' choices. According to a Gallup poll, for example, George W. Bush's competitive edge among regular churchgoers over his challenger John Kerry was 61 to 39 percent. Individuals who combine their strong faith with a conservative political view tend also to attach unusually high political importance to moral issues, such as abortion and gay rights. Currently, only 32 percent of regular churchgoers can imagine that they would ever be able to accept a compromise on the issue of abortion; this represents a decline from the 2000 election, when 41 percent felt similarly.

Religion and fundamental ethical and religious convictions seem to be more and more important in the United States, which is quite surprising in light of a strong historical tendency toward pragmatism. At the same time, this form of religiosity is different from those found in Germany or in other parts of Europe. To Americans, religious rites and procedures, doctrines, dogmas, and institutions are not as important as personal spiritual experience. This tendency was already noticeable in the Great Awakenings of the eighteenth and nineteenth centuries, and it became especially apparent in the twentieth century with the rapid rise of the Pentecostal churches. Religion is used as a stage for individual and collective experience to a much greater extent in the United States than in Europe. That Pentecostalism, as opposed to more mainstream Protestant denominations, is currently experiencing an upswing (for instance, in nondenominational megachurches) is striking because periods in the past that were marked by an increase in religious emotions were also times of profound political upheaval.

Religion shapes not only the private sphere but also politics in the United States in a manner without parallel in Germany or the other Western industrial nations. Many Americans value religion as a point of orientation and source of values. Thus, it is hardly surprising that in 2004, 72 percent of American voters answered yes to the question, "Should your president be a person of strong faith?" Although the question of religion provokes much stronger conflicts in American social and political discourse than it does in Germany, a majority of Americans still consider religion in general to be a sign of the "American way" and experience it as something basically positive.

What conclusion should we draw from this evidence? Is Germany more modern than the United States? Or is a new form of religiosity taking shape in the United States that is appropriate for the modern era and that will also reach Germany sooner or later? Does the American experience demonstrate that the path to modernity need not be linked to a decline in the importance of religion, as the example of Germany might suggest? Does Germany perhaps represent a special case in terms of religion?

RELIGION AND THE STATE

It is clear that legal history and the relations between the state and religious groups and organizations have played a decisive role in framing the trends described earlier. In Germany, the foundations of a state church were established in the sixteenth and seventeenth centuries, the likes of which do not exist in America. In the wake of the Reformation and other religious conflicts, several kinds of states took shape: alongside states with Catholic rulers, free imperial city-states, and ecclesiastical states, Protestant territorial states developed in which the sovereign also functioned simultaneously as the highest bishop, or *Summepiskopus*. After the establishment of the German Empire in 1871 under the leadership of Protestant Prussia, this traditionally close alliance between throne and altar affected all of Germany. It was not until the Revolution of 1918 and the formation of the Weimar Republic that this state of affairs changed and the Protestant institution of the high episcopate was dissolved. Social Democrats and liberals, who were active in both national and state governments, attempted to separate church and state. However, the political left was not able to win over a majority to such a secularist position. Lawmakers were able to agree only on a so-called limping separation, which established freedom of religion, and a cooperative relationship between church and state. The state obligated itself to allow Christian religious instruction as a required subject in state schools and to support religious schools and social institutions financially or otherwise to collect taxes specifically for the churches. For quite some time, the churches regarded this imperfect separation as a great success. If, however, one tracks the further development of this relationship from the perspective of the American experience, one could conclude that this partnership between church and state in Germany has, in fact, damaged the churches. A market for religion, one dependent on supply and demand, on competition, and on the relative attractiveness of its "products," does not exist in Germany, particularly because the Federal Republic's constitution, the Basic Law, is so similar to the constitution of the Weimar Republic on matters of religion. Despite legal incursions during the National Socialist era (1933–45), when the basic tendency of the regime was against the churches, the German tradition of a state church has remained alive and intact.

The situation in East Germany was very different. Although its constitution guaranteed freedom of religion, the state defined itself as atheist and undertook everything it could to estrange the population from the churches. This estrangement was accomplished only in part by direct pressure. Much more important was the introduction of alternative rituals like socialist "christenings" and secular coming-of-age celebrations.

Taking a longer historical view, we see that the religious landscape in the German territories was structured "from above" after the end of the Thirty Years' War and the Peace of Westphalia in 1648, whereas in the colonies of North America it was segmented horizontally. In the New World, instead of the confession of the ruling house determining the religious identity of the region, parallel worlds of different denominations were created through settlement, the taking of land, and the emigration of dissidents. When Roger Williams, together with his steadfastly Calvinistic followers, departed from the Puritans in the Massachusetts Bay Colony in 1636 and founded a new settlement in Rhode Island according to his religious principles, he established a mode of behavior that would profoundly shape America's religious-political history. He resolved a conflict by removing himself physically from its source.

Such actions unfolded as a consequence of living in a vast territory with few other European residents. Many contemporary observers of the colonial era interpreted the settling of Christian communities in the so-called wilderness as analogous to the biblical account of the Israelites' taking of land under Moses and Joshua, and the resultant limited compacts that incorporated a binding religious faith and a political hierarchy as a covenant with God, who also granted the settlers legitimate claim to the land they occupied. This line of thought prevailed both before and after the American Revolution. Alexis de Tocqueville (1805–59), for instance, perceived the roots of this political-religious formation of governance in the decentralized traditions of New England. He identified a communal code of practice, which placed great value on freedom in the face of both political and religious authority. This urge toward autonomy was accompanied, however, by a high degree of inwardly directed religious and ethical conformity. This combination of external craving for freedom and internal rigidity still characterizes the United States today.

The settlement of the American West altered the balance of individual religious cultures. The new territories developed into fields of experimentation for religious movements that defined themselves through "experience" and the active participation of a high percentage of laypeople. The established religious communities on the East Coast, such as the Episcopalians and the Presbyterians, developed more formalized administrative structures. Some religious communities distanced themselves from this formal model, and that act took on an overtly political dimension. It expressed itself in the form of skepticism toward an urban establishment, suspected of exploiting political institutions to further its own particular religious denomination. Of particular interest in this context were the Baptists, who, with their decentralized, grassroots form of organization, initiated a movement in which "religion from below" expanded and developed into a typical phenomenon of the American frontier. New religious movements, such as Mormonism, also conform to this model. With their exodus to Utah, the Mormons represent the typical American combination of religious separation and territorial mobility.

RELIGIOUS DIVERSITY, NATION, AND POLITICAL CULTURE

The United States defined itself early on as a land of immigration. Since the end of the nineteenth century, when the possibilities for territorial expansion had been largely exhausted, American society had to accept religious diversity as a social reality. National identity was derived from and supported by a mixture of civic and religious symbols. Germany, in contrast, was characterized by religious homogeneity and stability. Throne and altar had entered into an alliance. To be sure, the accelerated modernization of the German economy and society toward the end of the nineteenth century had contributed to the gradual wearing down of confessional boundaries. However, it was not until after World War II, in the wake of all the accompanying cultural, social, and political changes, that the denominational map of Germany changed strikingly. Various factors contributed to this situation: the arrival of more than twelve million refugees and displaced persons, the secularization policies of the East German state, the recruitment of "guest workers" starting in the 1960s, and, of course, the upsurge in the economy and the resultant culture of consumption. The system of denominational segregation in the public schools did manage, however, to continue in some parts of West Germany into the 1970s.

The confessional stability that persisted well into the twentieth century in Germany and the extraordinary movement in the open and pluralistic religious landscape on the other side of the Atlantic raise the question of the relationship between religion and political culture. How have the differences between denominations and religions influenced the political mentality, the culture, and, consequently, the everyday lives of Germans and Americans? Have they accentuated already existing tensions, or have religious tolerance and diversity helped mitigate conflicts?

Interestingly enough, denominational differences long generated much greater difficulties in Germany than the conflict between the religious and secular portions of the population. The early denominational schisms that obligated subjects to follow the confession of their rulers and that resulted in a high degree of confessional homogeneity within German states continued to have an effect into the nineteenth and twentieth centuries. Although industrialization and the accompanying increased mobility and urbanization brought Catholics, Protestants, and Jews closer together geographically, the existence of denominational enclaves continued to shape German history and still has an effect on the social environment of Germans today. The fault lines of religious conflicts have shaped not only Germans' worldviews, culture, and education but also their sense of social justice, sociability, economy, politics, and – with increasing impact – their attitude toward nationhood.

Whereas the Catholic Church in Germany has oriented itself more and more toward Rome since the mid-nineteenth century, German Protestants understood nationhood as an effective instrument of integration and at the same time one of demarcation vis-à-vis the ultramontane Catholics with a transnational perspective. In this way, the formation of the nation was tied together with the religious roots of Protestantism: the German nation was absorbed into the tradition of Protestantism and vice versa. As a consequence, the basically secular idea of nationhood took on, to a considerable extent, clerical – in this instance, specifically Protestant – characteristics. To be sure, the adaptation, reinterpretation, and appropriation of religious rituals and systems of meaning for nationalistic purposes or for the purpose of promoting nationhood are not specifically German phenomena. The "inventors of the nation" also drew successfully from other religious codes and symbols to establish new forms of community. The dictum of being chosen, which at present is often seen as primarily an American interpretation of the Old Testament, was at least until the end of World War I a general phenomenon of Western nationalism.

One important point of similarity in the political cultures of Germany and the United States in the nineteenth century was widespread anti-Catholicism. In the United States, this phenomenon provoked serious riots and even produced its own political party, the Know-Nothing Party. Whereas the ostracism of Catholics in the German Empire took place under state auspices, in the United States, Catholics were segregated socially largely as a result of migration patterns. Catholicism was the dominant faith among the late-nineteenth-century immigrants to the United States, who settled initially for the most part in urban areas and who determinedly maintained their ethnic and linguistic heritage. For this reason, they were perceived in many ways as the embodiment of "the stranger." Early anti-Catholicism among Americans was focused – as it was in the German Empire – on the ultramontane or "papist" orientation of the Catholic Church, but in the wake of the mass immigration of Catholics, the focus shifted in a more ethnocentric direction. American anti-Catholicism was embedded in a general nativism that expressed itself in a defensive attitude toward new immigrants and toward any non-Anglo–Saxon cultural influences. It reflected the resentments of people who were overwhelmed by the growing diversity and mobility of American society. The fact that American anti-Catholicism did not result – as was the case in Germany – in the formation of a separate space for Catholics is connected to the phenomenon of nativism as well as to the unofficial, unsanctioned character of American anti-Catholicism and the establishment of primarily ethnically based neighborhoods and districts. A "Catholic settlement" on strictly confessional lines that brought together believers of all national backgrounds – for example, Irish, Poles, and Italians – would have been unthinkable in the United States.

It was different in Germany, where the distance separating Catholics from the rest of the society was also perceived as a demarcation line between the state and a specific social milieu. In the *Kulturkampf* of the 1870s, the (Protestant) Prussian-German state subjected Catholic institutions and Catholics in positions of authority to repressive measures and curtailed their civil rights. This process stemmed from a particularly drastic set of circumstances. The process of nation-building in Germany unfolded not only by taking advantage of external "enemies" but also by identifying internal ones as well, and these enemies of the nation were defined not just by social and political criteria but also according to their religious and confessional affiliation. Germany's development diverged markedly from that of many other Western states in this respect. At least until the end of World War I, the term *evangelisch* (evangelical, or also Protestant, in German) was synonymous with *deutsch* (German), whereas *katholisch* (Catholic) and *jüdisch* (Jewish) were interpreted as designations for an un-German attitude or an unreliable kind of patriotism.

The way German Jews and Catholics reacted to this form of discrimination was very dissimilar. Whereas German Jews, who made up at this time about 1 percent of the population, attempted to modernize and denationalize their religion, the Catholic strategy for self-assertion tended toward traditionalism and compartmentalization. German Catholicism, branded as regressive, antiliberal, and antinational, managed to become tremendously cohesive by taking advantage – in a thoroughly modern way – of stabilizing institutions like associations, schools, and the press. This milieu also helped German Catholics to defuse the potential for conflict in their everyday lives generated by the broad process of modernization that was changing the whole country. Without a doubt, there were also Catholic liberals in Germany at this time and a cosmopolitan, educated Catholic middle class; however, the Catholic middle class remained a minority. Nonetheless, education and the belief in the promise of science played a much larger role in the self-definition of German Protestants and Jews, especially those in the middle class. Both religious groups adopted a positive attitude toward the social and technological modernization of society and its political liberalization as well.

Catholics of the Imperial era were perceived and categorized by other groups in German society, particularly by other confessional groups, as bound to tradition, emotional, lazy, subservient to Rome, and hostile to education. In fact, leading Catholic thinkers frequently deprecated "education" as a dangerous, objectionable innovation and in turn branded Protestants as rationalistic, godless, subservient to the state, and immoral. One significant consequence of this acrimony was that the number of Catholic children enrolled at institutions of secondary education long remained much lower than the corresponding numbers of Protestants and Jews.

The Catholic communities in Germany offered members of various social classes the opportunity to join together across class lines as a type of moral citadel against the liberal, Protestant-oriented nation. In this effort, Catholics at times made use of very modern social instruments, such as the participation of women or the political mobilization of broad strata of the society: for instance, through the formation in 1870 of the Catholic Center Party, which was originally conceived as a force of opposition to the process of state and societal modernization. In choosing not to follow the conservative–liberal tradition of electing only prominent citizens or of confining itself to a single social class, as was the practice of the Social Democratic Party, the Catholic Center Party distinguished itself from the other German political parties. In fact, it was one of the first people's parties, one, to be sure, that because of its exclusive focus on Catholic voters had a kind of built-in natural limit of expansion that accounted for approximately 30 percent of the voting public.

A typical feature of this phase of German social development was the politicization of religion by creating specific sectarian spaces with their own social and moral boundaries, which lasted well into the twentieth century. Roughly stated, Catholic voters preferred the Center Party or the Bavarian People's Party founded in 1918, which was the precursor party of today's Christian Social Union (CSU). Liberal and left-leaning liberal parties recruited their core voters primarily from the sphere of cultural Protantism, whose progressive, middle-class ideology also appealed to many Jews. The Social Democrats, in contrast, developed their own, above all nonreligious platform and concepts; almost 90 percent of its voters were secular Protestants who had distanced themselves from the church. These voting patterns survived into the early years of the Federal Republic. They were, however, altered somewhat by the fact that both of the newly founded Christian parties, the Christian Democratic Union (CDU) and the CSU, no longer defined themselves as Catholic but rather as nondenominational people's parties.

There is no counterpart to party identification along sectarian lines in American history because most conflicts have been regional or more broadly cultural. The Civil War was by far the most important conflict, generating far-reaching repercussions. It was understood, especially by white Southerners, as a struggle for a "way of life." In the South, a divergent form of religiosity had firmly established itself among the white population before the war. It found expression above all in enthusiasm, personal conversion experiences, and demonstrative piety. Thus, it was not by accident that Baptists, along with Methodism, developed into one of the most successful denominations in the region. The question of slavery in the South had already produced religious dissent, and the Southern Baptists and

Methodists had distanced themselves or even split from their respective churches in the North. In the South, both these denominations were originally more open to the participation of blacks in their church services than were the Episcopalians or the Presbyterians. However, because such participation was extremely attractive to black Americans, it was precisely this issue around which resistance to abolitionism began to coalesce in the white congregations of the South. The secession of the Southern Baptists created a completely independent denominational movement, which maintains itself still today as a distinct entity, at a considerable distance from the liberal world of the American Baptists and from the culture of the black Baptists.

Through the trauma of defeat in the Civil War, the unique religious path of the South was burdened with additional resentment. The changes forced on the South created animosity directed at a variety of perceived adversaries: at the institutions of the Union, at the culture of the Northern elites, at industrialization and urbanization, at Jews and Catholics, and, of course, again and again at blacks. In those areas where these resentments were joined by negative experiences of modernization, as was particularly the case during the Progressive era (roughly 1880 to 1914), they generated fertile ground for religious revivals. The same was true for the new territories and states that were being incorporated as the country expanded westward. These areas developed above all into spheres of experimentation and retreat for newly established religions and sects. Nowadays, the Mountain States and parts of the Pacific West are a stronghold of conservative Christianity that rivals the traditional "Bible Belt" of the South.

A decisive influence on the political and religious climate in the West and South was the image of the simple self-made man, who defends his family and attains economic prosperity with his own strength and adhering to God's commandments. The frontier experience was the incubator for the populism that flourished at the end of the nineteenth century. Populism was a protest movement against anonymous large institutions, banks, and bureaucracies, as well as against the national political establishment. Although many populists had originally profited from the winning of the West, they often felt overwhelmed by the economic transformation that took root around them. For this reason, populism frequently aligned itself with the innocent piety of believers in opposition to the liberal theology and cult of scientific progress espoused by the establishment. William Jennings Bryan, a three-time unsuccessful presidential candidate, demonstrated this appeal as late as 1925, when as a lawyer he attacked Darwin's theory of evolution in the famous Scopes trial. In his view, this teaching was a manifestation of technological arrogance over divine creation.

Traditionalism and agrarian populism were typical forms of protest among those whites who felt they had been left behind in the general process of modernization taking hold throughout the country, but particularly in the South and West. In their religious tendencies, however, they often appeared similar in manner to another group of discontents – namely, the black Americans who, still remembering the nightmare of slavery, were further uprooted and traumatized through agrarian crises, racial violence, and migration to the North. These disadvantaged segments of society provided fertile ground for the emergence of experimental, small-sized congregations as well as for occultism and syncretism.

Pentecostal forms of Christian fundamentalism and belief in the biblical Apocalypse found widespread resonance among both white and black congregations at the turn of the century. The quest for spiritual security, identity, and religious fervor formed the common denominator of these movements, which were also characterized by the renunciation of the rational world of economic discipline. By the same token, these religious movements – similar to the Catholic environment in Germany at the time – cannot be interpreted simply as antimodernist. Using expressive, emotional forms of exhortation, unconventional rituals, the integration of women into their services, and the application of the mass media, these movements developed unique religious practices that did not spread to older, more established congregations until much later.

In Germany, in marked contrast to the United States, religiously expressed opposition to modernization was institutionalized in a rigid organizational structure and ultimately became a considerable obstacle to democracy. In 1918, national Protestantism lost its centuries-old position of being the main religion in Germany identified with the state and was suddenly confronted with two opponents: the aforementioned ultramontane Catholicism and the "godless" labor movement. Although some Protestants became strong pillars of support for democracy and for the process of political and social modernization taking place in Germany, the more conservative, national Protestant congregations developed a posture of opposition to the Weimar Republic and at the same time demonstrated a pronounced receptivity to National Socialism. Among the Catholics, there was a greater potential for resistance to the Nazi ideology. This potential was based less in a fundamental immunity to the racist and anti-Semitic elements of this ideology or in any particular affinity to democracy. Rather, it was above all a response to the anti-Catholic aspects of National Socialist agitation; it also represented the attempt of the Catholics to defend the traditional religious institutions of the church against external attacks.

Nevertheless, Nazism, with its ideology of the "*Volk* community," began to penetrate the boundaries of organized religion in Germany during the years of Hitler's rule. Its most effective weapon in this regard was the ideology of racism, which took hold of ever wider circles of the population and led eventually to the annihilation of European Jewry. This ideology was accompanied by periodic efforts by the Nazi state to de-Christianize German society. These efforts included limiting religious instruction in public schools and then the complete abolition of confessional schools in 1941.

The reaction of the German churches to National Socialism, which offered a widely appealing alternative to Christian rituals, remained ambivalent. The 1933 Concordat between the Vatican and Nazi Germany conveyed to Catholics the feeling of having attained a legal safeguard for their religious activities; conversely, for the Nazi regime, it legitimized the antisocialist stance that it shared with the Catholic Church. Only later when the regime began to attack Catholic institutions did a tentative resistance emerge, which called into question the integration of the Catholic faithful into the Nazi cause; however, it never developed into a broad-based, effective resistance.

Protestantism during the Nazi era was also characterized by conflicting tendencies. Here, the spectrum of response ranged from the "German Christians," whose orientation was clearly in favor of National Socialism, to the "Confessing Church," which in several aspects was critical of the new regime and never accepted the "synchronization" (*Gleichschaltung*) policies by which the Nazis attempted to gain totalitarian control over the individual and then the whole society. Both churches succeeded partially in providing a niche of religious observance to those of conscience, and both also generated some individual resistance. As institutions, however, they failed almost completely in many areas. This is true, for instance, with regard to the protection and rescue of European Jews.

The decisive rupture that precipitated the disintegration of Germany's religious topography was not, however, National Socialism itself but rather its downfall and the end of World War II. In the eastern part of the country, the new socialist state raised atheism to the level of an official doctrine, whereas in the west, the victorious powers decided temporarily to entrust the representatives of the German churches with important tasks and political authority and at the same time to reinstate the churches as viable moral institutions. In June 1945, the CDU was founded. The new party defined itself explicitly as nondenominational; however, for quite some time, it was Catholics who set its tone. The party was anchored not only in the Catholic Church's claim to moral leadership but also in recent demographic changes: with the loss of the eastern zones of Soviet occupation, which were for the most part Protestant, and with the influx of Catholic refugees after the war, roughly one-half of the population in the western zones of occupation was now Catholic. With these developments, German Catholicism outgrew its earlier status of a minority religion. This change in status was reflected not insignificantly in the Basic Law of 1949 and in legislation enacted during the early years of the Federal Republic in which the influence of Christian, in particular Catholic, ideas was clearly visible. The inclusion of the word "God" in the preamble and many of the articles of the Basic Law reflected well the orientation of Catholic social teachings, as did the declaration of the fundamental right of marriage and family and the protection of religious education in public schools. Even so, the German bishops were disappointed in the Basic Law because it renounced the 1933 Concordat with the Vatican and only partly adopted the Catholic position on the rights of parents in raising children. Nevertheless, the new political order had the support not only of the trade unions but also of most churches.

A far-reaching re-Christianization of West Germany, as one might have expected, did not take place. With the gradual extension of the welfare state, the growing social and geographic mobility of the population, the various emancipation movements of the 1960s, and the influence of the Second Vatican Council, the Catholic subculture in Germany started to erode more and more, such that at a certain point one could speak of an internal pluralization of the Federal Republic.

In North America, "mainline" Protestantism was one of the most important forces of cultural development. It included the Episcopalians, Congregationalists, northern Methodists and Baptists, Reformists, and, to a lesser extent, the Lutherans. From the nineteenth century on, adherents of these denominations occupied more or less exclusively the preferred positions of power among political, economic, and cultural elites. Since the Civil War, the great majority of U.S.

presidents have been Protestant, as have been the majority of senior government officials. This is not at all surprising when one considers that many of the elite East Coast universities were shaped by tenets of liberal, moderate Protestantism. In contrast to its German counterpart, however, this dominant Protestant culture made only sparing use of its informal sources of power. One reason for this was the fragmentation of this culture among so many different churches, and another was the success of the "Social Gospel" as a reform movement driven by both Christian and ethical impulses. Many churches were engaged in the construction of cultural and welfare networks and coupled this engagement of behalf of the disadvantaged with criticism of political corruption and the moral degradation characterizing the large cities. In so doing, they offered not only material assistance but also an interpretation of deprivation as something primarily ethical and spiritual in nature. The most visible expression of this religious mission was the intensified anti-alcohol campaign carried out by mainline Protestants that culminated in the Eighteenth Amendment to the U.S. Constitution and the beginning of Prohibition in 1919. Despite massive support from the women's movements and from evangelicals, Prohibition had little success and was repealed in 1933. Its repeal marked a temporary cessation of serious attempts to use the repressive power of the state to enforce laws on the nation driven by the social ideals of mainline Protestantism, which espoused moderation, self-control, and familial responsibility.

Even after the defeat of Prohibition, social welfare still remained a major concern of the mainline churches; however, it lost its religious complexion. It was promoted increasingly by lay professionals who were largely indifferent to the character of the sponsoring organization, whether it was Jewish, Catholic, secular, or state. This professionalization of social activitism and community work tended to strip away the denominational distinctions and also transformed their formerly religious core. A growing segment of the clergy was now being educated in secular colleges and universities attended by the rest of the population, which had two effects. It acquainted future members of the clergy with members of other denominations, opening up the possibility of ecumenical contacts. However, it also increased the distance between the clergy and laypeople in their demoninations and, by so doing, impeded the development of an elite religious subculture.

Significant differences developed not only among the denominations within mainline Protestantism but also between this large grouping and more fundamentalist groups over the course of the twentieth century. Evangelical Christians, for instance, had supported Prohibition during the 1920s but not the social and political activities of the Social Gospel movement. Their theology, which was based primarily on personal salvation through Jesus, was not in synch with this movement, nor was the predominantly rural location of their adherents. In selecting their clergy, most evangelical congregations did not follow the academic path but rather hired leaders who had the "Spirit" and who had often been educated at parochial institutions. For this reason, their clergy often had little or no understanding of the scientific and technological worldview of the universities and other institutions of higher education. This lack of understanding in turn drove the evangelicals toward social separatism, as illustrated by the efforts of fundamentalist Christians to ban the teaching and open discussion of Darwin's theory of evolution in public schools. Many believed it was more important to cultivate a sense of belonging and a common search for salvation than to have social or political engagement for its own sake.

World War II and the Cold War provoked two diametrically opposed reactions in the religious sphere. In the liberal wing of the Protestant denominations – and, after John F. Kennedy's election in 1960, increasingly among liberal Catholics as well – engagement with the international scene accelerated; involvement with the Third World through Peace Corps activities and international ecumenism were part of this development. In contrast, conservative Protestants mostly confined themselves to the lives of their own congregations; however, because they were critical of "modernism" and permissiveness in society at large, they became part of the Cold War consensus.

Black Christians experienced the shameful contrast between the lofty ideals that the U.S. government espoused internationally and the racism that existed in their own country. The international media raised public awareness of the divergent worldviews of the various religious subcultures involved in the conflict between defenders of segregation and the activists of the civil rights movement. That movement also had an impact in Europe, where it generated a similarly progressive, grassroots democratic movement that was also internationally oriented. Christian values and commitments shaped and fostered this movement to a considerable degree, as the history of church congresses clearly documents. In this environment, denominational adherence rapidly lost its political significance. As early as the 1930s, the New Deal coalition of Franklin D. Roosevelt demonstrated that it was possible to marshal the support of very different religious groups, ranging from the Southern evangelists to black congregations, from Jews to Catholics.

The religious development of the United States up until the Eisenhower years can be summarized as follows. From early in the nation's history, there was a parallel development of denominational subcultures, some of which, such as the Catholics and the Jews, moved from positions in the social and cultural margins to the center of American society. The dominant religious–political faction made little use of its power. The geographical distance between different subcultures and denominational groupings continued to alleviate social conflicts; the passivity and self-isolation of evangelical and other more traditional Christians represented the extremes of this tendency. Nevertheless, a diverse and vital religious landscape continued to be a central element of American society and everyday culture.

RELIGION, SOCIETY, SOCIAL ISSUES, AND NEW CONFLICTS

The challenges of modernity – the disruptive consequences of industrialization and urbanization – were similar for both Germany and the United States; however, the strategies for coming to terms with these problems were very different on each side of the Atlantic. The three important differences between the American and German religious pathways into the modern era were the depth of denominational ruptures, the variety of religious offerings, and the degree of separation between church and state.

In Germany, in contrast to the United States, a successful socialist labor movement emerged in the nineteenth century; by roughly 1900, it had developed into a mass movement. To the lower classes in the industrialized regions, it offered alternative rituals and systems of meaning that went beyond religion, and often it operated in a decidedly anticlerical fashion. Socialist tendencies in the United States after 1900 were not expressed in a similar movement because of the weakness of American pressures for secularization.

In the United States, the "class question" was often considered within the context of ethnic or religious identities. In the very fluid American society, it was principally the religious congregations that offered security, shelter, models of identification, and social welfare services. Thus, the groups that had been disadvantaged by the process of industrialization frequently articulated their social concerns within the sphere occupied by religion and the church.

To be sure, the Catholic Church in Germany did fulfill some of these social and economic functions. It attracted a considerable portion of the lower classes and supported them through social institutions and organizations, such as the journeyman associations initiated by Adolf Kolping (1846–50), the Caritas welfare organization (1897), the People's Association for Catholic Germany (1890), and the Christian Unions (1899). However, the majority of German workers were Protestants, and it was not until relatively late that the Protestant Churches recognized the ever-present social problems as issues to be addressed by their own efforts. Many of the Protestant initiatives that were effective in the long term, such as the Inner Mission or the Bethel Institutions founded by Friedrich von Bodelschwingh (1831–1910), rested on concepts of Christian benevolence and patriarchal welfare that predated the social and emancipatory movements of nineteenth-century Germany and were essentially counter-undertakings to modern industrial society. They answered the needs of the modern worker only at a very rudimentary level. The same was true of cultural Protestantism, which did in fact combine both liberal and Christian values, but attracted followers primarily from the lower middle classes. Nevertheless, cultural Protestantism and Pietism were two important bases of religious socialism, which addressed social issues through a comprehensive appeal to all religious confessions in Germany. Karl Barth (1886–1968) and Paul Tillich (1886–1965), who after his emigration to the United States enjoyed considerable popularity back in Germany, were both prominent theological representatives of this movement.

The official Protestant Church remained largely uninvolved with the expansion of the working class and the advance of urbanization in Germany. It showed little or no understanding of the economic problems faced by members of the urban lower classes; this situation was exacerbated by the fact that there was a shortage of pastors in the working-class districts. Furthermore, the labor movement fulfilled the workers' need to make sense of their lives and to build communities often more effectively than the churches did. The remnants of Bismarck's strategy of weakening the Social Democratic Party and labor movement by introducing social welfare legislation favorable to workers and thereby establishing the beginnings of the modern social welfare state also further curtailed the church's realm of responsibility.

The social upheavals during World War II and the postwar period and the search for new values and political orientation appeared to enhance the prospects of Christian socialism in the 1940s and 1950s. This was clearly noticeable in the CDU's Ahlener Program, developed in 1947, which was based on Catholic social doctrine and backed by prominent figures like Oswald Nell-Breuning, S.J. The program proposed a mildly anticapitalist vision for the new (West) Germany. This vision, however, soon faded from sight, as the CDU committed itself more and more to the promise of economic liberalism. The Catholic component of the program was secondary, although it was reflected in the party's goal of a family-friendly social policy and in the preferred status of the confessional welfare associations. Left-wing Protestants had limited political importance in the early Federal Republic; their primary focus was on the politics of the peace movement.

Whereas social issues in modern-era Germany were addressed predominantly by organized labor and by the state, Americans had to rely for the most part on individual resources. In addition, family networks in the United States were less intact and effective than in Germany, where society was less mobile and social relationships more stable. Thus, only the religious groups in many instances could offer Americans support. Religious activity and congregations had always been a fixture of American life, and the chance to meet a kindred spirit within a religious group existed in almost every community.

The basic tendency of religious development in the United States remained associative, not institutional. Characteristic in this regard were new religious amalgamations, secessionist movements, switching denominations, and even religious entrepreneurship, including some forms that had emigrated from Germany. Many sects emerged that encompassed not only the full spectrum of apocalyptic movements but also black churches, Anglican traditionalists, and offshoots of Mormonism, Unitarianism, and Christian Science.

Many of the new religious associations fulfilled functions similar to those of the labor movement in Germany. They offered points of orientation, solidarity, and assistance to many who were overwhelmed by the fast-paced, unpredictable nature of modern American society. They also offered opportunities to participate, which — similar to the Catholic Center Party and the Social Democratic Party in Germany — fostered the exercise of democratic practices and modern methods of communication. Innovative techniques and means of communicating were often tested first in a religious context before they found use in the field of politics; for example, the interweaving of messages of salvation, tele-fundraising, and entertainment as part of large events. The Pentecostal preacher Aimee Semple McPherson, for example, was among the very first in the 1920s to use the radio, mass publications, and popular music to spread her religious message. Today, the performances of many American preachers of modern mega-churches, some of which have their own TV stations, seem like a combination of a mass political event and a management training seminar.

In Germany, the question remains as to whether the continuing loss of importance of the German labor movement will have religious implications. Furthermore, the relevance of the state's program for the "nationalization of culture," which attempts to convey a secular canon of knowledge through the public schools, is under scrutiny. Here, once again, we encounter a paradoxical phenomenon. On the one hand, the subject of religion continues to be a secure fixture in the public-school curriculum in most German states. The crucifix, especially in southern Germany, is still part of the standard set of classroom furnishings. In addition, discussions have begun on making Islamic religious instruction available in public schools in addition to Catholic and Protestant instruction. The overall role played in the German educational system by parochial or other private schools nonetheless remains relatively limited.

In the United States, in contrast, manifestations of religion were always an integral part of community life, and in the public schools they took the form of mandatory school prayer, which was eliminated by a Supreme Court decision as late as the 1960s. This state of affairs seems to be changing: the reinstatement of creationism in the curricula of some public schools and the rising interest in home schooling demonstrate that the dominance of the state and of secular forces in public education is being challenged and that the religious diversity of American society can no longer be universally equated with a peaceful coexistence of very different confessional persuasions. One of the reasons for this development can be found in the noticeable decline in membership over the past few decades in mainline Protestantism, in contrast to the rapid growth of Pentecostal and evangelical congregations. In direct competition with passionate, emotional forms of worship that seem to offer answers in an increasingly more complex, unsettling, and disorienting world, the more cerebral and established denominations of mainline Protestantism are losing their attractiveness. Furthermore, the geographic demarcation of the different denominations has begun to vanish. In today's American suburbs, evangelical Christians live in the same neighborhoods as Jews, Catholics, and nonbelievers. Cultural differences and antagonisms reveal themselves more easily and can erupt into localized conflicts. Increasingly, these conflicts have been expanding and taking on national significance, such as the cases involving school texts and curricula. Since the end of the 1970s, the emergence of the large bloc of evangelical and fundamentalist Christians from political passivity has been driving this development.

During the civil rights movement of the 1950s and 1960s, the traditional alliance between Southerners and the Democratic Party began to break up, and the protest and freedom movements that followed drove conservative Christians more toward political action. A crucial phase in this process of politicization was marked by the 1973 U.S. Supreme Court decision legalizing abortion, *Roe v. Wade*, and by the passionate debates surrounding the issue of rights for homosexuals. Both events contributed to the emergence of a new kind of ecumenism. Opposition to one or both of these two issues has united conservatives and others within almost all Christian denominations and has appealed to non-Christians (e.g., some Muslims and Jews) as well. Leading this opposition, however, are the evangelical and Pentecostal Christians, who have in their arsenal highly efficient methods for distributing their message via the most modern means of communication. Their efforts to mobilize their followers extend into the sphere of leisure activities, such that their adherents need hardly ever leave the bosom of their church and the company of their fellow believers. Mega-churches offer fitness and child care centers, dating clubs, and religious travel tours; they sponsor print media, Internet presentations, and radio and TV shows.

No longer are members of enthusiastic fundamentalist congregations primarily from marginal social groups or backward rural communities. Evangelically oriented universities and colleges are successful in attracting a broad cross-section of the student population, and leading positions in government, business, and the military are now frequently occupied by adherents to fundamentalist strains of Christianity. When the earnestly religious continue to demand that basic elements of Christian doctrine be incorporated into public-school curricula and into judicial decision making, these demands no longer fall on completely deaf ears. Media and science, areas that until now have been considered immune to this kind of religious influence, have come under attack with increasing frequency by evangelical politicians, who characterize the worldview of the natural sciences and "secular humanism" as just one possible view among others.

The continued peaceful coexistence of different denominations within the religious landscape of the United States is no longer assured, marking in some ways a return to the nineteenth and early twentieth centuries. Some understand the impact of conservative Christian groups, who see their particular moral orientation as the only "American way of life," as simply a function of their concentration in certain regions of the country, their specific political affiliations, and their focus on a few issues. Yet, surveys find that the majority of Americans define themselves as religious and also expect a certain degree of religiosity from their politicians; however, at the same time, most still object to any overt introduction of religious content into the political sphere. Religion is and remains for most American citizens a private matter – one, to be sure, that like others is also subject to the laws of a specific marketplace.

RELIGION AND THE MARKETPLACE

In Germany, everyone was, and still is for the most part, born as a Catholic or a Protestant, less frequently as a Jew or a Muslim, and increasingly as a nonreligious person. Unless one explicitly renounces one's religious affiliation, one also dies as such. Despite increasing urbanization and mobility, the rate of interconfessional marriages has historically been low: less than 10 percent during the German Empire and only 5 percent higher during the Weimar Republic. It was not until after the founding of the Federal Republic that a different kind of attitude toward marriage slowly began to evolve. Around 1950, roughly one-fourth of all Germans entering into marriage chose a partner from a different denomination or, very infrequently, from another religion. This increase in intermarriage, however, hardly affects at all the fact that in Germany religion or denominational affiliation is treated as a kind of birthright. Each German honors and preserves this connection for the most part, even when the degree of his or her own personal religious commitment approaches zero. Many Germans today still balk at the thought of converting to another denomination, for example, through marriage, or at renouncing their church membership altogether. This behavior also stems from the fact that church membership alone ensures each congregant the right to claim Christian rites at life's critical junctures, such as birth, marriage, and death. Only in East Germany, where until 1933 the population was predominantly Protestant and there was a strong labor movement, did this tradition of religious loyalty begin to fade. After 1945, its further deterioration was strongly fostered by the political authorities, and by the end of the 1950s, many East Germans were officially leaving their churches. This was, however, very much a decision against religion as a whole – one that would have a significant impact on later generations – and not in favor of another religious or confessional affiliation.

In contrast to this tradition, religious engagement in the United States can be traced back primarily to a voluntary and individual decision. Many Americans view themselves as spiritual seekers open to new religious loyalties, frequently several times over the course of their lifetime, and thus discover themselves anew any number of times. Their voluntary action and their conscious choice of specific religious alternatives tend to generate a readiness to participate actively in their religious life, a readiness that congregations also count on. In Germany, the so-called church tax is deducted automatically by the state as part of the overall federal and state income taxes; thus, it is not connected to any conscious act of the individual tax-paying church member. The state in turn also supports church institutions through organizational and financial means. In the United States, religious communities survive exclusively through the activity and financial engagement of their members. Moreover, this longstanding state of affairs strengthens the tradition of understanding one's religion as a form of services rendered and of accepting at the same time a degree of competition in terms of which religion markets itself most effectively, makes the best use of modern media, and in general best satisfies the needs of its "customers." Worship services broadcast over TV, charismatic pastors, and mass events in sports stadiums have characterized the religious landscape in the United States over the past half-century. In this respect, the rise of fundamentalist traditional Christianity seems paradoxical because, on the one hand, it fosters the formation of a rather rigid religious community. Through the use of its own media outlets, leisure activities, and educational institutions, it facilitates an insular lifestyle, separated for the most part from the secular "mainstream culture." On the other hand, this same fundamentalist community skillfully takes advantage of the modes of presentation and market strategies that are so ingrained in the modern culture of consumption.

It is precisely in this context that the most obvious symptoms of an anti-liturgical attitude toward religion become evident. Many Americans value above all the life-enriching spiritual rewards of their faith and the intensive communal experience they encounter in charismatic worship services. They are less interested in the identity of organized churches that distinguish themselves from others through their specific liturgy and theology. In place of a commitment to a firmly established religion, many Americans have opted for a general, loosely defined, traditional Christian sensibility constructed from their own subjective spirituality and the experiences nourishing that spirituality. New forms of piety and active religious engagement have taken shape in recent decades in Germany as well, partly as a response to the rapidly shrinking number of traditional churchgoers. Since the 1970s, rock concerts in houses of worship, lively church congresses, and engagement in the peace movement have demonstrated not only the potential for religious reform and modernization in Germany but also the role that churches played in the waning years of the GDR as a center for communication and political opposition and as a foundation for the establishment of a democratic political culture. The spread of religious sects and the "New Age" movement of the 1980s are also part of this same phenomenon. Other American developments, such as the aforementioned forms of religious entertainment and religious marketing, have, however, at least until now, not found much resonance in Germany.

Given some of the features that generally define a modern society, such as the significance of the marketplace, flexible membership associations, individualization, and also participation, the American religious landscape seems to correspond to these criteria much more than its counterpart in Germany. This correspondence is strengthened when mobility is also considered a factor. For example, the American dream is based on the myth, successfully renewed again and again, that social mobility is possible, and anyone, even the poor immigrant, can work his or her way up to the higher echelons of society. More traditional religious communities do continue to exist, but they are less widespread and have a higher degree of internal fluctuation than corresponding communities in Germany. There is still space and opportunity in the United States for small, especially pious communities, like the Amish or the Hasidic Jews, to live and maintain themselves as separate enclaves.

The loss of vitality and sense of community caused by internal migration and immigration in the United States and the accompanying insecurities and social instability experienced by the nation as a whole have been cushioned only slightly by state intervention. Much more attractive for many Americans have been the communal solidarity and security promised by grassroots organizations, and in this regard, religious groups have played an especially prominent role. As noted previously, they have made and continue to make inroads practically everywhere, even in the most remote towns. Wherever they have not yet penetrated, there have been radio and later TV preachers ready to fill the void since the 1920s.

The need for community also arose in Germany, even though it experienced markedly lower rates of migration and immigration than in the United States during the twentieth century. This need was met either by the organized labor movement, by a network of civic associations, or by a religiously based Diaspora community and the organization representing that community. It was not met by individual religious communities competing among themselves. Furthermore, the German welfare state, which was created during the German Empire under Bismarck and was fostered to a considerable degree by the Federal Republic after 1949, tended to prevent the formation of new kinds of religious communities along the lines of the American model. The state increasingly ameliorated areas of social need, leaving for the churches' attention only such niches that had been neglected by the state; for example, the care of disabled persons and, since the late 1950s, the new group of labor migrants known as "guest workers" (*Gastarbeiter*). To what extent the current forced restructuring of the welfare state, which points toward a downsizing of state responsibility and benefits, can provide a new sphere of activity for religious congregations promises to be an interesting question for the future.

In the United States, religion has continued to have a more significant effect on social integration. During the course of internal migrations, immigrant communities were frequently characterized by religious "founding fever" and by various types of new loyalties. The migration of black Americans from the South into the northern industrial cities during the first half of the twentieth century produced numerous cultural and religious innovations; for example, the Black Muslim movement. The westward migration from the Great Plains during roughly the same period, most notably during the Dust Bowl of the 1930s, of agrarian elements of the population favored the formation of a similarly fertile religious fundament in California among whites. Parallel to these movements, the establishment of secular communities took place primarily on the two coasts in university towns and centers of the service industries. These communities were populated by highly qualified professionals and academics from both inside and outside the United States. This pattern of migration was not, however, repeated in the more recent internal migration, in which from 1960 on many Americans have moved from the old industrial centers of the Rust Belt to the new growth centers in the Sunbelt. In this more recent migration, the tendency has instead been that many of the newly arrived middle-class residents have adapted to the conservative climate of their new home base, which has had an impact not only on their political but also their religious preferences. The congregations of Southern Baptists and Pentecostals have been growing in part through the conversions of former residents of the northern states.

This same tendency toward adaptation may well have contributed to the fact that the United States today is defined by distinct, strongly contrasting regions of different political and cultural influence. Along the coasts and the northern border to Canada, we find the "blue states" with generally a more liberal and secular orientation, whereas the other states, the conservatively oriented "red states," are perceived broadly as bastions of strong religious engagement and as electoral strongholds of the Republican Party. This rough geographic grid does not, however, reflect fully the current social and political makeup of the country. For instance, it does not take into consideration that people with opposing worldviews do in fact engage with each other in their neighborhoods, especially in the suburbs of the large cities. Even conservatively religious communities must adjust to more dissent – coming from outside but also from within. In addition, the tendency toward religious "shopping," trying out new forms of worship and being willing to change loyalties, is growing within nearly all denominations. The increased immigration from non-Christian countries of origin and the resultant significant renewal of religious diversity in the United States have strengthened this trend.

Thus, the differences between the German and American paths of religious development are striking, yet there are also recognizable points of convergence. For instance, the importance of a worldly, educated Protestantism as the core of an elite culture has declined noticeably on both sides of the Atlantic. In both countries, the consequences of urbanization, democratization, and mass consumption spurred new spiritual needs and yet posed challenges for religion.

Clearly, the history of modernization in both of these countries was more than merely a history of the decline of religion and the religious. Anyone who takes an interest in religion cannot apply uncritically to either Germany or the United States the widely used dichotomies of traditional versus modern, irrational versus rational. Nevertheless, religion and the modern era were never so deeply, intrinsically connected in Germany as was and quite obviously still is the case in the United States. Particularly in the case of the United States, we see that the thesis of secularization does not provide any universal explanations for the development of Western societies. In the last two centuries, striking cultural developments have occurred in the sphere of religion that have allowed us to understand religion as an effective bulwark against the challenges of the modern era. In this respect, religion and religious behavior have remained a constant and perhaps indispensable accompaniment to the process of transformation that has been taking place since the Enlightenment and the Industrial Revolution. During this period, the binding character of religious values, the bonding force of religious institutions, and the forms of religious practice have changed repeatedly and at times quite significantly. These factors themselves were part of the transformations described earlier and, in this regard, despite certain similarities and many examples of one country's development influencing the other's, we see reflected in the sphere of religion two very distinct and different paths into the modern era.

Further Reading

Bergen, Doris. *Twisted Cross: The German Christian Movement in the Third Reich, 1933–1990* (Chapel Hill, 1996).

Clark, Christopher, and Wolfram Kaiser. *Culture Wars: Secular–Catholic Conflict in Nineteenth-Century Europe* (Cambridge, 2003).

Ericksen, Robert P., and Susannah Heschel, eds. *German Churches and the Holocaust* (Minneapolis, 1999).

Gross, Michael B. *The War against Catholicism: Liberalism and the Anti-Catholic Imagination in Nineteenth-Century Germany* (Ann Arbor, 2004).

Heschel, Susannah. *The Aryan Jesus: Christian Theologians and the Bible in Nazi Germany* (Princeton, 2008).

Hockenos, Matthew D. *A Church Divided: German Protestants Confront the Nazi Past* (Bloomington, 2004).

McLeod, Hugh, and Werner Ustorf, eds. *The Decline of Christendom in Western Europe, 1750–2000* (Cambridge, 2004).

Meyer, Michael A., et al. *German-Jewish History in Modern Times*, 4 vols. (New York, 1997).

Ruff, Mark Edward. *The Wayward Flock: Catholic Youth in Postwar West Germany, 1945–1965* (Chapel Hill, 2005).

Smith, Helmuth Walser, ed. *Protestant, Catholics, and Jews in Germany 1800–1914* (Oxford, 2001).

Sperber, Jonathan. *Popular Catholicism in Nineteenth-Century Germany* (Princeton, 1984).

Steigmann-Gall, Richard. *The Holy Reich: Nazi Conceptions of Christianity, 1919–1945* (Cambridge, 2003).

Steinhoff, Anthony D. "Religion and Modern Europe: New Perspectives and Prospects," *Neue Politische Literatur* 53 (2008): 225–67.

Ward, W. R. "Guilt and Innocence: The German Churches in the Twentieth Century," *Journal of Modern History* 68 (1996): 398–426.

4

Law: Constitutionalism and Culture

MANFRED BERG AND DIETER GOSEWINKEL

Some years ago in a public debate, the U.S. Supreme Court justice Antonin Scalia rejected indignantly the notion that international and foreign law could be of significance for the U.S. Constitution: "We don't have the same moral and legal framework as the rest of the world, and never have. If you told the framers of the Constitution that what we're after is to do something that will be just like Europe, they would have been appalled." In Scalia's words, we see mirrored the unvaryingly influential perception that America is not only different from the Old World but also morally superior to it. This notion of exceptionalism is particularly evident in the popular culture of constitutional law. The Federal Constitution of 1787 calls forth unparalleled civil and religious admiration, and the principle of original intent – the binding of the courts to the intentions of the Founding Fathers – is more widely accepted in the United States than anywhere else in the world.

Given the impressive continuity of American constitutional history – especially when compared to the German experience – this acceptance and admiration are quite understandable. For the past 220 years, the Constitution has provided the institutional framework for political life in America. During the same period, Germany experienced a series of governmental systems and revolutionary ruptures, including two dictatorships. In the United States, the primacy of constitutional law as the "supreme law of the land" (Article VI, Section 2) was a constant from the beginning, whereas in Germany the "supremacy of the constitution" did not really take hold until after the caesura of 1945, and then only in the Federal Republic of Germany. Until then, the state had been of central importance to public law in Germany – it was not by accident that it was termed *Staatsrecht*, state law – whereas American constitutionalism has its roots in the protection of individual freedom vis-à-vis the power of the state.

Consequently, when we consider the effect of constitutional law on economic development in these two countries, we see that in Germany state intervention into the economy was never particularly controversial, whereas in the United States the authority of the federal government in economic matters has been highly contentious since the early nineteenth century. American constitutional law, even up to the present day, has not developed any binding material aims of the state (*Staatsziele*), as they have been formulated in the Federal Republic's constitution, the Basic Law (*Grundgesetz*), with respect to human dignity, equality of the sexes, protection of marriage and the family, the principle of social responsibility, and the protection of basic civil rights (Articles 1, 3, 6, 20, and 20a). This synthesis in Germany of constitutional law, human rights, state authority, and social responsibility, which took shape after World War II, is frequently seen as the more modern legal framework. However, one can also argue that the main reason the U.S. Constitution has remained so adaptable is because it leaves the regulation and legislation of public life to the political process, for the most part.

A German–American comparison must also take into account that German constitutional developments after 1945 were greatly influenced by American ideas and policies during the postwar occupation. Even if it is inaccurate to speak of an Americanization of German constitutional law in that period, the legal foundations of the Basic Law and the establishment of a constitutional court with far-reaching authority reflect unmistakably American influences. Nonetheless, a number of characteristic features of the Basic Law, ranging from its historically conditioned openness to international law to its incorporation of the law of nations and its transference of sovereign rights to supranational institutions (Articles 24 and 25), have no counterparts in the U.S. Constitution, which continues to rely to a considerable extent on the notion of a democratically legitimated national sovereignty.

Their culturally and historically conditioned differences notwithstanding, the German and American constitutions still exhibit some important similarities, such as their emphasis on the rule of law, federalism, and the separation of powers. Moreover, like most modern states, both countries have developed sometimes self-contradictory "cultures of rights." On the one hand, citizens want to see their rights and freedoms protected from governmental arbitrariness and they complain about bureaucracy and red tape; yet, on the other hand, they have high expectations regarding the performance of their government and its judicial system, including the performance of the constitutional court.

A historical comparison should not serve the purpose of proving the superiority of either the German or the American model. Rather, it should illustrate how the two constitutional cultures have reacted to the challenges of the modern era. How do we see the economic and social changes and conflicts of each society, the growing demands for political influence and social participation, and the expansion of spheres of governmental control reflected in constitutional law? How were minorities integrated and basic human rights protected? How has constitutional law either helped mitigate or exacerbated social and political conflicts? Was constitutional law an active factor in the modernization of the society, or did it simply adjust after the fact to changed social realities?

HISTORICAL AND INSTITUTIONAL FOUNDATIONS

The Constitution of the United States has its origins in the desire to establish strong national institutions that would provide the young republic with stability and the capacity to act. That this experiment has endured for more than two hundred years; that it was able to deal with the country's continental expansion and its rise as a political, economic, and scientific power; and that it has also accommodated the development of a multiethnic society is proof to Americans of the ingeniousness of their Founding Fathers, the drafters of the Constitution. How has it been possible to continually adapt this short eighteenth-century document to the demands of a modern society?

Because of the high hurdles to amending the Constitution – namely, a two-thirds majority in both houses of Congress and a subsequent ratification by three-quarters of the states – explicit changes to its text have been possible only in exceptional cases. Since the passage in 1791 of the Bill of Rights, the first ten amendments to the Constitution, only seventeen more amendments to the Constitution have been approved. Among them, only the three amendments passed after the Civil War, confirming the abolition of slavery and the civil and political equality of the freed slaves, have signaled a fundamental transformation of the American constitutional order.

In contrast to German legal culture and its pronounced tendency toward codification, the modernization of American constitutional law has taken place, for the most part, through case law adjudicated by the courts, in particular by the highest court, the Supreme Court. Indeed, and with good reason, not only Supreme Court justices but also legal scholars have claimed repeatedly that the Supreme Court is in fact the Constitution because it is charged with the task of constantly interpreting anew and making concrete the Constitution's fundamental principles. The Supreme Court assumed the authority for judicial review, for rigorously scrutinizing legislation regarding its compliance with the Constitution, in 1803 in the famous case of *Marbury v. Madison* even though that power was not expressly mentioned in the Constitution. The principle of judicial review has become the foundation of modern constitutionalism; it was not adopted in Germany, however, until after World War II.

The U.S. Constitution initially amounted to little more than a fledgling government's collection of rules and regulations that had little bearing on the everyday lives of the citizenry. During the first half of the nineteenth century, however, the Supreme Court handed down a number of judgments that laid the groundwork for a modern federal government. For instance, it strengthened the power of Congress to regulate commerce between the states (Interstate Commerce Clause, Article I, 8; *Gibbons v. Ogden*, 1824), which later would be interpreted as granting the federal government far-reaching economic and political authority. The infamous decision in the *Dred Scott v. Sandford* case (1857), which declared the congressionally approved prohibition of slavery in territories west of the Mississippi unconstitutional, demonstrated that action by the Supreme Court could do more to inflame than resolve political conflicts.

In the end, the Constitution was not able to provide a politically acceptable solution to the sectional conflict over slavery that played an increasingly central role in American political life from 1820 onward and led to the secession crisis of 1860–1. Whereas the Southern states viewed the Constitution as a compact between sovereign individual states, President Abraham Lincoln and the majority of Northerners considered it to be an indissoluble union created by the American people themselves. This question was resolved by the Civil War, which contributed powerfully to modernization and nationalization of American constitutional and legal culture. The Civil War and Reconstruction arguably constitute the only phase of U.S. constitutional history that is comparable to the constitutional ruptures that Germany experienced.

The sweeping constitutional changes ushered in by the Civil War bore most directly on the approximately four million black slaves who were finally freed by the Thirteenth Amendment in 1865 and, in the Fourteenth Amendment, were declared citizens of the United States with the right to equal protection of the law. The Fifteenth Amendment (1870) affirmed the right of all citizens regardless of "race, color, or previous condition of servitude" to vote (gender was not mentioned, and women were not guaranteed the right to vote for another half-century). The three Civil War amendments signaled a new understanding of the Constitution: it was no longer considered to be the untouchable expression of the will of the Founding Fathers but rather a document that could be amended to carry out political and social reforms. The Fourteenth Amendment in particular was to have a tremendous influence on twentieth-century views on citizenship and equality. These amendments were understood and applied very narrowly at the time they were ratified. The individual states feared the loss of their legal authority, and the prevailing racist *Zeitgeist* led rapidly to the virtual annulment of the civil rights of blacks. The achievement of these rights remained incomplete for more than one hundred years; it was one of the great tasks of modernization to be carried out by the U.S. Constitution.

The Civil War also led to a strengthening of federal power, especially the power of the executive branch. We see this in the introduction of a compulsory military draft and in the curtailment of certain freedoms guaranteed by the Bill of Rights. Even more significant were the economic initiatives undertaken by Congress during the war: it introduced new import duties, a uniform paper currency (the "greenback"), and a national income tax. It also authorized the construction of the transcontinental railroad and the allocation of federal land to settlers in the western territories (Homestead Act, 1862).

Modern German constitutionalism has its origins in the states (*Länder*), in federalism. As was the case in the United States, the first constitution to be valid throughout Germany, the Imperial constitution of 1871, was preceded by many earlier state constitutions. The tradition of sovereign territorial states in Germany was longer, more established, and more influential than in the United States. The Bavarian constitution of 1818 and the Prussian constitution of 1848–50, for instance, embodied traditions that had been developing for more than a half-century, before the constitution devised by Otto von Bismarck in 1871 established the national unification of Germany.

The Imperial constitution of 1871, enacted against the background of Prussia's victory over France, was a union of German princes, not a constitutive act of a sovereign nation. Whereas the preamble to the U.S. Constitution of 1789 proclaims, "We the People of the United States . . . do ordain and establish this Constitution for the United States of America," the constitution of the German Empire begins, "His Majesty the King of Prussia in the name of the North German alliance, His Majesty the King of Bavaria . . . enter into an eternal union." The constitution of the Weimar Republic (1919) opened with, "The German People, united in its tribes . . . " It was not until the Basic Law of 1949 that the political structure of Germany was established on the basis of the people's sovereignty.

The strong federal and monarchic traditions, the frailty of the democratic principle, and, indeed, the dictatorial usurpations of power that mark German history also help explain why the Germans have never made their constitutions the objects of cultic admiration. During the period of the German Empire, the day of national celebration was not associated with a seminal document, as with the Fourth of July and the American Declaration of Independence, but rather with a military event: the day of the decisive battle against the French in Sedan on September 2, 1870, which led to the founding of the German Empire.

Furthermore, until the middle of the twentieth century, the constitution in Germany did not have the status of a basic legal standard that established the political order, overruled all other legal authorities, and could prevail against all other organs and agencies of the state. In the United States, by contrast, the "primacy of the Constitution" found expression in the famous phrase of Supreme Court Chief Justice John Marshall in the *Marbury v. Madison* decision of 1803: "fundamental and paramount law of the nation." There was simply nothing comparable to that idea in German legal thought. The Imperial constitution of 1871 permitted changes to be made to it through the normal legislative process without a qualifying majority vote, which made it possible for lawmakers to achieve political ends outside the jurisdiction of the written constitution. In German constitutional scholarship, the expression "primacy of the constitution" was viewed as a notion of North American constitutional law and as something quite foreign to German law. In the German legal tradition, the constitution was simply one law among many. The de facto "primacy of the lawmaker" was reinforced by the conscious decision to do without a constitutional court.

The dualism between constitution and law reflected the unresolved question of sovereignty in German constitutionalism. This question was at the heart of a constitutional conflict in Prussia in the years 1862–6. The smoldering conflict between monarchical and democratic legitimacy affected both the standing and the political muscle of the Prussian constitution. It was understood not as a consummate legal order but rather as a framework for the political process. As a result, it was primarily programmatic. It set the standards of political culture, which then, through the process of open political debate, were given concrete expression in decisions. The limits of an individual's freedom were determined not by basic rights but rather through the political decisions of a legislative majority in parliament. In the same fashion, the legislative authority of the German Empire did not prescribe the development that produced a welfare state, but it did enable this development by permitting the establishment of rules and regulations uniformly throughout the empire.

The catastrophes of National Socialism and World War II brought an end to this tradition of constitutionalism in Germany. The Basic Law of 1949 vested sovereignty in the German people and expressly linked all powers of the state to the Basic Law. With the founding of the Federal Constitutional Court, the drafters of the Basic Law created an institution that bore a striking resemblance to the highest court in the United States and that was equipped with similar far-reaching authority, in particular with regard to judicial review. After 1945, the primacy of the Basic Law over all legislation ensured that decisions on basic values would be made in favor of fundamental civil rights, the rule of law, and the welfare state. Consequently, the German constitution became, like the U.S. Constitution, the immediate source of legitimacy that was to guarantee political stability and promote social justice.

CHALLENGES OF THE MODERN ERA

Faced with the precipitous pace of change that American society experienced in the decades after the Civil War – brought about by extensive industrialization, urbanization, and mass immigration – American politicians and citizens were increasingly prepared to accept regulation of economic and social life. The federal government and the states began to prescribe railroad freight tariffs, minimum wages, and working hours on the basis of their traditional police powers, which obligated them to safeguard public order and welfare. In response, the courts, especially the Supreme Court, responded with intensified activism. Between 1875 and 1900, the Supreme Court declared federal laws to be unconstitutional – before 1860, only 2 had been struck down – and state courts overturned nearly 100 regulatory measures. Most of the laws ruled unconstitutional had aimed at checking the power of large business interests. In 1895, for example, the Supreme Court circumscribed the antimonopolistic Sherman Antitrust Act, and in another ruling, it annulled the introduction of a federal income tax.

To protect against legal encroachments on private property, the Supreme Court invoked the doctrines of substantive due process and freedom of contract. Until as late as the 1930s, the court limited the guarantee of an inviolable core of substantive rights to the protection of private property. Only later did the court use its powers to strengthen civil rights and liberties. It was from the same doctrine of substantive due process that the Supreme Court evolved the freedom of contract in relation to the signing of labor contracts: employers and employees, in the view of the court, had the right to negotiate the terms of employment without governmental interference. This understanding of the freedom of contract not only made it difficult for labor unions to press for collective bargaining but also impeded the passage of legislation on occupational health and safety. In the highly controversial judgment of *Lochner v. New York* (1905), for example, the conservative majority on the Supreme Court quashed a law that limited the working hours of bakers to ten hours per day.

The critics of this decision were particularly incensed that the majority of the court had set aside a labor law that had been unanimously passed by the New York State legislature. Still, the Supreme Court did not back away entirely from trying to rein in industrial capitalism. Three years after the Lochner ruling, it decided unanimously to uphold an Oregon labor ordinance that set the workday for women at a maximum of ten hours. The court used the argument that protecting the health of women as mothers was in the public interest of the nation (*Muller v. Oregon*, 1908). This decision was noteworthy because it was supported by statistical data and medical findings, which documented the dangers to health caused by long working hours. For this reason, *Muller* is now considered to be a breakthrough for modern "sociological jurisprudence," which takes social realities into consideration in deciding legal questions.

Racism was one social reality that the Supreme Court, like the white majority of the population, was not yet prepared to confront in the late nineteenth and early twentieth centuries. Rather, it justified discrimination against the African American minority with a formalistic interpretation of the Civil War Amendments. The situation of black Americans had been worsening steadily since the end of Reconstruction. Already in 1883, the court had decided that the special injunctions for the protection of former slaves were no longer necessary: the "preferential treatment" afforded these citizens by lawmakers would now have to come to an end (*Civil Rights Cases*). Subsequently, the Supreme Court confirmed in 1896 in *Plessy v. Ferguson* the authority of individual states to enforce racial segregation, as long as the facilities for whites and blacks were of equal quality. With the "separate-but-equal" doctrine, the court bestowed on aura of constitutional respectability on an apartheid regime that lasted into the 1960s. The fact that the majority of the court expressly invoked "racial instincts" in explaining why the Constitution could not forcibly impose social equality of the races underscores how deeply biological concepts had penetrated American constitutional thought.

Racial segregation and the imposition of restrictive immigration limits for immigrants from Asia and Eastern Europe signaled the mounting uneasiness of the dominant Anglo-Protestant culture with the growing ethnic pluralism of American society in the early twentieth century. The attempt in 1919 to institute the prohibition of alcohol by using the Constitution as an instrument of social discipline failed miserably and ushered in a legendary heyday for organized crime. Americans introduced Prohibition with the Eighteenth Amendment and then terminated it without further ado in 1933 with the Twenty-First Amendment. A lasting legacy of the Prohibition era was the expansion of the jurisdiction of the federal criminal police agency that had been created in 1908 as the Bureau of Investigations and has been known since 1935 as the Federal Bureau of Investigation (FBI).

Faced with the explosion of crime during the 1920s, the Supreme Court moved to increase the investigative authority of the police. At the same time, however, it also approved legislation that strengthened basic civil rights and freedoms by extending the Bill of Rights to the individual states for the first time (*Gitlow v. New York*, 1925). The court still adhered to the traditional interpretation of the freedom of speech guaranteed in the First Amendment, such that government institutions were not allowed to exercise censorship yet were encouraged at the same time to prosecute vigorously any incidents of free speech related to violence or to a threat to public order and safety. Fear of revolution and war hysteria during the twentieth century led repeatedly to drastic curtailments of the civil rights and freedoms of Americans, and most of these measures were fully approved by the Supreme Court. Without a doubt, the internment of Japanese Americans during World War II was a severe breach of the civil rights of loyal citizens. The use of the term "concentration camp" to describe these internment centers is, however, completely inappropriate because the treatment of the internees was in no way comparable to that of the prisoners in the camps that the Nazis maintained in Germany and Eastern Europe. In contrast to Germany, the United States never saw the state succumb to the temptation of a totalitarian negation of all constitutional freedoms and safeguards, even during times of crisis.

From this perspective, criticism of the Supreme Court for its resistance to governmental intervention in the economy during the New Deal must also be tempered. The administration of Franklin D. Roosevelt instituted a program in response to the devastating economic crisis of the Great Depression that was revolutionary by American standards: it entailed imposing federal regulations on production, prices, and working conditions. The architects of the New Deal invoked the interstate-commerce clause and the constitutional responsibility of the U.S. Congress for the general well-being of the country (general welfare clause, Article I, 8) as the legal basis for their actions. The court, however, saw in these programs an expansion of executive power that ran afoul of the Constitution and, in 1935 and 1936, declared crucial core portions of the New Deal legislation to be unconstitutional. The United States found itself on the brink of a constitutional crisis. Arguing with antiquated doctrines, a highly conservative Supreme Court seemed to be attempting to derail a program of economic recovery and welfare modernization that both the Congress and a popular executive were energetically promoting.

After his triumphal reelection in November 1936, Roosevelt applied pressure on the court by introducing a plan for "constitutional reform" that would have allowed him to appoint six additional justices to the Supreme Court. Although Congress did not approve this plan, a majority of the court did finally realize that their permanent blockade of Congress and the executive was becoming unworkable, and in 1937 they allowed the New Deal legislation to pass and take effect. Furthermore, after a brief grace period, seven of the justices resigned from the court, ostensibly for reasons of age. Their resignations gave Roosevelt the opportunity to reshape the court by appointing new liberal justices who would continue to influence decisions of the court for decades to come.

The end of so-called laissez-faire constitutionalism and the strengthening of the federal government's jurisdiction and authority in economic matters have often been interpreted as the long overdue modernization of American constitutional law. Scholars have also noted a trend toward unification in other areas of the law. In light of the increasing professional demands on attorneys, nearly all the states by 1940 had made completion of an established course of legal study a requirement for sitting their bar exams. Before then, it was often possible for candidates to take bar exams without even the equivalent of a high school diploma. In 1923, the private American Law Institute was founded with the goal of facilitating a homogenization and simplification of case law and state legislation, both of which were becoming increasingly complicated and unmanageable. Its recommendations, however, found only very limited resonance with self-confident judges, who continued to defend their broad jurisdictions based in traditional common law. It was not until after World War II, in particular with the introduction of the Uniform Commercial Code and the Model Penal Code, that uniform concepts for civil and criminal law were developed. Because civil and criminal law fall under the jurisdiction of the states, however, there still exists a multitude of special laws and regulations, unique to each state.

The "legal realism" movement emerged in the early decades of the twentieth century in response to the oft-charged sterility of case law. Its proponents wanted to see judicial decisions give explicit legal recognition to social and political values.

Such a radical break with tradition was not possible, but the realist movement helped a "sociological jurisprudence" grounded in social data win support among jurists, especially in the decades immediately following World War II.

In contrast to the United States, individual civil rights and basic freedoms were not recognized at the federal level in Germany before 1949. For this reason, these rights and freedoms did not become a force for political change as in the United States even though Germany experienced similarly rapid, almost revolutionary, economic development and a broadening of political participation on the part of its citizens during the second half of the nineteenth century. Compared to the constitutions of the individual German states and those of other countries, the Imperial constitution of 1871 was a meager organizational statute. Its major purpose was to provide the constitutional framework for a newly created political entity. In accordance with the principle of the primacy of the law, the extension of individual freedom was not accomplished through the recognition of basic rights but rather through a series of laws passed by the Reichstag. The laws adopted from the North German Federation on the free movement of labor (1867) and trade (1869), which included currency regulations and provisions for patent and copyright protections along with measures to promote free trade, helped secure and systematically extend economic freedom for individuals. The late nineteenth century saw a series of measures to codify German law, including the promulgation of a criminal code and a civil code, the creation of an Imperial high court, the implementation of uniform criminal and civil procedures throughout the Empire, and the establishment of the Imperial Patent Office. Together, these steps laid the foundations for the rule of law in Germany.

It was not constitutional decisions on basic values but rather the intensive activity of imperial lawmakers in the Reichstag that created the preconditions for what the historian Michael Stolleis has called the "internal founding of the Empire through legal unification." The protection of individual freedom and property lay in the hands of the Reichstag, which acted to make any encroachments on these elementary rights dependent on the enactment of a law. There were, however, two sides to the increased legislative activity of the later nineteenth century. On the one hand, it strengthened the sphere of freedom of the individual in line with the liberal idea of the rule of law. On the other hand, this activity marked the beginning of a growing trend on the part of legislators to use law as a means to transform social conditions: the beginning, in other words, of the modern "interventionist state." Lawmakers, not the constitutional order or a constitutional court, gave legal form and direction to the accelerated social changes that accompanied Germany's rapid industrialization.

Germany experienced profound demographic and social change between 1850 and 1920 as it underwent the transition from an agrarian to an urban, industrialized society. The population doubled and the aggregate national income tripled. From 1880 on, its leading industrial sectors achieved faster growth than their counterparts in Britain and France, the country's most important economic competitors. In contrast to the United States, where the constitutional order was based on the liberation from agrarian and colonial hierarchies, in Imperial Germany there was a tension between the remnants of an antiquated feudal society and feudal privileges, and the new egalitarian mass democracy then taking shape. New social groups and classes emerged and began to question the conventional privileges and institutions. The Social Democratic Party, the political representative of the labor movement, stood in sharp opposition to the bourgeois-liberal and conservative-feudal political forces in the Reichstag. A new class of salaried employees began to organize politically and to position itself between the working class and the ranks of the civil service.

At the beginning of the twentieth century, the social and political tensions within Germany's legislative bodies could no longer be contained by compromises. The conflicts increasingly affected the political structure of the empire. The Reichstag pressed to extend its influence into areas of governance that had hitherto been the prerogative of the monarchy. In a constitutional system that had been established in large part to organize the state and that lacked a constitutional court to steer constitutional developments, these unresolved political conflicts became politically explosive and detonated in revolution at the end of World War I.

Whereas the Supreme Court played an active role in shaping and monitoring important social and economic legislation in the United States, the Imperial governmental administration and the Reichstag set the course of economic and social policy in Imperial Germany. The interventionist state began with new intensity and determination to reshape German society during the Imperial Era and during the period between the world wars. Until 1918, the state was subject to comparatively few constitutional constraints. The accomplishments of the interventionist state included groundbreaking and widely influential social welfare legislation as well as laws governing new technologies and technological advances in areas such as transportation and communications. Other laws focused on freedom of action within the economic sphere. Public law increasingly supplanted civil law and became responsible for addressing the challenge not only of applying standards of legal authority but also of balancing competing interests, such as those in the areas of cartel and patent law.

German courts were tasked with interpreting the laws according to their purpose and not measuring them against any higher rights or values, much less with deciding their constitutional validity. In contrast to legal practice in the United States, German judges were not seen as making decisions in concrete cases of dispute but rather as using scientific determination of objective judgments based on general principles in the tradition of Roman law. This view of the role of jurists resulted in the establishment of high standards for the education and certification of lawyers and judges. They had to complete an academic course of study and pass rigorous state entrance exams for acceptance into the legal profession. These requirements contributed to the development of an elitist class consciousness among the legal profession. The practice of choosing judges through public elections, which many American states adopted at this time, would have been quite unimaginable in Germany.

The attempt to balance social legislation, interpretive jurisprudence, and governmental administration in Germany was thrown into crisis during World War I, and that crisis eventually led to dictatorship. The Weimar Republic based Germany's constitutional order unambiguously on democratic sovereignty for the first time. Moreover, the new constitution of 1919 incorporated a wide spectrum of basic rights and social, economic, and cultural guarantees that extended beyond the classic freedoms. The Weimar constitution incorporated a number of fundamental legal decisions that, taken together, could have provided the foundation for a new understanding of the role of the constitution. Such an understanding found growing support among legal scholars during the Weimar Republic's existence. A number of authors advocated interpreting the Weimar constitution as a fundamental "decision" that had higher authority than any other source of law in Germany. This view was controversial, however. Although some judges and legal scholars supported it, a strong positivist movement clung to the traditional interpretation of the constitution.

The Weimar Republic was not in a position to resolve the crucial question of the scope of constitutional jurisdiction. Unlike the United States, Germany was dealing not only with catastrophic social conditions caused by World War I and the international economic crisis but also with deep social divisions and a crisis of confidence in liberal democracy, which in the end was no longer supported by a majority of the population. Whereas the New Deal produced a bundle of reform legislation that was approved by Congress and, later, by the Supreme Court, the German government struggled with political and economic crisis largely by means of extraparliamentary emergency laws. The exhaustion of democracy and parliamentary government ended with the suspension of the constitution.

The governmental takeover by the National Socialist German Workers Party (NSDAP, or Nazi Party for short) and the establishment of the *Führerstaat* set in motion an irreversible process of dissolution of the constitution. It resulted in a dictatorial system that lasted until 1989 in eastern Germany, where National Socialism was replaced by communist ideology after the collapse of the Third Reich in 1945. The National Socialist regime, undisturbed by the fact that the Weimar constitution was formally still valid and in force, systematically removed the separation between law and politics. The gradual disempowerment of the Reichstag and the dissolution of the states (*Länder*) removed all barriers protecting individual citizens from the regime. The regulations that the National Socialist regime passed in the form of laws determined the scope of individual freedom according to criteria of race, political belief, and social utility. The interventionist state quickly reached a new extreme with the Nazi dictatorship. This progression was particularly noticeable in the economic sphere, where the needs of the regime's planning – above all, its program of rearmament – resulted in an unprecedented level of dirigisme.

In practically all areas of law, the interpretation and execution of laws and edicts were oriented toward the ideological aims of the regime. Race became a central organizing principle in German law as it was represented by the Nuremberg Laws of 1935, which divided German citizenry between those who were of "German or related blood" and thereby entitled to the status of a citizen of the Reich (*Reichsbürger*) and German nationals who did not have this supposed racial character and were therefore without legal protection against discrimination or repression. In other words, the German racial state used law as an instrument to formally legitimize dictatorial power and to disenfranchise groups within German society that did not fit within the regime's vision of racial homogeneity. When individuals' freedoms were called into question, it was impossible for them to appeal to any higher authority protecting fundamental civil rights. Only in the realm of property rights did the regime allow a degree of freedom so as not to endanger private enterprise, which was the driving force behind the Nazi economy and arms industry.

National Socialism did away with the independence of the justice system, transforming it into a compliant instrument of power under the authority of "the Führer as the highest judge in the nation." The disenfranchisement and murder of millions of people for racial and political reasons before and during World War II showed that the German state, with its extreme centralization and dictatorial concentration of power, denied the law's function as a check on political opportunism. The primacy of politics, not the constitution, prevailed. At no time were Germany and the United States more distant from each other constitutionally than during the National Socialist dictatorship. After 1945, the subservience of the law to the political institutions of the German Democratic Republic's ruling party would also stand in marked contrast to the American constitutional order.

MODERN CONSTITUTIONAL DEMOCRACY

By the middle of the twentieth century, a liberal constitutional culture had been established in the United States that was characterized by the pragmatic tendencies of sociological jurisprudence and by heightened expectations regarding the government's regulatory capacity at the national level. The federal government assumed more responsibility for promoting greater economic equity and protecting civil rights and freedoms. Between 1953 and 1969, the Supreme Court under Chief Justice Earl Warren became a bastion of this new liberal culture. Through its decisions on a wide range of issues, including racial questions, voting rights and political representation, protection of privacy, the relationship of church and state, and the rights of the accused, the Warren court developed an activist vision of its role. In that vision, constitutional law was to serve as a motor for social modernization; accordingly, the Warren court did not hesitate to enforce fundamental rights and freedoms against the will of the political majority. Even today, the Warren court epitomizes the ideal of modern constitutionalism for its admirers; in the eyes of its critics, it embodies the elitist arrogation of legislative power by the judiciary.

With the case of *Brown v. Board of Education of Topeka, Kansas* (1954), the most significant and at the same time most controversial ruling of the Warren court, the Supreme Court prohibited the separation of races in public schools and therewith signaled the end of the separate-but-equal doctrine. *Brown* was, moreover, virtually a manifesto of liberal constitutional interpretation, which consciously broke with the past and explicitly used "modern" scientific findings. According to Warren's argumentation, which was based on psychological experiments, forced segregation produced a feeling of inferiority in black schoolchildren, constrained their intellectual development, and thus robbed them of their right to equal opportunity in obtaining a quality education. Racial segregation in education was consequently deemed "inherently unequal" in the court's famous formulation. Explaining that the educational system is the foundation of a democratic society and its institutions, the court went on to declare segregation a hurdle to modernization that harmed the nation as a whole.

The violent protests unleashed against the *Brown* ruling demonstrated that constitutional jurisprudence could, contrary to intent, intensify rather than resolve political conflicts. Because of its powerful position within the American system of government, the Supreme Court was never completely removed from political controversy; with the polarization of American society during the Warren Era, however, the politicization of the Supreme Court took on a new quality. Conservatives and liberals alike have been struggling ever since to exercise control over this institution whose authority, they believe, ultimately determines not only the interpretation of the Constitution but also the basic political and ideological orientation of the nation.

Above all, it was the rulings prohibiting school prayer in public schools (*Engel v. Vitale*, 1962; *Abington v. Schempp*, 1963) and legalizing abortion (*Roe v. Wade*, 1973) that many Americans regarded as massive assaults on their fundamental religious and moral beliefs. But although conservatism has regained cultural hegemony in the United States since 1970s, and although Presidents Nixon and Reagan both appointed traditionalist justices to the Supreme Court, there has not been a fundamental backlash in the court's position on controversial social issues. The comparatively strict separation of church and state is essential if for no other reason than the remarkable religious pluralism in the United States. Abortion is still legal, although some limitations have been imposed. Similarly, "affirmative action" laws to secure educational and employment opportunities for minorities also remain in force even though this issue is still highly contentious. Significantly, however, the constitutional justification for affirmative-action policies no longer rests primarily on the argument that such policies are a form of redress for historical injustices but rather that it is in the interest of society today to promote ethnic and cultural diversity in public and private institutions.

The division of the Supreme Court into conservative and liberal wings reflects the polarization of the country at large since the late 1960s. Simply put, two different constitutional cultures now confront each other: a conservative/traditionalist culture that defines America economically as a market society and insists on the rights of the majority to see its moral and religious values guaranteed by law, and a liberal culture that favors state supervision of large-scale economic interests and a high degree of protection for civil rights and freedoms.

Liberal commentators' criticism of the court under Chief Justice William Rehnquist (1985–2005) was at times alarmist but not completely unjustified. The majority of the Rehnquist court did, in fact, ignore their own principles, especially the principle of judicial restraint. That was clearly evident in the case of *Bush v. Gore*, which determined the outcome of the 2000 presidential election. The fact that President George W. Bush had the opportunity to appoint two new justices during his second term of office greatly concerned liberals, who feared that the Supreme Court could become the ideological spearhead of the conservative movement. Recent research on the influence of court decisions on social and political developments suggests, however, that the Supreme Court has in fact only a limited ability to either advance or retard social modernization.

In the case of the death penalty, its opponents among the justices argued in the early 1970s that, in light of evolving moral and humanitarian standards, this form of punishment violated the constitutional prohibition of "cruel and unusual punishment" (Eighth Amendment; *Furman v. Georgia*, 1972). In Germany, after the experience of the National Socialist reign of violence, the Basic Law explicitly denied legislators the possibility of introducing the death penalty. American opponents of capital punishment were able to secure only a moratorium on its use. Against the background of an upsurge in violent crime, the death penalty again found overwhelming support among the American public after the expiration of a moratorium in 1976. The fact that the United States has distanced itself from the legal cultures in other Western democracies on this issue does not disturb proponents of the death penalty, who say that the democratically determined will of lawmakers in the individual states is decisive. It must be noted, however, that a majority of the Supreme Court did in fact recently rule that sentencing mentally retarded offenders and minors to death constituted cruel and unusual punishment, and they referred explicitly to foreign and international law in their decision (*Atkins v. Virginia*, 2002; *Roper v. Simmons*, 2005). Whether these decisions represent the beginning of the end of the death penalty in the United States remains to be seen.

The pronouncements of the Supreme Court during the second half of the twentieth century, in particular those relating to civil rights, have had the effect of continually raising the expectations of American society vis-à-vis its legal system. Between 1960 and 1980, the number of cases that the Supreme Court heard doubled, and this was just the tip of the iceberg. There was talk at this time in the mainstream media of a "law explosion." In 1978, the magazine *U.S. News and World Report* complained that "Americans in all walks of life are buried under an avalanche of lawsuits." In 1960, there was one lawyer for every 620 inhabitants in the United States; at the beginning of the twenty-first century, there is one for every 300, the highest density of lawyers anywhere in the world. These legions of lawyers and the expansive field of liability law, which is widely considered outside the United States to be absurd on account of the frequently astronomical monetary settlements it produces, reflect a new trend in American legal culture. Pointing to the expectation that every wrong must be righted and every loss compensated, the legal historian Lawrence Friedman argues that a culture of "total justice" has taken root in the United States. At the center of this concept of justice stands, as before in American legal culture, the protections of individual freedom and property rights, not, as in Germany, a state interest in distributive justice. The introduction of social rights in American legal culture could well have explosive consequences. Americans by and large have shown little enthusiasm for "programmatic rights" and a clear preference for legal enforcement of their rights through the court system.

The new West German state created after 1945 from the Western Allies' occupation zones was the exact opposite of the National Socialist dictatorship. The constitutions of the individual states of the Federal Republic each contained a catalog of basic human and civil rights that had binding, comprehensive authority over all state organs and institutions, including the judiciary. The Basic Law of May 23, 1949, the Federal Republic's constitution, enshrined human dignity as an inalienable human right in its first paragraph. The separation of powers, in particular the independence of the legal system, was raised to the status of an immutable principle. For the first time in German constitutional history, the primacy of the constitution was comprehensively guaranteed. At the same time, the drafters of the Basic Law created safeguards to ensure that democracy and parliamentary government would not be able to maneuver themselves into a state of immobility, as had happened with the Weimar Republic. Extremely rigorous requirements were imposed for amending the new constitution, and protective barriers were created to defend it against attack. The guiding principles behind the Basic Law – the inalienability of human rights, the rule of law, the welfare state, and federalism – were secured "eternally" and protected against any alteration (Article 79, par. 3). In a sharp break with the past, the Federal Republic was designated a substantive constitutional state based on fundamental political and ethical values.

It was almost inevitable that this crucial turning point in constitutional history would lead to the establishment of an institution that, like the U.S. Supreme Court, would take on the role of guardian of the constitution. The Federal Constitutional Court assumed the powerful position, unprecedented in German history, of judicial monitor of the executive and legislative branches of government. Two new instruments contributed in particular to its ability to fulfill this monitoring function. First, the Basic Law established that the entire legislative process would be subject to constitutional regulation through the Federal Constitutional Court. Second, citizens who believe that their basic civil rights have been violated in some way by the state can file complaints directly with the Federal Constitutional Court. The court has gradually assumed a key position, similar to that of the Supreme Court in the United States, in the implementation and continued development of the fundamental principles of constitutional government.

In taking as a model the constitution adopted by the Frankfurt National Assembly of 1848–9, the so-called Pauluskirche Constitution, the drafters of the Basic Law were drawing on a precedent that bore noticeable American influence. But nowhere was the Basic Law's reliance on the American model more evident than in its provision for the Federal Constitutional Court. The establishment of the court represented arguably the most decisive, far-reaching modernization of German constitutional law after 1945, and it was the result not only of critical engagement with the German legal tradition but also of appropriation from American tradition, which had gained a certain political and cultural hegemony during the postwar occupation.

The strength of the Federal Constitutional Court did not stem solely from the provisions of the Basic Law. The court had to contend with the weight of tradition and to assert itself in handing down rulings. Many politicians in the ranks of the government viewed the court, whose members were not appointed by the government but rather selected by a parliamentary committee, as a thorn in the side that served the interests of the parliamentary opposition. They thus tried to put pressure on it and to influence the choice of its members. During the 1950s, the opposition appealed to the court to take its side on the great foreign policy issues of the day, namely rearmament and integration within the Federal Republic's Western alliance. At the same time, the court saw itself under pressure from the Adenauer government to approve governmental policies and decisions. Nevertheless, it was able to maintain its independence during this time, just as it did two decades later during the debate on the policies toward the Soviet bloc and relations with the German Democratic Republic (GDR) pursued by the Social Democratic–Liberal governing coalition led by Chancellor Willy Brandt. In its 1973 ruling on the Basic Treaty with the GDR, the Federal Constitutional Court proved to be the guardian of the constitutional mandate for German unity, a mandate it was called upon to interpret again in 1989 amid the social and political tensions that accompanied the process of unification.

The judges of the Federal Constitutional Court have contributed to the interpretation and development of the fundamental principles of the Basic Law with other far-reaching decisions. In 1961, for instance, they struck down a measure to create a television network under control of the federal government and reaffirmed the primacy of the states in regulating broadcasting. In the Maastricht Decision of 1993, the court applied the Basic Law's requirement for democratic governance in deciding whether the Federal Republic's participation in the process of European integration was constitutional. In a series of rulings, the court made the social welfare provisions in the Basic Law more precise and thereby laid the basis for individuals to claim entitlement to a minimum standard of living. It made an important contribution toward solidifying the Federal Republic's economic order by allowing lawmakers room to maneuver in enacting economic reforms. Its 1979 ruling on employee participation in management decisions (*Mitbestimmung*), for example, was important in defining how far lawmakers could draw on economic forecasts in shaping policy to address sweeping economic change.

The Federal Constitutional Court has had its most enduring influence in the area of civil rights. Beginning with its 1957 *Lüth* decision, in which the court determined that the call for the boycott of a film by the former Nazi propagandist, Veit Harlan, was covered by the right to freedom of expression, the judges developed a new concept of civil rights as part of an "objective scale of values." This view led well beyond the classical defensive function of civil rights and freedoms to an interpretation of civil rights that assigned a protective duty to the state. It was in the area of basic rights that what the legal scholar Bernhard Schlink has called "the dethronement of constitutional theory [*Staatsrechtswissenschaft*] by the constitutional court [*Verfassungsgerichtsbarkeit*]" is most evident. In similar fashion to their counterparts on the U.S. Supreme Court, the members of the Federal Constitutional Court formulated new civil rights in a number of their decisions, such as the right to "informational self-determination" in their ruling on the national census of 1983. Again like the Supreme Court, the Federal Constitutional Court has not shied away from political and social controversy. For example, it held to the view that abortion should, in principle, remain unlawful and punishable but, at the same time, by allowing broadly formulated exceptions to that prohibition, it opened the way to a widely acceptable compromise on a deeply divisive issue. In 1992, when the court, following American precedents, decided to interpret the freedom of expression very broadly and declared the sentence "Soldiers are murderers" not to be defamatory in all instances, it met with sharp public criticism. The public responded similarly three years later, when the court interpreted the presence of crucifixes in public schools as a possible violation of the freedom of religion of non-Christian pupils.

In such disputes, the Federal Constitutional Court, again like the U.S. Supreme Court, touched on taboos and the supposed cultural consensus of the majority, which it subordinated to a liberal, pluralistic standard. The fact that state-enforced neutrality on religious matters extends beyond Germany's two traditionally dominant Christian denominations and encompasses other religious groups, such as Muslims and atheists, is not easily accepted by those who see the foundations of German constitutional culture in Christian beliefs and principles. As in the abortion debate, the court has unexpectedly found itself taking sides in social conflicts. These conflicts did not, however, escalate into "culture wars," as in the United States, where, for example, militant anti-abortion activists have on occasion resorted to violence.

Growing transnational mobility and cultural pluralism have given rise to ever more frequent conflicts over rights in Germany. On points of tension between law and multiculturalism, the Federal Constitutional Court has been widely accepted as a mediator role, as evidenced by the broad public approval of two recent rulings. In 2002, it allowed Muslim butchers to perform ritual slaughters, a long-disputed practice that animal rights groups in particular had opposed. In the fierce controversy over the wearing of head scarves in public schools, the court narrowed the conditions under which a prohibition might be possible in a 2003 ruling, adding a reminder that religious pluralism arising from social change might be reason for lawmakers to rethink the issue.

In contrast with the Supreme Court, the Federal Constitutional Court does not directly reproduce the fault lines of the political camps in Germany. Its members are selected according to a system of proportional representation tied to the relative strength of the various parties in the Bundestag, and the court itself is divided into two chambers, each with its own areas of competence. As a result, the court conveys an impression of pluralism and neutrality, and that impression helps preserve its legitimacy and its standing as an arbiter of disputes and defender of the constitution. Whether this represents a "modernization" of German constitutional law depends on the standard being applied.

There can be no question that the Federal Constitutional Court has established and substantially strengthened the primacy of law, the awareness of the limits of political power, and the fundamental importance of basic civil rights for a free society. But the court has also assumed a role within the political process in Germany that goes beyond interpreting the Basic Law. On occasion, it has made decisions on major political issues, cast as constitutional controversies that the country's lawmakers have been unable or unwilling to settle. In 1993, 2005, and again in 2009, for example, the court had to rule on the compatibility of European integration with the Basic Law. In 1994, it was called on to decide the highly controversial question of whether the Bundeswehr troops could be deployed outside the territory of the NATO alliance.

This development reflects an older German tradition, namely the desire for a purportedly neutral referee, for an "objective, factual" ruling that can claim a higher legitimacy than a partisan political decision. The Federal Constitutional Court itself must ensure that it exercises self-restraint and does not enter into direct competition with the governmental bodies created to make political decisions. The court successfully demonstrated that self-restraint on two occasions, once in 1983 and again in 2005, when it upheld politically and constitutionally controversial decisions by the then-chancellors to dissolve the Bundestag by votes of no confidence. If one examines the development of the German legal system over the past century, it is quite apparent that public law on the whole and constitutional law in particular have become increasingly significant. The establishment of the primacy of the constitution as the paramount law of the land through the institution of a constitutional court marks a deep transformation that connects the German and American legal systems more closely than they had ever been in the past.

With regard to the central tasks of constitutional law – the establishment of a consensus on ideas of justice and the maintenance of social and political peace – the politicization of the U.S. Supreme Court in recent decades is particularly striking. Its decisions have been affected by the polarizing force of major social and cultural controversies more noticeably and more frequently than those of the Federal Constitutional Court in Germany. Consequently, in closing, the question presents itself as to whether the German adaptation of the American doctrine of the primacy of the Constitution has come to function more effectively as a stabilizing force for the peace of the society in Germany than it has in the United States. Arguably, the deep-seated rights consciousness that has become a cornerstone of American political culture over more than two hundred years of constitutional history continues to put a much higher degree of popular pressure on the U.S. Supreme Court than is the case with its German counterpart.

Further Reading

Berg, Manfred, and Martin H. Geyer, eds. *Two Cultures of Rights: The Quest for Inclusion and Participation in Modern America and Germany* (New York, 2002).

Böckenförde, Ernst-Wolfgang. *Recht, Staat, Freiheit*, 2nd ed. (Frankfurt, 1992).

Dippel, Horst. *Die amerikanische Verfassung in Deutschland im 19. Jahrhundert. Das Dilemma von Politik und Staatsrecht* (Goldbach, 1994).

Eberle, Edward J. *Dignity and Liberty: Constitutional Visions in Germany and the United States* (Westport, 2002).

Friedman, Lawrence M. *American Law in the 20th Century* (New Haven, 2002).

Gosewinkel, Dieter. *Adolf Arndt: Die Wiederbegründung des Rechtsstaats aus dem Geist der Sozialdemokratie (1945 – 1961)* (Bonn, 1992).

Grimm, Dieter. *Deutsche Verfassungsgeschichte 1776–1866* (Frankfurt, 1988).

Hall, Kermit L. *The Magic Mirror: Law in American History* (New York, 1989).

Huber, Ernst Rudolf. *Deutsche Verfassungsgeschichte seit 1789*, vols. 1 to 8 (Stuttgart, 1960–90).

Kelly, Alfred, Winfried A. Harbison, and Herman Belz. *The American Constitution: Its Origins and Development*, 2 vols., 7th ed. (New York, 1991).

Krakau, Knud, and Franz Streng, eds. *Konflikt der Rechtskulturen? Die USA und Deutschland im Vergleich, Publications of the Bavarian American Academy* (Heidelberg, 2003).

Schwartz, Bernard. *History of the Supreme Court* (New York, 1993).

Stolleis, Michael. *Geschichte des öffentlichen Rechts in Deutschland*, vols. 1 to 3 (Munich, 1993–9).

Stolleis, Michael. *Konstitution und Intervention* (Frankfurt, 2001).

Wahl, Rainer. *Verfassungsstaat, Europäisierung, Internationalisierung* (Frankfurt, 2003).

5

Welfare: Entitlement and Exclusion

DANIEL LETWIN AND GABRIELE METZLER

The welfare state is both a child and a defining feature of the modern age. Of course, welfare provision – the marshaling of collective resources to address a range of material hardships and social needs – existed long before the industrial era. But it was with the rise of industrial capitalism that the nation-state first emerged as the chief purveyor of social welfare. Conceived to afford citizens some protection from the uncertain, often unforgiving swirl of market forces, the modern welfare state unfolded at various times, in various forms, and with varying aims and impacts from one country to the next.

To examine the history of any welfare state – still more, to compare different ones – is to raise a host of questions. How, in this or that country, has welfare been defined? What has been the array of goods, services, and protections contained within it, and for which people, toward what ends, and by what mechanisms has welfare been dispensed? In what measures has the welfare system either advanced or subverted ideals of democracy, equality, and solidarity? How has it challenged or reinforced existing barriers of class, gender, or ethnicity?

How Germany and the United States tackled such questions is essential to their respective encounters with modernity. A comparative study calls forth its own particular batch of questions. Some are distinctive to the German experience: Why did the welfare state take root there so early – that is, so soon after its formation as a nation and after its industrial takeoff? What accounts for Germany's ongoing, indeed expanding, commitment to national welfare provision even as it passed through a jarring succession of political systems? How did Cold War welfare policy vary between East and West Germany?

Above all perhaps, interest in the German welfare state has been animated by a broader issue – the peculiarities of Germany's encounter with modernity, its *Sonderweg*, or distinctive path. According to this paradigm, the Germany of the industrial age remained a land marked by the prevalence of preindustrial values, the dominance of preindustrial elites, and the weakness of democratic structures. The peculiar tensions between the modern and the premodern, the industrial and the preindustrial features of Imperial Germany figured prominently in long-term explanations of the rise of Nazism, with Nazi social policy in turn traced to the paternalistic and authoritarian features of Bismarck's welfare state. More recently, the historical ambiguities of the German welfare state – its complex mix of progress and discipline, social rights and repression – have been interpreted more as a variant on the transnational character of modernity, a modernity whose pathological potential was realized in Nazi Germany but could easily have arisen – and to some degrees may have – within other welfare states as well.

Historical inquiry into the American welfare state, meanwhile, has been fueled by an assortment of concerns distinctive to the United States: from political culture and party alignments to labor affairs, race relations, the roots of poverty, and the dynamics of gender in American society. Interest in the American welfare state has, however, centered above all on its famous (or notorious) limitations – manifest not only in its late arrival but also in its meagerness, narrowness of scope, multiplicity of exclusions, and unmatched deference to market forces. It is hardly surprising that many observers question the very existence of an American "welfare state" as such; hence, they use such qualified formulations as "semi-welfare state," "reluctant welfare state," "welfare state laggard," "incomplete welfare state," or "truncated universalism." Scholarly emphasis on the weakness of American welfare sits oddly alongside popular images of a bloated, bumbling, insatiable "beast," diverting the savings of hard-working citizens toward an abject, dependent poor. ("Didn't need no welfare state!" as disaffected 1970s icon Archie Bunker would growl each week on TV in the *All in the Family* theme song, "Those Were the Days.") Unarguably, when examined against earlier modes of social provision in America, the rise of a national welfare state – particularly with the "Big Bangs" of the New Deal and Great Society – appear significant enough. Still, the lateness and "lite"-ness of the American welfare state are what dominate historical attention. The ghost of American exceptionalism haunts the field. In this variant, the questions arise: Why no universalist welfare state? Why no "social citizenship"? Why such breezy acceptance of poverty and inequality? And why such scant protection from the play of market forces?

Although the *Sonderweg* and the American exceptionalism paradigms each tend to highlight differences between the German and American welfare states, an intriguing blend of difference and commonality runs through their histories. Each welfare state has had its own fluid mix of high vision and grubby pragmatism, expansiveness and exclusion, empowerment and repression, alleviation of inequality and reinforcement of hierarchy. How these dualities played out in the two lands, we suggest, had much to do with the comparative evolution of the nation-state in German and American society.

FORMATION OF WELFARE STATES, 1880–1945

Traditional forms of social provision long preceded the advent of the modern welfare state. Preindustrial welfare was geared above all to the relief and oversight of the poor. In both the German states and colonial America, responsibility for the dependent poor fell first and foremost to family. What needs could not be handled by kin or private organizations became the obligation of local governments or parishes.

In both Germany and the United States, the nineteenth century brought mounting strains on this system. The rise of large, unruly cities overwhelmed local schemes of welfare. The spread of commercial agriculture and industrial production sowed new kinds of risk and hardship, marked by rural displacement, irregular employment, long hours, low wages, and perilous work. Across the industrializing world, sustenance was turning less predictable, the contrasts between poverty and affluence more stark, and class conflict more visible.

The foundation of the modern welfare state was laid in Bismarck's Germany, with the passage of a series of compulsory social insurance laws covering illness (1883), industrial accidents (1884), and disability and old age (1889). Subsidized to a modest extent by the state, these new modes of provision drew chiefly on joint contributions from employers and employees, who managed the funds collectively. Animating these measures was a wish to weaken the oppositional Social Democrats and secure mass loyalty for the new state, along with a commitment to sustain and stabilize industrial growth. Indeed, this top-down state-centered approach remained one of the salient features of Kaiserreich-vintage welfare.

Whatever its motivations – and however halting and piecemeal its formation – the birth of the German welfare state was a watershed moment. Not only was the extension of benefits tied for the first time to a national state but social insurance also brought a new outlook to the dispensation of welfare. Going beyond the stigmatization and degradation characteristic of traditional poor relief, the new approach recognized the material risks endemic to industrial life and created a legitimate claim to benefits. By compelling employers, workers, and the public each to absorb some portion of the social risks inherent in wage labor, the Bismarckian program sought to stem the flow of vulnerable workers into the ranks of the poor (and/or the socialists). The new insurance schemes were part of a wider range of social-policy innovations designed to regulate the market forces then budding around the Atlantic world, thus staking out a middle ground between laissez-faire individualism and socialism.

The social insurance benefits launched in the 1880s were neither lavish nor universal. They were conceived as the entitlement not of citizens but rather of employees – and only a fraction of the workforce at that, favoring the male industrial worker. Although access to social insurance would remain more or less workplace-based, eligibility for each form of welfare – public assistance and compulsory insurance – would soon start to expand. Landmark moments included the insurance law (*Reichsversicherungsordnung*) of 1911 and, of course, the massive state mobilization of World War I.

It was in the turbulent Weimar period that the German welfare state truly came of age. The Weimar Republic defined itself as an active welfare state, enshrining a variety of social rights in its 1919 constitution. The welfare state was strengthened substantially in the decade that followed through legislation on unemployment benefits, labor courts, labor exchanges, an eight-hour day, rent levels, health care, housing projects, and new public-assistance schemes. Thus, to the formative features of the Bismarckian welfare state, Weimar policy affixed the beginnings of social citizenship.

In the United States, meanwhile, the welfare state was conspicuous by its absence. If America had preceded most of Europe in the extension of voting rights and public education, the social dislocations of the late nineteenth century brought little movement toward the kind of welfare state then taking root in Germany. With the exception of Civil War pensions, social provision remained chiefly the domain of private charities and community-based mutual associations or, where there was public welfare, local government. Visions of social insurance made little headway. That left public assistance – which, if anything, was growing more penurious than ever, reflecting a newer, more hard-edged view of poverty in Gilded Age America.

Prospects for an American welfare state looked up at the turn of the twentieth century with the rise of Progressivism, a variant of the social reform current then surging through the Atlantic world. At its more radical edge, a cohort of social scientists, politicians, unionists, women's activists, "enlightened" business figures, and assorted others began advocating European-style – not least, German-style – plans of social policy.

By transatlantic standards, however, Progressive campaigns for a national welfare state bore little fruit. To be sure, a broad menu of social reforms came under consideration – and many took effect – in Progressive-era America: abolition of child labor, public mediation of labor disputes, and housing codes, to name but a few. But such policies turned more on regulation of the market than on the deployment of social resources to protect the vulnerable against the risks and hardships of industrial capitalism. Although modest steps in the area of welfare provision were taken – on the plane of social insurance, workers' compensation; on the plane of public assistance, aid to poor mothers (or "mothers' pensions") – these programs were limited by their meager funding, their often elaborate barriers to access (including location, racial and ethnic background, and perceived moral character), and their precarious reliance on state or local government. The bulk of social provision in 1920s America remained confined to private channels: either community institutions or an emerging set of paternalistic employers.

Why did the Progressives fail to deliver a welfare regime on the order of contemporaneous systems arising in Germany and elsewhere? Some explanations are particular to the Progressive period. A pre–World War I flash of interest in public health insurance, for example, was anticipated, coopted, and otherwise deflected by big medical, insurance, and employer interests. Whatever momentum may have been gathering for a German-style system of social insurance was derailed by the Great War (and demonization of all things German). Had the exigencies of war in the United States approached, in scale and duration, those experienced overseas, perhaps an American welfare state would then have materialized.

Or perhaps not. For the failure of an American welfare state to arrive at this moment can be (and has been) attributed to a variety of circumstances not confined to that era: broad opposition from corporate interests, the absence of a spirited or concerted demand from labor, fragmentation of workers along racial and ethnic lines, resistance from a doggedly laissez-faire judiciary, and the stumbling blocks posed by the nation's exquisitely divided and decentralized polity. Then there is that familiar assemblage of welfare-unfriendly attitudes – individualism, reverence for the free market, antipathy to state intervention, lack of patience or sympathy for the poor – held to be ingrained in the nation's political culture. In some combination or another, these more lasting (to some, even timeless) factors would continue to frustrate prospects for expansive welfare provision in America.

Still, Progressive-era social policy offered some precedent for a future welfare state, if only by affirming a positive role for government in addressing social hardships. Along the way, the Progressive era saw the gestation of an army of activists, policymakers, and professional experts committed to one or another vision of social welfare – a network that would lay the groundwork for and have a hand in crafting an American welfare state a generation later. Particularly prominent was the part played by women, typified by a diverse band of "maternalists" – cast alternately as hearty crusaders and austere elitists – who fostered the mothers' pensions programs. Indeed, more than the poor per se (or the prospective poor per se), it was women who came to be recognized as the group especially entitled to social provision and protection. Long overlooked in traditional, labor-based studies, the maternalists have been restored by feminist scholars to a central place in the origins of the American welfare state.

In key ways, though, America's embryonic welfare programs mirrored the German approach. Consider its Bismarckian, two-tier structure; although in America, it was so much more starkly gendered – that is, workers' compensation (i.e., social insurance) for men, as breadwinning workers; Mothers' Aid (i.e., public assistance) for women, as mothers. As in Germany, incipient forms of American provision bore the classic ambiguities of the Progressive age – the impulses alternately to empower the poor and to regulate them, to break down social inequalities and to elaborate them, to stabilize the social order and to render it more just. As Progressive reformers on both sides of the Atlantic embraced concepts of social engineering, older differentiations between the "deserving" and "undeserving" poor were modernized; they were no longer based on a traditional moral economy and work ethic but rather on modern, "rational," science-based criteria to determine who was entitled to receive welfare – or, for that matter, to reproduce – and who was not.

These tensions between empowerment and condescension, beneficence and control would take dramatic new turns in each country in the 1930s. In both Germany and the United States, existing modes of provision faced staggering tests with the global depression. In comparing their responses, it is the differences that spring most readily to mind. In Germany, a newly expanded welfare state was sent reeling by mass unemployment; by the early 1930s, the last Weimar governments were left cutting unemployment benefits and dispatching growing numbers of jobless onto local relief rolls. Meanwhile, the United States had scarcely any welfare state to lose (although existing sources of provision – private and public – were likewise soon exhausted). Under the force of the global depression, German politics hurtled rightward, culminating with the rise of National Socialism, whereas American politics was pushed leftward with the advent of the New Deal.

In Germany, the demise of social democratic governance – and the eventual triumph of the Nazis – was marked by the suppression of civil and labor rights, the denial of welfare to the socially and politically "undeserving," and the harnessing of social policy to a sensationally racist, repressive vision of the nation-state. The New Deal, in contrast, heralded an expansion of social rights. With hardship so pervasive, with recovery so elusive, with millions so manifestly "deserving" of aid, with existing safety nets so frayed, and with welfare's customary opponents so discredited, the drive for a national welfare state proved irresistible. Prompted by a mix of grassroots movements and top-down efforts from policymakers, Progressive-era reformers, and a segment of big business, New Deal welfare initiatives included direct relief and public jobs programs, the right of workers to organize, and federal minimum wage and maximum hours codes. But it was above all the Social

Security Act of 1935 – with its introduction of a federal commitment to old-age pensions, unemployment insurance, and poor relief – that marked the birth of the American welfare state.

Yet, trends in German and American social policy were not so cleanly divergent as they may first appear. After all, neither National Socialism nor the New Deal was anchored in laissez-faire principles. To the contrary, both were statist enterprises, with deep roots in Progressive traditions of social engineering. It bears mention that as the national welfare state came at long last to America, it hardly vanished in Germany. Without overlooking the breadth and brutality of Nazi repression, we can detect an egalitarian thrust to the regime's social policy as well. To cement the loyalty of the Aryan masses to the Nazi *Volksgemeinschaft*, it combined populist appeals with the implementation (for "deserving" groups) of various assistance programs and public works projects (especially for youth) and the extension of welfare to new groups, such as artisans and the self-employed. Even as the Nazis claimed to have reinvented the welfare state, there was a remarkable degree of continuity.

In form and function, it should be added, the New Deal welfare state borrowed heavily from the Bismarckian model. The Social Security Act established at the national level the two-tier, social insurance/public assistance approach that had been prefigured in the Progressive era. Compulsory social insurance was, as in Germany, work-based (not citizen-based) and contributory (funded jointly by employers and employees rather than from general revenues). And, as in Germany, no shame attended the "earned" benefits of old-age and unemployment insurance. It was public assistance – now dispensed most conspicuously through Aid to Dependent Children (an outgrowth of the state-based Mothers' Aid programs) – that would retain the stigma of an unearned "handout," its recipients rigorously screened for proof of destitution and "moral probity."

Finally, any temptation to juxtapose neatly the contraction of social rights in Nazi Germany and their expansion under the New Deal runs up against the elaborate shortcomings of welfare provision in the United States. Needless to say, social policy under the Third Reich was singularly harsh, with access to provision restricted by political and "racial" criteria; women facing growing barriers to welfare (not to mention compulsory sterilization and abortion); and workers' charity associations curtailed, eliminated, or incorporated into Nazi enterprises. Yet, America's nascent welfare state was not without its own myriad coercions, exclusions, and inequalities. As in Germany, welfare often was provided in the form of public works projects that, although securing workers a modest income, were also aimed at disciplining them. Moreover, the fruits of social insurance flowed disproportionately to whites, to men, and to the more affluent strata of American labor. This pattern owed in part, as in Germany, to its nonredistributive approach and in part to the multitude of occupations officially excluded from old-age and unemployment insurance: mainly trades – such as agricultural labor, domestic work, laundry services, teaching, and nursing – in which women and/or minorities predominated. Recurring in other areas of New Deal social policy, these exclusions represented the price extracted by business, Southern elites, and other conservative interests for their acceptance of New Deal provisions. For those consigned to public assistance, aid was typically low and, at best, grudgingly dispensed.

These broad areas of similarity – both during and preceding the 1930s – should not obscure some vital differences between the German and American welfare systems, however. The budding American welfare state remained significantly more modest in scope and levels of provision than its German counterpart. Although far-reaching reformers sought a lasting system of economic planning and public employment, New Deal measures along these lines were gradually phased out. Visions of national health insurance were likewise rebuffed, as they would continue to be for the seven decades to follow.

A further contrast between the German and American welfare states – one hardly confined to the New Deal/Nazi era – turns on the very different balances they struck between the different levels of government in the dispensing of provision. It is no small irony that if the repressiveness and limitations of welfare under the Third Reich were inseparable from its basis in a centralized state, the repressiveness and limitations of the New Deal welfare state were closely linked to the decentralized scheme of American provision – that is, to welfare's deep embeddedness in state or local bureaucracies.

"GOLDEN AGE" AND CRISIS

It was in the postwar era that the modern welfare state really established itself around the Atlantic world. In one country after another, the scattered, makeshift forms of provision that had cropped up over the previous sixty years now matured into comprehensive welfare states. However these systems may have differed in vital particulars, their development signified broad acceptance of the state's role as a modifier of the market economy. During the quarter-century following World War II, Germany and the United States would each enter this "golden age" of welfare-state expansion.

Although Germany's division into two separate states complicates analysis of the welfare state in the postwar era, both East and West Germany had one aspect in common: more than in other countries on either side of the Iron Curtain, the East and West German systems of social security were shaped by the Cold War. Indeed, the status, identity, and very legitimacy of the East and West German states depended on their performance in providing social welfare guarantees.

From the beginning, West Germany defined itself as a welfare state – a *demokratischer und sozialer Bundesstaat* (democratic and social federal state), according to its constitution, the Basic Law. The Bismarckian tradition of a two-tier welfare state, with a stratified system of compulsory insurance, was resumed – cleansed, of course, of the racial and ethnic discriminations introduced by the Nazis. West Germany's market economy was tempered with the essential attribute "social." There was broad consensus, shared by the two major political parties, that the state was responsible for promoting social justice and social security. Meanwhile, the system of cooperation between labor and employers was reestablished and advanced.

Focusing first on immediate needs, the reemergent welfare state was hardly equipped to deal with the heavy burden that had piled up over six years of "total war." Ad hoc measures were taken to support those in need. To prevent social unrest, particularly among the millions of ethnic German expellees from Eastern Europe, social policy was aimed at the reconstruction of justice and a sense of community, as exemplified in 1952 by the *Lastenausgleich*, the so-called equalization of burdens. Legislation in this field sought to compensate expellees for their material losses and thereby bring about a fairer distribution of the burdens that total war and the Potsdam agreements had inflicted on the German population.

With the economic boom that began in the 1950s came a systematic expansion in the scope and very concept of the German welfare state. Starting with the introduction in 1957 of the index-linked "dynamic" pension, the enhancement of welfare went on to encompass more generous public assistance, shorter working hours, and improved unemployment benefits. Peaking in the early 1970s with the expansion of the pension scheme, this enlargement of West German welfare provision was accompanied by a new conception of social and political rights. That does not means, however, that gender inequality was eliminated. If the crude bio-political interventions of the Third Reich were discontinued, they were replaced by West Germany's "soft" gender-related social intervention (exemplified in the taxation of spousal incomes, which discourages female full-time employment).

The provision of welfare in the German Democratic Republic (GDR) was based on very different assumptions. For a variety of reasons, economic performance and, accordingly, standards of living and welfare provision in the GDR never reached West German levels. The policy of the regime may be characterized as a mix of carrot and stick: on the one hand, the ruling Socialist Unity Party (Sozialistische Einheitspartei Deutschlands, or SED) was anxious to secure mass loyalty through social control and surveillance, an approach that subordinated the social and political rights of workers (as of all citizens) to the party's interest; on the other hand, the regime guaranteed job security, health care, child care, and sports and other recreational facilities, the provision of which was mainly based in the workplace. Its self-conception as a work-based society (*Arbeitsgesellschaft*), in which the identity of state and citizen alike was tied to employment, distinguished East Germany from its West German counterpart. They also differed with respect to gender: the East German welfare state encouraged female employment through the provision of generous maternity leave and day care for children. With respect to women, then, East German welfare bore a closer resemblance to the Scandinavian model than did that of West Germany, whose focus on financial transfers rather than the provision of social services (such as day care) put gainfully employed women at a disadvantage.

America found its own place in welfare's "golden age." Although no major new elements were added, social insurance and public assistance each underwent quiet expansion in the 1950s and early 1960s as eligibility widened and benefit levels rose. The second "Big Bang" of welfare growth came in the mid-1960s, with Lyndon Johnson's Great Society programs. In the arena of social insurance, old-age benefits were notably increased and universal entitlements enlarged to include Medicare, a federally funded system of health coverage for the elderly. Johnson's War on Poverty likewise enlarged benefits for the poor and created new modes of public assistance, such as Medicaid, food stamps, and (some years later) Supplemental Security Income. In addition to these forms of public assistance, the War on Poverty spawned a cluster of initiatives to elevate the needy – with considerable effect both on levels of poverty and the conditions and civic status of the poor.

Of course, the content and legacy of the War on Poverty have hardly been uncontroversial. From the outset, critics on the right denounced it as bloated and wasteful, a drain on public resources, a perverse reward for laziness, and an intrusion on the autonomy of markets and individuals. Intensifying this reaction was the swelling magnitude – and shifting demography – of public assistance. The War on Poverty was largely targeted – and was widely perceived as being targeted – toward the hardships of African Americans. The stigmatization and "racialization" of welfare went hand in hand, drawing on and feeding the perception that hard-working whites were footing the bill for indolent blacks. Here is one of the striking divergences in German and American social policy in the quarter-century after World War II: even as "race" was expunged from the discourse on welfare in post–Nazi Germany, it came increasingly to frame the discourse on welfare in the United States.

Less visible in public discourse, although prominent in scholarly treatment, have been critiques stressing how modest the War on Poverty was. Critics high-light the growing divide between the two streams of provision established by the Social Security Act. Although eligibility was broadened and benefits increased for both social insurance and public assistance, this two-tier structure continued to mirror, if not magnify, the unequal stations of women and men, minorities and whites, and the poor and the nonpoor. Social insurance, ever the locus of the "deserving" (largely nonpoor) recipients, absorbed the lion's share of the increase in public benefits. Aid to Families with Dependent Children, ever more the realm of "undeserving" claimants, remained especially reliant for its funding and dis-bursement on state and local government, where provision remained particularly ungenerous – in amount, accessibility, and spirit. In contrast to the postwar Ger-man welfare states, the American version was exceptionally minimal in both levels and breadth of public provision and exceptionally lacking in popular support.

Equally divergent, if less conspicuous, were the balances struck between public and private provision. Whereas the private realm diminished as a source of social welfare in West Germany, in postwar America there was a dramatic expansion of private, employer-based benefits, encouraged by a web of federal subsidies and regulations. Employees in the more privileged, largely unionized areas of the workforce came to enjoy company retirement packages (supplementing federal old-age benefits), along with employer health-care plans. Workers in the low-wage, non-union sector, by contrast, languished, receiving minimal coverage, if any at all. In lieu of universal entitlements, then, increasing portions of welfare flowed through private channels, generally bypassing those in greatest need.

In essence, the bifurcation of postwar American labor – between the upper working and middle classes on the one hand and the lower working class and the poor on the other – corresponded to two vital splits within the welfare state: that between "public" and "private" provision and that between social insurance and public assistance. Each of these splits would help frustrate prospects for a more generous social policy. First, the substantial private benefits enjoyed by the upper ranks of American labor sapped popular demand for expanded public benefits, such as national health care. Second, the continual growth of the public assistance rolls – comprised largely (and, in the eyes of many, overwhelmingly) of African Americans – exacerbated white alienation from the welfare state.

Still, on each side of the Atlantic, the expanded welfare states of the 1950s and 1960s enjoyed a momentum that seems astounding today. "[T]here are no signs, outside of marginal groups mostly centered in the United States, of a disposition to curb the welfare state," the philosopher Harry Girvetz could write in 1968. "It rides the wave of the future." Within a few years, as postwar prosperity flagged, neoliberal critics of the welfare state would be riding that wave across the industrial world.

In West Germany, as the oil crisis of 1973 put an end to the "economic miracle" and limited the state's room for maneuver, the welfare state came under mounting pressure. After years of full employment, German society now faced the specter of unemployment and rising expenditures on welfare. Reactions, however, were ambiguous: although social security underwent some cuts, its architecture remained by and large unaltered. In some aspects, it was even expanded; for example, through the introduction of credits into women's pensions for child rearing.

In East Germany, the welfare state followed a quite different course. There, public provision, housing in particular, was expanded significantly in the 1970s. However, the commitment of the East German state to full employment, even in times of recession, drained resources from other arenas of social need, such as the elderly and disabled. In the end, the weaknesses of the East German welfare state hastened the demise of the GDR.

Although it may be argued that the economic crisis of the 1970s hit the more generous European welfare states hardest, diminishing resources and rising opposition would also exhaust welfare expansion in the United States. There, several developments corroded belief in the capacity of government to uplift national life. Some of these trends, such as the oil crisis, were experienced globally. Others – Vietnam, Watergate, and the social divisions of the past decade – were particular to the United States. For many Americans troubled by the material insecurity and moral uncertainties of the time, the welfare state offered a ready scapegoat. Although the public-assistance rolls continued to expand amid the downturn of the 1970s, a number of War on Poverty programs were defunded or dismantled.

The crusade against welfare was ratcheted up during the Reagan years. Social Security (i.e., old-age insurance) proved too popular to confront head on, but "welfare" (i.e., public assistance) underwent sustained rhetorical attack and often steep cuts. Meanwhile, pressures intensified to push recipients into the paid labor force, thus completing an about-face in the original expressed premise of Aid to Families with Dependent Children – that mothers ought to stay at home. But the Reagan cutbacks soon hit the limits of public acceptance, yielding by the mid-1980s (as in West Germany) something of a stalemate that discouraged either expansion or retrenchment of welfare spending.

The political upheaval of Eastern Europe during 1989–90 opened a new chapter in the history of German welfare. Ever since, the accelerating mobility of capital and labor across national borders has presented a major challenge to the historical model of the nation-state and therefore, to the welfare state as well. Yet, globalization has not been the only challenge faced by Germany's post–Cold War welfare state. When unification brought East Germans directly into the West German welfare system, Germany, in a way, stemmed the neoliberal trends of the time. Although a mix of public and private provision has always been a salient feature of German welfare, the share assumed by public institutions has grown continuously from the 1880s on. This trend began to slow in the 1970s but resumed in the 1990s as German unification triggered a rise in social spending. The traditional German welfare state was expanded by the introduction of long-term nursing-care insurance in 1994. However, these expansions, together with rising unemployment rates, spurred a sharp increase in welfare expenditures that could not be covered by revenues from the new East German *Länder*. Public debt increased and taxes rose.

These after effects of unification did not cause the financial crisis of the German welfare state, but they did aggravate the pressures it has faced since the 1970s. Germany today confronts a new set of demographic dynamics – an aging population (together with increasing costs of health care), low birth rates, and new sources and a growing volume of immigration, rendering the politics of the welfare state increasingly "ethnicized." German society, which had lived out middle-class ideals since the 1950s, has become more polarized in ways that mirror to some extent the bifurcation of the American working class. Moreover, global competition and the opportunity to transfer production to other countries have compelled (or, at least, enabled) employers to scale back their own forms of welfare provision. The consensus, going back to the age of Bismarck, that the social costs of industrial society should be borne evenly by employers and employees has come under question, encouraging reductions in employer provision. The most radical reform has been the introduction in 2000 of privately funded pension schemes, ushering in a new balance between public and private welfare. Whether this change really marks a final break with the Bismarckian tradition remains to be seen.

In the United States, the assault on welfare persisted into the 1990s. Bill Clinton rode to the White House in 1992 as a self-professed "New Democrat" – a term signaling a repudiation of Great Society liberalism and a pledge to "end welfare as we know it." The "Gingrich revolution" of 1994 both fanned and coarsened antiwelfare sentiment, paving the way for the "welfare reform" long demanded by conservatives. Under the 1996 Personal Responsibility Act signed by Clinton, federal welfare funds were delivered as block grants to the states, which were authorized to impose strict conditions (above all, some manner of work) and time limits (both short term and cumulative) on welfare eligibility. For the first time, a federal entitlement – that of poor parents and their children to economic assistance – was rescinded. Defenders of this landmark legislation greeted sharply diminished welfare rolls as evidence of a renewed work ethic displacing the old culture of "welfare dependency"; critics denounced that view as complacent, myopic, and oblivious to the deprivations resulting (or bound in time to result) from the contraction of public assistance. Either way, retrenchment would continue to meet stiff resistance in the United States, as it would in welfare states generally. As with the German welfare state, prospects for the American variant were far from certain during the first decade of the twenty-first century.

CONCLUDING THOUGHTS

Throughout their respective careers, the German and American welfare states have each in its own way been regarded as an aspect of its country's "exceptional" path through modernity, giving rise to narratives that stress the contrasts between them. Still, the histories of German and American welfare did not unfold in isolation, and the shifting interplay between the two and, more broadly, between the United States and Europe deserves attention.

During the formative years of modern social politics, the preponderance of transatlantic influence flowed westward. European models of regulation and social provision seldom traveled uncontested or unaltered to Progressive-era America. A variety of social, political, and cultural obstacles noted earlier served to curtail the European influence. Even those most receptive to foreign examples tended to regard their source with some skepticism – not least, toward those programs and ideas coming out of Germany, a country whose fabled mix of efficiency and authoritarianism left Progressives alternately impressed and apprehensive. Still, the impact of German social politics was everywhere apparent – from the almost obligatory training of American social scientists at German universities to the prominence of German social insurance among the overseas programs studied by American reformers.

World War I marked the beginning of a decades-long receding of the German impact on American social politics – along with a gradual reversal in the flow of transatlantic influence. Whatever interest Weimar social initiatives may have stirred across the ocean tended to be eclipsed by the general prosperity of 1920s America. Indeed, the mystique of American "Fordism" – with its exaltation of productive efficiency – found no small resonance in war-torn, crisis-ridden Europe. The interplay of American and German/European social policy grew still more complex amid the global crisis of the 1930s. If New Dealers remained somewhat intrigued by state responses abroad (not excluding those of Nazi Germany), the fragility of social provision (not to mention political democracy) overseas further diminished Europe's stature. Indeed, if any program emerged around the Atlantic world as a beacon of social innovation, it was the New Deal itself.

By the end of World War II, transatlantic exchange in matters of social policy was all but dead; the old Progressive connection could scarcely survive the strains of the 1930s and 1940s. If the war-ravaged countries of Europe responded to the promise of comprehensive risk-sharing welfare plans of the sort sprouting up from Britain to Scandinavia to the two Germanys, such schemes found less resonance in the prosperous, globally dominant United States (even as aid from the latter underwrote the revitalization of European social policy). In postwar American policy circles, Keynesian, growth-oriented solutions came to overshadow more social democratic alternatives.

In the 1960s, fiscally based conceptions of social policy and the welfare state, so prevalent in President Johnson's Great Society, had a deep impact in Germany. During the 1960s and early 1970s, these Keynesian notions amalgamated with traditional German thought on welfare to form a very distinctive set of political ideas, based on Western (i.e., Anglo-American) conceptions of the state and its relation to society. In this sense, the flow of transatlantic ideas had been unmistakably reversed and, to this day, trends in American thinking on welfare hold considerable sway in Germany – only now, those views involve the promotion not of growth-driven welfare state development as much as crisis-driven welfare-state retrenchment.

Despite a long history of interaction, striking contrasts between the German and American welfare states have persisted, whether the seminal character of the welfare state in Germany versus its lateness in the United States, its persistence in

Germany versus its sporadic development across the Atlantic, the generosity of benefits in Germany versus their meagerness in the United States, or the overall receptiveness accorded the welfare state within German society versus the broad opposition evident in America. A key factor in explaining these divergent trajectories is the relation between welfare and the nation-state. From the beginning, the German welfare state – building on a tradition of collectivism rather than individualism and on confidence in the state rather in the self-regulating forces of the market – has been a major instrument in the creation and reassertion of national unity and identity. Already notable in the Kaiserreich, this dynamic would continue through the twentieth century. After 1918, the welfare state served as a means for the renewal of national legitimacy, helping Germans cope with the challenges of defeat in war, political collapse, and social upheaval. For its part, the Nazi regime invoked the Bismarckian welfare tradition to shore up its hegemony (bending that tradition, of course, to its own social and political agendas). After 1945, the link between a strong welfare state and (West) Germany's self-identity, pushed further by the exigencies of the Cold War, contributed to the striking persistence of welfare institutions through times of deep social change. After 1989, under very different circumstances, the welfare state facilitated the process of unification. Ultimately, then, the continual presence of a robust welfare state, even through such sharply disjunctive periods, is not as unexpected as it may first appear. In fact, it was precisely the instability of German polity and society from the late nineteenth through the late twentieth centuries that time and again gave the welfare state such a vital role in the reestablishment of national cohesion.

In America, by contrast, the forging (and reforging) of the nation-state has been more peripheral than central to the history of welfare. Without question, the big spasms of welfare state-building of the New Deal and Great Society eras each heralded a bold recasting of the relation between citizen and state. But the United States had passed its critical moments of state formation and preservation – that is, the 1780s and 1860s – long before it entered the ranks of modern welfare states. Although New Deal welfare was designed largely to stabilize the social and economic order, it was never so integral to the nation – its creation, survival, or revival – as its German counterpart would be to German nationhood in the 1880s or in subsequent epochs of national crisis.

Attention to German and American exceptionalism may tend to obscure some noteworthy similarities between their welfare states, however. First – lest we forget the obvious – each provided significant protection from the hardships and uncertainties of modern society. Another similarity, one that has only just begun to be noticed, concerns the overall magnitude of social provision in America relative to that in countries, including Germany, across the Atlantic. Inquiry into the American welfare state has traditionally focused on its relative paltriness, but some have begun to question whether welfare provision in the United States has been so minimal after all. By traditional measures – that is, levels of public spending as a proportion of gross domestic product – American welfare provision has long trailed far behind that in Germany. When, however, we widen the focus to include private, especially employer, provision (such as health care, pensions) and nonspending governmental provision (such as tax policy, regulation, government credit and insurance, and so forth), the gulf between America and European countries in aggregate welfare provision narrows dramatically, at times completely. Yet, America's "private welfare state" benefits primarily the upper strata of the labor force and thereby perpetuates inequality. If widening the picture to encompass private benefits alerts us to the magnitude of American welfare provision, it also confirms the lopsidedness of its distribution.

Another similarity between the German and American welfare states lies in their common limitations, particularly in contrast to the "social democratic" model. Unlike the universalist Scandinavian conceptions of welfare, both the American and German systems of social insurance have been based on employment. The principle of equivalence (contributions/benefits) has functioned to preserve the social status of the contributing individual rather than to promote social equality. Although surely ameliorative with respect to the hardships of industrial capitalism, the German and American welfare states have each remained nonegalitarian, mirroring and reproducing social and economic inequalities – along lines of gender, occupation, ethnicity, and race – in their respective societies.

Today, it is not yet clear if the traditional model of the German welfare state can survive the multilayered crises it is facing or if it will instead converge with the American model, as indicated by the liberalization of markets (both capital and labor), in the course of which the focus of state activity has been shifting from the protection of labor to the promotion of work. It is hard to decide if the label "Americanization" fits these processes. In a way, both welfare states have entered into a "race to the bottom." However, it seems more likely that the German welfare state will be reformed along the paths other Western European states have already taken and that new forms of social provision within the European Union will emerge sooner or later.

As in present-day Germany, the outlook for welfare in twenty-first–century America remains both ambiguous and uncertain. Social insurance and aid to the needy (public and private) each face ongoing retrenchment. Ballooning federal deficits in the wake of the Bush tax cuts and the prodigious increase in post–9/11 military spending have strengthened the hand of conservatives set on shrinking the welfare state still further. Yet, signs remain of an abiding attachment to core aspects of the welfare state, a sentiment that politicians may test at their peril: witness President George W. Bush's stillborn campaign following his 2004 reelection to expand the assault on welfare onto the long inviolable zone of Social Security.

After the end of the Cold War, the accelerating process of globalization, with its fluid migration of capital and labor, has strained the fabric of Western societies. In both Germany and America, the welfare state was one of the salient institutional features of industrial society, the product of their respective races to modernity. Whether it will survive in postindustrial societies and whether Germany – or rather Europe – and the United States will embark on competing postmodernities remain to be seen.

Further Reading

Esping-Andersen, Gøsta. *The Three Worlds of Welfare Capitalism* (Princeton, 1990).
Gordon, Linda. *Pitied but Not Entitled: Single Mothers and the History of Welfare, 1890–1935* (New York, 1994).

Gordon, Linda, ed. *Women, the State, and Welfare* (Madison, 1990).

Hacker, Jacob S. *The Divided Welfare State: The Battle over Public and Private Social Benefits in the United States* (New York, 2002).

Hentschel, Volker. *Geschichte der deutschen Sozialpolitik (1880–1980): Soziale Sicherung und kollektives Arbeitsrecht* (Frankfurt, 1983).

Hockerts, Hans Günter, ed. *Drei Wege deutscher Sozialstaatlichkeit: NS-Diktatur, Bundesrepublik und DDR im Vergleich* (Munich, 1998).

Hong, Young-Sun. *Welfare, Modernity, and the Weimar State, 1918–1933* (Princeton, 1998).

Koven, Seth, and Sonya Michel, eds. *Mothers of a New World: Maternalist Politics and the Origins of Welfare States* (New York, 1993).

Katz, Michael B. *In the Shadow of the Poorhouse: A Social History of Welfare in America* (New York, 1986).

Klein, Jennifer. *For All These Rights: Business, Labor, and the Shaping of America's Public–Private Welfare State* (Princeton, 2002).

Lieberman, Robert C. *Shifting the Color Line: Race and the American Welfare State* (Cambridge, 1998).

Metzler, Gabriele. *Der deutsche Sozialstaat: Vom bismarckschen Erfolgsmodell zum Pflegefall* (Stuttgart, 2003).

Mink, Gwendolyn. *The Wages of Motherhood: Inequality in the Welfare State, 1917–1942* (New York, 1995).

Noble, Charles. *Welfare as We Knew It: A Political History of the American Welfare State* (New York, 1997).

Piven, Francis Fox, and Richard A. Cloward. *Regulating the Poor: The Functions of Public Welfare* (New York, 1993).

Ritter, Gerhard A. *Der Sozialstaat: Entstehung und Entwicklung im internationalen Vergleich*, 2nd rev. ed. (Munich, 1991).

Ritter, Gerhard A. *Der Preis der deutschen Einheit: Die Wiedervereinigung und die Krise des Sozialstaates* (Munich, 2006).

Rodgers, Daniel. *Atlantic Crossings: Social Politics in a Progressive Age* (Cambridge, 1998).

Sachsse, Christoph, and Florian Tennstedt. *Geschichte der Armenfürsorge in Deutschland*, 3 vols. (Stuttgart, 1983–92).

Schmidt, Manfred G. *Sozialpolitik in Deutschland: Historische Entwicklung und internationaler Vergleich*, 2nd rev. ed. (Opladen, 1998).

Skocpol, Theda. *Protecting Soldiers and Mothers: The Political Origins of Social Welfare Policy in the United States* (Cambridge, 1992).

Stachura, Peter D. "Social Policy and Social Welfare in Germany from the Mid-Nineteenth Century to the Present," in Sheilagh Ogilvie and Richard Overy, eds., *Germany: A New Social and Economic History* (London, 2003): 227–50.

Steinmetz, George. *Regulating the Social: The Welfare State and Local Politics in Imperial Germany* (Princeton, 1993).

6

Immigration: Myth versus Struggles

TOBIAS BRINKMANN AND ANNEMARIE SAMMARTINO

The most potent symbols of American immigration are the Statue of Liberty and Emma Lazarus's illustrious poem, "The New Colossus." Embossed on a bronze plaque affixed to the statue's pedestal in the early 1900s, the poem reads, "'Keep ancient lands your storied pomp!' Cries she, with silent lips. 'Give me your tired, your poor, your huddled masses yearning to breathe free. . . .'" This poem was written during a time of unprecedented immigration to the United States. Between 1900 and the start of World War I, approximately thirteen million people arrived on America's shores. Lazarus's poem and the statue with which it is so closely associated symbolize how America was then and continues to be a beacon to immigrants around the world. Even after the reorganization of the Immigration and Naturalization Service as part of the new Department of Homeland Security, immigrants are coming in record numbers to the United States.

Germany has no comparable symbols that celebrate immigration as a crucial part of its history. Indeed, Germany seems to be the very opposite of a nation of immigrants. Although Germany has received migrants in growing numbers since the late nineteenth century, it did not develop a coherent long-term policy for regulating their integration until the twenty-first century. Until recently, leading German officials repeatedly declared that Germany was and is not an *Einwanderungsland*, or country of immigration. Whereas every child born on American soil is an American citizen, this never was and is still not the case in Germany, as even today, citizenship is partially based on proof of "German" descent.

Is it possible, then, to characterize the United States as a classic country of immigration and Germany as the opposite until very recently? Does the Statue of Liberty, known around the world as a symbol of immigration and openness, stand in contrast to the image of the "dark-skinned" *Gastarbeiter*, the migrant recruited from abroad to work temporarily in West Germany but who ended up staying? Does this inclusion versus exclusion story really hold up? Was American immigration policy really as open as Germany's was restrictive or nonexistent?

A closer examination reveals that the image of an exclusive and restrictive German immigration policy is not entirely accurate. Nazism has cast a long shadow onto the German past, and too often German interactions with foreigners, legal and otherwise, are viewed solely as precursors to Nazi genocide. Yet, closer scrutiny belies this simplistic teleology. For example, the thorough medical screening of millions of transmigrants from Eastern Europe in Germany before 1914 was a direct consequence of American legislation against "undesirable" immigrants. Thousands of migrants in transit were deported from Imperial Germany back to Eastern Europe because American immigration inspectors might deny them entry. Limiting the numbers of Polish "guest workers" before 1914 was surely xenophobic, but no more so than American restrictions on Chinese laborers after 1882. Or, to give another example, Germany did not have an official policy regarding political asylum before 1949, but seekers of political asylum often were able to find a safe haven on German soil.

America's story is also more complicated than Lazarus's poem suggests. The image of Lady Liberty opening her arms wide to the "yearning masses" is compelling but obscures a much more troubled and complex history. Ironically, Ellis Island, one of the most potent symbols of the American immigration story, is closely connected to immigration restrictions. Few visitors to the national monument and immigration museum are aware that Ellis Island was closely associated with the development and implementation of stringent immigration restrictions.

The history of migration in America and Germany is a multifaceted story. Rather than a choice between two paths to modernity – one marked by openness and tolerance and the other by xenophobia and violence – this chapter presents the American and German paths as parallel, if not equivalent, developments.

BEFORE WORLD WAR I: OPEN DOORS VERSUS DESCENT-BASED CITIZENSHIP

Between 1870 and the early 1920s, roughly twenty million people migrated to the United States, mostly from Eastern and Southern Europe but also in smaller numbers from Mexico, Canada, and parts of East Asia. These immigrants encountered Americans who themselves were overwhelmingly immigrants or second- and third-generation descendants of immigrants.

This mass migration had an immediate and sustained impact on the United States. Around 1900, some of the largest American cities had a majority of foreign-born residents. A comparison of Berlin and Chicago is instructive. Berlin was about the same size as Chicago around the turn of the century. Largely as a result of transatlantic migration, Chicago's population more than doubled from five hundred thousand to more than a million in a time span of only ten years, between 1880 and 1890. In the 1890s, 80 percent of Chicagoans were either foreign born or children of foreign-born migrants. Admittedly, this was one of the highest proportions in the United States, not least because Chicago at the time was a rapidly growing economic hub. Like Chicago, Berlin also expanded rapidly and became one of the world's largest and economically most dynamic cities, but foreign-born migrants and their children comprised less than 10 percent of its population.

Around 1900, immigrants visibly dominated many American urban neighborhoods: New York's Lower East Side was home to perhaps five hundred thousand Jews and also a sizeable Italian community. Large German communities resided in Chicago's northwest side. San Francisco's Chinatown was already a tourist destination. After the 1906 earthquake, however, the potential spread of the "Mongolians" (as the leading Oakland newspaper put it) beyond a clearly confined urban space and across the San Francisco Bay alarmed politicians. In some cities, one immigrant group was dominant, like the Germans in Milwaukee and the Irish in Boston. Even though German, Jewish, and Italian immigrants appeared to be large and homogeneous groups to many Americans, migrants came to America with rather diverse backgrounds. Germans, for instance, shared little apart from a common language, and they did not easily come together in their new home country.

The story of American immigration is also a story of German transmigration, and the histories of the two states are linked by their problematic relationship to migrants from Eastern Europe. According to the migration scholar, Aristide Zolberg, a transatlantic perspective reveals that the rigid German policy toward "suspicious" transmigrants can only be understood in the context of America's "remote border control." Although the period of massive German immigration to the United States had come to an end by the close of the nineteenth century, after that time many Eastern European immigrants passed through Germany on their way to America. It was no coincidence that the German authorities opened control and disinfection stations along Germany's eastern border, near large railway hubs, and in the ports of Hamburg and Bremen soon after 1890, for it was then that the United States began to send back suspicious migrants, mostly people who were poor and ill. Consequently, the large steamship companies that were responsible for covering their return passage costs refused to take certain people on board. Moreover, Russian authorities often declined to readmit "their" citizens. After 1891, many Eastern European migrants were turned back at Germany's eastern border or before they reached the ports on the North Sea, long before they reached America. The outbreak of cholera in Central Russia and in Hamburg in 1892 led to even more stringent controls. As a result of American pressure, Germany required migrants from Russia to undergo obligatory disinfections after 1892. In 1894, the U.S. Immigration Commissioner applauded the German transit control system because Germany was "protecting itself against undesirable immigrants . . . and at the same time protecting us."

German cities themselves became the temporary or permanent home of many Eastern European Jews. Although the authorities sought to limit such immigration, it remained relatively easy for Eastern European immigrants to find a way into Germany. Germans reacted primarily with disdain and distaste, and, aside from the efforts of some German Jewish organizations, little effort was made to integrate them into German society.

Poles were another sizeable migrant group. Many were employed on Prussian agricultural estates, and they comprised a high percentage of mine workers in the Ruhr Valley. The state was caught between conflicting priorities. On the one hand, Germany needed the labor provided by the Poles but, on the other, the state faced public agitation to limit the number of these "dangerous" foreigners. In 1884–5, bowing to public pressure, Bismarck ordered the deportation of forty thousand non-naturalized Poles (among them many Jews) from Prussia. Yet, this act inspired such criticism from the owners of large agricultural estates that the policy was rescinded in 1888. Thereafter, the authorities developed a sophisticated control and rotation scheme for foreign agricultural laborers. Jewish and other Eastern European immigrants who did not work on the Prussian estates did not enjoy this "protection." Thousands were expelled across the eastern border between 1904 and 1906, even though the situation for Jews in the Russian Empire had become increasingly precarious.

The right-wing press and nationalist agitators in this period expressed fears that Germany was subject to *Überfremdung*, to "over-foreignization." Even the liberal Max Weber said that "a Slavic flood that would entail a cultural regression of several epochs" was threatening Germany. The increasingly influential German nationalist right mobilized fears of an onslaught of Slavs and Jews to push through more stringent border control and surveillance measures as well as to pass a new citizenship law. Whereas U.S. citizenship is based on the principle of residency or *jus soli*, the 1913 German citizenship law enshrined the principle of *jus sanguinis* or descent. Local officials had considerable leeway, however, in granting citizenship to naturalization applicants; the restrictiveness of this law masked a much more complex reality.

The doors of the United States were open to most migrants from Europe until 1914, but America's more restrictive post–World War I policies had their origins in the nineteenth century. The United States responded to the growing immigration of non-"whites" – persons not originating in Britain and Northwest Europe – by excluding certain groups during the second half of the nineteenth century. Immigration policy, hitherto the responsibility of the states, was moved into the domain of the federal government and Congress. In addition to persons who might become a "public charge," the 1882 Chinese Exclusion Act explicitly targeted a specific group of immigrants. In the following years, the ban on immigration from China was tightened, and Chinese aliens living in the United States were subjected to severe restrictions. In 1891, against the background of rising immigration and nativist pressures, a new federal agency was created, the Immigration Bureau, and much more stringent controls on America's borders were introduced. Ellis Island was by far the largest of a number of immigration reception centers set up in the early 1890s in the wake of the reorganization of immigration policy. These reception centers were extralegal spaces that anticipated contemporary internment facilities at international airports for unwanted migrants.

On January 2, 1892, an Irish teenager, Annie Moore, became the first migrant to enter the new reception center on Ellis Island. This day was her birthday, and she was presented with a golden ten-dollar coin for the occasion. Not all migrants were treated as kindly. The migrants who followed Annie were checked by inspectors for contagious disease with the goal of establishing whether they would be able to support themselves rather than becoming a public charge. Inspections of third-class passengers were invasive and often humiliating; before World War I, first- and second-class passengers, in contrast, were checked only superficially on shipboard rather than on Ellis Island. Admittedly, even the stringent controls for third-class passengers at Ellis Island stopped few Europeans from immigrating to the United States before 1921, but they served as a blueprint for future immigration restrictions. Migrants from Asia faced much more severe treatment. At Angel Island, opened in 1910 in the San Francisco Bay, many aliens, mostly Chinese, were interned for lengthy periods.

Immigrants and their descendants had to contend with more than just inspections and the possibility of internment and even deportation. During the nineteenth century, Catholic immigrants encountered a barrage of discrimination and violence in their new land. Anti-Semitic stereotypes were widespread among settled and recently arrived Americans even if direct violence against Jewish immigrants remained rare. Racially "different" migrants – from China, Japan, and the Philippines as well as from Latin America – who arrived after the 1880s suffered much abuse. Chinese immigrants in particular frequently became victims of violent persecution throughout the West. In one incident, a mob killed twenty-eight Chinese immigrants in a Wyoming mining town in 1885. In the same year, a wave of riots against Chinese immigrants flared up across the Pacific Northwest.

Immigrants often encountered hostility in the United States, and more than a few returned home, but the wave of migration in the late nineteenth and early twentieth centuries transformed American society. By 1914, America was less "white" and less Protestant and much more diverse and pluralist than it had been a half-century earlier. More importantly, the processes of cross-ethnic immigration and Americanization were and continue to be closely related. As America became a country of immigrants, what it meant to be "American" changed. This was not the case in pre–World War I Germany. Even though some immigrants made Germany their temporary or permanent home, dominant notions of German national identity became more rigid and exclusivist. Immigrants in Germany did not remake German culture and remained for the most part outsiders. In contrast, many immigrants successfully made America "their" home, undercutting "Anglo-American Americanism" as an exclusionary and hierarchical understanding of ethnic and religious groups. However, it would not be until the 1960s that a majority of Americans would accept ethnic or cultural pluralism, a term incidentally coined by the German Jewish immigrant Horace Kallen in 1915.

TURNING POINT: WORLD WAR I AND ITS AFTERMATH

The Great War marked a caesura in the history of migration worldwide. The all-encompassing nature of the conflict led states to restrict the out-migration of their citizens and the in-migration of potentially dangerous foreigners. The erection of legal barriers to entry changed migration policy in both Germany and the United States.

Germany and many other combatant countries introduced large-scale surveillance of resident foreigners. These measures ranged from the imposition of passport and visa restrictions to internment. The enactment of travel and migration restrictions meant the end of an era of relatively free movement across borders. Germany also used its 2.5 million prisoners of war (POWs) as a labor reserve to compensate for the loss of its own men to military service. At the same time, many foreign workers became forced laborers almost overnight.

The relatively open American doors also began to close after 1914. Although neither world war was fought on U.S. territory, both led to more restrictive American immigration policies. In 1917, tens of thousands of mostly German immigrants, including naturalized immigrants, were interned as enemy aliens. In the same year, Congress passed a restrictive immigration law by an overwhelming majority. In addition, several prominent left-wing activists were interned, stripped of their American citizenship, and deported to Europe shortly after the war. Ironically, quite a few of the expellees, most famously Emma Goldman, were interned and deported from Ellis Island. The function of the reception center was thus reversed. The decline of immigration after the war had made space available on the island, and until its closure in 1954, it would primarily serve as an internment facility for suspicious and unwanted persons. For many, the Statue of Liberty had been their first impression of the New World; for some, it was the last.

The crisis of the international political system, combined with economic recession, made it easy for many Americans in the isolationist 1920s to see migrants as an economic threat or as dangerous radicals, emissaries from a world convulsed in revolution and bloodied by war. Europeans, including Germans, were hardly more likely to welcome immigration. After 1917, immigrants to the United States were required to have a passport and a visa – a huge problem for many refugees from Eastern Europe. European states had already begun to demand passports and visas in 1914, but many wartime and postwar migrants did not possess these documents. Moreover, many Eastern Europeans lost their citizenship when the Romanov, Hapsburg, and Hohenzollern empires collapsed. New nation-states such as Poland had little interest in boosting the size of their potentially dangerous minority communities, especially Jews and ethnic Germans, meaning that applications for citizenship could sometimes drag on for years and were often rejected. Meanwhile, refugees fled shifting borders that put them in the "wrong" nation-state or revolutions that brought the "wrong" ideology to power.

By the mid-1920s, statelessness had become a growing problem. Although the League of Nations addressed this issue by introducing so-called Nansen passports, statelessness prevented many refugees from moving across the new borders in East Central Europe – and to the United States. In his novel *Pnin*, the Russian-born writer Vladimir Nabokov, himself a stateless emigrant living in Berlin during the 1920s, wrote about the hurdles facing stateless migrants in interwar Europe: "the dreary hell that had been devised by European bureaucrats (to the vast amusement of the Soviets) for holders of that miserable thing, called the Nansen passport (a kind of parolee's card issued to Russian émigrés)."

World War I and the ensuing military conflicts in Eastern Europe uprooted huge numbers of people. Many of these migrants were Jewish, Catholic, Orthodox Christian, or Muslim, and a substantial number were poor and "dark." Some had left-wing sympathies. In other words, they were precisely the kind of immigrants whom many Americans already loathed. The 1917 Russian Revolution stoked the anxieties of Americans worried about a left-wing takeover at home, international political crisis, and an uncertain economic outlook, all of which provided the already strong anti-immigrant lobby with decisive momentum.

In 1921, Congress significantly reduced immigration. Annual national quotas were established. There were no quotas for Jews, Gypsies, and other minorities; rather, they were subsumed within the quotas for their countries of residence. These quotas created a hierarchy explicitly favoring "white" immigrants from Northern and Western Europe and excluding "dark" migrants from Eastern and Southern Europe as well as Asians and Africans. The new legislation also made "illegal immigration" a criminal offense. Ironically, this definition made it much easier to exploit Mexican agricultural workers as cheap and easily disposable "wetbacks." Tellingly, the U.S. Border Patrol was established in 1924 to prevent border crossing not by Mexicans but by illegal Europeans and Asians.

The Johnson–Reed Act of 1924 reduced the quotas even further. It also shifted responsibility for granting immigrant visas from U.S. immigration inspectors to consular officials in the migrant's home country, often leading to excruciatingly long waiting periods.

Whereas the oceans that surrounded the United States afforded it the luxury of making decisions about whom to let in, the states of continental Europe had to contend with large-scale migrations after World War I that they could control only to a limited degree; John Hope Sullivan counted 9.5 million refugees as late as 1925. The aftermath of war, revolution, and territorial redistribution in Europe provoked a refugee crisis of unprecedented severity. As the postwar upheavals were concentrated in Eastern Europe, Germany became one of the major receiving countries for refugees. In the four years after 1918, approximately one million ethnic Germans from territories ceded to Poland, France, Belgium, and Denmark moved to Germany. In addition, more than a half-million former citizens of the shattered Russian Empire, including many ethnic Germans and Jews, found safe haven in Germany from revolution, civil war, persecution, and famine. These numbers say little about the constant movement of people and their countless individual tragedies. Many refugees spent years in different camps across Europe as they awaited permission to immigrate. Some managed to get into the United States just before the restrictions were enacted; many were stuck for years in makeshift camps and settlements in Germany and Western Europe; others stayed in Germany for years before moving on or back after the political situation in Eastern Europe had stabilized somewhat.

Fears of Bolshevism and large-scale refugee immigration encouraged countries across Europe to maintain their wartime restrictions. In Germany, new attempts to establish a national registration system for foreigners and to strengthen the border failed as the government did not possess the resources to implement such costly measures. German authorities asserted that a majority of immigrants coming to Germany after the war were Jews; in fact, Jews comprised only a small percentage of the total number of migrants. Descriptions of economic and political crisis in the East and the difficulty of maintaining border controls often went hand in hand with diatribes about the combined threat posed by Eastern European Jews and Bolshevism. Jewish refugees and migrants faced a new form of radical anti-Semitism in Germany. Anti-Semitism and anti-foreigner sentiment formed a dangerous and mutually reinforcing spiral that persisted throughout the existence of the Weimar Republic.

German policy toward foreigners in the Weimar Republic can be characterized as doubly protectionist, reflecting both economic and nationalist motives. But protectionism alone cannot explain German actions and attitudes toward migrants. For example, Germans from across the political spectrum supported a de facto (if not de jure) policy of asylum for Russian refugees fleeing civil war and revolution. These refugees were concentrated in the German capital and, at its height, the Berlin Russian community may have had as many as 360,000 members. For many Germans, the anti-Bolshevism of these Russian émigrés made them more palatable as a foreign presence on German soil.

Germany was doubly affected by the new American immigration policy. Other countries in the Western Hemisphere followed the United States and soon tightened their immigration policies. The annual immigration quotas for Germany were generous, but the restrictions placed on Eastern European immigrants by countries in the Western Hemisphere meant that many potential transmigrants were permanently or temporarily "caught" in Germany, unable to complete their westward journey. During the Depression, American consular officials were ordered to be especially vigilant. The United States took in more Jewish refugees from Nazi Germany than any other country, approximately one hundred thousand. Nonetheless, U.S. officials turned down thousands of visa applications by German Jews for the flimsiest of reasons. Only in 1939 was the German quota fully filled for the first time; for many German Jews, it was too late.

GENOCIDE, ETHNIC CLEANSING, AND SLAVE LABOR VERSUS INTERNMENT AND GUEST WORKER PROGRAMS

The ambiguities of Weimar Era attitudes toward migration disappeared with Hitler's seizure of power in 1933. Nazi Germany not only implemented policies that led to mass murder but also directly and indirectly uprooted and permanently displaced millions of people across East Central Europe. The Nazi regime placed further restrictions on immigration. It used racial criteria to distinguish between "Germans" and "non-Germans," stripping Jews, in particular, of their German citizenship. After the Hitler–Stalin pact of August 1939, the regime resettled ethnic Germans in East Central Europe on a massive scale. In 1939–40, for instance, Baltic Germans were settled in the western part of Poland. This "Germanization" policy also led to the expulsion of thousands of Poles and Jews. Germany's wartime economy demanded millions of workers and, between 1939 and 1945, hundreds of thousands of Western and Eastern Europeans were deported to Germany as forced laborers and subjected to extreme brutality.

Nazi racial ideology and German labor needs formed a devastating combination that encouraged the exploitation of forced labor. The forced-labor regime geared up in March 1940, when the Reich Security Main Office (RSHA) of the SS instituted a system for the complete control of Polish conscripted labor. Poles were forced to live in separate camps, away from the German population; they had to wear a "P" on their clothes, were forbidden to have any contact with Germans outside the workplace, and were banned from public pools and public transportation. They were paid the lowest legal wages.

Restrictive as these measures were, they were only a harbinger of the brutal system of forced labor yet to come. This harsher phase began with the war against the Soviet Union in June 1941. In part as a result of the harsh treatment of Soviet POWs, which resulted in more than three million deaths, Germany began to employ Soviet civilian workers. These workers were lured to Germany with false promises of good housing and food, but the reality that greeted them was far different. They were segregated from the German population in closed residence camps. At all times, Soviet workers had to wear a badge marked "OST" (East). If the workers broke this and other arbitrary rules, they faced draconian punishments. As the war dragged on and German losses mounted, the German economy became ever more dependent on foreign labor. Soon, even the pretense of recruitment was abandoned and, by 1942, German soldiers began kidnapping civilians and sending them to Germany to work. By the end of 1944, 20 percent of all workers in Germany were foreigners.

In 1942, the concentration-camp system was reorganized. All inmates were forced to work for the German war effort under atrocious conditions that resulted in huge death rates. In Auschwitz, the industrial mass murder of Jews was combined with systematic slave labor. The concentration-camp population greatly increased after 1942, as more and more people from the occupied areas were forced into the system. Several new camps were created during the next two years, and Germany was covered by a dense web of branch camps, which were often attached to large industrial plants. Toward the end of the war, the system completely collapsed, with devastating consequences for the inmates who suffered "evacuations," death marches, and ever-shrinking food rations. Soviet, British, and American forces encountered thousands of dying inmates and many more unburied bodies as they liberated the camps.

After entering the war in late 1941, the United States again interned "enemy aliens" on a large scale. Although several thousand Germans and German Americans were arrested, the main targets of the internment policy were second-generation American citizens of Japanese ancestry (Nisei) and not yet naturalized first-generation Japanese immigrants (Issei). The government unleashed an anti-Japanese propaganda campaign that popularized racist stereotypes and described the Nisei and Issei as potential collaborators with the enemy. At least 120,000 Japanese Americans were deported to remote internment camps in desert areas in the western United States in 1942. It took until 1988 for the U.S. government to belatedly apologize for the gross violation of the Nisei's constitutional rights.

In the West and Southwest, Mexican laborers increasingly replaced Americans who were serving in the war (or were interned). In 1942, the United States and Mexico initiated the so-called Bracero program, under which Mexican workers were allowed into the United States on temporary work contracts. Most were employed as agricultural laborers and were guaranteed a modest minimum wage. The number of workers accepted through the program varied from year to year, reaching a peak of roughly 450,000 in the late 1950s; the program was abolished in 1964.

The harsh U.S. immigration policy toward Jewish refugees from Germany before World War II partly explains why, after the war, the United States briefly opened its doors to many displaced persons (DPs) from across Eastern Europe. However, whether these individuals collaborated with the Nazis or were victimized by them played no role in American immigration policy; in fact, only a minority of the DPs admitted to the United States were Jewish refugees or survivors of Nazi persecution. Ironically, people who had benefited from Nazi policies – ethnic Germans from Eastern Europe, Lithuanians, Latvians, Croats, and others – formed perhaps the largest part of the approximately 450,000 DPs admitted between 1945 and 1952. Given that many Lithuanians, Latvians, and Croats had collaborated with the Nazis, this was a particularly bitter pill for Jewish refugees and other survivors of Nazi persecution. Many of the Jewish refugees had to wait for years in DP camps, mostly in Germany, albeit under American protection. In another sad quirk of fate, many of them had to live in proximity to DPs from Eastern Europe, some of whom had been complicit in the Holocaust.

AFTER 1945

The postwar West German state was more tolerant of immigration, but, at the same time, it imposed heavy restrictions on immigrants who sought German citizenship. Because of continuing conflicted attitudes toward labor migrants, citizenship policy in West Germany was more restrictive after 1945 than it had been at any point prior to the Nazi ascension of power. Nevertheless, since 1945, West – and now unified – Germany has been one of the numerically greatest recipients of immigration in the world. If it ever were true, the idea that Germany is "not a country of immigration" no longer holds any statistical validity.

The end of the war in 1945 left Germany in ruins. In addition to confronting a severe housing shortage, a practically nonexistent economy, and starvation, Germany also faced a massive influx of refugees displaced by the war and postwar convulsions. There were approximately forty to fifty million refugees in Europe as a whole, and occupied Germany housed seven to ten million of them. The first group of immigrants consisted of former POWs, civilian forced laborers, and concentration-camp inmates. Although many of these people found their way to their homes, 1.7 million DPs remained in the Western occupation zones alone at the end of 1945. In addition to the DPs, Germany received ethnic German refugees who fled the advancing Soviet troops at the end of the war or were expelled from the areas that Germany had ceded to the Soviet Union and Poland.

The expellees in the Soviet occupation zone faced much resentment, but they assisted in infrastructure rebuilding and also aided in the economic development of what became the German Democratic Republic in 1949. However, the Soviet occupiers and the East German Socialist Unity Party (Sozialistische Einheitspartei Deutschlands, or SED) barely recognized the expellees as a defined group. At the end of the 1940s, the SED simply announced that "the naturalization of resettlers in the Soviet zone of occupation is complete."

In the West, by contrast, the expellees served as an important and influential political-interest faction well into the 1970s. Ethnic German immigrants were automatically granted German citizenship as a result of the 1913 citizenship law that remained in force after 1945. Here, as in East Germany, the expellees were quickly, if not necessarily easily, integrated economically. However, unlike East Germany, the West German state acknowledged the claims of the expellees to the territories they had left in Eastern Europe. Indeed, West Germany did not accept the 1945 territorial revisions until 1970. Nonetheless, as in East Germany, there were social frictions created by the sudden influx of large numbers of people with different customs and mentalities. One peasant expellee who married a resident German explained, "The [native] peasant women pay no attention to me here. I am a refugee, and so there is a barrier between us."

Between 1949 and 1961, approximately 2.5 million East Germans left for the West. West Germany did not recognize East Germany as a sovereign state and regarded all East Germans as German citizens. By erecting the Berlin Wall, the East German regime closed the last remaining loophole, reducing the number of *Übersiedler* (migrants) from the East to a trickle – until the fall of 1989. It is less known that *Übersiedler* also moved in the other direction. Between 1949 and the late 1960s, approximately five hundred thousand West Germans moved to East Germany; two-thirds of them were, however, return migrants. Although some of these *Übersiedler* were expelled, most stayed and received East German citizenship.

Despite the addition of six million new mouths to feed as a result of the expellees' immigration, the West German state reached full employment by 1961. In that year, too, East Germany built the Berlin Wall, effectively ending the influx of new labor upon which the West German state and its booming economy were dependent. West German industry was still hungry for more labor and, as a result, the Federal Republic began to import laborers from Southern Europe. West Germany had already signed an agreement with Italy authorizing the importation of Italian laborers to assist with the "reconstruction" of German industry in 1955. Similar agreements followed with Spain and Greece in 1960, Turkey in 1961, Portugal in 1964, and Yugoslavia in 1968. By 1974, four million non-Germans were living on West German soil, and 10 percent of the country's workforce were foreign labor migrants.

The economic recession of the early 1970s led to increased political pressure to limit the influx of these *Gastarbeiter* (guest workers). The formal limit on labor recruitment in 1973 did not actually end immigration as much as it changed the character of the foreign population in West Germany. Between 1973 and 1989, the foreign population in the Federal Republic increased from four million to almost five million, although the number of foreign workers actually fell from two and a half million to two million. This demographic shift was a result of supposedly temporary resident aliens deciding to settle in Germany and sending for their families. Although their continued residence was not foreseen in the planning for the guest worker program, unlike in Wilhelmine or Weimar Germany, there was no serious discussion of their expulsion. More importantly, the *Gastarbeiter* enjoyed social rights early on. This constituted not only a distinction from prior German practice but was also different from the American Bracero program. Like other Germans, the *Gastarbeiter* had access to health care, and like other fully employed German workers, obligatory contributions entitled them to German state pensions and unemployment benefits. In contrast, Braceros did not have access to comparable benefits in the United States.

East Germany had a somewhat analogous program that brought in foreign contract workers from socialist countries such as Cuba, Angola, and Vietnam. Most of these workers were isolated from the rest of the population, however, and they were forced to leave once their contracted time expired. Unlike in West Germany, the treatment of contract laborers by the East German state could be harsh: female Vietnamese contract laborers, for instance, were not allowed to become pregnant. If they did, they had to return home immediately or have an abortion.

It is difficult to assess the degree to which foreign workers became integrated into the host culture of either of the two Germanys. Certainly, neither German government encouraged their integration or acceptance. Indeed, the very term *Gastarbeiter* was used to demonstrate that these foreigners were not immigrants but rather temporary "guests." Despite these challenges, German Turks in particular have created a vibrant social and cultural life in cities such as Frankfurt, Stuttgart, and Berlin. Furthermore, many of the *Gastarbeiter* who applied for citizenship and their children eventually became German citizens.

Yet however much resident foreigners may have gained some legal rights and social benefits in Germany, cultural acceptance of non-Germans has lagged behind. This is particularly the case with respect to Muslims in Germany. Now, almost fifty years after the first Turkish "guest workers" moved to Germany, local, state, and national governments are just beginning to tackle issues such as the training of imams in Germany, Muslim burials and other rites such as ritual slaughter, and the provision of religious instruction for Muslim children in state schools, which is available for Christian and Jewish students. There is strong resistance in several parts of Germany to the erection of mosques in city centers or residential neighborhoods. Tellingly, several large mosques can be found instead on the outskirts of German cities, often next to malls or industrial areas. Terrorist attacks, supported only by a tiny minority of Muslims in Germany, have exacerbated the perception of Islam as a diffuse threat. In addition, the reluctance of the state and society to accept Muslim residents as Germans has contributed to widespread ignorance about Islam.

In this respect, Germany resembles its European neighbors, where the situation for Muslim minorities is in some cases even more difficult. In Denmark, for instance, Muslims can only be buried as Protestants because the Lutheran state church does not allow Muslim cemeteries. In France, the secular state makes it often difficult for Muslims to set up cemeteries. America's long tradition of religious pluralism and clear-cut separation of church and state may serve as a model for Europeans to help them integrate their Muslim minorities. Muslim immigrants, especially from the Middle East, have faced discrimination in the United States since 2001, but as the dominant face of the immigrant in American politics remains Hispanic, anti-Muslim sentiment has not necessarily translated into anti-immigrant sentiment; after all, many Muslims in America are African Americans, not immigrants. Furthermore, the expression of their religion is not an issue for the American state. Although subject to pervasive discrimination by society and the state after the attacks of September 11, Muslim immigrants have often found it easier to integrate into the pluralistic American society than have their co-religionists in Europe.

In addition to labor immigration, asylum has been another vector for the immigration of non-ethnic Germans to West Germany. As a result of German guilt about the Nazi past, the Basic Law (Grundgesetz) as drafted in 1949 had a particularly generous asylum policy: Article 16 guaranteed asylum for anyone suffering political persecution. Nonetheless, until the 1970s, few people applied for political asylum. Ethnic Germans have had an easier path to Germany. In the 1980s, increasing numbers of asylum seekers were joined by ethnic Germans from Eastern Europe and the Soviet Union, so-called *Aussiedler*. Many of these *Aussiedler*, especially those who arrived in the mid-1990s, were Germans quite literally in name only. Although they gained German citizenship automatically, they continue to face grievous difficulties with integration into German society. East Germany had also offered political asylum to members of certain groups, especially left-wing activists from Latin America – most prominently, Chilean supporters of Salvador Allende who fled the country after Augusto Pinochet's violent takeover in 1973.

German attitudes toward immigrants after reunification in 1990 remain conflicted. In 1994, partly as a result of the arrival of a large wave of refugees from the conflicts in Yugoslavia, the Bundestag essentially abolished the generous asylum clause, supposedly to close a loophole for illegal "economic migrants." Efforts to liberalize immigration did not make much progress even after a Social Democratic/Green Party coalition government came into office in the late 1990s. In 2000, the German government adopted a "green card" program to bring several thousand young information-technology professionals from Eastern Europe and South Asia to Germany. Only a handful of professionals applied, however. In contrast to the American green card, which guarantees permanent residency and is often the first step to full citizenship, the German green card turned out to be a "red card" because it did not provide permanent residency and explicitly excluded the possibility of obtaining German citizenship.

Germany, like its European neighbors, needs more immigrants to revive an aging society and save its ailing pension systems. German officials have finally, if belatedly, acknowledged Germany's past and present as a country of immigration. In a 2000 speech, President Johannes Rau stated that "leaving a homeland and adapting to a new culture is a story that has been repeated throughout history – in the history of Germany too" and, crucially, "promoting immigration is a prime task for our society." Nevertheless, popular resistance to immigration remains strong. Only after years of negotiations did Germany finally pass an immigration law, which took effect in January 2005. For the first time in modern German history, a law allows for the immigration and naturalization of persons who cannot claim ethnic German descent. However, it has opened Germany's door to immigrants only to a very limited degree. For instance, asylum seekers and refugees are still not permitted to work and are forced instead to rely on welfare as long as their status is pending, a process that can drag on for years. This mandated reliance on welfare not only provokes popular discontent among poorer Germans; it also closes a crucial path to integration. It is hardly understandable from an American perspective, where hard work has traditionally been viewed as an important avenue into American society. If Germany has become – indeed, always was – a country of immigration, its recognition of that fact has been intermittent at best.

Germany's story during the past forty years has been one of a fitful and gradual coming to terms with immigration. In contrast, the United States has, on the surface at least, had a substantially more generous immigration policy. The Johnson administration overhauled and liberalized U.S. immigration policy in 1965, supplanting the racist quota laws that had been in place since the 1920s. As Roger Daniels, a leading historian of American immigration, has remarked, President Lyndon Johnson "for once, underplayed the importance of a piece of legislation for which he was responsible," when he stated in 1965, in front of the Statue of Liberty, that the Hart – Celler act was "not revolutionary." Each country, including Mexico, received relatively fair annual quotas. In addition, the act made it possible for relatives and persons needed as workers to bypass the quotas altogether. The lawmakers envisaged a rise of immigration from Europe. However, West European economies were booming and emigration from Eastern Europe was severely restricted. Rather unexpectedly, the quotas and the bypass possibilities boosted migration from East and South Asian countries as well as from Latin America. The predicted annual cap of 290,000 immigrants proved unrealistically low. During the 1970s, the numbers of immigrants, most of whom were non-Europeans, reached twice that number, and it has continued to climb steadily. Indeed, at the opening of the twenty-first century, immigration rates reached the level of the period just after 1900.

In the wake of the terror attacks of September 11, 2001, America has become much more concerned about protecting its borders. Self-styled "Minutemen" patrol the border with Mexico, individual communities have restricted access to government services to both legal and illegal immigrants, and raids have sent many illegal immigrants home from jobs in which they had enjoyed tacit acceptance in the past. In addition, the Immigration and Naturalization Service (INS) was reorganized. The newly created Department of Homeland Security has imposed new immigration restrictions and more thorough checks, targeting certain groups, although the overall rate of immigration has not significantly declined.

In addition to America's officially sanctioned (i.e., legal) immigrants, there are a substantial number of illegal immigrants, whose work has become crucial to the American economy. The quota system, especially in the case of Mexico, has proved to be a huge constraint on legal immigration. The history of immigration restrictions, coupled with the tradition of tapping a pool of seemingly unlimited cheap labor south of the border for low-wage jobs, explains the huge rise in "illegal" migration to the United States, particularly since the late 1970s. Illegal migrants work in America's fields and factories and even take care of American children. As of 2005, there were more than ten million illegal immigrants living and working in the United States; another million arrive each year, overwhelmingly from Latin America.

The illegals are a very real and important part of American economy, but they inhabit a legal gray zone and can indeed be described as social "ghosts." Although many illegal immigrants have lived in the United States for decades and often have legal spouses and children, they face serious social and legal restrictions. Illegal migrants cannot organize against exploitative employers; they cannot easily visit their homes and families; often, they have to avoid medical care even if they are able to afford health insurance; and they are easy targets for blackmail. Not only are illegal migrants highly vulnerable to criminal victimization, not to mention racially motivated violence, but they are usually unable to go to the police when they are victimized.

Of course, the "illegal migrant" is a legally defined construct. The American government spends huge sums to enforce a nonenforceable border. Hundreds have died in the deserts of Arizona and New Mexico after the controls along the urbanized areas of the border in Texas and California began to be more strictly enforced in the early 1990s. In recent decades, illegals have been employed in the expanding service sector, more are coming from Central America, and they have increasingly moved away from the border – following middle-class Americans to the shopping malls and restaurants in suburbia and exurbia across the nation. But wherever they live, they have to enter and leave through the back door.

Why does the United States not simply liberalize work migration from Mexico and other Latin American countries? After all, many Latin Americans living in the United States are perfectly legal immigrants, a fact that is often ignored in the American immigration discussion. What would be economically feasible, and make the lives of millions of clandestine migrants easier, is difficult to achieve politically. Most Americans oppose an official lifting of the "Tortilla Curtain." Latin Americans are seen as competitors for jobs; according to popular belief, huge numbers already take advantage of social services such as education and welfare, and they are associated with crime, notably drug smuggling. An amnesty for illegal immigrants already living and working in the United States is a hotly debated topic; however, both major American parties object to a liberalization of policy toward new immigrants. In 2004, the Bush administration proposed a guest worker program as a solution to the continuing illegal migration. Aspiring migrants would be offered a legal path into America as guest workers, but only for a limited time period and with no option to apply for permanent residency while in the United States. This concept, as many commentators quickly recognized, closely resembled the older Bracero program. After three previous bills had stalled in Congress in 2005 and 2006, even a widely supported compromise, the 2007 Immigration Reform Act, failed to pass in the Senate. In addition to instituting the guest worker program and providing funds for reinforcing the U.S.–Mexican border fence, this act would have offered most of the then-twelve million undocumented migrants a chance to become legal immigrants. In 2009, President George W. Bush acknowledged the failure to pass the immigration reform act as one of the biggest regrets of his presidency.

It is noteworthy that the United States has allowed de facto guest workers to enter the country legally for many decades. Highly skilled or seasonal workers can apply for nonimmigrant visas (H1B or H2B), which are valid for a limited period. Yet, the quota for H2B visas for seasonal workers is often exhausted before the end of each year. Unlike the proposed guest worker program, these visas do offer the possibility to apply for permanent residency (the so-called green card) and eventually citizenship. The H1B/H2B scheme resembles the German *Gastarbeiter* program and could be the basis for broader immigration reform in the United States. Admittedly, *Gastarbeiter* were expected to return to their home countries, but they enjoyed social rights and could apply for citizenship. A new Bracero program, as envisioned by the Bush administration, is likely to fail so long as labor migrants are deprived of the possibility of becoming permanent residents and eventually citizens.

The issue of illegal work migration has a parallel in the German and European case: America's Southwest could be compared to Germany's East. Before World War I, Germany wished to seal its long eastern border but could not; at the same time, it was dependent on Polish migrant labor. With the collapse of the Soviet empire in 1989, the border between East and West once again became more porous. Meanwhile, the United States currently engages in a futile attempt to control its long Mexican border while being simultaneously dependent on the illegal immigrants who cross it despite these enforcement attempts.

CONCLUSION

There is no German counterpart to the image of the Statue of Liberty welcoming the "huddled masses" to America's shores. Yet, behind the myths of American inclusion and German exclusion lurks a much more complicated portrait of two nations struggling with the challenges and opportunities of immigration.

The image of the United States as a beacon of freedom and tolerance for immigrants is a myth. From its earliest days until the present, forces of exclusion, deep-rooted racism and discrimination, and even brutal violence, especially against "non-white" immigrants, have been part of American history. For most of the twentieth century, U.S. immigration policy was restrictive, and the most deserving refugees and immigrants were excluded. Still, American immigration history proves the enormous potential of immigration from around the world. In America, immigrants have not encountered an exclusive *Volk*, tied to a romanticized ethno-cultural myth from the past, but rather a republican project influenced by Enlightenment universalism and oriented toward the future with a strong pluralistic ethos. Ethnic groups are not perceived as minorities but as distinctive parts of the dynamic and pluralist American mosaic. Since the late nineteenth century, immigrants have made America "their" home. Hyphenated identities are really an expression of a deeper link between a specific ethnicity and America. A good illustration of this mutually reinforcing and dynamic relationship between seemingly particularistic and overarching American narratives is the foundation or "home-making myth." Immigrants have successfully inserted their memory into the public memory of America by constructing their own foundation myths, which range from Columbus, who has been claimed by Italian, Jewish, and Spanish Americans, to the participation of different groups in the American Revolution, the Civil War, and beyond. Another illustration of this relationship is the rise of ethnic American food in and especially beyond America during the twentieth century. Pizza or bagels are quintessentially American, and yet their appeal is defined by their ethnic roots.

In contrast, Germans have never accepted immigration as part of their national identity, even as the long twentieth century bears witness to the reality of a large population of immigrants living and working on German soil. In Germany, as in many other countries, immigrants were and often still are expected to accommodate to their respective host societies, although prejudice has made such assimilation difficult, if not impossible. Germans have rarely been entirely hospitable to migrants, but except for the Nazi years, they cannot be characterized as being completely unwelcoming either. As in the United States, economic, political, social, legal, and cultural imperatives all complicate any simple narrative of the German encounter with immigrants.

Today, both America and Germany stand at a crossroads. In Germany, the immigration law of 2005 seems to be a turning point, although its full significance remains unclear, and President Rau's vision of German recognition of immigrants is more a dream than reality. In 2008, Chancellor Angela Merkel attended a swearing-in ceremony for new citizens that heavily borrowed on the American model, symbolically demonstrating her commitment to the inclusion of immigrants. Nevertheless, the number of foreigners who became German citizens that year declined to its lowest level since German reunification in 1990. Meanwhile, America faces contradictory impulses – on the one hand, a desire to shut its borders to illegal immigrants and turn inward following the terrorist attacks of 2001; on the other, a newly mobilized immigrant population eager to claim its own stake in a pluralistic America, on display in massive demonstrations by immigrants and their supporters who flooded onto America's streets in 2006 to protest anti-immigration legislation then making its way through Congress. The election of Barack Obama as the first African American president seemed for many to open a new chapter in American history. President Obama, himself the child of an immigrant (albeit one who returned home), has insisted on the importance of comprehensive immigration reform that would provide a path to citizenship for long-term illegal immigrants. However, at the time of this writing, it is too early to know how successful he will be in achieving immigration reform that assuages fears of unrestricted borders while acknowledging the plurality of America's past and present.

Further Reading

Bade, Klaus J. *Migration in European History* (Oxford, 2003).

Bayor, Ronald H., ed. *Race and Ethnicity in America: A Concise History* (New York, 2003).

Chin, Rita. *The Guestworker Question in Postwar Germany* (Cambridge, 2007).

Daniels, Roger. *Coming to America: A History of Immigration and Ethnicity in American Life* (New York, 1991).

Fahrmeir, Andreas. *Citizenship: The Rise and Fall of a Modern Concept* (New Haven, 2008).

Gabaccia, Donna R. *We Are What We Eat: Ethnic Food and the Making of Americans* (Cambridge, MA 2000).

Fuchs, Lawrence. *The American Kaleidoscope: Race, Ethnicity, and the Civic Culture* (Hanover, 1990).

Herbert, Ulrich. *A History of Foreign Labor in Germany, 1880–1980: Seasonal Workers / Guest Workers* (Ann Arbor, 1990).

Higham, John. *Strangers in the Land: Patterns of American Nativism, 1860–1925* (New Brunswick, 1955).

Higham, John. *Send These to Me: Immigrants in Urban America* (Baltimore, 1975).

Hoerder, Dirk. *Cultures in Contact: World Migrations in the Second Millennium* (Durham, 2002).

Hoffmann, Lutz. *Die Unvollendete Republik: Zwischen Einwanderungsland und Deutschem Nationalstaat* (Cologne, 1992).

Klausen, Jytte. *The Islamic Challenge: Politics and Religion in Western Europe* (Oxford, 2005).

Lucassen, Leo. *The Immigrant Threat: The Integration of Old and New Immigrants in Western Europe since 1850* (Urbana, 2005).

Marrus, Michael R. *The Unwanted – European Refugees in the Twentieth Century* (New York, 1985).

Ngai, Mae M. *Impossible Subjects: Illegal Aliens and the Making of Modern America* (Princeton, 2003).

Øverland, Orm. *Immigrant Minds, American Identities: Making the United States Home 1870–1930* (Urbana, 2000).

Reimers, David M. *Other Immigrants: The Global Origins of the American People* (New York, 2005).

Tichenor, Daniel J. *Dividing Lines: The Politics of Immigration Control in America* (Princeton, 2002).

Wertheimer, Jack. *Unwelcome Strangers: East European Jews in Imperial Germany* (New York, 1987).

Zolberg, Aristide R. *A Nation by Design: Immigration Policy in the Fashioning of America* (Cambridge, MA 2006).

7

Masses: Mobilization versus Manipulation

W. FITZHUGH BRUNDAGE AND KONRAD H. JARAUSCH

Since the Jacksonian Era, American intellectuals have generally hailed the broadening of political participation as a sign of ineluctable progress and unparalleled historical importance. Some commentators voiced reservations about the pace and extent of democratization, but their voices were countered by those, like Theodore Parker, an important influence on Abraham Lincoln, who interpreted American history since the Revolution as demonstrating the superiority of "a government of all, for all, and by all." In contrast, many more European observers, like Gustave Le Bon, were more skeptical of the mass age, fearing the emergence of demagogues through the gullibility of "the mob." Terrorized by the Nazi and communist dictatorships, Hannah Arendt, a German émigré on American soil, formulated her disappointment in the promise of expanding democracy thus: "Totalitarian movements are mass organizations of atomized, isolated individuals." These contrasting judgments not only exemplify distinctive historical experiences between the Old and New Worlds, they also circumscribe the range of consequences of a transformation that intensified around the beginning of the twentieth century.

Instead of simply constituting a success story, the experience of mass politics suggests two contradictory readings. On balance, the record of mobilization in the United States supports an optimistic assessment because during the course of the twentieth century, the political system came closer to reflecting the diversity of the nation's population and interests than at any previous time. Despite pitched contests over who could participate in public life, the mass mobilization of constituencies was an essential facet of American public life throughout the twentieth century. In many ways, this development appears to have been both emancipatory and democratic in effect, as exemplified by the campaign for women's suffrage before World War I, the industrial labor movement during the 1930s, the civil rights movement of the 1960s, and the environmental movement more recently. Some elements of the German story also support such a positive representation. During the semi-constitutional empire, the universal male suffrage of Reichstag elections extended participation and prepared the ground for the liberal constitution of the Weimar Republic. After the dark interlude of the Nazi dictatorship and the continuation of repression under the communists in the East, the re-democratization of the Federal Republic ultimately succeeded in turning the longing for participation back into a parliamentary direction.

Yet, there is much evidence as well for a more skeptical assessment of this trajectory that emphasizes exclusion and manipulation. On closer inspection, American mass politics has also generated many reactionary movements, ranging from the Ku Klux Klan during the 1920s to the anti-abortion movement since 1973, and it has not prevented the emergence of oligarchic politics. In Germany, the breathtaking rise of the Nazi movement in the early 1930s as well as the concurrent popularity of the Communist Party showed that an antirepublican majority of the electorate could actually abolish a democratic government. As *Mein Kampf* demonstrates, Hitler was obsessed with the issue of gathering mass support for his illiberal policies, turning hopes for participation into hollow forms of acclamation and thereby using his charisma to manipulate rather than liberate his followers. The radical antifascism of the communists ironically led to another one-party dictatorship, that of East Germany's Socialist Unity Party (Sozialistische Einheitspartei Deutschlands, or SED), that used some of the same methods to whip up the crowd – albeit for opposite ideological ends. The rise of popular participation has therefore been a contested process rife with contradictory consequences.

To resolve this paradox, it may be useful to divide the development of modern mass politics into several periods, even if the transatlantic chronologies sometimes diverge considerably. A first period, centered around the transformation from a politics that was dominated by networks of local notables to mass organizations on a national scale that sought to expand the suffrage, could be located roughly from the 1880s to the end of World War I. A second period, dealing with the expansion of participation to virtually all members of the community that produced dictatorial counter-movements focused on acclamation, could be said to have lasted from the 1920s to the generational rebellion of the late 1960s. A final period, which involves the ambiguous experiences of mature democracy with universal rights but declining participation rates and flare-ups of extraparliamentary politics, would extend from the 1970s to the present. Such a periodization not only suggests similarities of development on both sides of the Atlantic but also highlights the increasing disparity during the middle period.

Because transatlantic comparisons demand analytical categories to illuminate similarities and differences, four guiding questions structure the following reflections:

1. Who participated in mass politics and on what basis? This question addresses the attempt of previously excluded groups to gain a voice in the political process.
2. What were the principal sites of mass politics? This question involves the location of conflict, which shifted from "civil society" to parties and parliaments, only to spill once again into extraparliamentary arenas.
3. What were the chief aims of mass mobilization? This question involves efforts to protect individuals from repression, to obtain social security as well as economic opportunity, and eventually also to realize such goals as racial and gender equality.
4. How did the developments in the United States and Germany influence each other?

This line of inquiry shifts the perspective from a comparison to transnational influence. In Germany, the ideals of American democracy formed a positive model, but their negative aspects could also fuel a blinkered anti-Americanism. Similarly, in the United States, progress in democratizing Germany would be seen as validation of its own system, but the National Socialist and SED dictatorships also served as cautionary examples.

At the beginning of the twentieth century, the political struggle revolved around making the American and German systems more inclusive, although these systems differed markedly in the degree to which the voices of citizens were heard. Without question, the scope and influence of mass politics in the United States during the late nineteenth and early twentieth centuries were vastly larger than in Germany. In no German cities did democratic politics comparable to the American practice prevail. Likewise, state governments and legislatures in the United States, which were centers of political innovation in the era before the mid-twentieth-century consolidation of federal power, responded to democratic pressure to a degree unmatched in any of the *Länder* in Germany. Moreover, even during the era of the so-called robber barons in the United States, when J. P. Morgan, John D. Rockefeller, and their ilk were alleged to have run roughshod over democratic principles, the influence of American elites in politics was strikingly smaller than that of their counterparts in Germany. Robust political parties in the United States sometimes did the bidding of elites but could also be swept up by populist impulses. In sum, the United States and Germany entered the twentieth century with very different experiences with mass, democratic politics.

Nevertheless, the direction of political change in the two countries was similar in several important regards. The American form of government was a republic with an inclusive language of public life and a general acceptance of the diversity of civil society. Reflecting both the democratic impulses and racial assumptions of antebellum ideology, the electorate in 1890 included virtually all native-born white men. The political parties of the age were so adept at mobilizing this electorate that at no subsequent time in the twentieth century did such a large proportion of eligible voters routinely turn out on Election Day. In Imperial Germany, by contrast, political rights were also growing but remained more restricted. As a concession to the national liberal movement for unification, Chancellor Otto von Bismarck had conceded universal male suffrage to the citizens of the Reich, who thereafter voted in elections for the parliament, called in neo-medieval fashion the Reichstag. But in the empire's semi-constitutional order, this body only had legislative and budgetary powers, and the Kaiser reserved the right to appoint the chancellor, control the military, and conduct foreign affairs.

On both sides of the Atlantic, actual participation in politics remained circumscribed by considerable restrictions of citizenship. In the United States, the federal system sanctioned substantial exceptions to citizenship rights, including the enforcement of the Reconstruction-era constitutional amendments. Not only were African Americans systematically disenfranchised in much of the former Confederacy but also many categories of immigrants, including both Chinese and Japanese, were deprived of access to citizenship. Moreover, half the nation's population – women – lacked formal political rights. In Imperial Germany, the differing franchises of the states were even less liberal. The largest member, Prussia, which controlled about three-fifths of the population, had a "three-class-suffrage" in which votes were apportioned within electoral districts according to the amount of taxes paid. For instance, in rural East Elbia, a handful of large landowners, called Junkers, constituted the first class; several hundred townspeople, consisting of the propertied and educated middle class, comprised the second category; and tens of thousands of landless laborers occupied the bottom group.

The pressure to abolish these restrictions came from mass organizations that were dissatisfied with the limited nature of the traditional "politics of notables" (*Honoratiorenpolitik*). In the United States, groups like the Knights of Labor and the Populist movements of the 1880s and early 1890s clamored for a greater voice for "producers" (i.e., all those occupations that contributed to the wealth of the society) against "parasites," like lawyers and speculators. Moreover, the women's suffrage movement and the United Negro Improvement Association campaigned for an extension of formal voting rights beyond white males. In Germany, the nascent Social Democratic Party and its supporting trade unions were especially important in organizing public demonstrations to demand electoral reform for workers and women. Similarly, the Catholic minority that gathered in the Center Party as a result of the *Kulturkampf* tried to gain a larger voice in the political process by making itself indispensable. In both countries, the drive for an extension of participation was spearheaded by precisely those groups that felt excluded from the political process and underprivileged in a social and economic sense.

In response to the clamor for inclusion from below, traditional elites sought to create a mass basis for maintaining their own ascendancy. Reactionary groups, resenting any liberalization, also began to fight back. In the United States, nativists campaigned to restrict immigration, and white Southerners revived the Ku Klux Klan to intimidate blacks. In Germany, where the power of elites remained substantially greater than in the United States, the various parties of the right, such as the Conservatives and the Free Conservatives, began to sponsor various kinds of mass organizations with the aim of assembling a popular following and competing more effectively in elections. A plethora of rightist groups such as the Army, Navy, and Colonial Leagues; the Pan-German League; and the anti-Slavic HTK-Association therefore created a base for nationalist and anti-Semitic causes, initiating an ideological competition for the allegiance of the masses who were growing interested in politics. In both countries, the government used national holidays like the Fourth of July and the Kaiser's birthday to hold military parades with colorful uniforms, shiny weapons, bands playing, and officers on horseback to reaffirm patriotic loyalties as well as shore up the existing order.

In the United States, legislatures were the primary site of the emergent mass politics because they determined the rules of the political game. State legislatures and municipal governments became centers of political innovation and mobilization as a result of campaigns by both political "machines" and reform-minded groups intent on turning popular politics to their advantage. By the early decades of the twentieth century, pressure from these sources brought about changes in the U.S. Congress as well, such as the direct election of U.S. senators.

In both countries, civil society produced numerous voluntary associations that mobilized like-minded groups for common causes, thereby expanding the actors in public life beyond the confines of the electorate. In the United States, some groups, especially women's organizations like the Women's Christian Temperance Union, adopted a nonpartisan strategy to lobbying. During the early twentieth century, organizations committed to everything from public health to juvenile justice reform pioneered new and sophisticated forms of lobbying. In Germany, the counterpoint to the massive trade-union movement was provided by two employers associations, the CVDI and the BDI, which lobbied heavily for adoption of business-friendly policies, even if they sometimes clashed over issues like protective tariffs. Among the middle class, professional organizations of lawyers, physicians, teachers, and engineers proliferated, all of which wanted to make sure that their clientele got its wishes adopted through laws passed by parliament. Thus, despite the breadth and energy of the voluntary organizations that participated in civil society, electoral politics remained at the center of mass politics.

The slowness of the federal legislature to respond to popular desires, however, forced insurgent movements to adopt an extraparliamentary strategy, dramatizing their causes in the public so as to force change from without. In the United States, the most striking instance of this process, as noted, was the Populist movement, a largely agrarian insurgency of the 1890s that won broad support across much of the rural South and Plains States. The movement seemed poised to challenge the established political parties in the elections of 1896, but without a proportional system of representation, the Populist party could achieve its goals only through either cooption by one of the existing parties or outright victory. When the Populists fused with the Democrats, they not only surrendered many of their principles or saw them coopted but also underscored the apparent futility of third-party politics in the American system. In Germany, the new mass organizations first tried to dominate the public space to demonstrate the overwhelming nature of their support. The purpose of Socialist marches, with banners flying and members singing and walking in closed ranks, was to impress a public with the power of a labor movement that could no longer be ignored.

The ultimate aim of this "politics of the street" was the expansion of participation in the political process. In the United States, public discourse focused on the protection of individual freedom within a mass democracy dominated by large, impersonal forces. In the presidential campaign of 1912, Woodrow Wilson, the Democratic candidate, advocated a "New Freedom" that purportedly would offer the American electorate greater individual autonomy in the face of the threat of economic and political concentration (in the form of business "trusts" and labor unions). In Germany, the chief goal of mass mobilization was the extension of civil rights to create a parliamentary government. Because the Conservatives opposed concessions to the masses and the National Liberals and the Center Party were unsure what to do, it was the Progressive Party and the Social Democratic Party that clamored for expanding franchise rights. However, the domestic deadlock stymied Prussian electoral reform until the masses took matters into their own hands and rebelled against the military quasi-dictatorship in the November Revolution of 1918.

Behind the campaign for extending participation lay the struggle for a better life through individual exertion or through collective social reform. In the United States, the legacy of nineteenth-century laissez-faire ideology, focused on individual "liberty" as the sacred principle of democracy, was so strong as to inhibit collective action and to make the country generally unreceptive to the spread of socialism from the continent. Even when the Progressives campaigned for social improvements like municipal reform, they were careful to couch their appeals in language that was consonant with the rhetoric of American individualism. The common refrain was that mass mobilization and collective goals were necessary to empower individual citizens in an age of mass society. The stronger heritage of state power in Germany, in contrast, inspired conservatives like Bismarck to initiate a social policy of accident, health, and unemployment insurance to stop Marxist subversion. The liberal middle-class parties that dominated city governments had no compunction about employing a professional civil service as guardians for housing reform, better transportation, and so on. The labor unions and the Social Democratic Party therefore had little difficulty in calling for state action to improve the lives of the poor.

During this formative era of mass politics, there was considerable transatlantic interaction. Just as English communitarianism and German radicalism had exerted influence on currents of reform in the United States before the Civil War, so too a generation of "transatlantic brokers" foraged through Europe during the late nineteenth century, looking for solutions to the problems that vexed the modernizing United States. Among these cosmopolitan reformers who studied in Germany during the 1890s were, to name only a few, Frederic Howe, John R. Commons, Richard T. Ely, and W. E. B. Du Bois. That experience "knocked the provincial blinkers off a cadre of young Americans." Looking on Germany as a sociopolitical laboratory, American reformers became students of everything from zoning policies in Berlin to socialist housing in Vienna. Of course, the American disciples of European reform did not wield political power commensurate with their ambitions because few of them engaged in mass politics. Nevertheless, they framed the debate about social politics that would, to a great extent, dictate the evolution of the American state well into the New Deal era.

From the Revolution of 1776 onward, American democracy served as a model for those restive spirits in Central Europe who wanted to democratize their own states. Although the educated were often skeptical of the lack of cultivation of the New World, the common people had no such inhibitions and looked with admiration at the democratic experiment that they hoped to emulate in time. Whereas elaborate treatises tended to warn of the leveling consequences of extending participation, popular pamphlets embraced the American example with enthusiasm — an image that was also supported by letters from emigrés. Especially during the revolution of 1848, the radical democrats looked to America for models of self-government, and many fled across the Atlantic once the revolution failed. The Social Democratic Party had more difficulties with transatlantic borrowing because consumer capitalism eventually came to serve as an alternative model to socialist revolution. Because of ambivalent feelings of both attraction and repulsion, propagandists on both sides during World War I had little difficulty accentuating negative clichés by turning the Germans into militaristic "Huns" and the Americans into greedy "Yanks."

WIDENING PARTICIPATION

During the middle of the twentieth century, the movement to widen political participation in both countries was ultimately victorious – but this period also witnessed the greatest divergence between the United States and Germany as the former perfected its democracy while the latter fell prey to two dictatorships. In the United States, virtually all of the most pernicious gender and racial obstacles to political participation by adults were removed by ratification of the Nineteenth Amendment in 1920 and the passage of the Voting Rights Act of 1965, respectively. Soon after the Voting Rights Act was enacted, the voting age was lowered to eighteen. Participation in formal politics expanded more during these five decades than during the previous century and a half of the nation's history. This dramatic expansion of American democracy was both a consequence and stimulant of mass politics. Indeed, much of American public life and formal politics during the twentieth century was given over to coming to terms with the implications of the expansion of democracy.

In Germany, the Weimar Republic, born in defeat and revolution, also made a resolute attempt to realize democratic aspirations, but its eventual failure paved the way for the rise of the Nazi and communist dictatorships. Its constitution abolished all restrictions of class and gender, therefore allowing universal participation. Women not only received the vote but could also run for office and claim full citizenship. On the state level, the different limitations were ended as well, so that the regional and national suffrages became equally liberal. However, proportional representation allowed political fragmentation and permitted the rather considerable antirepublican minorities on the left (communist) and on the right (National Socialist) to compete using democratic means for illiberal ends. Because large sections of the public rejected the Versailles peace and the policy of fulfillment, and the economic crises of hyperinflation and the Great Depression fractured the underlying civil society, Weimar eventually turned into a "Republic without Republicans." Within an illiberal electorate, the chance for universal participation was insufficient to create a stable parliamentary government.

Based on its liberal traditions, the United States was more successful in broadening identities and in creating more inclusive conceptions of citizenship during this period. After 1924, when new immigration restrictions dramatically reduced the number of immigrants, public discourse surrounding citizenship displayed a new tolerance toward the nation's diverse populations and cultures. At the same time, the liberal politics of Franklin Delano Roosevelt (FDR) promoted new ideas about "Americanness" to create a broader base for the Democratic Party beyond immigrant Catholics and white Southerners. To achieve that goal, Democrats sought to retain the allegiance of longtime supporters while at the same time winning over rural Midwestern Protestants and Northern African Americans. Faced with the challenge of uniting diverse and competing interests, FDR resorted to a political rhetoric that emphasized the common needs and aspirations of all Americans. This expansive "civic nationalism" embraced the nation's immigrants, lauding them as ardent Americans whose ambitions and patriotism were indistinguishable from those of other Americans. The simple but crucial point is that this new ascendant "civic nationalism" encouraged Americans to imagine themselves as a single national community united by culture and values.

The Nazis, by contrast, sought to overcome the fragmentation of the Weimar Republic by combining elements of popular mobilization with strong leadership and by sponsoring a racial nationalism that excluded allegedly hostile groups from the national community. Hitler did not consider the Nazi party a regular party but talked incessantly of "our movement," which suggested direction and dynamism at the same time. The concept of a *Volksgemeinschaft*, a national community, similarly embraced inclusiveness and participation. In practice, the leadership principle (*Führerprinzip*) meant a strict top-down hierarchy, and the thorough "coordination" (*Gleichschaltung*) of organizations eliminated the independence of civil society. Actually, the mythical union of the people was based on severe exclusions of a political (anticommunist, illiberal) and racial (Jews, Roma, Slavs) nature that deprived the discriminated groups not only of their citizenship rights (as in the purge of the bureaucracy and the implementation of the Nuremberg Laws) but ultimately also of their lives. Although they practically abolished parliament, the Nazis retained plebiscites, turning participation into mass acclamation to validate Hitler's continuing charisma.

In its pursuit of an antifascist communist ideology, the German Democratic Republic ironically resorted to similar political devices because it also became a one-party dictatorship. In contrast to the Nazis, the SED was never really popular, having to govern as a minority and rely on the tanks of the Red Army as the workers' uprising in 1953 demonstrated. The communists also talked about participation but defined democracy in Rousseau's sense as implementation of the *volonté générale*, with the leading party deciding what the people ought to want. An educational or welfare dictatorship would guide the *demos* and take care of its needs. Nonetheless, the SED also insisted on popular participation through its own mass organizations, in which citizens were compelled to be active to demonstrate their good faith in the system. The creation of a "national bloc" of antifascist parties, which distributed parliamentary seats before elections were held, reduced voting to a meaningless act of "folding ballots." Except for the churches, no space for an independent civil society in the GDR remained.

Only with the establishment of the Federal Republic in 1949 did a liberal definition of participation return in western Germany. Shocked by the extent of Nazi crimes, the architects of the Basic Law, the Federal Republic's constitution, wanted to prevent the self-dissolution of democracy in the future by correcting the Weimar Republic mistakes. The new constitution made it impossible to abolish human rights, added a 5-percent hurdle to parliamentary representation, weakened the power of the presidency, and excluded plebiscitary elements. The revival of politics from the bottom up – beginning with home towns, extending to states, and only then to the federal level – also tried to focus participation on areas in which citizens could gain a sense of controlling their own affairs. The Federal Republic was a "representative democracy" that distrusted grassroots movements and privileged decisions of elected representatives so as to gain independence from the changing sentiments of an immature electorate. As a result, the Bundestag grew more aloof than the preceding Reichstag, and the "Bonn Republic," as the Federal Republic was informally known, proved more stable than its predecessor. Nonetheless, it took several decades for the restored democracy to strike roots.

In the United States, meanwhile, the emergence of modern mass culture both facilitated and encouraged mass politics. The sites of American mass politics were decisively affected by the mass media, which promoted a shared culture cutting across ethnic, class, and racial lines. The unprecedented corporate consolidation of the still relatively young mass media, including radio, movies, and later television, eroded many of the remaining cultural boundaries that had sustained the nation's "island communities." To take one notable example, swing music during the 1930s became so pervasive that it provided the soundtrack to Merrie Melodies cartoons, fueled the popularity of Texas swing, dominated the airwaves, and inspired the fusion of Klezmer music and jazz that became known as Yiddish swing. By the late 1930s, swing music had left its imprint on virtually every form of popular music and every community of listeners in the nation.

In Germany, the media were a crucial element in both supporting democracy through free speech and legitimating dictatorship through propaganda. Weimar's press landscape was highly diverse, torn by partisan disputes and competitive in its variety of formats. The "reactionary modernism" of the Nazis was particularly adept at using modern tools like radio and film to spread the message. The Nazis' chief propagandist, Joseph Goebbels, understood how to reach a mass audience. Hitler's magnetic speeches were broadcast over the air to an audience that was compelled to listen in schools, factories, or town squares, and newsreels celebrated real and imagined Nazi victories. At the same time, the streets were filled with parades of some of the many uniformed Nazi Party auxiliaries, marching and waving flags to suggest popular unity behind the regime. East Germany's communist regime used most of these techniques as well. The SED held weekly indoctrination hours to bring its members up to speed on the latest ideological developments. Only the Federal Republic restored press freedom and created an independent radio and television system, capable of expressing diverse views and criticizing the government.

If the mass media facilitated mass politics, the maturation of the broker state of the New Deal era placed a premium on the mass mobilization of political-economic blocs. In the United States, skepticism and even hostility toward mass organizations gave way to a recognition of the value, even necessity, of competing interest groups. In the new calculus, the state would adjudicate the competing goals of organized labor (the name itself is suggestive), consumer groups, and business. Although this model of governance encouraged mobilization of organized interests, it simultaneously worked to yoke those interests to the state and, when possible, to the Democratic coalition. The Townsend and Share the Wealth campaigns for federally funded pensions during FDR's first term, for example, were quickly coopted by the Democratic Party; similarly, the industrial labor movement quickly joined the Democratic coalition rather than remain a separate site of mass politics.

In the successive regime changes of the twentieth century, German mass organizations, representing competing interests, also played a crucial role. During the Weimar Republic, the politics of the street intensified, assuming a quasi-civil war character because of the various communist insurgencies and the rightist putsches of Kapp and Hitler. Paramilitary organizations attached to the mass parties, such as the Social Democrats' Reichsbanner, the Communists' Rotfront, and the Nazis' Sturmabteilung, flourished and engaged in pitched battles for control of beer halls, streets, and market squares. In the Third Reich and the GDR alike, all mass organizations were "coordinated," that is, controlled by the ruling party to serve as transmission belts of official ideology. Participation in them was mandatory to show one's support for the regime, and the ruling party used them for purposes of public acclamation. Only the Federal Republic restored the freedom of association within civil society, which led to a proliferation of groups lobbying the Bundestag in favor of their particular interests. The practice of consulting all major social factions before making decisions established a kind of "neocorporatism" in politics.

Two American mass mobilizations that proved resistant to the gravitational pull of formal politics and that tried to establish "counter-institutions" were the civil rights movement and the student movement of the 1960s. African Americans were compelled by their pariah status in the South to think creatively about sites for and modes of mass mobilization. They considered older black civic institutions in the region too rife with class divisions or too bound up in the established order of interracial politics to serve as foundations for aggressive or inclusive activism. Consequently, the new grassroots organizations and campaigns launched by the Student Nonviolent Coordinating Committee (SNCC), the Southern Christian Leadership Conference (SCLC), and other groups often stood in opposition not only to the segregationist civic institutions of the South but also to national political institutions and civic organizations. The battle at the 1964 Democratic Convention over the recognition of the Mississippi Freedom Democratic Party, a black insurgency against the established Democratic organization, exposed the challenge to conventional political institutions and procedures. Inspired by this example, student radicals during the 1960s displayed a similar skepticism toward the nation's political traditions and institutions. Looking to the university campuses and new grassroots collectives, activists imagined new institutions that would promote meaningful "participatory democracy."

The German counterpart to this grassroots effort to establish an alternative mass politics was the "extraparliamentary opposition" (Außerparliamentarische Opposition, or APO). Drawing on both a postwar tradition of mass resistance to rearmament and the ideological inspiration of the New Left, union members, leftist Protestants, and students activists coalesced in the late 1960s in a broad-based protest movement. Their opposition focused on the governing coalition's proposal of so-called emergency laws (*Notstandsgesetez*) that would allow government to function in the event of natural catastrophe or nuclear war because they considered this project reminiscent of the presidential emergency decrees that had toppled the Weimar Republic. When the Bundestag passed a watered-down version of the law despite a demonstration attended by several hundred thousand angry citizens, the movement collapsed. The concurrent wave of student activism that borrowed its methods of sit-ins and teach-ins from the American civil rights movement caused much uproar in the universities but did not have much more institutional success. Ultimately, the victory of the Social Democratic–Liberal coalition in 1969 and

Chancellor Willy Brandt's promise to "dare more democracy" pulled most of the protesters back into regular politics.

With formal participation within reach, the goals of mass politics shifted to the provision of a good life. Among the signal developments during the New Deal in the United States was the widespread expectation that the state would ensure security and opportunity for its citizenry. Driven by the suffering unleashed by the Great Depression, the nation's planners during the 1930s stumbled toward a new economic vision that fused the capacity for mass production with mass consumption. This new conception entailed a substantial policy shift toward increasing the spending power of American citizens so as to make consumer demand the force driving production and investment. The passage of unemployment compensation and pensions during the New Deal and the GI Bill after World War II marked the beginnings of a sustained expansion of public programs to promote consumption. That such benefits were recognized as rights, not as paternalistic rewards or alms doled out by charities, had far-reaching implications. Based on the postwar prosperity, observers and planners alike concluded that social and economic advancement could proceed without structural changes in capitalism or divisive state management of the economy. More and more Americans presumed that the creation of a "consumer republic," in which the state compensated for the flaws of capitalism, would settle the most pressing conflicts that had previously vexed the nation.

Because of its drastic ruptures, German politics also aimed at creating a sense of security against the vagaries of economic upheaval, albeit while assigning an even stronger role to the state. The suffering of World War I created a need for healing the physical and mental wounds of the participants. Hyperinflation, rationalization, and the Great Depression put a premium on finding a way to provide a secure livelihood that allowed people to share the benefits of a nascent consumerism. The Weimar Republic failed to a considerable degree because its chaotic politics managed to extend benefits to some previously underprivileged groups but proved unable to insulate the majority of the citizens from the ill effects of the Great Depression. Learning this lesson, the Federal Republic nonetheless gambled on unleashing the forces of the market with Ludwig Erhard's currency reform of 1948 and his "ordoliberal" policies that gave the state an active role in maintaining the smooth operation of free-market mechanisms. The resulting "economic miracle" gradually convinced doubters of the importance of competition, while providing the means to finance the extension of the welfare state to an even larger group of World War II victims. Moreover, it allowed for the rapid expansion of consumption to the masses and the development of a nonelite popular culture in the media, which provided a more colorful and attractive lifestyle than the drab egalitarianism of the East.

These programs of mass consumption achieved their intended aims in both countries to an impressive degree. In the United States, inequalities of wealth narrowed substantially, rates of poverty fell, and personal incomes rose among historically disadvantaged groups, including African Americans. Against the backdrop of an ideological struggle against Marxism, which purported to promise a future bereft of inequalities, liberals were responsive to constituencies who appealed to the federal government to remove longstanding obstacles to their full and equal participation in the nation's economy. The remarkable burst of legislation of Lyndon Baines Johnson's Great Society was the culmination of the reimagining of the state that had begun three decades earlier. The German extension of the welfare state, based on a market economy, had even greater success in healing the wounds of war, reducing class distinctions, and providing buying power for mass consumption. The huge transfers of the Equalization of Burdens Law, the indexing of pensions, and the expansion of free education that culminated in the early 1970s created a material floor of preconditions for participating in democracy among the underprivileged strata.

Yet, the embrace of "security" and "opportunity" as societal goals did not automatically promote the democratization of American institutions and mass politics. To the contrary, anxieties over security, specifically national security, repeatedly restricted political discourse. Organized labor, civil rights activists, New Left groups, and other social justice organizations endured harassment and denunciation from public officials who stoked public fears of communist subversion, as they used expanded police and national security powers that the federal government acquired during the Cold War to suppress dissent. Similarly, critics of social justice proved adept at invoking the rhetoric of "opportunity" to castigate politically mobilized disadvantaged Americans as "special interests." By 1964, when Barry Goldwater ran a quixotic campaign for the presidency against Johnson, the conservative critique of entitlements as a threat to individual responsibility and freedom was already codified. Subsequent initiatives, such as affirmative action, were easily folded into a gathering conservative backlash.

In the German context, the dictatorships also offered a bargain that promised domestic and foreign security in exchange for giving up political freedom. The Nazis' domestic propaganda made it seem that public works like the building of the *Autobahnen* were providing full employment, and the secretive rearmament program promised to restore international respect. The price for this bargain with Hitler was his unleashing of World War II. Although its economic effects were for a time masked by the exploitation of the defeated during the initial victories, the terror of Allied bombing, the fighting within the Reich's borders, and the ensuing occupation brought that suffering home to the German people, which they had visited before on their neighbors. Burned by this experience, the German Democratic Republic chose recipes from the radical wing of the labor movement by initiating a policy of expropriation of the landed elite and of the leading entrepreneurs so as to construct a planned economy. This system subsidized basic foodstuffs, housing, and transportation on a minimal level and provided work for everyone, whether or not it was needed. Initially, this approach proved fairly popular, but in the long run it was unsuccessful in enabling the economy to make the leap to high technology and to provide modern consumer goods. The GDR's security mania led to a militarization of society, the building of the Berlin Wall, and secret police repression.

During the middle of the twentieth century, interaction between the two competing forms of mass politics also increased – albeit not always in a constructive sense. Not surprisingly, the two dictatorships embraced rightist and leftist versions of an anti-Americanism that construed democratic U.S. mass politics as the central enemy. Despite the Nazi fascination with American technology, the Third

Reich appealed to long-held prejudices of the cultivated elite against U.S. popular culture, denouncing it as inferior. Hitler's belligerent posture was not lost on
FDR, whose image of Germany retained traces of World War I hostility. Nazi
propaganda appealed to crude racial prejudices against Jews and blacks, which
escalated into open hostility with Hitler's declaration of war in December 1941.
Mutual stereotyping reached a new climax when FDR derided the Third Reich
as a danger to Western civilization and Goebbels denounced the United States as
the center of the world Jewish conspiracy. The GDR, firmly in the Soviet camp,
continued this anti-American propaganda, albeit with a leftist twist that attacked
NATO as well as American imperialism in the Third World. However, despite
SED prohibitions, American popular culture attracted young people, who found
the music and lifestyle of the New World more palatable than the official Soviet
model.

The two German democracies were more receptive to American influences
and opened themselves to a process of Americanization in all walks of life. The
Weimar Republic was in effect a stepchild of Wilsonian idealism, not just because
the defeated elites wanted to ward off a harsh peace but also because democratic
internationalism seemed to be a lesser evil than Bolshevism. Moreover, American
mediation in reparations issues with the Dawes Plan created some breathing space
for economic recovery and international reconciliation. The Weimar Republic
thus provided a stage for an initial wave of Americanization in areas as diverse
as business and culture. Having little alternative to integration with the West,
the Federal Republic resumed the pattern of "catch-up modernization," largely
according to American blueprints. It helped that German experiences with the
GIs turned out more positively than those with Russian soldiers. The American
example proved attractive not only to those adults who wanted protection from the
Soviet menace and a recovery of business opportunities but also to those young
people who were fascinated by rock n' roll and relaxed lifestyles. Hollywood's
dreams of peace and prosperity had a profound impact on the German public
because those disappointed in the Nazi promises were looking for new definitions
of a good life. The Americanization of the Germans was therefore largely voluntary
and benign, even if critics continued to harp on the shortcomings of American-
style mass democracy. Except for the creative contribution of Hitler's refugees to
American arts and sciences, virtually all influence went therefore from the United
States to Germany during this period.

DISCONTENTS OF DEMOCRACY

During the last third of the twentieth century, the central question was what kind
of use citizens would make of their expanded participation rights. Disappointingly,
mass politics in the United States was characterized by striking contrasts between
the unprecedented size and inclusiveness of the electorate and the decline in
actual rates of participation. The inclusive, consensual mass politics of the New
Deal era was replaced by a very different model of political participation: issue
politics. Expressing a backlash against the consequences of too much democracy,
the strategy of the George W. Bush administration exemplified the effort of a
committed ideological minority to reshape the tenor of public life in a more

conservative direction by exploiting the disinterest of the majority. Only around one issue – "the War on Terror" – did the Bush administration strive to mobilize the nation and insist on unity. To a remarkable degree and for at least five years after September 11, 2001, Bush and his allies succeeded in forging a national consensus regarding the appropriate steps necessary to defend the nation. In other areas of politics, public debate was largely given over to wedge issues that polarized public debate and typically mobilized only impassioned single-interest voters. Even in the 2004 election, which was perhaps the most divisive presidential election in at least three decades, fewer than 100 million of America's 222 million voting-age citizens cast ballots.

German mass politics experienced a similar paradox, albeit with a somewhat higher level of voter participation of about four-fifths in national elections. After the formal establishment of democratic institutions in the postwar era, a process of "inner democratization" was necessary to make the discredited elites and the skeptical populace accept parliamentary government. The children who had grown up in the Bonn Republic went one step further and demanded a "democratization of democracy," that is, a radical extension of participation into all areas of life, including the school, the workplace, and public service. Yet, this effort to extend the meaning of democracy from a set of political arrangements into cultural attitudes and interpersonal behaviors produced angry criticism from conservative theorists, who rejected such enlarged notions of participation as a violation of the Basic Law, which envisaged representative, not participatory, democracy. Although in a formal sense parliamentarianism prevailed, its defenders were eventually discredited by a series of corruption scandals, leading to a rising disgust with politics in general that lowered participation rates in the Federal Republic as well.

Despite the alarming degree of voter apathy, a form of activist mass politics nonetheless continues to influence American public life. One legacy of the protest movements of the 1960s has been a proliferation of causes that espouse and practice participatory democracy through grassroots mobilizations for liberal or conservative ends. The antinuclear movement of the 1970s and early 1980s, for example, exerted considerable influence over national energy policy despite its inchoate organizational structure. Similarly, groups ranging from the Million Man March organized by the Nation of Islam to the Promise Keepers, a national Christian all-male, mega-revival movement, have yoked highly sophisticated methods of grassroots mobilization to the defense of "traditional" moral values. Perhaps no group more fully exemplifies the power of grassroots activism to shape national political debate than the anti-abortion movement, which has compelled both political parties to take a stand on a deeply divisive issue that many politicians undoubtedly would have preferred to ignore. Another illustration of the potent fusion of grassroots mass politics and single-issue politics was the proliferation of plebiscites on divisive issues that eroded the governing authority of legislatures in California, Oregon, and elsewhere.

In Germany, similar single-issue groups, called new social movements, have pursued grassroots mobilization as both a means and a goal in itself. Prompted by concerns over environmental disasters, discrimination against women, and the nuclear arms race, a series of local citizens' initiatives created extraparliamentary protest networks because the established people's parties had largely ignored their fears. Through confrontations over the building of nuclear power plants, initiatives to create women's shelters, and peace rallies, activist citizens sought to generate enough public pressure to move the formal parliamentary machinery. In this endeavor, they were helped by an increasingly critical media that redefined its role from mouthpiece of the establishment to guardian of unconventional views. However, such grassroots initiatives ran head-on into the rigidity of the political class, which had carefully coopted all traditional mass organizations, so that employers and labor representatives were heard on economic decisions, churches influenced family policy, and so on. Although on a local level, "citizens' movements" (*Bürgerbewegungen*) had considerable success in defending neighborhoods, the creation of the Green Party refocused participatory efforts back onto existing parliamentary channels.

Because of oft-discussed "disillusionment with big government," American public life has in recent years drifted toward the privatization of public responsibility. The rise of gated communities with private security forces, the restrictions on behavior and speech in shopping malls, the campaign for school vouchers to subsidize private schooling with public funds, and the intense hostility to any nationalized health plan were just a few of the manifestations of the erosion of public life and suspicion of government initiatives. Almost certainly, the "hollowing out" of public institutions and the proclivity of Americans "to bowl alone" have been exaggerated. However, it is telling that even while liberals decried the erosion of the activist state of the New Deal order, they failed to offer a viable alternative program that could overcome popular disillusionment in public institutions, especially skepticism about the capacity of the state to fulfill its obligations. Not even the communitarian movement, which centered more on social control than on social justice, was able to reinvigorate the political process. Because neither events nor ideology, except for the trauma of global terrorism or a near catastrophic economic crisis, have provided a brake on the balkanization of public life, it is unclear whether contemporary Americans have the capacity or the interest in using mass politics to expand democracy.

In West Germany, an intensive contest developed over the aims of mass politics from the 1970s on. The majority of the population was content to preserve "the German model" of neocorporate consensus-building among different social forces that had long guaranteed political stability and rising prosperity. However, an activist minority instead sought to realize postmaterial values such as the preservation of the environment and gender equality. Growing frustrated with the lack of responsiveness of the parliamentary process, these activists demanded an expansion of plebiscitary instruments, such as referenda, in the hope that these would force the government to follow their lead. Although some state constitutions did allow citizens' initiatives, the Bundestag and the Federal Constitutional Court continued to balk at such devices, until the electoral success of the Greens during the 1980s compelled the established parties to incorporate elements of the protest into their programs. In East Germany, the nascent opposition started to demand real human rights – foreshadowing that remarkable "democratic awakening" of 1989 that would bring the SED dictatorship crashing down. Although East German intellectuals sought to reform socialism and find a third way between communism and Western parliamentarianism, East German citizens in their demonstrations and the March 1990 election opted overwhelmingly for traditional forms of democracy, such as the Basic Law and the social-market economy, as guarantors of a better life.

Transatlantic interaction has intensified in recent decades – although both systems have continued to exhibit large structural differences that have inhibited influences from the outside. In the civic movements, German protesters adopted many of the nonviolent techniques of the civil rights movement because some of them had been exchange students on American campuses. In election campaigns, there has also been a noticeable transfer of U.S. methods, starting with polling of focus groups, going on to the personalization of the contest in lead candidates, and extending to the use of advertising techniques to package messages like commodities. Nonetheless, German electoral contests have remained more centered on political parties and ideological messages because the mixed proportional and electoral district system makes for more programmatic coherence as well as popular participation than the winner-take-all system in the United States. Because of its sense of superiority and exceptionalism, American politics has, in contrast, been quite reluctant to accept any inspiration from Europe, whether in regard to multilateral foreign policy, international law, or social solidarity. Despite increasing structural similarities and direct transfers, it might be better to speak of a limited convergence on a common type of representative mass democracy, challenged by recurrent protest movements.

PARADOXES OF PARTICIPATION

In the long perspective of the twentieth century, the democratic vision of mass politics has undoubtedly triumphed over its authoritarian or dictatorial alternatives. In this competition, American democracy had the great advantage of possessing a revolutionary tradition, a set of representative institutions, and a republican rhetoric that had universal appeal. In contrast, the Imperial German counter-model that combined executive power and military strength with limited participation and welfare support proved less attractive on an international scale. Whereas American democracy managed to remove some of its remaining internal barriers, the Weimar Republic's attempt to advance democracy failed, and the Nazis instituted a dictatorship based on Hitler's charisma, the leadership principle, and organizational control, thereby substituting acclamation for real participation. This alternative had some advantages in winning the initial campaigns of World War II, but in the long run, its repression, exploitation, and racial genocide aroused most of the world against it. Although less bloody, the antifascist dictatorship of the SED that claimed to act in the name of "the workers and peasants" similarly repressed its own population. After the double liberation of 1945 and 1989, the Germans therefore returned to a modified version of the American model without, however, buying into its manifest problems.

Although participation increased during the last one hundred years on both sides of the Atlantic, the rise of mass politics ought not to be told as a linear success story. On a very basic level, the two German dictatorships demonstrate that formal rights of participation are essential for democratic self-government. Montesquieu's careful emphasis on institutional balance therefore trumps Rousseau's emphasis on the presumed general will. But the American example also repeatedly shows that within a liberal constitution and parliamentary framework, illiberal minorities can succeed in disenfranchising less-favored parts of the population like women, immigrants, and blacks. In addition to securing the legal bases for participation, it is therefore important to create a political climate that enables citizens actually to make use of their rights. The lack of such a climate is the source of some current problems of neocorporate mass democracy in a media age because big interest groups can determine political decisions and effective media campaigns can sway public sentiment against what might be the real needs of the electorate. Moreover, the fate of various protest movements points to the difficulties of dealing with issues such as abortion in which aroused minorities seek to enforce their prescriptions on skeptical majorities. Therefore, one danger lies in voter apathy that makes possible minority rule within mass democracy.

The increasing variety in sites of political contestation has produced a similarly ambiguous result. No doubt, the development from local mass rallies to national media broadcasts has decreased physical confrontation in the streets and made it possible to reach a larger number of citizens simultaneously through the airwaves. In addition, the proliferation of information sources from rumor and modest newssheets to elaborate newspapers, TV and radio newscasts, and Internet link-ups has enhanced a concerned public's ability to find out about problems and to voice contending opinions. At the same time, however, the communication revolution has enlarged the possibility of commercial exploitation and political manipulation, especially when the media fail in their task of criticizing government, such as in the aftermath of the terrorist attack of 9/11. Similarly, the repeated attempts to mobilize people for protest have had local successes in preventing ill-advised highway or housing projects, but such networks have only been able to influence national politics intermittently and have proven unable to sustain themselves in the long run. The decisions by the Schmidt and Kohl governments to ignore the hysterics of the peace movement in the early 1980s is a case in point that demonstrates that grassroots mobilization is not automatically superior to representative government.

The evolution of the aims of mass politics also has led to somewhat paradoxical consequences on both sides of the Atlantic. The initial push sought to increase participation because only through broader access to political decisions could citizens who had to pay taxes and serve in the military make sure that their wishes were respected. Initially, the demand for greater inclusion was motivated by the desire to escape the dictates of necessity by securing adequate food and shelter, so as to survive wars and depressions. Because the elites were not about to give up their privileges, the exploited had to demand enfranchisement of the majority. Unfortunately, populist movements could, if goaded by demagogues, also turn violent and repressive, paving the way for dictatorships of the right and the left, which found new political, ethnic, and racial groups to exclude. Both the Nazis and communists offered a bargain that promised rising standards of living in exchange for political acquiescence, thereby turning the masses into passive subjects. Ultimately, capitalist democracy proved better able to meet people's basic needs, increase the benefits of consumption, and offer entertainment through popular culture. Ironically, during the last several decades, this democratic deal has been challenged by advocates of postmaterial values who redefined the good life in terms of ecology, equality, and peace. Yet, unlike during the Great Depression, neither the recent financial meltdown nor the rise of a left populism with Die Linke (The left) have been able to shake allegiances to representative government, as the reelection of Angela Merkel in 2009 showed.

Behind the rise of mass politics, therefore, lies a much-abused dream, promising that the extension of participation will bring about a more humane world through self-government. Needless to say, the catastrophic first half of the twentieth century underlines the brutal betrayal of this hope because not only democracy but also dictatorship were products of the mass age. Fortunately, in the second half of the twentieth century, self-government prevailed on both sides of the Atlantic, even if the struggle over its precise form continues to the present day. For Americans, the main challenge was to live up fully to their own professed ideals. The discrepancy between their rhetoric and performance was one abiding source of self-criticism at home and anti-Americanism abroad. For the Germans, the chief task was to emulate the better elements of the U.S. model without losing some of their own preferences for a stronger role of the state in providing welfare or culture in the bargain. An optimistic reading, reinforced by the election of Barack Obama, would find some confirmation of a Habermasian view that an expanded public sphere would bring about more equality, peace, and justice. But the negative experiences of the century also caution against taking the advance of liberty for granted and rather suggest that its lofty aspirations ought to be treated as a challenge, which each successive generation has to meet anew.

Further Reading

Anderson, Margaret Lavinia. *Practicing Democracy: Elections and Political Culture in Imperial Germany* (Princeton, 2000).

Arendt, Hannah. *The Origins of Totalitarianism*, new ed. with additional prefaces (New York, 1968).

Bark, Dennis L., and David R. Gress. *A History of West Germany*, 2 vols. (Oxford, 1989).

Brinkley, Alan. *Voices of Protest: Huey Long, Father Coughlin, and the Great Depression* (New York, 1982).

Brundage, W. Fitzhugh. *The Southern Past: A Clash of Race and Memory* (Cambridge, 2005).

Cohen, Lizabeth. *A Consumer's Republic: The Politics of Mass Consumption in Postwar America* (New York, 2003).

Dawley, Alan. *Struggles for Justice: Social Responsibility and the Liberal State* (Cambridge, 1991).

Fraser, Steve, and Gary Gerstle. *The Rise and Fall of the New Deal Order, 1930–1980* (Princeton, 1989).

Fulbrook, Mary. *Anatomy of a Dictatorship: Inside the GDR, 1949–1989* (Oxford, 1995).

Gerstle, Gary. *American Crucible: Race and Nation in the Twentieth Century* (Princeton, 2001).

Jarausch, Konrad H., and Michael Geyer. *Shattered Past: Reconstructing German Histories* (Princeton, 2003).

Jones, Larry, and James Retallack. *Elections, Mass Politics and Social Change in Modern Germany* (Cambridge, 1992).

Kershaw, Ian. *Hitler*, 2 vols. (New York, 1999–2000).

Lindenberger, Thomas. *Strassenpolitik: Zur Geschichte der öffentlichen Ordnung in Berlin, 1900–1914* (Bonn, 1995).

Markovits, Andrei S., and Philip S. Gorski. *The German Left: Red, Green and Beyond* (New York, 1993).

McCormick, John P., ed., *Confronting Mass Democracy and Industrial Technology: Political and Social Theory from Nietzsche to Habermas* (Durham, 2002).

Parker, Theodore. *Works of Theodore Parker*, vol. 6 (New York, 1907).

Patterson, James T. *Grand Expectations: The United States, 1945–1974* (New York, 1996).

Pfaff, Steven. *Exit-Voice Dynamics and the Collapse of East Germany: The Crisis of Leninism and the Revolution of 1989* (Durham, 2006).

Rodgers, Daniel T. *Atlantic Crossings: Social Politics in a Progressive Age* (Cambridge, 1998).

Sneeringer, Julia. *Winning Women's Votes: Propaganda and Politics in Weimar Germany* (Chapel Hill, 2002).

8

Market: Consumption and Commerce

HEINZ-GERHARD HAUPT AND PAUL NOLTE

American GIs hand out chewing gum, chocolate bars, and cigarettes in occupied Germany; West German youngsters in the 1960s and 1970s are fascinated by the images of American pop and protest culture; Coca-Cola and McDonald's dominate everyday life in Western Europe. As these developments attest and countless other ubiquitous images underscore, aside from its influence on world power struggles, there is hardly a sphere that modern America and its global influence throughout the twentieth century have affected as deeply and as penetratingly as the world of mass consumption. We seem to have a clear winner in the contest to shape the modern era: the United States emerges as the pioneer of the market-driven society, especially with respect to consumerism. It is a phenomenon that, in addition to its economic impact, fundamentally changes or even invents in many ways the culture of everyday life, the concept of lifestyles, and the world of images and symbols that characterizes the modern era. Bundled into the term "Americanization" is the notion of a one-way street, running from West to East, from which the Germans constantly received new impulses of modernism emanating from the United States, without ever being able to counter them with their own.

On closer inspection, however, this picture becomes more complex. In fact, we can easily call up images of a successful transfer of consumer goods from Germany to America; German luxury cars parked in front of American garages, for example, and German kitchens sparkling in American households. Products "made in Germany" have long had the reputation in the United States of being not only at the cutting edge of technology but also embodying the latest stylistic innovations. Thus, we see that the cultural dimension of consumerism in these two countries is also reciprocal. Viewed historically, the conventional images of German–American commercial consumption are clearly concentrated in the period since World War II when the political ties between the Federal Republic and the United States were at their strongest. However, the question arises as to whether the lead that America enjoyed since the late nineteenth century in establishing the modern, commercialized, and urbanized society was so obviously dominant or whether this competition with Germany toward a consumer society was more evenly matched.

The examples previously cited reveal other fault lines in this comparison. The German protest movement during the 1960s and 1970s contrasted the notion of permissive Americanism with that of unsophisticated respectability espoused by German parents, while at the same time it reacted vehemently not only against then-prevailing American political power but also against the materialism and con-sumerism of American culture. The acceptance and rejection of "Americanism" in Germany were already closely linked in earlier periods: in the 1920s, for exam-ple, but also during the Third Reich. However, criticism of consumer society is by no means an invention of the "more traditional" or even the "more culturally conscious" Europeans and Germans. In fact, the mass consumption of the twen-tieth century has been a controversial topic in its own homeland, in the United States itself, as many forms of modern consumer politics and protest movements against consumerism were invented and put to the test there.

These are the central questions and themes of a comparative history of con-sumerism and market-driven society in Germany and the United States, and they are treated more systematically in this chapter. If we understand consumption in its relation to the modern market economy as the acquisition and utilization of goods, then we see that in the course of the nineteenth century on both sides of the Atlantic, the consumer society gradually replaced the needs-based economy, which in its various forms was frequently tied to a local or regional market. With the advent of industrial mass production, the consumer society produced durable goods and distributed them to customers through new marketing channels, such as networks of newly created retail sales outlets, organized and supplied by large commercial firms.

Before the eighteenth century, consumers were part of a very limited social stratum. It expanded initially to include the middle classes and then gradually the entire population. The nexus of commercial consumption and luxury, which had characterized the seventeenth century in Europe, gradually dissolved, transforming consumption and commercial markets into forces that shaped both society and culture. The "mass culture" of the twentieth century, with its many facets ranging from mass advertising to leisure activities to music, from a technically advanced standard of living to the individual realm of "self-fashioning," is based on the two pillars of media penetration and consumerism.

Thus, we see reflected in consumer society a multidimensional history of the "dash toward modernism" that characterizes our era. Mass consumption has pro-duced new economic and social environments, transformed landscapes, and created new destinations for modern consumers, such as department stores and shopping malls. How did this process unfold in two different countries, which in their respective conceptual designs as universal "middle-class" societies are basically quite similar? It remains to be seen whether the first impression of America as having a lead in this race into modern consumerism can be validated. Clearly, however, the image of a Germany simply lagging behind every American inno-vation by two to three decades is false. The strength of specific traditions in both countries has been repeatedly expanded by far-reaching political decisions. Economists have termed this a "path-dependent" outcome and, in the realm of consumer research, scholars have borrowed language from the comparative analysis of welfare states and speak now of differing national and continental "consumption regimes."

One can argue that, in terms of the development of consumerism, the United States actually did take the lead well into the nineteenth century because the British colonies of North America, in contrast to the territories of the Holy

Roman Empire on the continent, were already tied into global networks of consumption and were in fact part of an "empire of goods." This perception may be erroneous, however, because the research on the history of mass consumption in the United States and Germany is still asymmetrical. Since the 1980s, the terms "consumer society" and "consumer culture" have been important themes in American historical studies; in Germany, their discovery is more recent, and accordingly, the scholarly literature is thinner. This fact is rooted again in a deep cultural distinction between the two societies. The United States developed early on an image of itself as a consumer society and a consumer economy, whereas the economic culture in Germany, even after 1945, remained in both the Federal Republic and of the GDR a culture of industrial production – despite, in the latter case, the people's consumption regime that dominated in the post-1945 years and that made promises to its people of achieving specific living standards. Only in the last two decades has a fundamental change taken place in this respect. Even with the economic crisis of the 1930s, the rise in affluence and abundance in the United States has been relatively continuous, at least when compared to the repeated fractures, catastrophes, and periods of privation in German history, especially the years 1916–23 and during the existence of the GDR, which on one level can be viewed as a systemic experience of deprivation. One could conclude from such observations that these two distinct strands of economic development are now moving closer to one another. Let us see if this is in fact the case.

SITES OF CONSUMPTION

The modern market-oriented society is like a web that has been woven ever more tightly over the past two hundred years. In the eighteenth century, it linked the commercial centers of Boston, Philadelphia, New York, and Charleston along the Atlantic coast of the British colonies in North America and, likewise, the points of transaction for continental European trade in the Holy Roman Empire, which were located more toward the interior in cities like Cologne, Frankfurt, and Leipzig. In the nineteenth century, the Industrial Revolution established a new model. The intersections of industrial production, especially those represented by the heavy industries of coal and steel, became particularly prominent and were supplemented by the new network of communication and transport created in just a few decades by the railroads. Pittsburgh and Chicago in the United States and the Ruhr River region and Berlin in Germany are examples of this early highly industrialized phase of market-oriented society and its regional connections.

At the turn of the twentieth century, once again a new model emerged and began to establish the characteristic intersections and social movements of the consumer society – a society whose regional integration, landscapes, and emblematic structures were increasingly shaped by the economic and cultural significance of private consumption. Cities promoted themselves as centers of mass consumption. The attributes of consumption defined traffic and trade routes from the inner cities out toward agrarian provinces. Everyday life was influenced more and more by advertising for consumer goods on building facades, along major highways, and at transportation hubs, like train stations and airports. This was true in equal measure for the United States and Germany, despite characteristic differences. In the early stages of the modern consumer society, roughly from the 1880s until World War I, the similarities seemed to prevail. Yet, soon thereafter, and with full impact perhaps not until after World War II, each nation opted for a different path, and instead of a gradual convergence, we see rather two distinct parallel developments.

During the last third of the nineteenth century, the two countries' comparability in terms of economic consumption stemmed from a similar point of departure. In contrast to France and England, neither Germany nor the United States was then an integrated national society with a corresponding economic sphere. Instead, during the 1860s and 1870s, they each experienced significant crises in their movement toward national integration. In the United States, this phase was marked by secession, civil war, and the difficult period of Reconstruction; in Central Europe, it was attended by the Prussian–Austrian civil war and the founding of the German Empire under Prussian leadership. The apparent resolution of these crises – the successful settlement of territorial and constitutional issues of confederation – ushered in on both sides of the Atlantic an economic boom period that had already begun earlier in the century in Paris and London. It entered into the history books in Germany as the *Gründerjahre*, or "Founding Years," and as the "Gilded Age" in the United States. These compelling epithets conceal a common task of paramount importance in both countries: in a time of growing global economic competition (in which Great Britain had clearly dominated until then) and in the face of unresolved problems of cultural integration (the North–South conflict in the United States and in Germany the still fragile union of previously independent states that still resisted Prussian hegemony), each nation strove to achieve as rapidly as possible the national integration of its economy, transportation system, communications networks, and society.

Both of these young nations also had at their disposal – as no other country in the world had at this time – the economic, demographic, and cultural resources necessary for accelerated growth, which catapulted them both by the start of World War I into world leadership positions. Both were expanding societies, not only in an external sense with their respective imperialistic and colonial ambitions but even more so internally because by 1890, the United States had lost its frontier, its western boundary of settlement expansion. Both societies were moving rapidly toward urbanization and metropolitan culture: around 1900, Berlin and Chicago were generally viewed by contemporaries as twin cities. The new sites of mass consumption developed first in the large cities and then radiated out into the agrarian regions. The latter movement occurred certainly earlier and in more pronounced fashion in the United States than in Germany, first because of the larger, continental dimensions of the country, and second because of the relative youth of the agrarian settlements compared with the centuries-old farming-village structures in Central Europe. Consequently, the role already played in the United States in the 1880s by mail-order trading companies like Sears, Roebuck and Company and Montgomery Ward was considerably greater than in Imperial Germany. There was one primary reason for this larger role: mail-order businesses based in metropolitan hubs and distribution centers like Chicago answered the modern consumer needs not only of agricultural communities but also of those located in the thinly populated, commercially underdeveloped hinterlands.

The decades around 1900 constituted the robust beginning of the modern consumer society. This takeoff phase was stimulated less by innovations in production – although a number of new technical, industrially produced everyday wares, such as the razor with changeable blades, and then a little later the first electric household devices significantly propelled the consumer market. In fact, it was much more a revolution in business administration that drove the consumer society, both in an internal economic sense and externally in strikingly new forms of representation, namely by way of advertising and public programs designed to foster consumption. In place of the independent salesman, there emerged large firms and enterprises, such as the aforementioned mail-order businesses. Even while the salesman still managed to supply the demand of his geographically limited circle of clients in his specific market sector, whether in groceries or clothing accessories, the department store developed in both countries from around 1890 on into the leading symbol of a new world for consumers.

Both Berlin and Chicago were imitators in this aspect of consumer culture because Paris had long since blazed this trail and, with a lead of approximately three decades, was the undisputed department-store pioneer. The adoption of this innovation in Germany and the United States took place almost simultaneously, with the United States achieving perhaps a slight lead. The department store was not, however, a direct "import" from France; it happened rather as a result of individual salespersons enlarging their businesses or converting their wholesale businesses, which hitherto had been the domain only of large firms, into retail businesses and thus servicing their clients as end users. In a second phase, which again took hold in both countries before World War I and began to flourish during the 1920s, the individual department stores expanded through franchising into department-store chains. Here, it is interesting to note that the local or regional character of the chain-store enterprises remained intact longer in the United States than in Germany and persists in some cases until today: for example, until only very recently, Filene's was rooted in Boston and New England, whereas firms like Karstadt or Hertie in Germany expanded nationally at an earlier stage.

In the department stores and – particularly in the United States – in the large mail-order houses, various aspects of the new consumer society converged. The practice of stimulating demand through an overwhelming flood of new products replaced the old system of simply meeting the demand at hand. A whole universe of everyday goods and merchandise was packed into the range of products offered by a single firm and displayed on its floors, in its departments, or on the pages of its catalog. Consumption was geared increasingly to aesthetic appeal, generated through advertising and product presentation. The huge department stores at the turn of the century, like Wertheim and KaDeWe in Berlin, Macy's in New York, and Wanamaker's in Philadelphia, virtually "invented" many techniques to effectively display their wares in showroom windows and, through the use of light, color, and placement, to accentuate their aesthetic appeal. Already somewhat earlier – in the 1880s, and here again strikingly parallel in both countries – the standardization of products had begun. As "brand names" and branded products, they were unmistakable, inspired customer loyalty, and could be marketed universally on a national scale. When shopping in New York or Baltimore, one no

longer bought a bar of soap but rather, to use one of the first very popular brand
name products, one purchased "Sapolio"; in Germany, consumers did not buy
just any cornstarch or spice but rather shopped everywhere for the same-looking,
same-tasting "Maggi" or "Mondamin."

In the period leading up to World War I, both the United States and the
German Empire appeared to be roughly at the same stage of development in their
progress toward becoming modern consumer societies. At this point, they were
both leaders in a global trend that hitherto – roughly until 1870–80 – had been
led by England and France. In this period, the United States seemed to move
ahead of Germany in a number of sectors, such as advertising and marketing, and
in the development of new forms of retail distribution. It also took the lead in
mail-order retailing, price standardization, and, somewhat later, in the invention of
self-service shopping. Germany led the way in other areas, especially with respect
to the national integration of markets and enterprises. American firms with a
national presence from the Atlantic to the Pacific coast were slower to develop
than their counterparts in Germany, due presumably above all to the great physical
distances involved. This slower pace was true not only in the retail sector but also
in other areas of the economy, such as banking. Although the grocery stores of
the A&P chain, the Great Atlantic and Pacific Tea Company, already carried the
goal of national expansion in their name, national chain stores, particularly in
the foodstuffs sector, did not begin to dominate the markets until after 1914.
By that time, Germany had generated new and different forms of distribution,
such as the retail cooperative and the consortium of independent retailers, like
EDEKA, the purchasing syndicate of German merchants founded in 1905. Like
American chain stores from this period, these retailers provided the German
consumer with a unified and standardized presentation in design, advertising, and
range of products; however, their administrative structure was quite different from
the privately owned, centrally administered enterprises that predominated in the
United States.

Herein may lie one reason for the increasing differences in consumer culture
that began to develop after World War I. The war itself and its economic and
social consequences also played a role in creating those differences. During the
war and the following years, the progressive unfolding of capitalism and the consumer society continued in the United States in a much more steady and stable
fashion than in Europe; it even entered into a boom phase, the first stage of technical, mechanized mass production with its attendant modern lifestyle. Because
of economic stagnation and inflation, the European countries and, in particular,
Germany fell behind in this respect, not only compared with America but also
with their own level of development in 1913. Toward the end of the war in
1916–17 and during the first years of the Weimar Republic, the consumer society
and market in Germany were marked less by glistening department-store facades
and attractive home furnishings than by hunger, protests against price increases,
crises in the supply chain of consumer goods, black markets, and a geographic
shift in population. The large cities with their economic draw were no longer able
to integrate the agrarian population from the hinterlands but rather became very
conscious of their fundamental dependency on the food being produced in these
agrarian regions.

It was not until the middle of the 1920s that this crisis in the metropolitan centers of Germany was gradually overcome. Berlin in particular, as the capital of the "Golden Twenties" – or "Roaring Twenties," as it was known in the United States – then began to develop a new commercial charm for consumers. American businesses had in the meantime taken advantage of the weakened European economy and had penetrated German markets, including consumer markets, with, for example, the expansion of the Woolworth's department store chain. The American automobile industry also began at this time to establish itself in Germany, beginning in 1925 with a Ford plant in Cologne. Even setting aside the consequences and effects of the war in Europe, it became apparent that the typical large American enterprise based on private capital was in a much more advantageous position to expand internationally than retail cooperatives and the loose consortia of traditional retailers in Germany. During this same period, U.S. firms were also expanding noticeably within their own national boundaries, both in terms of vertical and horizontal integration of retail operations and the national integration of retail markets. Consequently, from their more or less equally competitive positions in the struggle for markets before 1914, a pronounced asymmetrical relationship between Germany and the United States began to develop, and its cultural component soon found expression in the catchphrase of "Americanization."

Another change that transformed the American consumer society starting in the 1950s had even deeper, more far-reaching effects, especially on urban planning and the structure of American cities. Until then, the U.S. market economy and its consumer culture had been concentrated in the large metropolitan areas around densely populated inner cities. This focus of development followed a basic pattern that corresponded fairly directly to that of European cities at this time. This was particularly true of cities on the East Coast and for some Midwestern cities, such as Detroit and Chicago. After World War II, however, a new phase of urban development and residential planning took hold in the United States and was repeatedly strengthened and sustained by the federal government: the growth of the American suburbs began in earnest. What started as a suburbanization of living quarters, as a migration of middle-class inner-city residents into commercially attractive, single-home developments on the periphery of the cities, soon also precipitated a suburbanization of the consumer society as well. This transformation was already well underway by the mid-1950s. The driving force behind this momentous shift in development was, of course, the ascendancy of the automobile in American society, with the corresponding loss of significance for rail transport, in terms of both long-distance national freight transport and regional, urban commuter rail traffic. The dramatic increase in the private ownership of cars and the simultaneous expansion of the interstate highway system for truck transport essentially destroyed the old structure of the market and consumer society that was focused on the urban centers and downtown areas of cities like New York and Chicago.

The old pattern of organization was replaced by a virtual network, in which any point, as long as it lay next to a street or highway, could, at least in principle, assume a function of central importance. Within only a few decades, the inner-city centers of commercial activity during the classical era of the consumer society began to decay. Prominent locations of retail businesses, such as large department stores, had to be sacrificed along with their cultural ambience. In their place, two new types of consumer centers emerged from the suburban setting: the strip and the shopping malls, both of which shaped the new "vernacular landscape" of the modern consumer society. The strip can be viewed as a further development of the classical main street model in a provincial town. Gas stations, motels, businesses, and the not-to-be overlooked fast-food restaurants, of which McDonald's was a pioneer, all lined up along the thoroughfares and main suburban highways, each surrounded by generously proportioned parking lots. Frequently, the customers did not even have to leave their own cars to fulfill their needs as consumers: they could simply roll down the window and be serviced by a drive-through restaurant or other type of business.

The suburban shopping mall established, for all practical purposes, a new decentralized commercial center for consumers. The typical configuration of such a mall included several "anchor" businesses – large department and clothing stores – together with a multitude of specialized retail shops, businesses, and eateries, all connected by a series of wide, gallery-like interior passageways, so that many thousands of customers could be accommodated at the same time. The shopping mall also took over some of the public, noncommercial functions of the classically modern European city, functions that typically were separated from the areas of commercial consumption but were located nearby in other parts of the inner city. These functions included halls and structures for public events and meetings, as well as the public space of the street itself, which as a shopping venue and a connecting path between businesses became part of the commercial space. Not by accident, this transformation of commercial consumption led to legal and political conflicts regarding the boundary between the public and the private sphere. Another aspect of this conflict was its inherent social stratification. White middle-class consumers gravitated toward the shopping malls in the suburbs, which tended to isolate them from the economically less advantaged and from African Americans in particular.

Contrary to the widely accepted notion of an Americanization of Western Europe and in particular of Germany after World War II, we see instead in this socially significant development of consumer culture the emergence of something akin to a new special-case scenario for America in the modern era. In any case, it is an example of different trends and approaches intersecting and influencing each other in a rather complex manner. It is true that between the late 1940s and the 1970s, there was in West Germany an undeniable movement of the consumer culture toward the overpowering cultural paradigm of the United States, which had at the same time also assumed hegemonic political power. This movement was manifested most noticeably through the proliferation of American products and lifestyles, which from their origin promised the consumer a taste of the "American way of life," as in the infamous cases of Coca-Cola and blue jeans. The Americanization of German consumer culture and lifestyles worked in this way to undermine a certain stiffness and bourgeois conventionality that had characterized everyday German culture from the middle of the nineteenth until the middle of the twentieth century. It also contributed to a lessening of class and social boundaries in German society, which had always found familiar expression in habits of consumption. Another characteristic feature of postwar German society was the transformation of what one might term distant dream destinations or "imagined spaces of consumption." The dream world of luxury, indulgence, and affluence was no longer to be found in the old colonial spheres, not in Africa or in the Orient, but rather in America, and especially in the American West. This shift from an oriental to an American point of reference for consumers can be traced quite clearly in the marketing campaigns for luxury articles like tobacco and cigarettes. Here, for example, in the case of a leading brand of cigarettes, we witness the Americanization of the camel, which, through the wonders of advertising, is transported from the Arabian desert to the "Wild West" of the American frontier.

All these changes and refinements of German consumer culture were made possible by a fundamental economic reality: the unrivaled prosperity of the postwar decades. Thanks to this upswing, the Federal Republic – like many other European countries – was able to achieve a high degree of affluence for a large segment of its population and to reach the historic level of mass consumption that the United States had experienced already in the 1920s. This prosperity entailed establishing the typical technical basis for mass consumption and its attendant lifestyle: the electrification and automation of the average household with the introduction of refrigerators, washing machines, and electric mixers and toasters. More so than in other West European countries, the private automobile in the Federal Republic became an almost indispensable form of transportation – comparable only to its significance in the United States – and came to symbolize an unlimited individual freedom of movement. This process of technical and economic proliferation was also highly charged in a cultural sense. Furthermore, it was anchored in political decisions; namely, the firm commitment of the political elites to a universal expansion of commercial consumption, indeed, even to a conceptualization of prosperity, security, and freedom – of everything, in other words, for which the Federal Republic stood – in terms of mass consumption. This consensus was shared by proponents of the "social-market economy" like Ludwig Erhard and by leaders in the Federation of German Trade Unions.

In opposition to the powerful momentum behind this consensus, we see emerging in Germany a distinctly divergent geographic pattern of consumption and lifestyle. In contrast with development in the United States, the inner cities – the classical downtown areas – retained their dominant position; they remained intact as centers of commercial consumption. The reconstruction of destroyed cities after World War II and the urban-renewal projects since the 1970s, which have been oriented largely toward conserving the character of the older cities, have actually enhanced the core of the German city as a center of commercial activity. With the introduction of pedestrian zones and shopping arcades, small and mid-sized German cities have attempted to imitate the basic patterns of design for commercial areas in the large cities. At the same time, an increasing shift of residential development to the suburbs also produced a corresponding shift and suburbanization of commercial consumption; however, suburbanization has occurred on a much smaller scale than in the United States. To go "shopping downtown" is still today a commonly used phrase in Germany as well as a typical pattern of consumption.

Only since the 1980s has there been a noticeable increase in the development of commercial zones on the urban periphery in the Federal Republic; perhaps the most significant pioneer in this regard was, however, not an American enterprise but rather the Swedish household furnishings firm IKEA. Well-established German furniture retailers also followed this trend, as did large building-materials and home-improvement centers, as well as some of the members-only, wholesale warehouse "consumer markets" – the German version of Costco or Sam's Club. Just how ambiguous this Americanization of German consumer culture has remained is illustrated by the recent failure in the German market of an American giant in this field, namely Wal-Mart. Despite early pioneering efforts in the realm of suburban shopping-center design, such as the Main-Taunus Center in Sulzbach near Frankfurt (1963) and the Rhein-Ruhr Center in Mülheim/Essen (1973), as well as subsequent developments like the Weser-Park in Bremen and the CentrO in Oberhausen, the American model of the suburban shopping mall never really established itself in Germany. It is true that after German reunification in 1990, new suburban shopping centers very rapidly emerged in what had been East Germany; for instance, one mall is in the Leipzig/Halle region. This transformational development of a new, booming, purely market-driven society overlapped again very soon with the trend toward a determined revival of the inner-city shopping-center model, a trend that was both championed and regulated by political forces and one that marks a clear distinction with parallel developments in the United States.

Starting in the 1980s, this same trend toward commercial development of the inner city has also gained a certain traction in the United States. Consequently, the past two decades, the boundary between the inner-city and suburban-development trends has blurred and the instances of the two trends intersecting have increased. The renovation of Union Station in Washington, D.C., for example, and its redesign as a shopping and restaurant center bear a striking similarity to the (later) renovation and conversion of the main train station in Leipzig into a multistory shopping mall. It is also significant that America's newest, fastest-growing, and most deeply symbolic destination for commercial consumption and excess, namely Las Vegas, has since the 1990s established itself in the middle of this suburban, car-addicted nation as a huge yet pedestrian-friendly, inner-city shopping and entertainment center.

Of course, Las Vegas has also become a catchword for a kind of modern, consumer-oriented cityscape. Such cityscapes were in essence "cities of commercialized consumption" on a national, indeed continental, and to some degree even global scale. They formed around compact centers that nevertheless seemed to emit an almost magnetic attraction, and they fostered a new synthesis of reality and imagination – of radical market-driven consumption together with the allures of the leisure industry. Hollywood was a pioneer in this field, followed soon by the Disney theme parks in Anaheim near Los Angeles and Orlando, Florida, and, of course, by Las Vegas. It is interesting to note, however, that the boundaries of the larger American shopping malls, which also function as gigantic entertainment centers, such as the Mall of America in Minneapolis, have become fluid in some respects. One reason may be that the consumer- and market-oriented character of American society is displayed so directly and openly that it has become an integral part of the "vernacular landscape," something that in Germany, despite the neon signs of gas stations and fast-food restaurants looming ever higher, has definitely still not happened.

Perhaps the contrasts in the United States are simply much greater than in Europe. The glamour of the major centers of consumer culture in the United States, whether urban, suburban, or post-suburban, as in the case of Las Vegas or the new "edge cities" like Tyson's Corner in Virginia, simply cannot mask the existence of relatively neglected fringe areas, of marginalized regions of commercial consumption. For most of the twentieth century, much of the old South in the United States remained a marginalized region, a backwater of the modern consumer society, comparable in Germany perhaps only with the agrarian, commercially underdeveloped East, which was uncoupled geographically from the West in 1945. For four decades, the GDR remained a special case, a politically and ideologically prejudiced territory of commercial consumption, in which, nevertheless, the reality of consumption, just like the desire to consume, was a momentous social force.

MARKETS, MARKET REGULATION, AND CONSUMERS

The history of the consumer society can be recorded as the development of a society in which consumers, acting as a sovereign entity, decide whether to select or reject consumer goods and maintain their freedom in the face of paternalism and regulations imposed by the state. Indeed, this credo of the market economy has characterized numerous studies. Particularly when Europe and the United States are compared, the United States is adorned with the nimbus of consumer autonomy, whereas the restrictive consumer conditions that limit the mass market and consumers' freedom of choice in Europe are emphasized. The authorities in the United States responsible for facilitating mass consumption were viewed during the interwar period and after 1945 as creating an "irresistible empire" (Victoria de Grazia), which, from its position of strength, swept away governmental obstacles and social privileges and distinctions. This same "empire" also attempted to clear the way – also in Germany – for an unencumbered mass market with its own laws of autonomy for both producers and consumers.

State-imposed market regulations were a feature of the history of German production and consumption in the twentieth century. This can be illustrated in exemplary fashion by considering the history of the German handicraft and retail trades. Under the influence of industrialization, the competition of large corporate enterprises, and the revolution of production techniques, master craftsmen demanded protection from the state for their livelihood and independence, after they had finally lost their previously protected guild status throughout Germany in the 1860s. They were particularly successful in achieving these demands, especially during the period of the German Empire. Through legally binding regulations, not only were the certified master craftsmen guaranteed the exclusive right to train apprentices, they also obligated themselves through a two-thirds majority vote to become organized in trade associations. For their part, the guilds were responsible for the content and regulation of the examinations for the skilled and master craftsmen's certificates and for monitoring the quality of the professional training

and of the work itself. In 1934, after prolonged pressure from the master craftsmen and their national organization, the German Federation of Craftsmen, the
so-called Comprehensive Certificate of Competence was introduced. It effectively
limited free access to the technical professions and guaranteed master craftsmen
a monopoly within the labor market. During World War II, however, National
Socialist authorities intervened massively in the established structure of the technical professions. They strongly favored enterprises that used modern, streamlined
production methods. In the 1950s, the East German government continued the
tradition of state control of labor relations but with a different goal: the collec-
tivization of the labor market. At the same time, the Federal Republic – defying
the rhetoric about the social-market economy – officially codified in 1953 the
obligatory Certificate of Competence for the rank of master in all the skilled
trades. This state of affairs remained in effect through all the various changes in
labor relations during the rest of the twentieth century, and it was not until 2005
under the government of Gerhard Schröder that the Certificate of Competence
was dropped in a number of professions. This move, it must be said, was motivated
in part by pressure to conform to European labor standards.

The measures to regulate the skilled trades were guided by the ideal of a corporate society in which the middle class was ascribed a central and stabilizing
function for German society as a whole. Nevertheless, state interventions were
crafted not only according to this middle-class ideal but also with the interests of the technical and retail-trade professions, as well as those of consumers,
in mind. The introduction of laws governing shop closing hours and the closure of businesses on Sundays curtailed the freedom of retail business owners,
and male and female employees were guaranteed rights in an area of labor relations in which the collective organization and defense of respective interests had
proven difficult. From this perspective, it is understandable that both churches
and labor unions protested against the liberalization of these closing-hour laws,
which, when compared to international standards, have tended to draw laughs. In
the end, through price controls and government control of specific sectors of the
economy, state authorities also intervened repeatedly in consumers' freedom of
choice.

During both world wars, laws regulating consumption were introduced specifically to address situations of scarcity and, in 1950, German consumers still had
the "freedom" to choose between products, the prices of which were controlled
exclusively by the state. In the following years, the governments of both German
states phased out price controls, with the exception of prices for agricultural products, which had been manipulated by the state since the end of the nineteenth
century.

The tendency of German government authorities to constrain the free market
has been frequently contrasted with the American tradition of economic liberalism.
On closer inspection, however, we see that it is not so much the degree of state
intervention into the market of producers and consumers but rather the logic
behind such interventions that differs. Consequently, in light of the relatively weak
workers' movement in the United States and the politically powerful interests
of big business, safeguards for workers in smaller firms, for instance, were less
important there than in Germany; it was not until the New Deal of President

Franklin D. Roosevelt that these safeguards were backed up with state support through legislation like the National Industrial Recovery Act (NIRA), passed in 1933, and the National Labor Relations Act (NLRA) of 1935. The middle-class ideal behind German state interventions into the economy was also a factor in the United States, where it played a somewhat different role. Accordingly, small, locally established, independent businesses were to provide high-quality, low-priced products for well-paid workers with solid purchasing power. It was not ideals motivated by class consciousness or conservative social ideas that shaped this vision of an economy based on small businesses but rather the autonomous strength of consumers and their interests that fueled this vision. These same interests played a role in the failed attempt in the late 1930s to impose state controls on the expansion of retail chain stores.

In the United States, the state did not attempt conservative structural interventions in the economy. Rather, in the realm of consumption, the country's "prohibitionary legal culture" (G. Cross) repeatedly forbade the consumption of particular products for certain periods of time; there is no direct equivalent of this trend in German legal culture. Even if specific pieces of American legislation, such as the Pure Food and Drug Act of 1906, could conceivably also have been passed in Germany, the legal background was very different. There was no systematic policy directed toward specific products, nor was there a recognized need to educate and enlighten German consumers, as was the case in the United States. It was possible in the United States to justify the prohibition of certain products to the American public in terms of protecting the family, struggling against the temptations of consumption, and as a means of educating consumers. The prohibition against alcohol, which a number of churches and other organizations had long demanded, finally became law with the enactment of the Eighteenth Amendment to the Constitution in 1919. The era of Prohibition, however, quickly ran its course, and the Eighteenth Amendment was repealed in the early 1930s. With such acts of ethical demarcation, various groups within American society attempted again and again through morally charged campaigns to combat or contain the excesses of the modern era.

The movement to shield children from viewing certain TV programs, which began in the 1970s, and the growing concerns about obesity are other examples of campaigns designed to inform consumers and influence their freedom of choice. This kind of public relations work carried on by consumer organizations has clearly had a stronger impact in the United States than in Germany and has also resulted in significant state support for the organized interests of consumers.

MEASURES OF CONSUMPTION: CONSUMPTION AND SOCIAL DIFFERENTIATION

The American model of a one-class market, which understands consumption as an integrating phenomenon in terms of social class, began to have an impact, especially after 1945, in Europe and in particular in Germany. It found its equivalent in Helmut Schelsky's thesis of a "flattened middle class society," which was developing in the Federal Republic and in which commercial consumption was an important factor in the process of integrating the German worker into the middle class.

However, the members of the middle class in Germany were for a long time during the twentieth century less engaged in consumer politics than their American counterparts and were rather more the beneficiaries of state patronage. One of the reasons for this was that the development of German democracy was not linked directly to the unfolding of a self-organized, self-conscious, and financially strong class of consumers. Already during the period between 1880 and 1914, the Progressive movement in the United States had linked the cause of civil rights with that of consumer rights. Especially in the interwar period during the New Deal, consumers experienced a political upsurge that never took place in Germany. Franklin D. Roosevelt wanted them not only to be represented institutionally in the government but also through their purchasing power to help pull the American economy out of crisis. In the 1930s and during World War II, the sensible, informed, and organized consumer embodied all the virtues of the good, conscientious citizen. This consumer was supposed to become the backbone of American society, and through his or her access to consumer products, a broad-based equality of opportunity was to unfold. Such concepts did not emerge in Germany until after 1949 when they became apparent, for instance, in Ludwig Erhard's slogan of *Wohlstand für alle*, "prosperity for everyone," although in this case, they were not accompanied by the powerfully egalitarian attributes they had summoned up in the United States before 1945.

These two societies, Germany and America, differed not only in their political definitions of the middle class as a vehicle of commercial consumption but also, more importantly, in the social reality of the social strata. Even if the entire population in the United States was not able to participate fully in the middle-class consumer economy, the social basis for it was still much greater than in Germany. To be sure, at the beginning of the 1930s, one-fifth of all American families had no sink in their kitchens, two-fifths had no electricity, and one-third did not possess an automobile. In the "land of unlimited possibilities," these possibilities were obviously limited, at least for parts of the population. Still, the level of affluence, as measured in household appliances and automobiles, was clearly higher than in Germany, where during the same time period, a privately owned car represented a luxury item for a small minority of the population. The standard of living of an average Detroit worker in a Ford plant at this time contrasted noticeably with that of a skilled craftsman in Germany. American workers could afford radios, record players, electric irons, and frequently – even if they had to use credit – their own automobiles, whereas their German counterparts transported themselves on bicycles or, at best, motorcycles.

The differences in these two consumer cultures revealed themselves not only in the fact that broader segments of the society profited in the United States from their engagement in the consumer economy but also in the manner in which the distribution of consumer goods developed in different parts of these two societies. In Germany, this distribution, as well as the exclusion of certain parts of the population from it, was guided, by and large, by social and professional criteria. Thus, at the beginning of the twentieth century, the possibilities for consumption and the resultant standard of living of skilled workers or craftsmen in Germany were noticeably greater than those of minor clerks, who, together with unskilled workers, generally had difficulty making ends meet. White-collar employees, in particular those who were unmarried and residing in cities, emerged, especially during the Weimar Republic, as the mainstream of a new consumer society, oriented toward both cultural and material consumption. Their significance for Weimar society was greatly exaggerated by the contemporary press, above all by Siegfried Kracauer. In the United States, these differences in income and patterns of consumption were also pegged to social criteria, but ethnicity and race were often more decisive. For instance, the black population often had to defer to white customers, use separate restrooms and entrances, and so became dependent on their own consumer institutions until the final decades of the twentieth century. Even in times like the Depression and during World War II, when blacks conformed to the modes of behavior expected of good citizens and worthy consumers, their discriminated status did not change substantially. Indeed, because of their enforced deference to whites, they experienced their marginalized social position even more intensely. Even though in recent decades advertising and the fashioning of consumer products have been targeted to the black population, notably the black middle class, using elements of their music, their dance styles, and their clothing fashions, this has not fully revolutionized their economic situation as consumers because many other blacks are still poor, indeed the poorest segments of American society.

In both the United States and Germany, the development of a broad-based consumer society was in no way dependent on the dismantling of traditional gender roles. This statement might seem surprising because in both countries during times of war and crisis, women played a crucial role as a social and economic force. When, for instance, German authorities attempted during World War I to blame food shortages and the miserable conditions of the civilian population at first on housewives and their lack of foresight and care, a groundswell of protest resulted and other, more logical scapegoats, such as speculators and profiteers, were named as culprits. In the United States, women assumed positions of importance in the consumer movement during the 1930s and 1940s and demanded laws to protect against price-gouging and to foster better institutional representation for consumers. They also participated more than German women in commercial boycotts, the most memorable of which was perhaps the meat boycott of 1936. In so doing, they created significant inter-urban and regional connections between consumer groups. During World War II, they supported price controls, and their political engagement was sought with slogans like "Lady, it's your war, win it!" In the period after the war, there was, however, less for them to win, because the "Consumers' Republic" they lived in was characterized by legislation such as the GI Bill of Rights (a law to facilitate the reentry into society of returning soldiers) that tended to reinforce male dominance in the society at large. The income-tax structure had the same effect because it favored the model of the male breadwinner. In Western Germany after 1945, the political discourse surrounding consumer affairs also had little effect on the traditional division of labor between the sexes; if anything, it reinforced this division.

The pace of development of a mass-consumption society depended in the end on either side of the Atlantic on the frequency of crises and on the responses to these crises. The level of development in Germany before 1914 can justifiably be compared with that of the United States. In German cities at this time, we can also see the beginnings of an expansion of consumer culture. Household finance records from a variety of different social groups indicate that in addition to major outlays for food and groceries, which were still the dominant expenses, there remained in the average household limited sums available for clothing, personal hygiene, and entertainment. In the following decades, it was, however, impossible to satisfy the society's needs and desires for consumer products. Between 1917 and 1919, and in part also during the period of hyperinflation in 1923, the households of low-wage earners again experienced food shortages and hunger, and the standard of living of white-collar workers declined precipitously. During the Depression and the years after 1945, large segments of the German population experienced hunger, which was by no means always accepted with resignation; it also provoked public protests. These protests were understandable because these periods of scarcity clearly revealed the winners and losers in economic development: on the one side were property owners with tangible assets, and on the other were wage earners. The American situation, despite a partial collapse of the value of real wages during World War I and the Depression of the 1930s, developed much more evenly and was characterized by a significant expansion of internal markets.

World War II produced very different results on the two sides of the Atlantic. In the United States, it generated full employment and a shift in politics and the economy that favored a lessening of class and social distinctions. During the period from 1938 to 1950, economic consumption in the United States rose by 70 percent, whereas in Europe during the same period, it sank on average by 3 percent. Between 1941 and 1944, the average American household income increased by 24 percent and, more importantly the income of the poorest 20 percent of households rose three times as much as that of the top 20 percent of households at the other end of the economic spectrum.

In Germany, there was no equivalent to this expansion of middle-class consumption as a result of the war. The National Socialist regime was confronted with the dilemma of maintaining the support of the population by providing a steady stream of necessary consumer goods while financing a massive rearmament in preparation for war. In some areas, such as leisure activities and the production of radios, they were able to offer consumers a reasonably broad spectrum of choices; however, the satisfaction of other consumer demands had to be postponed until victory in the war had been achieved. The Nazis' ideological bond to the *Volksgemeinschaft*, the *Volk* community, symbolized in the weekly stew they prescribed for everyone, was incapable under wartime conditions of expanding or even maintaining the prewar range of possibilities offered to consumers. The GDR also failed in this respect. Compared to West Germany, it was always at an economic disadvantage and was never able to establish an egalitarian class of consumers, even though the experience of living with shortages of consumer products was shared by large segments of the population into the 1970s. It was, however, not possible for a broad-based identification to emerge with the socialist principle that each person should receive (and consume) according to his or her needs, as long as the party elites determined in authoritarian fashion what those needs were.

CONSUMER CULTURE AND CRITICISM: REFLECTION AND POLITICIZATION

Market society and consumption have changed the Atlantic societies in the twenti-eth century not just in terms of their "hard" structural conditions; that is, through the formative power of economic exchange and the social framework created by this exchange. The increasing penetration of market conditions from the realm of production into the private sphere and the evolution of mass consumption into a universal social phenomenon have initiated a course of reflection in which con-sumer society has become the focus of a process of cultural acquisition. The term "cultural acquisition" is used here in the broadest sense – in a spectrum rang-ing from emphatic approval, through cautious doubt, to fundamental criticism and also in very different forms of articulation: from the desk of an intellectual writing critically about consumer culture to the street in which a demonstra-tion of social protest involving consumer issues is taking place. When reflecting on the social and political implications of economic consumption in a transat-lantic context, it is not as easy to arrive at clear value judgments as one might expect from a purely German or European perspective, in which the United States often appears superficially as a country with an "affirmative" consumer culture. Instead, when viewed more intensively, we see again a host of complexities and "competing modernities": similarity and distinction, archetype and copy, and, perhaps most significantly, a broad realm of overlap and transfer, which shaped in particular the period between the 1940s and the 1970s. Whether the two paths have again separated since then is difficult to say and, empirically, is still an open question.

During the phase of the "classic modern era" in any case – that is, from the turn of the century until the 1930s, when the infrastructure of an urban mass consumption society emerged – the unfolding of this society progressed on either side of the Atlantic more or less along the same lines. In Germany, as in the United States, the rapid pace of social changes accompanying the advent of the consumer society caught the eye of contemporary observers and culminated in expressions of either euphoria or repudiation. Cultural criticism regarding the overwhelmingly material aspect of the new consumer society, concern about the destruction of traditional social relations, and morally tinged misgivings with respect to the new wealth of corporate capitalism and the corruption of everyday life through rampant commercial consumption were all voiced not just in Central Europe but also in the United States. In America, these doubts were also rooted in a specific social, cultural preindustrial society – as it were, in a Tocquevilleian society (Alexis de Tocqueville). Moreover, after World War I, in the 1920s and 1930s, the voices criticizing consumer culture were probably even louder in the United States than in Germany. Paradoxically, the more muted criticism in Germany was due in part to the wave of Americanization that engulfed Europe in the 1920s and generated a growing fascination with the "American model," whereas in its country of origin, this phenomenon provoked a yearning for the past and produced an often noted mood of skepticism, a mood somewhere between "progress and nostalgia" (Lawrence Levine). In a 1924 article in the *Atlantic Monthly*, the journalist Samuel Strauss coined the term "consumptionism" to describe the changes that he was observing in the modern era. With this term, he anticipated a number of the central themes that developed later in the transatlantic criticism of consumer culture, such as the inherent pressure to produce something new for the sake of novelty alone, the pressure to create surplus and waste without any redeeming social value, as well as the danger of eroding classical democracy through consumption and replacing it with a system of purely technical-economic rationality.

Strauss's criticism was linked to strands of the American interpretive tradition, in particular to the vision of a "democratic capitalism," of a capitalism supported by the small and independent producers; this vision had been handed down from Jefferson at the end of the eighteenth century on into the twentieth century. Avoiding the temptation to overly generalize regarding these movements and their respective social contexts, it is, however, still possible to identify three common elements in this American tradition: first, the willingness to accept without hesitation capitalism and its market society as long as they operated "fairly" and respected the rights of individuals and small property owners; second – and here we frequently see differences with Germany – the emphasis on democratic principles; and third, the willingness to organize politically into self-interest groups instead of merely appealing to the state and its moral obligation to regulate commerce and social affairs.

At the beginning of the twentieth century, this basic understanding by American consumers of their own situation apparently contributed to the fact that dissatisfaction with and criticism of consumer culture and the market economy evolved into constructive forms of social engagement and the formation of political interest groups by consumers and workers. The role played by the National Consumers League and, equally important, the independent engagement of women in such causes were significant indications of this development. As in Germany, the self-confidence and self-empowerment of American consumers were anchored early on in the workers' and trade-union movements but soon expanded beyond these limits in the United States. The model of the "citizen consumer" was developed from various perspectives within the intellectual circles of the New Deal by leading thinkers of the day, such as Robert S. Lynd; it was incorporated into the economic theories behind the New Deal and also influenced state and federal politics. In Germany, this model, which included a system of corporate interests that exerted control and regulation over markets and supplanted the role played by citizen consumers as independent, democratic actors, was opposed by the state itself toward the end of the imperial period.

Beginning in the 1940s, and in Germany after the collapse of the Third Reich, the cultural dimension of the consumer society entered a new phase on both sides of the Atlantic. The intellectual arguments against consumerism were characterized by new dynamism and incisiveness, and these arguments carried over increasingly into new kinds of social/political protest movements. Furthermore, in this phase, the transnational connections between the United States and West Germany were especially close. Despite its novelty, this new phase harbored certain affinities to the past as well. In the Federal Republic, for instance, the new criticism of the consumer society, apart from its primary political-ideological focus, also incorporated older elements of criticism directed at the modern era in general. In addition, some complex continuities existed between aspects of consumer politics during the Third Reich and the emergence of the consumer society in the Federal Republic. In this context, Ludwig Erhard is a particularly prominent example and, in fact, from two different perspectives: on the one hand, there was an institutional connection, stemming from his early activity in the Society for Consumer Research in Nuremberg during the National Socialist period, and, on the other, there was an intellectual link from his rather elaborate economic concepts expressed during the early days of the Federal Republic. These varied from a conservatively critical rejection of the mass-consumption society to an optimistic vision of mass consumption embodied in his previously cited slogan, "prosperity for everyone."

The classic expression of transatlantic research into the consumer society during this phase is Max Horkheimer and Theodor W. Adorno's study *Dialektik der Aufklärung* (The Dialectic of Enlightenment), which emerged from their exile in California during the 1940s. In many ways, this study marked the birth of a new stream of social criticism, to which many prominent German and American scholars were to contribute. The essence of this work can be summarized as follows: "enlightenment" in the "cultural industry" is consummated as "mass deception." This interpretation of the modern consumer society determined to a considerable degree the direction of American and German research into this topic for several decades. The immediate experiential background of this study was the West Coast of the United States; however, its critical, theoretical thrust revealed unmistakably its European/German roots. Here again, it is often difficult to distinguish between its adherence to the "leftist" Marxist tradition of criticism of capitalism and its debt to the "right-leaning" tradition of middle-class, humanistic (*bildungsbürgerlich*) criticism of the culture of mass commercialization. Two decades later, with the appearance of Herbert Marcuse's *One Dimensional Man*, we encounter a very similar combination of viewpoints: this major groundbreaking study took its place alongside Horkheimer and Adorno's book as one of the central works of the German–American New Left movement. A liberal, American pendant can be seen in David Riesman's study *The Lonely Crowd*, which appeared in 1950 (and eight years later in German translation, with an introduction by Helmut Schelsky). When the full spectrum of perspectives on the topic at this time is considered, we see that the critical discussion of the consumer society began to move to the left and, in so doing, often took advantage of typically conservative topoi. Some of Jürgen Habermas's early essays in the journal *Merkur* clearly illustrate this tendency.

At the same time, conservative voices in this debate were transformed into friends of consumerism and all the more so when they recognized that the leftist criticism of the consumer society harbored a fundamental criticism of contemporary Western society. They felt obliged to defend the capitalistic system against this critique. Whereas leftist liberal thinkers like John Kenneth Galbraith criticized this society with works like *The Affluent Society* – the German translation of the title used the term *Überfluss*, surplus, making the criticism even more pointed – conservatives like David Potter celebrated the abundance of the prosperous 1950s as a fulfillment of the American mission and an embodiment of the American character. In all these different viewpoints, with their various intersections and oppositions, we see a very close connection between German and American contributions to the discussions and research on consumerism, both in terms of the history of the relevant concepts and the personal networks of the scholars involved.

In the 1970s, this phase of radical intellectual debate and criticism of the consumer society began to subside in the United States, as well as in Germany, although perhaps somewhat later. This can be interpreted as an indication that the debate had focused on a late phase of the transition into a fully developed consumer society – in other words, on its birth pains rather than on its downfall or self-destruction. Just as important, however, is the time frame in which forms of action associated with this consumer criticism took place; in this respect, it is clear that they started and unfolded earlier in the United States than in Germany. In both countries, consumer politics as the politics of individual consumers moved to the forefront of political action and debate. Commercial consumption became "the issue" but was also the instrument of change in a multitude of new social movements. In the United States, we see this in the civil rights movement in the 1950s and early 1960s. The fight against racial segregation moved from the workplace to the lunch counter. In this way, the civil rights movement reached back unmistakably to the older, pragmatic, and radically democratic tradition of using consumption as a means to effect political change.

Since the 1970s, the consumer-protest movement has taken on an additional, more fundamental significance – not as a protest with the aid of consumption but rather as a protest against commercial consumption itself, against the dominance of material goods and the psychic constraints of the modern consumer society in general, from which parts of the younger generation were seeking to escape. In both the United States and the Federal Republic, this variation of protest established itself much more than the protest "with" consumption. It was rooted in the critique of capitalism and commercial consumption from the student movements of the 1960s and unfolded at first "romantically" in the hippie movement and later more pragmatically in the environmental movements, including those of considerable significance in Germany associated with the Green Party. The prominence of so-called postmaterialist concepts in the "silent revolution," described early on by Ronald Inglehart, favored the spread of such forms of practical protest, and they influenced not only narrow circles of fundamentalists but also a broad spectrum of the educated middle class. Different varieties of "ethical consumption" began to take root that called into question the manufacturing conditions of consumer goods in developing countries, including minimum-wage standards, occupational safety standards, and the incidence of child labor, and in some cases opposed them through the use of consumer boycotts. This phase of discussion and political action focused on consumer issues has continued into the beginning of the twenty-first century. The scope of such protests is increasingly global, and their effectiveness is enhanced by technical innovations in communication like the Internet.

CONCLUSION

The relatively advanced status of research related to consumer affairs in the United States explains in part why the transfer of American goods, forms of trade, and marketing methods to Germany is better known and understood than similar movements in the reverse direction. Consequently, the impression of a one-way street can easily arise, by which American ideas and prototypes have penetrated Germany apparently unchecked, giving rise to the phenomenon of the "Americanization" or "Westernization" of the Federal Republic. Although this view undoubtedly encompasses important developments, it underestimates the effect of endogenous processes in the consumer society in Germany. It is possible, for instance, to understand the successful spread of self-service stores in Germany beginning in the 1960s as the imitation of an American model. One can, however, integrate this development into a more complex history, in which the American promotion of this form of retail sales failed in Germany, and it was only through the intervention of German retailers themselves and their strategies to streamline their own operations that the foundation was laid for the introduction of American-style self-service businesses. Concerning the social aspects of consumer culture and factors related to urban design, the influences since 1945 stemming from the Americanization of Germany were roughly equal to those of distinctly European/German origin. Although the transfer of German or European forms of commercial consumption to the United States was arguably less frequent than in the reverse direction, it was also much less researched until now. The role played in the second half of the nineteenth century by world's fairs, which were a showcase not only for industrial products but also for consumer goods, was in this context certainly just as important as the role of immigrants, who exported models and traditions of consumption back to their home countries.

In comparing these two consumer societies, the differences are not really revealed by just highlighting the striking contrasts, such as modern versus traditional or pioneer versus straggler. Rather, it is a case of differing approaches and modes of consumption and market development emerging from different historical and economic conditions on either side of the Atlantic. These conditions account for the structural hierarchy within which goods were produced for the consumer market in each society, as well as for the size of the national market, which in the United States, for instance, dictated different, larger, and more intensively networked forms of commerce and product development. They also reflect clearly the very different political paths followed by each society in the twentieth century: in distinct contrast with America, the modern German consumer society was shaped to a significant degree by two dictatorships, one during the Third Reich and the other afterward during four decades in eastern Germany.

Even if the development of the American consumer society was not spared by any means from economic crises and periodic losses of purchasing power, still these forces did not affect the budgets of average citizens and the supply of products from the consumer-goods industry as profoundly as they did in Germany at the end of both world wars. During these periods, the organized, currency-based exchange of goods broke down, and black-market exchanges proliferated to fill the vacuum. In light of the fact that Germany's economic development was certainly more crisis-ridden than that of the United States, it is not surprising that it was not until the 1960s in Germany that a middle class emerged that demanded a massive supply of durable consumer goods and launched therewith a revolution in consumer habits and tastes. We are speaking here, of course, of the Federal

Republic; developments among East German workers and skilled craftsmen at this time were naturally very different.

In contrast with the New Deal, during which the economic crisis of the Depression years was overcome in part through the active participation of consumers and their organizations, no such broad political representation of consumer interests emerged in Germany. The consumer cooperatives in Germany, which became successful by combining the needs and goals of consumers with active, internal participation in management discussions about profits and their distribution, lost their independence under National Socialism and, after 1945, were not able to regain their previous importance in the consumer economy. There was also nothing comparable in Germany to the political program launched by Ralph Nader, which focused exclusively on the protection and civil rights of consumers. This stems not only from the fact that in Germany the interests of manufacturers shaped the political debate more than those of consumers, but also because for most of the twentieth century, more attention was paid to the welfare and social well-being of citizens than to the actual range and availability of consumer goods.

At this point, one must ask whether in the globalization of commercial consumption the different national traditions have begun to blur. Are the differences between German and American consumer culture dissolving, and is the same thing happening in general to dualistic relationships, transitions, and rivalries in the contest for an optimal definition of what "modern" really means? To a certain extent, this is true. The globalization of consumer culture and the attendant emergence of new variations of "modern consumption" in China, India, and the Islamic world have the effect of making the Western, the North Atlantic approach appear more unified. Conversely, the collective experience seems to indicate that national cultures incorporating their own distinct market societies, modes of consumption, and forms of political conditioning are not so easily blended together. Moreover, the struggle surrounding globalization has projected the American paradigm of the modern consumer society – especially from the perspective of its critics – more sharply than ever onto the general consciousness. This is particularly true in Germany, where any consideration of consumer culture without the emblematic reference to Coca-Cola, McDonald's, and Starbucks is simply unimaginable and thus remains closely bound to an image of America.

Further Reading

Berghoff, Hartmut, ed. *Konsumpolitik. Die Regulierung des privaten Verbrauchs im 20. Jahrhundert* (Göttingen, 1999).

Cohen, Lizabeth. *A Consumers' Republic: The Politics of Mass Consumption in Postwar America* (New York, 2003).

Daunton, Martin, and Mattew Hilton, eds. *The Politics of Consumption: Material Culture and Citizenship in Europe and America* (Oxford, 2001).

De Grazia, Victoria. *Irresistible Empire: America's Advance through 20th-Century Europe* (Cambridge, 2005).

Fox, Richard Wightman, and T. J. Jackson Lears, eds. *The Culture of Consumption: Critical Essays in American History, 1880–1980* (New York, 1989).

Haupt, Heinz-Gerhard. *Konsum und Handel: Europa im 19. und 20. Jahrhundert* (Göttingen, 2003).

Siegrist, Hannes, et al., eds. *Europäische Konsumgeschichte: Zur Gesellschafts – und Kulturgeschichte des Konsums (18. bis 20. Jahrhundert)* (Frankfurt, 1997).

Spiekermann, Uwe. *Basis der Konsumgesellschaft: Entstehung und Entwicklung des modernen Kleinhandels in Deutschland 1850–1914* (Munich, 1999).

Strasser, Susan, et al., eds. *Getting and Spending: European and American Consumer Societies in the Twentieth Century* (Washington, DC, 1998).

Trentmann, Frank, ed. *The Making of the Consumer: Knowledge, Power, and Identity in the Modern World* (Oxford, 2006).

Wildt, Michael. *Am Beginn der Konsumgesellschaft: Mangelerfahrung, Lebenshaltung, Wohlstandshoffnung in Westdeutschland in den fünfziger Jahren* (Hamburg, 1994).

Zatlin, Jonathan. *The Currency of Socialism: Money and Political Culture in East Germany* (Cambridge, 2007).

9

Authority: Schools and Military

DIRK SCHUMANN AND JUDITH SEALANDER

In 1966, Stanley Herzon learned that his draft lottery number was 115, a possible ticket to Vietnam. He managed to fail his medical exam and remained convinced, decades later, that America's intervention in Southeast Asia had been a terrible mistake. Yet, curiously, this now-middle-aged businessman also felt wistful. He'd grown up "soft," he told an interviewer, "longing for the discipline" of military service.

Stanley Herzon's sentiment provides an iconic statement of modernity. Before the late nineteenth century, few would have thought that the state had the right, much less the duty, to discipline the young. The demographic and technological revolutions that produced modern societies by the end of the eighteenth century enlarged the reach of public institutions. But only during the past one hundred years were governments sufficiently powerful to regulate mass behavior in a comprehensive manner, at least in theory, as they could for the first time reach urban and rural areas, social classes, and ethnic groups in a similar way. From the time the United States was founded, the key to achieving this goal was a state-shaped definition of citizenship. The state could define citizenship, which helped it regulate mass behavior. "Good" Americans praised the free market, lauded individualism, and embraced the theory of equality, even if they did not always enact it as an ideal. Not surprisingly, expectations for "good" Germans were hardly as consistent. Obedient imperial subjects mutated into tolerant Weimar nationalists and then became fervent followers of Hitler. A denazified West Germany asked its citizens to support democracy; the German Democratic Republic wanted committed socialists.

Despite substantive differences, both Germany and the United States wanted public institutions to instill certain norms from childhood onward. During decades of sometimes bitter antagonism, the two rivals cooperated in usually unacknowledged ways to impose a new condition of modernity: state-controlled categorizations of entire populations. On both sides of the Atlantic, the economic, social, and emotional roles traditionally played by families shrank as state law displaced private choices and the rearing of properly trained citizens became a public obligation. Various public institutions tried to impart societal standards to the young. Juvenile courts implemented laws that defined deviant behavior, sending offenders to so-called reformatories. Schools and armies, however, were the most broadly important institutions, and for that reason they are the focus of this chapter.

Military conscription and mandatory school attendance affected the lives of most twentieth-century German and American children and young adults.

Schooling and military training sought to shape bodies and minds. Young people had to accommodate themselves to large organizations – to fulfill given tasks, to find their place in a hierarchy, and to respect and cooperate with others. Well into the twentieth century, those who taught and trained the young favored drill and punishment. The young were to learn more than mechanical discipline, however: they would also get to know and accept the prevailing values of the society in which they lived. Discipline did not necessarily exclude freedom. Citizens in a democracy would be guided by self-discipline to find the proper balance between exerting their rights and respecting those of others. Moreover, school education always contained an element of intellectual creativity that defied total control. Hence, the boundaries of discipline in the classroom and the military unit often were inexact and contested, particularly in the second half of the twentieth century.

But the idea that the state *could* dictate the daily routines of tens of millions of citizens under age twenty-five was peculiarly modern. Doing so required large bureaucracies, which developed gradually and expanded greatly after 1890. Compulsory education laws affected boys and girls under age eighteen. Armies, especially those primarily composed of draftees, were always young. Throughout the twentieth century, the average American draftee was rarely older than twenty-one. This was true for Germany too, except during the two world wars, when the reach of conscription widened to include the majority of men between ages eighteen and forty-five.

The crisis of total war, however, was the exception that reinforced the rule: it was the young the modern state most wanted to shape. Those under eighteen were the first to experience the full force of modernity's reliance on forms of discipline shaped by new professions. The fields of sociology, anthropology, and psychology all prospered as governments started to use their ideas, methods, and evidence. Intelligence could be measured, human "stock" could be improved, and society was the sum of its statistics.

At issue was the increasing salience of social science rationales to the construction of social order and the centralization of power within national governments. Relations among local, state, and national authorities were not without tension, and struggles for control interfered with government actions. Indeed, significant noncompliance on the part of the young themselves marked – and continues to mark – modern efforts at disciplinary control, particularly, but not exclusively, in the United States.

Despite being interrelated in many ways, the United States and Germany were more often competitors and, at times, bitter enemies than friends between 1890 and the middle of the twentieth century. American leaders claimed that mandatory schooling would broaden democracy, not inculcate "Germanized" obedience; a U.S. draft would not copy "Prussianized tyranny." In turn, German generals questioned the competence of the American military, and German pedagogues criticized the lenient methods of American schooling. Even after 1945, German leaders were opposed to imitating U.S. models. As thousands of students and teachers experienced American education firsthand, however, interest and amity replaced hostility and ignorance.

The United States and Germany competed with each other to define modernity, and it was a competition that twice culminated in bloodshed. Each society could exaggerate its images of the other, especially where the easily romanticized topic of social responsibility and the young was concerned. By the late twentieth century, however, Germany and the United States had come closer together. Both embraced "educational standards" movements as leaders of both countries worried about declining levels of student skills. Both tried, largely unsuccessfully, to integrate minority schoolchildren. Germany, which for generations had praised its military as the "school of the nation," faced a growing public debate about mandatory conscription. Some thought the American "volunteer army" provided a better model. These once-bitter competitors showed signs of a converging modernity.

EMERGING MODERNITIES: GERMANY AND THE UNITED STATES, 1890–1914

On October 16, 1906, an army platoon marching through Köpenick, a small town on the outskirts of Berlin, was stopped by a man wearing a captain's uniform. Declaring himself in command, he ordered the soldiers to occupy City Hall and arrest the mayor, who refused to hand over the keys of the municipal treasury. The "captain" was an impostor, but his escapade illustrated the overwhelming respect enjoyed by the military in Germany. After the wars of unification in the 1860s and in 1870–1, the military's prestige grew spectacularly; it was credited for creating the German nation-state.

Military values permeated German society in the late nineteenth century more than ever before, as all German states accepted the Prussian system of universal conscription. On the eve of World War I, the German army comprised more than 800,000 soldiers, the equivalent of 1 percent of its population at the time. Recruits initially had to serve for three years; after 1893, they had to serve for only two years. Some tried to dodge the draft by emigrating to the United States. As late as 1911, almost two-thirds of all recruits were still farm boys in their early twenties. They were judged by German leadership to be more physically fit and less likely to belong to the socialist labor movement than their urban counterparts. Only 6 percent came from big cities, although that was where more than 20 percent of the population was living.

For many recruits, this period of military service functioned as a crash course in modernity. As they entered the garrisons in the cities, they found barracks that were better lit and cleaner than their rural homes and featured such amazing technological innovations as indoor toilets. From the first day, however, recruits were subject to a harsh discipline that often included brutal and degrading treatment by superiors. Training emphasized physical toughness and relied heavily on formal drill. At the same time, though, it also took into account that modern warfare required smaller units to act with some degree of independence on the battlefield. All in all, many soldiers looked back on their military service with more pride than anger, regarding it as a test of manliness. Even staunch socialists were no exception. Military service could create or reinforce a basic adherence to emperor and nation, and this adherence could be joined to a variety of political positions.

In contrast to the German example, nineteenth-century Americans violently resisted conscription. In 1863, a massive draft insurrection paralyzed New York City. Thousands of people, led by young Irishmen who had fled the Great Famine, killed, looted, and destroyed transportation infrastructure. Politicians knew that immigrant adolescents were leading the riots, and the continuing arrival of European immigrants in the millions (mostly young and male) could be politically worrisome. What could keep the United States from the kind of disorder epitomized by the draft riots and violent labor protests? Expanded and consistently enforced mandatory schooling emerged as one answer. Jane Addams echoed the view of many prominent reformers when she argued that publicly supported education could inculcate habits of "self-discipline" and love of country, especially among the ethnically diverse peoples of America's crowded cities. A nation of immigrants risked disintegrating into quarreling tribes of strangers.

At no time between 1890 and 1914 was more than 15 percent of America's total population foreign born. The 800,000 newcomers who arrived each year gathered in the nation's big cities and lent credibility to the idea that the country's culture was under siege. Extension of compulsory schooling was an urban crusade, a response to the reality of cities where often one out of three adults was foreign born and a majority of children had parents who did not speak English. Although parochial schools took in many immigrant children, they operated on their own terms, emphasizing Catholicism and fostering, albeit unintentionally, the emergence of an ethnic rather than a general "American" identity. Because children born on American soil were automatically granted citizenship, reformers connected their worries about the future citizenry's competitive abilities to their high-pitched rhetoric about vanishing American traditions.

Germany was frequently the focus of anxious comparisons. The United States must rise to the "German challenge," many claimed. Whereas illiteracy in Germany had basically disappeared by 1900, it still hovered around 10 percent in the United States. Two-thirds of American children attended elementary school but, in numerous places, attendance was sporadic and public regulation haphazard. Controlled by local boards of education, "common schools" focused on basic computational and reading skills. In many states, school terms lasted three months at most, and parents were expected to pay a considerable portion of "public" school expenses. The vast majority of children left school entirely before age twelve. Fewer than one in five attended high school and, of that number, five out of six failed to graduate.

Americans dismissed compulsory military service as tyranny, but they by and large accepted compulsory, extended, and publicly financed education, in good part because it was sold as an engine of economic and social mobility. By the onset of World War I, new laws in almost all states required children to attend school for much longer periods of time, usually six to nine months a year, between the ages of six and sixteen. The state was also to be the final arbiter of curriculum, even if parents chose to send their children to private schools.

This legislative revolution led to a keystone of the twentieth-century mentality: children's education was too important to be a private matter. As with other ideas underpinning modernity, however, the gap between theory and practice was wide. Few U.S. cities had the money or personnel to keep close track of attendance. New York City assigned four men to the task, a laughable number given the city's size. This tiny staff was responsible for enforcing truancy laws for hundreds of thousands of children, now told by New York State to be in school until age sixteen. Frequently followed by hostile, jeering crowds of neighborhood adults, overwhelmed inspectors watched boys and girls duck down alleys or slip out backdoors. At least New York City *had* inspectors. Most other cities did not.

In contrast to this American ambivalence about mandatory education, Germany created a three-tier system that was tightly controlled by state governments. Most of the country's children between ages six and fourteen were enrolled in a free *Volksschule* for nine months a year. A small minority of pupils then went to a *Gymnasium* to prepare for university, and the remainder attended a *Realschule*, where they learned basic skills for white-collar work. Heavily state subsidized, the German school system doubled its number of teachers and enrolled more than ten million pupils by 1914. Worried American reformers were right; less than 1 percent of the German population was illiterate, at a time when an inability to read was a far greater U.S. problem, especially in the impoverished South, where some 20 percent of the population was unable to write. It was common for American workers to sign for receipt of their pay with an "X."

Educational disparities did exist in Germany, although they were less severe than in the United States. Children in the German countryside spent fewer days at classes than their city peers and were often taught in one-room schools. It did not help that rural Catholic priests and Protestant pastors also served as school inspectors. Frequently at odds with teachers, they wanted to have older children home when they were needed to help on the farm.

Clergy also reinforced the authoritarian character of curricula and classroom instruction after 1871. As was true in the United States, teachers were generally free to beat children for being lazy or recalcitrant. It was obligatory to portray the Prussian-centered, Protestant-dominated German Empire as the fulfillment of German history. In the Prussian East, with its large population of ethnic (and Catholic) Poles, school authorities even attempted to eliminate Polish language and culture from the classroom. As had similar "English-only" Americanization campaigns in the United States, these "Germanization" efforts triggered massive resistance.

Nonetheless, school instruction in both countries exposed millions of youngsters to expected norms of loyal citizenship, for the most part successfully. Still, better educated young citizens were also more able to develop an informed view of the world not congruent with that of any government. After all, in Germany, socialists and center-left parties continued to increase their share of votes in parliamentary elections and succeeded in 1912 in garnering almost a majority of votes, capping forty years of school instruction that glorified authoritarian nationalism. During the same era in the United States, the Socialist Party's influence peaked, as citizens throughout the Midwest elected socialist mayors. No school system anywhere among the many thousands of locally controlled American districts extolled socialist views on capital, labor, or the ownership of property, however.

MODERNITIES AT WAR: GERMANY AND THE UNITED STATES, 1914–1945

Turn-of-the-century Germany and the United States viewed each other warily, if at times with grudging admiration. Two world wars, separated by the rise of virulent fascism, would change them into bitter enemies.

World War I put the German war machine, built up since 1871, to the ultimate test. Only a few weeks after the outbreak of the war, the German army increased to the unprecedented size of three million men. During the next four years, more than thirteen million men – 85 percent of all German males between ages seventeen and fifty-two – became soldiers. More than ten million of them served at the front or in support units. Military service now became a key experience for an entire generation.

Discipline remained harsh in the German military. Officers tended to opt quickly for rigid punishments. Without prison cells near the front, they humiliated offenders by roping them to trees. Such methods maintained discipline through the first two years of the war but ironically paved the way for the erosion of discipline in subsequent years. After the appearance of the first signs of widespread dissatisfaction with the course of the war, military officials banned "tying" and reduced the number of punishable offenses. However, when the German spring offensive of 1918 failed to achieve a desperately sought breakthrough and hundreds of thousands of fresh American troops arrived in France, large numbers of German soldiers enacted a "covert military strike." Perhaps between 750,000 and one million soldiers tried to avoid the frontlines by "losing" rifles, jumping off transports, or finding a way to extend their hospital stays. Tens of thousands of other soldiers simply surrendered. The Revolution of 1918, which began with a mutiny in the navy, and the Armistice that same year only hastened the break-up of the military. The formerly mighty German army ceased to exist.

By 1917, the United States was a combatant nation, vowing to defeat the Central Powers and make the world safe for democracy. To do so, the Wilson administration imposed the first effective military draft in American history. From the war's outbreak in 1914, some alarmed U.S. leaders had campaigned for German-style universal military-training programs, taking pains never to utter the hated rival's name. How else could the United States instill a sense of responsibility among its native born and, even more important, among its millions of newcomers? A great number of immigrants, after all, had fled Europe to avoid military service. They were a "domestic menace" almost as serious as threats from without.

Demands for universal military training of all males between the ages of eighteen and forty-five never succeeded, although the campaign would be periodically revived. Instead, the Selective Service Act of 1917 pointedly excluded most aliens. Nonetheless, it dramatically extended traditional definitions of the obligations of U.S. citizenship: qualified males between the ages of twenty-one and thirty could be compelled to become soldiers. Under pressure from army officers who wanted younger recruits, Congress soon amended the draft to include ages eighteen, nineteen, and twenty. Unlike Germany, with its wide age range for soldiers in World War I, American draftees typically had not yet celebrated their twenty-first birthday.

Provost Marshal General Enoch Crowder, head of the new system, cited Civil War precedent regarding the draft. Bounties and legal purchase of substitutions would be forbidden. Five thousand local draft boards, run by civilians, would act as administrative agents. The public would no longer condemn federally imposed conscription as "un-American." Crowder was too optimistic. Nonetheless, Selective Service marked a momentous change. Seventy-five percent of the four million American doughboys were draftees.

The Great War's conscription transformed those individual lives. It also altered institutions, most importantly the American public school. Army testing of more than two million men, in fact, spurred a change crucial to the emergence of mature modernity: a faith in numeric judgments. The draft began the process because it opened the door to mass measurement. The idea that intelligence was quantifiable was not an American one, nor did it become the exclusive means by which children were tracked in school. It emerged from the laboratories at the University of Leipzig, to be refined by Frenchman Alfred Binet. For the rest of the century, nevertheless, the social-science calculation of intelligence would have its most significant consequences in the United States.

Early twentieth-century American psychologists were well aware of German and French work in this area; many had studied in Europe. However, the tests of "mental ages" they brought home took hours. In response to the U.S. Army's desire to identify potential officers, Stanford University professor Lewis Terman created simplified versions of these tests that large numbers of people could complete quickly.

Before the war, American leaders sought ways to organize a highly diverse population without sacrificing faith in the idea that American democracy offered each individual equal opportunity. Army-style mass IQ testing provided a method to do so. It also provoked a sense of crisis, as the military rejected one in three potential draftees. The most important disqualification category, weight, had nothing to do with mental ability. In a relatively poor population, great numbers of potential young soldiers did not meet the minimum weight of 105 pounds. Few Americans knew that specific detail. They were, however, shocked by the news that too many of the country's young were physically and mentally unfit. Institutional change was imperative.

Army group testing in 1917–18 had a profound impact on American society in two ways. For one, it reinforced the racist and eugenic thinking behind the federal legislation of the 1920s that severely restricted immigration. Then, also beginning in the 1920s, it helped convince thousands of local governments to increase property taxation and earmark the money for public education. Although state laws extending mandatory education generally preceded American involvement in World War I, the statistical portrait of young Americans, publicized by U.S. Army testing, led to greater state spending on education. Prominent educational theorist Ellwood Cubberley summarized the new imperative in a widely read book, published just at the war's end. An uneducated citizenry posed a public peril; the state had a fundamental right to compel schooling; American "civic righteousness" and "democratic unity" demanded it.

Expanded schools, established "for the sake of democracy," were never truly democratic, however. Not until the late 1960s did black and white children share classrooms in large numbers, much less friendships or shared values. Nor were children likely to leap the high hurdles posed by class. At the same time as the Great War spurred massive increases in funding for public schools, it also provided a vehicle – intelligence testing – that channeled children into different educational "tracks." The children of the prosperous studied math and English; the rest entered "vocational" classes.

Noncompliance characterized the first several decades of U.S. efforts to substitute school for full-time work for youths under age sixteen. Cities without truant officers did not enforce attendance mandates. States with tiny departments of education loosely supervised legally set curricula. Until the 1930s, the U.S. federal government remained small, in relative terms, and it certainly did not oversee education of the young, which was understood to be the proper function of local governments.

In alliance with thousands of local draft boards, the federal government *did* seek to oversee military conscription after 1917. However, like states that expected their residents would abide by new school-attendance statutes, the federal government initially assumed that citizens would freely participate in the draft. In fact, probably close to three million American "draft slackers" evaded the first national attempt at mass conscription. Some left the country but most probably stayed right at home and were never caught.

Much lower draft-resistance rates during World War II reflected the greater popularity of the war that Americans came to call the "good war." They also indicated the increased regulatory sophistication of more powerful government bureaucracies. In 1917, the only proof of age many Americans possessed was a hand-lettered entry in a family Bible. By 1942, public registration of births was nearly universal.

In 1917, a small professional American military became an organization of four million soldiers, mostly draftees. Then, in 1919, the Army rapidly demobilized, and the U.S. Congress abolished the draft. Nevertheless, conscription was less controversial after the war than it had been in April 1917 when the United States entered the war and Woodrow Wilson hesitated to propose the draft. After the Nazi invasion of Poland in 1939, the United States was once again a reluctant belligerent. However, in sharp contrast, legislators permitted resumption of a draft in 1940, fully a year before a formal declaration of war.

Three-quarters of the four-million-man U.S. Army assembled to fight the Great War were draftees, a figure that increased to more than 90 percent in the sixteen-million-member force created to defeat the Axis. In its new incarnation, a revived Selective Service copied the decentralized organizational model created in 1917, with the choice of recruits left in the hands of civilian volunteers, who now staffed more than six thousand local draft boards. All males between the ages of eighteen and sixty-five had to register. This time, resident aliens as well as citizens faced possible military duty. However, as was the case during the century's first major war, the U.S. Army considered the best potential soldier to be a young man between the ages of eighteen and twenty-one. It rarely accepted privates older than age twenty-eight. Older men and men with dependents made less effective inductees.

As they had during World War I, U.S. leaders argued that military conscription spread the burdens of national defense democratically. They also repeated their belief in its large-scale social efficiency. A conscription system would call those the nation *could* spare and keep others working at vital tasks. It worked as social discipline for the generation fighting the war and as social insurance for the future. As General James Harbord noted, a volunteer system would allow the "children of future America" to be "sired by stay-at-homes."

Germans, long accustomed to mandatory military training, did not bother with such debates. The turbulent years between 1914 and 1945 witnessed too much wrenching social and political change. Limited to the comparatively small size of 100,000 men by the Versailles Treaty, the Weimar Republic's Reichswehr became an army of highly skilled volunteer professionals. Although one million young German men joined paramilitary organizations and combat leagues associated with political parties, even more became members of sports clubs, preferring civilian to quasi-military discipline. However, German youths did not have the same range of options about school attendance. During the Weimar Republic, a compromise between the Socialist Party and the centrist parties made possible a reform of the German school system, making it less unequal and more comprehensive, extending mandatory schooling until age eighteen. Thus, all German youth who did not enroll at a *Gymnasium* or *Realschule* but entered an apprenticeship after *Volksschule* now also had to attend a vocational school. Moreover, although elementary schools retained their religious character, school supervisors everywhere were now selected and paid by the state.

Finally and most importantly, state governments abolished private institutions that prepared middle-class children for a *Gymnasium* and required all children age six and older to attend a *Volksschule* for four years. Determining where they would go after these four years in the three-tier system could have created the need for standardized intelligence exams similar to those used in America. Privately funded institutes for pedagogical diagnostics in Leipzig, Hamburg, Munich, Bremen, Berlin, and Mannheim did offer advice to teachers. They failed to gain traction, however. Germany had one single school psychologist before 1945. German educators considered their own skills sufficient to determine what was best for students, and they regarded advocates of psychological tests as unwanted intruders.

As was true in the United States, day-to-day reality in the classroom probably changed less than these restructurings suggest. Although about twenty thousand new school buildings were constructed during the 1920s, the huge disparities between city and countryside remained almost unchanged. In 1931, almost three-quarters of *Volksschulen* in rural areas still grouped pupils of all ages together in one or two grades. Education ministries imposed limits on corporal punishment and reduced curricula to mere guidelines to give teachers more flexibility. Hence, reform pedagogy, which emphasized encouraging the skills of each child, gained some ground. Political radicalization, however, thwarted further progress after 1930.

Surprisingly, the Nazi regime did not encourage teachers to use harsh methods to discipline their pupils. Instead, new regulations called for corporal punishment to be largely eliminated. Such leniency did not extend to pupils designated as Jewish by the regime; most had lost all rights to attend state schools even before deportations began in 1940. In addition, the regime reassigned, demoted, or dismissed any teacher deemed disloyal or Jewish; one-third of all female principals lost their positions. Hitler Youth gatherings, usually held twice a week, exposed students to the Nazi ideology.

During the war, many children were evacuated from the cities and sent to camps subject to close supervision by Hitler Youth leaders. The National Political Education Institutions (*Nationalpolitische Erziehungsanstalten*, or NAPOLAs) and Adolf Hitler Schools (*Adolf-Hitler-Schulen*) established to produce thoroughly committed Nazis, enrolled only a small fraction of all pupils, however. The NAPOLAs had no more than six thousand students in 1941. Hence, German schools under Nazi rule did not create legions of ideological zealots. When the regime was collapsing, very few young people heeded the calls of Nazi leaders to form *Werwolf* groups and fight a guerilla war against the Allies. Instead, many would soon prove receptive to the attractions of American culture.

Rebuilding a massive military force was a priority for the Nazi regime, which reinstated the draft in 1935 to restore the military to "a school of the nation for educating our youth in the spirit of willingness to fight and a love of the fatherland that is ready to make every sacrifice," as Minister of War Werner von Blomberg put it. As before 1918, all men between age eighteen and forty-five were eligible; they were usually drafted at age twenty for two years. Moreover, in 1935, all males between ages eighteen and twenty-five had to serve in the Labor Service for a half-year, mainly performing agricultural work, building roads, and supporting the construction of the Autobahnen. After 1936, membership in the Hitler Youth became mandatory for youths aged ten to eighteen.

Hence, German male youth entered the army familiar with Nazi ideology and paramilitary training. This familiarity helped make the military professionally efficient as well as largely loyal to the regime, especially as it grew rapidly during World War II. By 1945, eighteen million German men had served as soldiers, including many who were considerably older and younger than twenty; in 1943, even seventeen-year-olds began to be drafted. Women were excluded from military obligations, as in the United States. Massive government campaigns to encourage American women to join "Rosie the Riveter" as war workers were misleading; most female adults were stay-at-home housewives in the United States. By contrast, German women between ages eighteen and twenty-five performed one year of compulsory service (*Pflichtjahr*) in agriculture or domestic work after 1938. The Labor Service demanded an additional six months after 1939. Nevertheless, fearing a breakdown of morale at home, the regime never fully implemented a universal civilian draft for women during the war.

CONVERGING MODERNITIES? THE UNITED STATES
AND GERMANY AFTER 1945

For much of the twentieth century, images of the German enemy were ubiquitous in America. The generation that grew up hating the Hun brought up children who hated Hitler. Only after 1945 did Germany and America begin to converge as societies. Although few U.S. citizens could dissect the ideological differences between communism and Nazism, they certainly knew that the nondemocratic Soviet Union had fought with America against nondemocratic Germany. This alliance slightly complicated America's longstanding anticommunism. During the war, American officials had in fact promoted the falsehood that Russia was allowing its citizens greater political freedom.

That situation changed with the defeat of Germany and the onset of hostility between the United States and the Soviet Union. Within a frame of Cold War tensions, a divided Germany received skewed U.S. attention. The GDR remained a shadowy entity, hidden by the Iron Curtain. The United States and East Germany were ideological rivals, although East Germany set up a comprehensive school system that was superficially similar to the American educational system. By contrast, West Germany emerged as rehabilitated friend, and it and the United States moved closer together. In West Germany, schooling became more egalitarian and conscription less universal.

In turn, the United States took up some German traditions, including extended conscription. In both societies, state-issued documents marked the process of becoming an adult: birth certificates, school enrollment papers, national military registration cards. In the United States, that final piece of paper was a notable marker of modernity – acceptance of the first-ever American peacetime draft. The U.S. Congress extended conscription through 1947, responding to the military's needs for men to serve in occupied Germany and Japan. That itself was a departure from longstanding traditions. American wartime armies had historically disappeared soon after the end of fighting. In 1948, a year after the draft ended, President Harry Truman signed a new bill authorizing its resumption: Cold War policy demanded perpetual military readiness.

The U.S. public reacted calmly to these Cold War circumstances. In fact, peacetime conscription stimulated almost no public controversy at all despite the monumental change it symbolized. A boy's eighteenth birthday marked a new state obligation: registration for possible military service. Draftees fought in Korea and Vietnam, although volunteers outnumbered them in both conflicts. As late as 1968, the public continued to favor the draft. As part of his campaign for the presidency that year, Richard Nixon proposed an all-volunteer army. The idea went nowhere.

Within four years, however, conscription came to symbolize an increasingly unpopular war, even though only one in four soldiers in Vietnam was a draftee. Since 1917, thousands of local boards had chosen "doughboys," or World War II "GIs," or Vietnam-era "grunts." As in previous wars, the typical draftee was still young; the typical draft-board volunteer was a prominent middle-aged citizen. However, during the Vietnam War, in striking contrast to their behavior during previous wars, draft boards issued an unprecedented number of exemptions. After 1969, nearly one in ten registrants received a conscientious objector classification.

The draft emerged quite suddenly, as America tried and failed to avoid involvement in World War I. It ended just as suddenly, with the American failure in Vietnam. By ending the draft, Richard Nixon sought to end antiwar protests. The ones that most concerned him were not those in the street, where adolescents burned registration cards, but inside Selective Service's local board offices, where adults registered a more subtle anger.

When the Allies dissolved the Wehrmacht, Germans did not long for the reintroduction of conscription. Total defeat in World War II would create a broad antiwar consensus in Germany. With the rise of Cold War tensions, however, governments in East and West remilitarized. Against massive opposition,

Chancellor Konrad Adenauer's conservative government established a new West German military and reintroduced the draft. West German males who had turned eighteen were to serve for twelve-month periods.

The new Bundeswehr emphasized that its soldiers were "citizens in uniform." Unlike their predecessors in the Reichswehr and the Wehrmacht, Bundeswehr soldiers had the right to vote and to join political parties. Moreover, they received explicit instructions not to obey orders of an obviously criminal character. To ensure decent treatment, a *Wehrbeauftragter*, an ombudsperson responsible for considering soldiers' complaints, was to be appointed from the ranks of the Bundestag. Conscientious objection now became a constitutional right, although objectors had to prove their motives in a hearing and had to serve as *Ersatzdienstleistende*, as "replacement social workers," mainly in hospitals and nursing homes; those young German men who opted out of the military had to serve for a somewhat longer period of time.

These reforms sought to imbue the Bundeswehr with the democratic values it had been created to defend. Day-to-day reality in the barracks proved harder to change, however. The death of a young paratrooper at a training exercise near the town of Nagold in June 1963 revealed widespread abuse of recruits and spurred a national debate. Draftees, in particular those who had graduated from a *Gymnasium*, complained of boredom. The number of conscientious objectors, meanwhile, rose steadily. Until the mid-1960s, roughly 3,000 young men, less than 1 percent of those liable for military service, applied for conscientious objector status each year; in 1968, the figure rose above 10,000 for the first time. The Bundeswehr was no longer able to claim a mandate for teaching young West German men the discipline they needed to defend their country and prepare for adulthood.

Although the Nationale Volksarmee, East Germany's equivalent of the Bundeswehr, was established shortly after the war, the communist regime did not reintroduce conscription until after the construction of the Berlin Wall in 1962. In contrast to those in the West, East German recruits remained under tighter control, served for a longer period of time, were granted fewer furloughs, and had to wear their uniforms even when off duty. Because of pressure from churches, the regime allowed conscientious objectors to serve in construction units – as *Bausoldaten*, or "building soldiers." They did not have to work with weapons but were still under military discipline and had to wear a uniform.

The communist government in East Germany moved quickly to change the school system, replacing Germany's traditional three-tier structure with a comprehensive *Polytechnische Oberschule* (polytechnical high school). Only those deemed loyal to the state were able to aim for a university education, a small number that was never more than 10 percent of a given age cohort. In West Germany, in contrast, some 15 percent of the population studied at a university in the 1960s; this figure approached 20 percent by 1980. In the GDR, more than twenty-five thousand *Neulehrer*, young teachers who had undergone shortened training courses and were more committed followers of the regime than many of their older colleagues, entered the schools. Most teachers were members of the Socialist Unity Party (Sozialistische Einheitspartei Deutschlands, or SED), as were the overwhelming majority of school administrators. The establishment of a Ministry of Education in East Berlin further centralized government control of the school system.

School discipline was not to be enforced by physical punishment. Reality in the classroom did not immediately follow suit, especially in rural areas, where spanking one's children was normal practice in most families. The regime advocated methods that were different but no less rigid. A new youth organization, the Freie Deutsche Jugend (FDJ), was given a broad mandate to improve young peoples' performance at school and work. East Germany's rulers also created other institutions meant to solidify their grip on society and promote military values and discipline among the young. After 1952, the Society for Sport and Technology (Gesellschaft für Sport und Technik) provided paramilitary training for young people between ages fourteen and twenty-four. In 1978, fearful it might lose control of its youth in the wake of détente and youth unrest in the West, the East German government added *Wehrkunde* (paramilitary instruction) to the school curricula of the ninth and tenth grades. All pupils learned why the GDR needed a military, and boys spent two weeks in boot camp. Even in the 1980s, military training involved the teaching of hatred, directed at socialism's enemies in the West, including soldiers in Western armies.

Vietnam ended conscription in America, but America's similarities with Germany persisted. During conscription's half-century history, opponents warned that military-style forced discipline would produce Prussian-style tyranny. Yet, as the United States returned to a volunteer military system, a denazified West Germany became a model for the democratic treatment of soldiers. Did U.S. demands that its military be nonpartisan deprive volunteers of basic civic rights? Should it copy West Germany's willingness to allow active-duty enlisted personnel to stand for political office? Did West Germany embody the "ideal of civilian in uniform" while the United States made "mercenaries" of its own young men, depriving them of their full rights by limiting their rights to free speech and to political participation? Were soldiers in West Germany's conscript army more able to exercise their rights than the new members of America's all-volunteer force?

West Germany's new role as positive model extended to mandatory schooling as well. Neither society abandoned the idea that the state should compel its young to attend school, but doubts about the effectiveness of state-sponsored schooling united critics on both sides of the Atlantic. Since the early twentieth century, Americans had praised public schools as central to democracy. Under one roof, they said, children from many backgrounds would bond as fellow citizens. In fact, children in comprehensive schools had long been divided by intelligence testing and curriculum tracking.

Some felt that this division was a reality that had to be acknowledged. They argued that if the U.S. vision of a school where all students existed as equals did not exist, better to follow West Germany's example and improve vocational education. Since the days of the Empire, one school for all children had never been the rule in Germany. U.S. education analysts began to lavish praise on preparation given German teenagers. They admired Germany's vocational education, as it gave youths a good chance for adult success.

Stephen Hamilton was one such American observer, and a girl he called "Anna" was the product of high-quality German vocational training. Beginning at age fifteen, Anna worked in a large West German manufacturing firm's accounting department, while spending her afternoons in classes that provided additional training in purchasing and inventory control. By age eighteen, she accepted regular employment at the company, which already had invested in her long-term future and willingly subsidized an additional year of computer training. Anna's hapless American counterpart, in contrast, "was being turned out of school to sell candy, flip burgers, and pump gas." U.S. vocational tracks were underfunded, filled with obsolete equipment, burned-out instructors, and bored students, in Hamilton's estimation.

Ironically, just as American educators were increasingly attracted to the discipline, work ethic, and skill they attributed to German education, Germans themselves began to find their schools inadequate. After the collapse of Nazi rule, the West German school system had been rebuilt along traditional lines. American efforts to introduce middle school and high school in the American mold met with fierce resistance in West Germany. Methods of disciplining children remained rigid and included a teacher's right to hit recalcitrant pupils. However, a heated public debate about corporal punishment indicated that a growing number of parents, pupils, and pedagogues saw it as anachronistic and antidemocratic. At the same time, the *Volksschule* slowly began to lose its dominant position in the system. Whereas in 1952, 80 percent of thirteen-year-olds attended *Volksschule*, this share had dropped to 70 percent in 1959, as more and more pupils went to *Realschulen* or *Gymnasien*.

In the 1960s, the pace of change quickened. Pedagogues and politicians worried that too many talented youngsters were consigned at too early an age to *Hauptschule* in cities as well as in rural areas. Germany sent fewer adolescents to university than did most other highly developed nations. Could such trends doom the country to a noncompetitive future? As a consequence, *Realschulen* and *Gymnasien* underwent a massive expansion. In 1960, less than 30 percent of all pupils attended either *Realschule* or *Gymnasium*; by 1980, this figure had reached almost 50 percent, and the majority of these pupils were attending *Gymnasium*.

While some American educators were championing vocational training in Germany, West Germany was cautiously adopting American-style comprehensive schooling in experimental networks of *Gesamtschulen* from the 1970s on. In 1980, they accounted for 14 percent of *Gymnasien*. These schools consciously copied U.S. ideas about educating all children in one school. Some, such as the Holweide School in Cologne, even tried American teaching techniques, such as requiring teachers and pupils to work in teams. Even more tellingly, Holweide hired a school psychologist. After the war, U.S. occupation authorities had tried to introduce school psychology to West Germany on a broad basis. It took another twenty-five years, however, until each state had its own school psychology service. Occupation officials also promoted standardized testing, with more success. American-style IQ tests became a widely accepted tool in deciding who should attend which sort of school. As the walls in the three-tier school system showed some cracks, state governments used testing to further strengthen their control over the system, as did the federal government in America.

The United States became a – largely positive – point of reference in West German debates about education, in part because thousands of West German high school students and teachers had participated in exchange programs since the late 1940s. Methods of disciplining pupils liberalized in both countries, as corporal punishment was banned or became subject to tight restrictions and basic rights of pupils were acknowledged, however differently defined. Germany and the United States now used each other as models, something that reflected a convergence of anxiety. Both were aging societies with expensive systems of social services and declining percentages of youths aged eighteen or younger. Would the young fail themselves and the nation? Were they being failed by the systems of discipline invented to train them for citizenship in the twentieth century?

German and American leaders thought that a united, healthy, and well-educated population was vital to continuing economic competitiveness. Neither nation was confident that its young were growing up with even minimally sufficient skills. In the United States, alarming reports noted the numbers of high school graduates who had trouble deciphering bus schedules or correctly counting their change. American leaders loudly demanded a "turn" to rigorous academic standards, forgetting that historically they had never been imposed on all students. In 2001, the results of the first Program for International Student Assessment (PISA) study, which compared students' skills in reading, math, and science in thirty-one countries in Europe and the Americas, were shocking for Germans, as German students scored in only the medium to lower ranks. Ministers of education, although disagreeing about what political steps had to be taken, nevertheless accepted PISA as a new universal standard for measuring academic achievement.

German and American leaders agreed that greater government oversight would ensure that all children gained higher levels of competence in math, science, and language skills. In reality, although students were legally required to attend school, nobody knew what percentage of students was actually in school, much less whether they were mastering basic skills. Rising rates of truancy and violence, such as a student's shooting rampage in the East German city of Erfurt in 2004 that left sixteen other students and teachers dead, alarmed many Germans. A small but growing number of parents defied state authorities and taught their children at home. Experts recommended that teachers make greater efforts to address the individual needs and problems of their students; teachers criticized the multitude of legal regulations that made successful discipline so difficult. The tone of the debate was rather somber. Globalization, which placed a premium on high-quality students, increased pressure on educational systems. But by exacerbating class tensions, it also called into question what any public system could realistically accomplish.

CONCLUSION

Late-nineteenth-century German and American elites welcomed modernity with confidence. True believers in the powers of measurement and the possibilities of state-imposed discipline, they dramatically remade the lives of millions of children and youth. Their late-twentieth-century counterparts were far less optimistic about the abilities of the school or the army to shape future generations of ideal citizens.

Beginning with the young, citizens became numbers on scales of normalcy – with lives shaped by state-imposed standards. Yet, standards were in disarray, as was faith in the ability of state institutions. As Germany hesitantly experimented with American-style comprehensive schooling, some in the United States began to call the system obsolete. Was it time to reevaluate the skills that workers would need in the future? From the eighteenth through the mid-twentieth century, for instance, the ability to write had been crucial to success in societies where modernity depended on printed words. In the future, would speaking and listening be more important than reading and writing? Did developed nations need to reimagine new kinds of training for different versions of literacy and numeracy?

Germany had long praised its military institutions as schools for society. However, as the United States joined other Western nations and abandoned conscription, Germans too began to rethink an institution once central to modern German self-definition. No longer seen as necessary for defending Germany and the West against a Soviet invasion, the Bundeswehr struggled to reimagine its place in society. Reduced to fewer than 300,000 soldiers after 1990, the German military actually drafted only about one-third of eligible young males. Almost half in this age cohort now claimed the status of conscientious objector. This led some Germans to call for an "efficient" American-style professional military of "less expensive" volunteers. In reply, defenders argued that the draft guaranteed close links between society and the military.

This debate showed that Germans no longer saw the military as an essential institution for disciplining young people and integrating them into society. Not many disagreed with the late German chancellor Willy Brandt, who in 1969 had declared that the "school is the school of the nation." Whatever differences remained between the United States and Germany, on this crucial point, both societies converged.

In 1918, the U.S. federal Bureau of Education optimistically predicted that mandatory schooling of the nation's young would enable every citizen "to shape both himself and society toward ever nobler ends." General Enoch Crowder similarly thought that Selective Service would "unite the energies of all Americans" and produce a "virile national consciousness" among an entire generation of the young. By the late twentieth century, such statements sounded quaint. Nonetheless, citizens in a converging Germany and America had not abandoned a central tenet of modernity. They still believed that the young had state-mandated rights and state-sponsored obligations, although they did not always know how to guarantee these rights and how to define the obligations that came with them.

Further Reading

Chambers, John Whiteclay. *To Raise an Army: The Draft Comes to Modern America* (New York, 1987).

Flynn, George. *The Draft, 1940–1973* (Lawrence, 1993).

Frevert, Ute. *A Nation in Barracks: Modern Germany, Military Conscription, and Civil Society*. Transl. Andrew Boreham with Daniel Brückenhaus (Oxford, 2004).

Fuhr, Christoph, ed. *The German Education System since 1945*. Transl. Vera Heidingsfeld and Timothy Nevill (Bonn, 1997).

Kater, Michael. *Hitler Youth* (Cambridge, 2004).

Katz, Michael. *A History of Compulsory Education Laws* (New York, 1976).

Keim, Wolfgang. *Erziehung unter der Nazi-Diktatur*, 2 vols. (Darmstadt, 1995–7).

Lamberti, Marjorie. *State, Society, and the Elementary School in Imperial Germany* (New York, 1989).

Lamberti, Marjorie. *The Politics of Education: Teachers and School Reform in Weimar Germany* (New York, 2002).

Peterson, Carl. *Avoidance and Evasion of Military Service: An American History, 1626–1973* (San Francisco, 1998).

Ravitch, Diane, and Maris Vinovskis, eds. *Learning from the Past: What History Teaches Us about School Reform* (Baltimore, 1995).

Reese, William J., and John L. Rury, eds. *Rethinking the History of American Education* (New York, 2008).

Gender: Equality and Differences

EILEEN BORIS AND CHRISTIANE EIFERT

Traveling to visit relatives around 1900, the young painter Gabriele Munter, later a founder of the "Blue Rider" group, confirmed what her repatriated German mother had often recalled: American women were self-assured, full of initiative, athletic, and strong-willed. Most significantly, they had equal status with men. Münter was not alone in her praise for American gender relations. On her return home from the 1909 meeting of the International Alliance of Women, the well-known social policy expert Alice Salomon confessed, "If I am reincarnated as a woman, my only wish is to be an American." Other German feminist travelers to the United States in the years before World War I lauded the country as the land of the future. Women's equality seemed more advanced there than anywhere else in the world, especially than in Wilhelmine Germany.

In contrast, Americans noted that German women slept "silently in a home-spun cocoon," "content" to be a "leaderless and hopelessly domesticated group." In 1915, feminist Katharine S. Anthony countered this impression in the first English-language account of the German women's movement. Notions of women trapped by "children, kitchen, and church," she argued, misrepresented an edu-cated group of activists who fought for women's rights and for better maternal and child welfare. Indeed, Progressive women reformers, like anti-sweatshop cru-sader Florence Kelley and settlement founder Jane Addams, relied on German models in developing an American welfare state. Yet, the equation of German womanhood with the *Hausfrau* persisted into the twentieth century, temporarily replaced in the 1930s and early 1940s by a portrait of Nazi baby machines no less devoted to *Kinder, Kirche, and Küche*. After World War II, the *Fräulein* eager to fraternize with GI Joe and the plain but strong communist woman driving a trac-tor presented additional contrasts to the All-American Mrs. Consumer, unhappy housewife, and Hollywood vixen. Similarly, the German *pater familias* and Nazi storm trooper, no less than the greedy American businessman and sexually aggres-sive GI, provided diverse portraits of masculinity, subject to class and racial/ethnic differences, which both modernizing nations embraced. Gender performances in each were more complex, however, than such representations of womanhood and manhood suggest.

Historians of women have shown that Western capitalist societies generally shared a similar understanding of gender. These societies assigned wage-earning to men and caregiving to women, linking the first with employment and the second with unpaid domestic labor. With increased urbanization, intensified industrialization, and the development of consumer culture – key components of modernity – the contradictions intensified between such social constructions and lived experience. Taking advantage of such an opening, women and children gained the possibility of greater autonomy from the family, marking the decline of patriarchy. By the early twentieth century, social movements for equal rights grew stronger. But women did not experience modernity the same as men, even as some women, especially those who were not mothers, developed work and public lives similar to those of their male counterparts. Moreover, different nations came to modern – that is, to more equal – gender relations according to their own traditions.

For most of the twentieth century, the United States and Germany were political and economic rivals with contrasting political systems and welfare states. The centrality of segregation and racial discrimination and the subsequent African American freedom struggle in the United States and the consequences of racial politics – *Zivilisationsbruch*, or the "rupture of civilization" – in the Holocaust and state transformations under National Socialism and communism in Germany generated divergent paths to modernity. Gender relations proved no exception. The rights tradition in the United States provided a legal and political vehicle for women to advance in the workplace while having more children than was the norm in Germany. The residual welfare state in the United States, in which the state acted as the last resort when the private family and market failed, gave less support to families than was common in the various German states, with their corporatist traditions. More powerful male-dominated trade unions in Germany shaped social policy, upholding the family claim over individual rights. Indeed, an individualist ethos and a rights tradition shaped the state's relation to gender in the United States, promoting individual rather than group equality. However, the rising Protestant evangelical influence on politics by century's end celebrated family values over women's rights as individuals. The United States developed an independent women's movement, but German women entered the state more fully as representatives of political parties. Thus, although transatlantic exchange – of objects and people, popular culture and ideas – reinforced modern ideas of womanhood and manhood, gendered modernity in the United States and Germany nonetheless reflected divergent national cultures and experiences.

MAKING OF THE MODERN: 1890S–1930

During the first decades of the twentieth century, the contours of gender expanded in both nations. In the United States, however, race limited opportunities for African American and other minorities. Indeed, gender was racialized, with the very meaning of manhood and womanhood entwined with race, so that white womanhood remained the symbol of purity and black womanhood remained caught between two contradictory representations: the sexualized Jezebel and the desexualized mammy.

For white women in the United States, middle-class women in Germany, and urban women in both countries, increased access to education opened new perspectives; economic independence promised greater autonomy; and occupational opportunities arose in offices, department stores, schools, and professions. With the opening up of political parties in 1908, German women participated for the first time in the political determination of gender relations; four years later, the Progressive Party in the United States addressed women's issues, including regulation of factory working conditions and suffrage. Middle-class women organized for community betterment, conducting a transatlantic dialogue with those in the other nation on women's rights, economic justice, and peace. In their leisure time, women abandoned corsets to cycle, row, or swim. German women organized sports clubs beginning in the 1890s, and American coeds embraced the gymnasium, imported from Germany. By the 1920s, athleticism appeared to enhance rather than de-sex womanhood. These signs of change, however, could not hide the persistent and widespread consensus that the male-breadwinner family represented the most desirable gender arrangement.

Not only did economic restructuring reorganize the workplace, but it also contributed to the reconfiguration of gender. Whereas the household economy relied on the labor of all family members, breadwinning drew men and older children out to jobs organized by sex, age, and skill. Race was a potent factor in the determination of what kinds of people were hired for which jobs, especially in the United States. As the nature of work changed, masculinity was redefined; for women, the move into wage labor was itself a fundamental change. Where de-skilling of jobs had deflated manhood, industrial workers undertook re-masculinization by distinguishing themselves from women and those labeled as feminized men: the "clean" Anglo professional or the "dirty" Asian, Hispanic, or African American domestic servant. But the most belittled and feminized were also hypersexualized, as black and Chinese men appeared in the popular imagination as rapists or seducers of white women, fueling a culture of lynching and justifying the exclusion of immigrants. The white laboring man, made powerless by machines and scientific managers, appeared to be all body. Cartoonists contrasted his bulging biceps with the effete and bloated bodies of capitalists. The man in the Arrow Collar and dark suit, which hid his body, stood apart from shirt-sleeved laborers. White men in white collars – clerks, professionals, and managers – embraced a masculine domesticity that redefined refinement through cultivation of the strenuous life. Symbolized by Rough Rider Theodore Roosevelt, such men sought to toughen their bodies through sport and exercise outside the workplace. They also transformed the home into a masculine preserve through the straight-lined designs, living-room fireplaces, and wooden paneled dens of the Craftsman bungalow – homes built in leafy retreats from the urban core.

Whether from desire or necessity, women's march into the workplace further shifted the contours of gender. Abandoned and divorced wives lived outside the breadwinner–housewife model, securing livelihoods for themselves and sometimes for extended families. The working girl – young and single – became the prototypical women worker as the income-generating activities of both urban and rural mothers remained hidden. To be sure, modernity had an uneven impact, with a woman's work varying by place of residence, marital status, education, race, and ethnicity. Within the ethnic working classes, the family economy persisted, but possession of income enhanced the power of married women and encouraged daughters to insist on greater freedom from the family. Daughters used their wages to purchase cheap fashionable clothes or live on their own. The percentage of U.S. women who were employed outside the home increased from 14 percent in 1880 to about 25 percent in 1910. Still, a higher percentage of German women were in the labor force; their employment rate rose from 37.5 percent in 1882 to 45.9 percent in 1907. However, when home-based labor was included, the U.S. employment rate for women was at 40 percent and closer to that of Germany.

Women's greater economic independence generated greater sexual freedom and control over their bodies both within and outside marriage. The pre–World War I sexual revolution challenged the conventions of respectability embraced by middle and working classes in both nations. "Sex radicals," like Margaret Sanger and Emma Goldman, disseminated birth-control information and advocated "free love." Urban life facilitated heterosexual and homosexual encounters in public spaces such as dance halls, bathhouses, and interracial cabarets. In search of cheap amusements, working-class women "treated" male partners with sexual favors, blurring the boundaries between courtship and prostitution, a form of women's work that was increasingly subject to punishment by American and German municipal authorities and social reformers. College girls moved toward nonchaperoned dating. In contrast, black American clubwomen adopted a politics of respectability to counter persistent sexual slander and abuse. They sought to control the reputation of a race judged as wanton since the period of enslavement. This contrast between black and white middle-class women suggests that modernity did not necessarily translate into the public display of sexuality for all women.

The diversity of models for women's lives, to which the women's movement drew attention, coexisted with a crisis of masculinity that found expression in a hysterical fear of effeminacy, increased nervousness, and hypermilitarism. This crisis was more pronounced in Germany than in the United States perhaps because the United States lacked so strong a militarist tradition. Since the turn of the century, the German public had witnessed a more intense discussion of male homosexuality than in any other country. Opposing pathologization and criminalization of homosexuality, Magnus Hirschfeld believed that homosexuals represented a "Third Sex." But love between men appeared to endanger male privileges in state and society. Moreover, many insisted that modern man was sick; neurasthenia emerged as a reaction to demands for decisiveness, fearlessness, and self-assertion – that is, for manliness – in both Wilhelmine Germany and the United States. As with homosexuality, physicians attacked this condition for blurring the lines of gender. Female illness also emerged when women stepped out of their proper place, leading to sexual deviance and sexual atrophy.

German militarists devised more rigid gender images to combat such potential crossing of boundaries. The "struggle for existence" served as a trope for imagined communities of the male sex and the nation. Before World War I, the German officer elite presented itself as a caste, which would conquer an all-engulfing effeminacy. The remedy – a "hard war lasting several years," as the noted military historian and officer Colmar von der Goltz argued in 1907 – would at least establish unambiguous gender difference as a structural principle of society. American jingoists and imperialists associated manhood with war, with presidents quick to send troops to prove their manhood against "lesser" races.

It was thought that only a strict hierarchical division of labor between the sexes could preserve the family. Although marriage numbers in Germany rose, the birth rate dropped from 35.7 per one thousand in 1890 to 17.5 in 1930. The

U.S. birth rate also dropped but remained higher, with the white rate declining from 31.5 to 20.6 and the black rate from 48.1 to 37.5. Population growth in Germany came from immigration; the "new immigration" that had swelled the U.S. population ended with the National Origins Act of 1924, which restricted the entrance of immigrants from nearly everywhere except the Americas. The proportion of married women in formal employment rose in Germany to 29.1 percent in 1925; in the United States, still only a tenth of wives were in the labor-force. Married women's increased labor force participation limited the scope of the cult of domesticity enshrined in the new German Civil Code of 1900. The privileging of men in marriage law and social insurance represented a legislative attempt to reinforce a hierarchical gender system, which nevertheless continued to erode with war and economic instability.

Codification of American marriage laws reinforced Christian monogamy as the norm. The "companionate marriage" rooted in mutuality, sexual attraction, and equal rights represented a modern alternative to male dominance, although divorce rates began their ascent during this period. With children attending school, reinforced by compulsory education and bans on child labor, custody laws favored mothers over fathers. In response to male nonsupport, reformers sought to reim-pose breadwinning and homemaking roles onto deviant working-class families. They used special domestic-relations courts to go after male "slackers," who deserted rather than divorced their wives. Reformers further instituted mothers' or widows' pensions that rewarded the labor of childrearing as a service to soci-ety but made them unavailable to most African Americans and noncitizens. The meagerness of pensions forced recipients to earn additional income, undermining the domesticity such income supplements were supposed to preserve.

Labor policy, rooted in notions of protection, further embodied dominant gen-der roles. New York and other states inscribed the male family wage onto workers' compensation. Labor standards for women improved conditions only in female-dominated industries, but restrictions on night work, lifting, and occupational hazards placed barriers to women's entrance into more lucrative male trades. In its support for labor legislation designed only for women, the American Federation of Labor (AFL) displayed its gendered understanding of who should bring home the bacon and who should cook it. Women required state protection; men could take care of themselves through collective bargaining. The AFL asserted that men should earn a family wage large enough to support a wife and children, making it unnecessary for women to enter the workforce.

Similarly, the German *Arbeiterinnenschutzgesetze* (women workers' protective legislation) only affected the small number of women working in factories, ignoring those in agriculture and the service industries, thus reinforcing the inequalities between the modern industrial and agricultural sectors of the economy. Regardless of its effectiveness, protective legislation declared that it was the state's business to ensure women's availability for housewifery and motherhood. Women of color in the United States, valued as workers rather than as mothers, remained for most of the century outside such labor standards because they toiled in jobs uncovered by the law.

World War I shook German gender relations. Contrary to the hopes of militarists, the war not only failed to cement authoritarian structures, but it even facilitated their more rapid disintegration. To ensure victory, women replaced men who had traded civilian for military employment; at home, domestic labor compensated for the lack of goods. This exceptional situation lasted more than four years and could not simply be forgotten after the war was over and men returned to their former workplaces. The Revolution in 1918 brought suffrage to women. There was no going back to the prewar gender order, particularly in middle-class and conservative circles. Nonetheless, a longing lived on in the dreams and perceptions of Freikorps soldiers, who participated in the European and German civil wars as paramilitary guardians of order, distinguishing themselves by their brutality.

Entering combat n 1917, the United States experienced less disruption in daily life. Nevertheless, Woodrow Wilson's vision of making the world safe for democracy appeared hypocritical as long as women lacked the right to vote. Taking advantage of this political opening, suffragists succeeded in pushing through the Nineteenth Amendment in 1920, which finally enfranchised women. However, for African American women, race proved more salient than gender: it took the Voting Rights Act of 1965 to guarantee the vote to black men and women. Even though native-born women gained citizenship rights independent of their husbands in 1924, kinship relations still shaped immigration policy. These laws and regulations classified lone mothers as unemployables and thus potential public charges and judged some single women as prostitutes and thus undesirables. Gendered notions of proper labor further shaped acceptance of the movement of people across borders, a hallmark of modernity.

The German family, in contrast to most in America, emerged from the war conflict-laden and weakened. Although marriage rates rose as individuals searched for greater security, there were still large numbers of families without male breadwinners, women without mates, and children with fathers suffering bodily or psychological injuries. The "stab in the back" legend blamed defeat on homefront weakness personified by women and "effeminate" men, especially Jews and Social Democrats. This legend absolved frontline soldiers of responsibility and confirmed the existence of strong women and weak warriors. George Grosz, Alfred Döblin, Fritz Lang, and other artists dramatized female betrayal through images of sex murder. Their stylized figure of the sex murderer reflected a growing fear of violent criminals who were at once omnipresent and nondescript. They directed an increased sense of social insecurity against women, who seemed to benefit more than men from urbanization and white-collar work.

In the 1920s, a growing number of erotic representations of women in advertisements, posters, and book jackets helped spread the myth of the sexually independent "New Woman," both of the Weimar Republic and the Jazz Age in the United States. The American flapper symbolized a modernity marked by sexual rebellion that also saw ethnic variations, such as Mexican American bobbed-hair girls and "New Negro" women. The bathing beauties of the "Miss America" contest, a pageant first held in 1921, projected an ideal of glamour and sexiness that the American woman was told to combine with innate wholesomeness, talent, and service to her community. Other new women formed close same-sex networks, developing a lesbian subculture.

Chorus girls in the cabarets and vaudeville theaters of Berlin and New York displayed their bodies in the mechanical harmonies of the assembly line, offering more a demonstration of the benefits of rationalized labor than of eroticism. In contrast, African American expatriate Josephine Baker captured German hearts with her banana dance; admirers celebrated her as the embodiment of nature, Africa, and ecstasy, even as conservatives lamented her influence and storm troopers broke up one of her performances. Harlem dancers stood for uninhibited sexuality, and blues women oozed sexuality in laments over male wrongs. Yet, like Marlene Dietrich in *The Blue Angel*, Baker represented more: the frivolous and lascivious nudity of self-assured women. Such performers embodied a modernity that Germans equated with America. Nonetheless, German attitudes toward both America and modernity were highly ambivalent. Americans were more enthusiastic about the modern, especially technology, science, and the concept of the new. Those who doubted modernity disproportionately lived in rural areas, rejected Prohibition and evolution, clung to a patriarchal gender script, and embraced fundamentalist religion.

In the Weimar Republic, revolutionaries of the left adhered to representations of the strong man no less than did conservatives. The stylized half-naked communist warriors of KPD iconography expressed male stereotypes similar to those held by the National Socialists; these images reflected the longings of men who saw their masculinity imperiled. Demonstrations became militarized and political meetings erupted into brawls. The message was clear: the streets and, with them, the world belong to fighting men. In harmonious accord with the gender order, women supplemented men in the political arena as healers and caregivers, organizing welfare services for the various political parties. In the United States, by contrast, violence erupted not between political parties but in battles between male workers and police, as in Toledo and San Francisco in 1934 and Detroit during the sit-down strike in 1937. Women auxiliaries not only provided food but also smashed factory windows and ripped the clothes off strikebreakers, defying the script of proper womanhood. During the world economic crisis, German political parties, with their network of associations, offered men and women looking for work and meaning a mutually supportive community that the individual family often seemed incapable of providing. Left-wing parties in the United States, although weaker than in Germany, and unions also provided people with a sense of community.

DEPRESSION AND WARS: 1930S TO THE 1960S

In disrupting men's ability to act as providers, the Great Depression made it difficult for American and German families alike to live out the male breadwinner/female caregiver ideal. Not only did American restrictions on child labor propel wives and mothers into the labor market but also the nature of the economic collapse, which hit basic industry hardest, meant that women retained their jobs longer than men. Couples postponed marriage and pregnancy, with contraceptives becoming a big business. The normative preference for male breadwinning led the federal government to fire married women – leading some to divorce husbands so they could keep their jobs. By 1932, families seemed to be disintegrating, with rising desertion rates and a quarter-million teenagers leaving home prematurely.

Instead of transforming gender norms, the Depression acted as a conservatizing force. The link between personal and social revolution broke down, exemplified by the proletarian mother replacing the rebel girl as an icon of radical womanhood. Public arts projects celebrated the sexual division of labor, marked by the pioneer family, the manly worker, and the female consumer. The "children of the Depression" became the adults of the postwar period; they would seek to right the order of things by returning to female domesticity and male breadwinning.

In this context, the New Deal institutionalized the male breadwinner/female caregiver model. It created a welfare state that linked public benefits either to an individual's employment status or kinship to an eligible worker. Relief programs maintained gender and racial divisions by matching work placements to presumed class, race, and gender characteristics. Women found themselves assigned to sewing projects; men undertook public works. The Civilian Conservation Corps cultivated youthful manhood as well as trees. Discrimination often kept African Americans from obtaining work relief; Mexicans faced deportation. Major legislation covering collective bargaining and labor standards indirectly sustained white male breadwinning by excluding occupations dominated by white women and by men and women of color, such as personal services, agriculture, and nursing. Social Security also reflected gender norms. Survivor's insurance went to lone mothers only if their deceased husbands had contributed into the system. States sought to punish gender deviants, especially poor and sexually active single mothers, through regulations that disproportionately denied assistance to both the never-married and racial minorities. Under the burden of Jim Crow, the South stood as modernity's backwater, both in terms of the emancipation of women and the state provision of safety nets for those bereft of a male wage.

National Socialism promised security and order through the restoration of a stricter hierarchy between the sexes. It envisioned a mutually supportive, racially pure "*Volk* community," with the SS representing the ideal of "Aryan" manhood. Propagandistic films projected depersonalized men, dressed in black uniforms, marching in close formation and embodying violence. Synchronized movement made the SS, like the showgirls of the 1920s, parts of a machine that promised to relieve the burdens of individuality while maintaining individual masculinity. Notions of womanhood combined virulent antifeminism with the partial promotion of emancipation. Quantitative and qualitative improvement of the "*Volk* community" demanded that women, as potential childbearers, be removed from public life and skilled occupations and returned to the home.

Before the war, the German government encouraged women to enter agriculture or domestic service to fulfill their "Duty Year." When the war began, there was minimal pressure to mobilize *Volk* women for industrial employment; later, recruitment depended on structuring jobs so that women could continue caring for their families. The option of four- to six-hour days developed, tied to incentives like workplace nursery schools, nursing rooms, cafeterias, and a twice-monthly "housework day." Nonetheless, women's labor-force participation only rose 3 percent between 1939 and 1944, compared to a 32 percent jump in the United States from 1941 to 1945. The higher rate of female employment in Germany can be attributed to the numbers of women in the agricultural sector; the American statistics did not, however, take account of women's work on family farms. Without prisoners or foreign laborers to replace male workers who had gone to war, U.S. war production relied on women entering industry. The

American homefront also sought to accommodate the women's double day. Stores stayed open after work; prepared foods and commercial household services became available. The state financed child care centers but not to the extent needed, forcing mothers to take night shifts, leading to the phenomenon of latchkey children and fueling panic over juvenile delinquency. The organization of domestic labor remained privatized to a greater extent in the United States than in Nazi Germany.

This time, war disrupted the American landscape, with fifteen million internal migrants, "war widows" running households, and severe consumer shortages. Entrance into the war production workforce spiked female labor-force participation to 37 percent by 1944, whereas in Germany in 1942, nearly 41 percent of the labor force was female. Overall, the war strengthened family formation; divorce temporarily dropped, as did age at marriage, and the birthrate climbed. Leaving home for big cities or the military, homosexuals created new sexual communities. Despite being hounded by vice squads, a vibrant queer culture questioned gender conventions, especially in San Francisco and New York. Women's presence in the military, although as noncombatants, further challenged gender expectations but evoked old concerns about camp followers, "mannish women," and loss of respectability. Yet, here too race reared its ugly head, with black women's military service restricted to the replacement of black men, whom white military officials assigned to mess halls and other support functions.

The need for womanpower threatened "the democratic family" and its stay-at-home mom. Factories hired Rosie the Riveters only "for the duration." Still, women in slacks as well as those with rivet guns expanded the boundaries of womanhood. Although wartime propaganda portrayed overalls as glamorous, women themselves found both personal pleasure and sexual danger in previously masculinized workplaces. From the rebellion of zoot suiters and "pachucas" to the mixing of black men with white women on the shop floor, the homefront offered its own terrain of struggle. Race riots were both battles over scarce urban space, such as housing, and reactions to new gender and sexual encounters. Despite the temporariness of women's advance into better-paying jobs, the war years prefigured a new gender regime, the dual (male and female) breadwinner and female caregiver that would dominate the last third of the century for different reasons in the Germanys and the United States. Wage-earning mothers in the German Democratic Republic, like growing numbers of African Americans in the United States, reflected a parallel gender order: the female head of household. Such single mothers supported children without a husband.

When it came to replacing conscripted men, the German state applied measures that more consciously linked gender and racial criteria. European Jews of both sexes, male and female foreign laborers from occupied countries, and prisoners of war all were forced to labor in the armaments industry. The gender of exploited workers hardly influenced their assigned tasks. In this "equal" treatment of women and men, National Socialist racial policy showed itself simultaneously to be a gender policy. During the selection process at Auschwitz, young children, designated useless for labor, remained with their mothers to be gassed immediately.

Men and women found comfort in traditional understandings of family as they sought to survive ghettos and concentration camps. Surrogate families and "camp sister" relationships created the emotional and, above all, material preconditions for resisting dehumanization. In internment camps for Japanese in the United States, generational bonds often undermined the power of elders and fathers. Meanwhile, strong state penetration and surveillance undermined the ability of the *Volk* family to ensure mutual support, protection, and security. This partial process of family dissolution, encouraged in part by the importance placed on participation in National Socialist organizations, opened new opportunities for girls and single and married women to seek self-affirmation and expand their radius of action. Rising through the ranks of the League of German Girls or the Nazi Women's Organization also could compensate for sexual discrimination.

The sexualization of women persisted under National Socialism. Racism and homophobia, to be sure, marked Nazi sexual morality, but a certain liberalization also occurred, with "sexual freedom and satisfaction" becoming "the exclusive privileges of 'healthy' and 'Aryan' heterosexuals." Representations of naked bodies celebrated their beauty and purity. Women could divorce, with marital infidelity permissible toward non-Aryan spouses. At war's end, however, sexual violence replaced permissiveness. Soviet soldiers claimed the victor's right to rape. Reminded of their own acts during the war, German men insulted raped women, blaming them for their victimization and for sullying men's honor. To escape sexual exploitation or merely to survive, women entered relationships with individual soldiers, trading their bodies for protection and food. Some women in the U.S. occupation zone found these barter relationships most attractive, as American soldiers represented the desirable American way of life. Well into the 1950s, defeated German men lamented the striking decline of morals among their women, railed against sexual excesses, and found a new focus for their racism in African American soldiers.

After the Nazi dictatorship, the two German states developed concepts of gender relations and the family with the intent of breaking with the norms of the immediate past. In the German Democratic Republic, which propagated universal social equality as a central normative category, gender equality was defined as women's right to paid employment, not men's equal duty to perform housework. This meant that only women had to reconcile waged work with family labor. To lessen their double burden, women again were offered part-time jobs, child care, and a right to a monthly paid housework day. The saying that "it is good for a woman to be forced to stand on her own two feet" reflected the knowledge that the labor market could not do without female workers any more than the state could dispense with women having children. Therefore, in the GDR, the number of working-aged women in the labor force rose from 50 percent in the 1950s to 81 percent in 1988. The birth rate, however, dropped to 9.6 children per one thousand women by 1970. Discrimination against women in paid employment still continued in wages, occupational qualifications, and promotions. Husbands and fathers partially relinquished their status as family breadwinners to the state but retained their position as providers as long as the average female wage was insufficient to support a family. Ultimately, gender relations remained hierarchical and unequal.

The Federal Republic of Germany likewise proclaimed the equality of the sexes and prohibited gender discrimination. After March 1953, laws violating the requirement of equality were to be repealed. The Federal Republic, however, rejected gender equality as a structural principle for the family, interpreting the constitutional protection accorded to marriage and the family as guaranteeing traditional family structures. The Equal Rights Act of 1957 affirmed the model of the male breadwinner with housewife/supplementary-earner family. Only with the reform of marriage and family laws in 1976 and 1979 did the state abandon this model, although it continued to define marriage as a union between heterosexual partners. These formal declarations contrast with the United States, where a proposed Equal Rights Amendment stalled during the 1970s.

American women's wartime labors during World War II earned them no right to a job. Their inequality came from the structure of labor markets and civil society and from persistent racial discrimination, although some public policies exacerbated these factors. Union seniority systems privileged returning male veterans, and governmental definitions of full employment reinforced the notion that housework lacked economic value. With the end of the war, reconversion policies stressed family normalcy. Most public funding of day care ended within a year of demobilization. The GI Bill of 1944 – with housing, education, and job preferences for qualified veterans – not only shored up male breadwinning but also privileged whiteness and heterosexuality. Eligibility depended on receiving an honorable discharge, which was less available to African Americans and homosexuals. Such policies reinforced existing gender and family arrangements despite centrifugal social forces, including black and Mexican freedom movements demanding equal treatment in jobs, public accommodations, and voting. Dressed as if going to church, civil rights protestors adhered to conventional gender presentations from the 1940s to the time of the lunch counter sit-ins of the early 1960s. Besieged by white hecklers, they offered iconic representations of quiet manhood and respectable womanhood.

The early postwar/Cold War years placed fathers at the center of the family but also promoted family togetherness in new suburban enclaves. The gender ideal morphed into the "American Dream," which collapsed modernity into abundance, defined by home ownership made available to all through hard work and the end of discriminatory practices like restrictive covenants: clauses in sales contracts that prohibited selling property to racial and religious minorities. With national health measured in terms of proper gender relations, the American nuclear family positioned itself in the struggle against communism. Thus, Vice President Richard Nixon in the famous "Kitchen Debate" with Russian Premier Nikita Khrushchev in 1959 extolled the superiority of the American home, its appliances, and female domesticity. Nonetheless, popular psychologists blamed national weakness on overbearing moms, who emasculated their sons. "Modern women" were becoming "a lost sex," rejecting femininity in the rush for careers. White women were the objects of such antifeminist diatribes, but black women faced more detractors, who portrayed them either as "black bourgeoisie" pushing husbands into early graves or as matriarchs, breeding an "underclass."

During the Cold War, the nation remained caught between desires to harness all available "manpower," which demanded maternal wage earning, and to fulfill children's best interests through homebound motherhood. The postwar baby boom increased the white fertility rate to 3.53 children per women and the black rate to 4.52 by 1960. Rather than a retreat into domesticity, this period witnessed a new consumer economy, higher standards of living, and rising prices that led mothers into employment after their children entered school. By 1960, 40 percent of employed women were married, and more than a quarter of these women had children under eighteen. West Germany had slightly more women in the labor force, but a lower percentage were married; in 1961, nearly 49 of 100 employed persons were women, and 36.5 percent of them were married. Necessity continued to justify female employment but other rationales appeared as well, foremost of which were arguments for a strong economy, fueled by the wages of women consumers. However, unleashing American "womanpower" would require part-time and temporary work to reconcile domestic responsibility, national security, and labor-force demands. The "miracle years" in the Federal Republic also saw greater prosperity and rising female employment.

Perceptions of female difference – that women differed from men because they bore children and undertook the cultural and social assignment of household work – shaped American policy initiatives. Activist trade union women fought for maternity leave, child care, and a shorter workday, while demanding higher wages, an end to discrimination against married women, and greater participation in their unions. The President's Commission on the Status of Women in 1961 sought to overcome sex discrimination in employment, while maintaining familial and maternal activities. Throughout the post–World War II period, from the Women's Strike for Peace to the Parent Teacher Association and other voluntary organizations, women moved from the home into ever-widening arenas, relying on domestic ideology to redefine gender boundaries. Yet, not all activist women embraced this platform: supporters of the Equal Rights Amendment sought a more individualist notion of equality, and antifeminists rejected state interference in family arrangements. Fighting either for peace or for women's legal and professional rights, West German women, by contrast, redefined gender boundaries but remained tied to concepts of state protection that the women's liberation movement rejected.

Meanwhile, with the movement of the majority of Americans to home ownership after World War II, men had to balance family, employment, and public duty. Parenthood became "A Man's Job, Too!" When Jim Anderson returned from work, television viewers learned that *Father Knows Best*, but popular media simultaneously celebrated male rebels for their defiance of respectability and responsibility, whether James Dean, Elvis Presley, or Marlon Brando. As symbols of danger, men of color offered white men alternative masculinities; so did *Playboy* magazine in its promotion of "flight from commitment." The election of the youthful John F. Kennedy as president in 1960 represented a return to national vigor after eight years of Dwight D. Eisenhower, who suffered multiple heart attacks while in office. Kennedy's appearance, in fact, masked his own serious health problems. The reigning ideology associated national health with healthy marriages, promoting the trope of the personal as political. The women's liberation movement soon would embrace this conflation to challenge, rather than sustain, notions of female domesticity and inferiority.

In Germany, domestic ideology during the postwar years highlighted economic reconstruction as a new field for male heroism. Men would repair broken masculinities through the old script of family provision. Participation in the socialist as well as the consumer society turned on women's wage work as well, however. War widows preferred "unclemarriages" to legal ones to keep their pensions; securing and improving one's income counted more than sexual purity. Remilitarization in the 1950s offered well-known remedies and so contributed to the public debate over authoritarianism associated with earlier forms of militarism, including the Nazis. In East Germany, the defeat of the June 1953 uprising left men and women with little room for dissent against political norms promoted by the ruling Socialist Unity Party (Sozialistische Einheitspartei Deutschlands, or SED).

German gender imagery came under the influence of pop culture and mass consumption, both of which were associated with America and by no means ended at the Iron Curtain. From the mid-1950s, rock'n'roll intensified a youthful rebellion against familial and societal strictures and heightened adult fears that decadence and the decline of morals had become unstoppable. The wild dance style in which blue-jeans-wearing men whirled women through the air appeared as an assault on the traditional values that regulated gender and family relations in both nations. At the same time, though, conservative Christian values in Germany represented a break with the Nazi past; the slightest breath of sexual permissiveness and youthful autonomy tacitly recalled National Socialism. The breakdown of conservative gender images required all-out contestation, including continued criminalization of homosexuality in East and West, even though the Nazis also punished same-sex relations. American conservatives, led by Senator Joseph McCarthy, likewise focused on the homosexual menace as undermining both proper gender roles and national security.

RECONSTITUTING GENDER, WORK, AND FAMILIES, 1960S TO THE 2000S

During the last decades of the twentieth century, economic and political changes again challenged the gender order. Greater access to education qualified girls and young women for professions and an economically independent life. The widening circle of possibilities for women shifted the balance of power between men and women. Women gradually found their way into sectors of the labor market and career levels previously closed to them. In reaction, the German public blamed women university graduates for the nation's comparatively low birthrate in the 1990s. Those who assumed that education made women selfish affirmed the persistent validity of the family model of male provider/housewife mother. Policymakers conceptualized women as the indispensable core of the family, whereas men, abstracted as providers of finances, merely *had* a family.

Women provided the labor force for a growing service sector. In both nations, immigrants and noncitizens undertook private household labor and public cleaning, which enabled native-born women to move into higher-paying occupations. Although Germany had relied on Italian immigrants and migrants from annexed Polish territories in the nineteenth century, immigration to the Federal Republic during the years of the postwar "economic miracle" appeared to be something new. Even the increasing mobilization of married women for paid employment did not alleviate the labor shortage. As a result, young unmarried Greek, Turkish, and later Yugoslav "guest workers" were recruited for unskilled and low-waged women's work in the textile, clothing, and food processing industries. Pictures of thousands of male "guest workers" bringing along their wives, whom many German citizens identified with cultural backwardness, overshadowed the public presence of these young women migrants. (The woman wearing a headscarf would become a symbol of alien difference and cultural threat in the United States only after the September 11, 2001, terror attacks.)

In the United States, the civil rights movement opened up the nation's workplaces to African Americans and later to other racial/ethnic minority groups, but it also increased opportunities for white women. All American women benefited from the struggle against racial discrimination when equal rights policies expanded to include gender. There was no German equivalent to Title VII of the 1964 Civil Rights Act that prohibited discrimination in the workplace on account of sex, nor did the concept of affirmative action exist. In West Germany, the concept of gender difference – women's primary role as wives and mothers – continued to shape politics and guide public policy. In the East, the attempt to raise the birthrate to compensate for the high emigration rate led to workplace policies that accommodated motherhood. Unification ended the right to child care that had developed in the East for demographic reasons.

A new norm of wage-earning motherhood divided women from each other in the United States. Affirmative action opened up higher-paying jobs in blue-collar trades, usually associated with men, lifting thousands of women of color and their families out of poverty. The national welfare rights movement organized to defend the right of poor women to engage in motherhood. With African Americans moving into industrial and white-collar jobs, immigrant labor, especially from Mexico, entered the nation to clean houses and buildings, pick crops, and undertake heavy construction. Although the wage gap between the sexes narrowed, with women earning around seventy-seven cents to the male dollar at century's end, the earnings gap between professional and poor women, who were disproportionately women of color, widened. Women with resources took advantage of the globalization of domestic labor and found it easier to siphon off domestic duties, including childcare, to other women than to convince men to do their share or rearrange the workplace to accommodate family life. With more than 70 percent of mothers in the workforce, balancing work and family moved from a working-class problem into a general crisis. Parents who took family and medical leave or moved from full- to part-time work faced barriers to workplace advancement, with women placed on "the mommy track," a secondary tier of employment with limited promotion and lesser earnings; fathers who took time off for parenting were judged to be less committed to their jobs.

The sexual revolution of the 1960s may have unevenly transformed gender within families, but it initiated a thorough liberalization, commercialization, and politicization of sexuality in both West Germany and the United States. New women's movements formed and, in tandem with nascent gay and lesbian movements, radically challenged gender images and relations. These movements questioned the family as the ultimate expression of a fulfilled life. Meanwhile, contraceptives helped remove fear of an unwanted pregnancy, encouraging a more liberated sexuality. Urban and rural communes developed alternative living arrangements. The divorce rate rose sharply to one-third of all marriages in West Germany after 1976 when the parties no longer had to prove legal fault and could resort to the charge of irretrievable breakdown to obtain a divorce. The birthrate, after increasing in the 1950s, continuously declined after 1965 and, since 1972, has fallen below the mortality rate. In East Germany, marriage fell and divorce rose; although the birthrate increased slightly, it stagnated at 2.3 during the 1950s and 1960s, then dropped to 2.2 in the 1970s, and fell to 1.9 in the 1980s. By 1989, 52 percent of all babies were born out of wedlock, a sign of remarkable social and cultural change. The United States experienced a similar decline in birthrate: the urbanization of African Americans, women's labor-force participation, and availability of birth control lowered the birthrate to below replacement level. New immigrants from the Americas accounted for U.S. population growth.

Unlike in the Federal Republic, the two-paycheck family represented a new norm in the United States, although more women never married and a significant portion became single mothers, some from failed relationships and a few out of choice. Young heterosexual and previously divorced couples turned to cohabitation, rather than marriage, reaching 10 percent of all households by 2005. By then, less than half of all households consisted of a married couple. With no-fault divorce, half of all marriages ended in divorce; more households existed without children than with them. Same-sex relationships became more open, if not more demonstrative. Lacking the legal right to marry, same-sex couples suffered from economic disadvantage, as well as second-class citizenship, as more than a thousand legal provisions gave distinct benefits to married couples. Same-sex marriage remained a contentious political divide at the beginning of the twenty-first century.

Nourished by advances in higher education, legalization of birth control and abortion, and the ferment of the Vietnam War, a new feminism spread throughout the United States. Reacting to exclusion by their radical male counterparts, college-aged white, Latino, and African American activists embraced the inherent worthiness of being a woman and called on men to change their behavior, individually and institutionally. Alongside their men, women of color also fought against racial injustice, from police brutality to neighborhood demolition and job loss. Only white women could afford to think that "sisterhood is powerful" and to ignore how they benefited from race and class privilege.

The new feminists demanded equal rights, equal pay, and the end of discrimination, which by the early 1970s, the middle class appeared well on the way to achieving. They also insisted on control over their bodies and the elimination of sexism, which included stopping media portrayals that degraded and demeaned women and thus encouraged violence. A radical men's movement sought to take responsibility for such violence and to celebrate being a man outside the context of breadwinning. During the last third of the century, the sexual division of labor within households began to shift, with men doubling and women halving their hours of housework, although women still performed most routine family labor.

In both Germanys, a new feminist movement addressed topics similar to those in the United States, but it emphasized state protection of women. Feminism in Germany was less individualistic than American feminism, and this difference was most apparent when it came to abortion. In 1975, two years after the U.S. Supreme Court, in *Roe v. Wade*, upheld a women's right to abortion during the first trimester on the basis of the right to privacy, the West German Federal Constitutional Court declared for the human life of the fetus, striking down the legalization of abortion. However, it would allow abortion on the basis of protecting the woman from health threats as determined by a physician. GDR law, in contrast, permitted first-trimester abortions from 1972 onward. After unification, in response to protests by East Germans against the Federal Republic's more stringent abortion law, the new reunified German legislature passed a more liberal measure in 1992. This law also was invalidated by the court. A 1994 law was a compromise of sorts, although it tilted toward the "pro-life" position. It criminalized abortion, thus prohibiting state insurance coverage, but permitted women to terminate a pregnancy during the first trimester and reaffirmed support for funding child welfare and kindergartens. U.S. abortion policy in the decades after _Roe_ became more restrictive through state legislation that required parental or spousal consent, burdened clinics with specifications, and imposed waiting periods. Whereas Germany would fund abortions for women on welfare, the United States upheld a right to abortion but refused public funding, which made it difficult for women on public assistance to pay for the procedure. Meanwhile, a few pro-life extremists attacked abortion providers and bombed clinics, but most sought to limit, if not prohibit, the practice through legislation, voter referendums, and court decisions.

Politics remained a terrain for challenging the gender order. West German terrorist groups that emerged in the 1970s and 1980s placed themselves outside society and the gender order. Women's overrepresentation among their members fired media fantasies about "gun-toting women," suggesting an allegedly small step from emancipation to terrorism. Similarly, the Weather Underground, Black Panthers, and other self-styled revolutionaries, like Patty Hearst, in the United States challenged associations of women with nonviolence that the peace and antinuclear movements continued to reinforce.

Whereas West Germany rejected affirmative action in the workplace, it instituted quotas for equal representation of women in political parties. In 1984, the same year that the Democratic Party in the United States unsuccessfully ran a woman for the vice presidency, the parliamentary group of German Greens elected an all-female executive, which gained fame as the _Feminat_. With the election of Chancellor Angela Merkel in 2005, German discussions of female capability quickly died down. The number of women officeholders has remained small in the United States, although polls suggested that the nation was willing to elect a female president even if some conservatives like talk-radio commentator Rush Limbaugh lambasted Democratic women as hysterics or harpies. A woman commander-in-chief joined physicians, lawyers, and other professionals on prime-time TV, although ditzy girlfriends, wise moms, and hypersexual victims continued to populate the television airwaves.

During the 2008 presidential campaign, eighteen million people voted in the Democratic primaries for former First Lady and New York Senator Hillary Rodham Clinton, who was defeated by Barack Obama. Obama became the first African American to be nominated for the presidency by a major party and, in turn, to be elected president of the United States. The Republicans attempted to capture some of the women's vote that year by nominating Governor Sarah Palin of Alaska. Feminists were enraged over contradictory media portrayals of Clinton as a vulnerable, emotional woman or as not feminine enough during the campaign but laughed at comedian Tina Fey's mimicking of Palin, the folksy defender of rural white America and self-proclaimed hockey mom and barracuda with lipstick. The election showed that a woman candidate was not the same thing as a feminist candidate and that women voters could separate the advancement for women in electoral and other public office – as earlier seen in the appointments of Madeleine Albright and Condoleezza Rice as secretaries of state – from the promotion of policy issues benefiting the majority of the nation's women. Hillary Clinton became secretary of state under Obama.

By the 1980s, the New Right, drawing strength from resurgent Protestant evangelicalism, sought to reinvigorate a patriarchy that seemed to have succumbed to the combined forces of economic necessity and the mass women's movement of the previous decade. New men's movements, like the evangelical Promise Keepers and the black nationalist Million Man March, promoted the responsibility of fathers. Covenant marriages prohibited divorce, and promotion of virginity distinguished Christian courtship, as did a turn to modesty. No equivalent movement existed in Germany where the larger popular culture continued to sell sex through dating shows, music videos, and movies. In Germany, this American popular culture still exercised a strong influence, although, under EU encouragement, cultural transfer among European countries became more important. Secularization, especially in the GDR, was so widespread that Christian fundamentalism could not gain ground there, and the Islamic fundamentalism of many of its recent immigrants met widespread rejection. The tentativeness of objections to the institution of arranged marriage – criticized in the Muslim case as forced marriage – shows how normalized the power gap in gender relations remains in secularized German society. In contrast, during the 2008 U.S. presidential campaign, a more compassionate evangelicalism gained traction. Candidates Obama and Republican John McCain appeared before the Southern California Saddleback Church of Pastor Rick Warren, who sought to mobilize his congregation against world poverty and not merely condemn gay marriage.

Germans joined other Europeans in celebrating Obama as a cross between John F. Kennedy and Martin Luther King, Jr. The German press puzzled over what kind of manhood did the 47-year-old Illinois senator with a white Kansas mother and Kenyan father represent: Was he a superhero or an Uncle Tom, "the redeemer – or simply a seducer?" A relief from the parochial cowboy Bush, he was "smart," "attractive," and "cosmopolitan." By the inauguration, Obama had come to embody the new man, who both pushed for fatherhood responsibility and praised the work of single mothers, confident in his loving, indeed romantic, "equal partnership" with the strong, fashionable, and equally smart wife and mother Michelle – a portrayal that upended old stereotypes of the black family.

CONCLUSION

Viewed from the perspective of the past century, a common gender ideology has marked modernity, but contrasting national histories have shaped the development of male breadwinning, female domesticity, women's rights, open sexualities, and freedom from family claims. With regard to gender, politics shaped the divergent journeys to modernity undertaken by Germany and the United States. Throughout the twentieth century, the German welfare state improved provisions against social insecurities; it pioneered in the introduction of prenatal care and maternity leave. Germans turned to the political process to address the allocation of resources within and between families. Although family values and sexuality proved a terrain of political struggle in the United States, politicians paid homage to the family as private and thus not subject to political intervention. Nonetheless, public morality demanded interference into intimate life, as seen in governmental policy on abortion, welfare, and unmarried motherhood.

As we move into the twenty-first century, gender issues remain central to political life. The dissolution of the male-breadwinner family continues. Women's "rights" remain associated with participation in waged work, not the right to choose how to combine maternal work with economic survival. The ideal for white middle-class women has shifted from the domestic norm to some form of wage-labor motherhood, a combination that women of color in the United States have long had to juggle. It was widely believed that women too could become individuals, the autonomous individuals as envisioned by liberal theory, and, if they were unable to succeed, they were scolded for making bad choices. Compared to women, men found themselves with few acceptable alternatives to breadwinning. But forces of deindustrialization, deregulation, stagflation, and global competition were undermining the very economic and social protections that had buttressed the family wage and undergirded family security. In the most recent economic crisis, male unemployment has soared, with mainly lower-paying service-sector jobs, long held by women, remained available.

The process of modernization in Germany and in the United States might have been smoother without the fight for gender equality. Demands for inclusion of women of different classes and ethnicities often exposed the precarious balance established between men. On both sides of the Atlantic, gender images have represented inequalities, serving as symbols of threat and desire: the liberated, educated, and seductive American woman against the silently sleeping, silly German woman; the American father/defender of family and community versus the German authoritarian militarist. The longevity of these images diverts attention from the persistence of the model of the male breadwinner and female caregiver/supplementary income provider shared in both nations despite significant institutional differences. That the United States and Germany both embraced modern gender relations but competed with each other on the world stage underscores how gender reflects both global and national realities.

Further Reading

Boris, Eileen. "On Cowboys and Welfare Queens: Independence, Dependence, and Interdependence at Home and Abroad." *Journal of American Studies* 47 (2007): 599–621.

Boris, Eileen, and Lewis, Carolyn Herbst. "Caregiving and Wage-Earning: A Historical Perspective on Work and Family," in Marcie Pitt-Catsouphes, Ellen Ernst Kossek, and Stephen Sweet, eds., *The Work and Family Handbook: Multi-Disciplinary Perspectives and Approaches* (Mahwah, 2006): 73–97.

Chin, Rita, *The Guest Worker Question in Postwar Germany* (Cambridge, 2005).

Eifert, Christiane. "Women Entrepreneurs, 1950s–1980s: Wartime Leftovers or Indicators of Modernisation?," in Ralph Jessen and Jane Caplan, eds., *West German Modernity: State and Society in the "Bonn Republic"* (Oxford, 2010).

Faue, Elizabeth. *Community of Suffering and Struggle: Women, Men, and the Labor Movement in Minneapolis, 1915–1945* (Chapel Hill, 1991).

Feldstein, Ruth. *Motherhood in Black and White: Race and Sex in American Liberalism, 1930–1965* (Ithaca, 2000).

Hausen, Karin. "Mothers, Sons and the Sale of Symbols and Goods: The German 'Mother's Day'," in Hans Medick and David W. Sabean, eds. *Interest and Emotion: Essays on the Study of Family and Kinship* (Cambridge, 1984): 371–413.

Hausen, Karin, ed. *Geschlechterhierarchie und Arbeitsteilung: Zur Geschichte ungleicher Erwerbschancen von Männern und Frauen* (Göttingen, 1993).

Heineman, Elizabeth D. *What Difference Does a Husband Make? Women and Marital Status in Nazi and Postwar Germany* (Berkeley, 1999).

Heinsohn, Kirsten, Barbara Vogel, and Ulrike Weckel, *Zwischen Karriere und Verfolgung: Handlungsräume von Frauen im nationalsozialistischen Deutschland* (Frankfurt, 1997).

Herzog, Dagmar. *Sex after Fascism: Memory and Morality in Twentieth-Century Germany* (Princeton, 2005).

Höhn, Maria. *GI and Fraeuleins: The German–American Encounter in 1950s West Germany* (Chapel Hill, 2002).

Kimmel, Michael. *Manhood in America: A Cultural History* (New York, 1996).

May, Elaine Tyler. *Homeward Bound: American Families in the Cold War Era* (New York, 1988).

Meyer, Leisa D. "Interrupting Norms and Constructing Deviances: Competing Frameworks in the Histories of Sexualities in the United States," in S. Jay Kleinberg, Eileen Boris, and Vicki L. Ruiz, eds., *The Practice of U.S. Women's History: Narratives, Intersections, and Dialogues* (New Brunswick, 2007): 280–307.

Neuhaus, Jessamyn. *Manly Meals and Mom's Home Cooking: Cookbooks and Gender in Modern America* (Baltimore, 2003).

Schulte, Regina. *Die verkehrte Welt des Krieges: Studien zu Geschlecht, Religion und Tod* (Frankfurt, 1998).

Sklar, Kathryn Kish, Anja Schüler, and Susan Strasser. *Social Justice Feminists in the United States and Germany: A Dialogue in Documents, 1885–1933* (Ithaca, 1998).

Zaretsky, Natasha. *No Direction Home: The American Family and the Fear of National Decline, 1968–1980* (Chapel Hill, 2007).

zur Nieden, Susanne, ed. *Homosexualität und Staatsräson: Männlichkeit, Homophobie und Politik in Deutschland 1900–1945* (Frankfurt, 2005).

I I

Environment: Conservation versus Exploitation

CHRISTOF MAUCH AND KIRAN KLAUS PATEL

On the one side of the Atlantic, an almost endless territorial expanse and a state that stretches across a continent, encompassing all kinds of climactic zones; on the other, dense settlement in a single temperate zone. Here, there are urban landscapes and settlements without a center; over there are cities and villages whose history can often be read, like peeling an onion, back to the Middle Ages or even to classical antiquity: in almost no respect do the United States and Germany seem to differ as profoundly as in their respective patterns of settlement and in their treatment of the natural environment. At present, the United States is responsible for about one-quarter of global carbon dioxide emissions, whereas according to many rankings, Germany is one of the most successful of the leading industrialized countries in the field of climate protection. Nowhere in the world is there as much packaging and garbage as in the United States; in Germany, by contrast, an environmental consciousness receives significant support from state institutions and environmental political parties. Historically, Germans may have drawn repeatedly from the practices and ideas of the American environmental movement, but at first glance, it is the differences between Germany and America that are the most visible.

SURPLUS AND UNIFORMITY

"In the beginning all the world was America," wrote John Locke in his 1690 *Second Treatise of Government*, using America as a metaphor both for the state of nature and for a distant and isolated continent. Because European colonists perceived the New World's indigenous people also to be a part of nature, the American territory appeared empty and endless to them. They defined it as a *vacuum domicilium* and legally as a "wasteland." In the cultivation of a "wilderness" that in reality had been the Native Americans' hunting and farming grounds, the white settlers saw a project given to them by God. The early settlers saw this task as nearly unachievable and, particularly in the early colonial days, their main occupation was the struggle for simple survival. Entire generations imagined the continent to be limitless. Thomas Jefferson, for instance, believed the settlement of America would take a hundred generations. In the end, however, it took only five. Never in history were such vast amounts of land populated by immigrants at such a quick pace.

Early on, Americans devised strategies for imposing order on the "untamed" environment. The Northwest Ordinance of 1787 became the foundation of the land system that enabled the orderly surveying, sale, and settlement of public lands in the United States. Subdividing the continent into regular rectangular sections, it subjected the landscape to an organizing principle as clear as it was simple. Since then, endless lines and right angles have structured "American space," setting the mold for fields and settlements as well as street plans. To this day, each flight over the Midwest shows a striking landscape of geometry and parallel lines, suggestive of surplus land and uniform settlement.

The availability of surplus resources has meant that farmers hardly identified with the land that they worked, something that can be seen in the sequence of agricultural functions found for ground and soil. The lucrative tobacco plant, for example, only grows in fresh soil. After a few harvests, its yield and quality start to decline. For this reason, American tobacco planters moved often, pushing the frontier ever more to the West. On their former land, corn and grain farmers explored other variants of an ecologically unstable one-crop approach. The history of grain and cattle farming followed similar patterns of exploitation and migration, encouraging the move to the West, where the land was seemingly endless and certainly cheap. Most states had lost more than a third of their forests by 1850, Massachusetts as much as 60 percent. The motto of the wood moguls – "cut out and get out" – also applied to other branches of the economy connected with land management. Land was first of all a commodity, not what the Germans call *Heimat*: a "homeland" resonant with cultural meaning. The fast pace of purchasing land, developing it, building on it, selling it, and then resettling to a new area, and then repeating the same pattern, fixed the nature of land development in America. Economic priorities – in particular, gaining a connection to a market – were decisive; putting down social and emotional roots in the land was not. Benjamin Franklin was not entirely wrong when he complained that Americans were bad farmers because they had so much land.

The practice of dividing up land on a drawing board also damaged the environment. Instead of taking into account the local topography, plants were cultivated out in parallel rows. This method of planting, together with ignorance and the desire to maximize profits, led directly to erosion and soil exhaustion.

The federal government played an essential role in these developments. American myths of the freewheeling pioneer spirit – of yeoman farmers and lonely cowboys – are misleading. With the Louisiana Purchase of 1803, the United States expanded its territory by about two million square kilometers with the stroke of the pen. The federal government became the greatest landowner; and even when Washington sold off land, it could set the tone for later development. The government promoted a capitalist attitude toward using nature, from which speculators and big investors often profited but not the small-scale farmers.

Politicians in Washington have exercised immense power in shaping American environmental history. Interestingly, almost one-third of American territory and one-fourth of the productive forestland still belong to the federal government, land that it administers as "public domain." Natural disasters reveal the government's presence and importance to environmental affairs, more so in the United States than in Europe. In the wake of a Dust Bowl caused by overcultivation and with sandstorms dispossessing hundreds of thousands of people in the Great Plains – described by John Steinbeck in his novel *The Grapes of Wrath* – Washington intervened and showed the farmers alternative ways to work the land. Since 1979, the federal government has had the Federal Emergency Management Agency at its disposal, with 2,500 full-time employees and more than 5,000 volunteer workers. After Hurricane Katrina in 2005, Washington sent more than thirty thousand soldiers from active service in the National Guard to New Orleans, the largest civil occupation in U.S. military history. The federal government also figures prominently in the efforts to predict catastrophes and in the financial reconstruction of disaster zones. Indeed, in the course of the twentieth century, the development of sophisticated early-warning systems has led to a reduction in the number of victims of natural disaster; financial damage, however, has become considerably more severe, in part because the government has set aside extensive financial resources for major disasters. Some fifty million people in the United States live in hurricane-prone areas; Florida, despite being the state with the highest risk of hurricanes, has seen the highest growth in population until only very recently.

The transition to an energy system based on oil made for an unsustainable relation to the environment in the United States as in the rest of the world. After the major oil reserves were discovered in 1901 in Spindletop, Texas, the transition from coal to oil was unstoppable, and since the interwar period, Americans have been dependent on oil. The environmental consequences manifested themselves over the course of the twentieth century in tandem with population growth, urbanization, industrialization, and "automobilization." Energy use in the United States increased tenfold from 1900 to 2000; per capita energy use by the 1970s was three times greater than that at the beginning of the century. Neither the massive budget deficits, brought about chiefly by importing oil, nor the economic and ecological costs of oil disasters – like the sinking of the *Exxon Valdez* in 1989, which destroyed a bird and sea otter sanctuary off the coast of Alaska – have prompted Washington to reconsider its reliance on oil. Rather, the United States has sought political and, in emergency situations, military ways to guarantee the global oil supply.

A breathtaking economic and political – as well as social and cultural – dynamic of growth left the United States the only remaining superpower by the end of the twentieth century. This growth dovetailed with a remarkably rapid construction of national infrastructure. In the 1990s, American roads stretched to a length of some twenty-four million miles, equivalent to the combined length of all roads in Germany, Canada, Great Britain, Japan, France, Poland, Brazil, Hungary, Mexico, Italy, and China. In 2010, the American road network is still by far more extensive than that of the entire European Union.

The ecological dark side of America's economic success story includes rampant growth, pollution, extinct species, and, above all, a culture of wastefulness, with global consequences that may well be irreversible. During the Cold War, the United States produced dozens of millions of cubic meters of long-lasting nuclear waste. It has also caused environmental degradation outside of its own borders, as in Southeast Asia during the Vietnam War. Even the energy crisis of the early

1970s inspired only a limited rethinking of environmental questions: for a brief time in the 1970s, cars with good gas mileage were challenging the gas guzzlers; twenty years later, the SUV fashion was in full swing. Well into the twenty-first century, vehicles kept growing not only in size and engine power but also in gas consumption.

The richness, both real and imagined, of the U.S. natural resources has been a powerful driving force in American life. It propels the dynamism and flexibility of modern America. At the same time, however, it is also linked to the resulting problems of air, water, and soil pollution.

Germany, very much unlike America, was densely settled as early as the Middle Ages. In 1900, the German Empire had a population density of 107 people per square kilometer, which was about ten times higher than in America; a century later, even though it had not experienced nearly as great demographic growth, Germany was still seven times more densely populated than the United States. In part because of this high population density, Germans, like other Europeans, have extensive historical experience with limited natural resources. The loss of the forests as a result of wood consumption during the early modern period and the scarcity of coal around 1900 are but two of many examples of resource scarcity that shaped the collective experience of Germans.

An awareness of scarcity thus served as a counterforce to the uncontrolled use of resources over the course of German history. The opportunity for seemingly unlimited consumption was precisely what made North America so attractive for millions of emigrants: Europeans imagined the New World to be a "land of limitless possibilities," not least because of its abundant natural resources. In Germany, one could draw on the lessons of experience – which were powerful locally and which, historically, promoted strict regulation and effective supervision of resource use – such as punishment for overexploitation. In North America, by contrast, such lessons were quickly forgotten in the midst of rapid settlement and migration, as well as in the elimination of the indigenous peoples and with them their experience with natural resources.

Scarcity of resources led not only to a culture of moderation and thrift in Germany, however; it also had explosive, devastating consequences. Imperial Germany's pursuit of overseas colonies and, even more so, the Nazis' vision of securing additional *Lebensraum* were driven by thirst for resources of all kinds. At least twice in its history, Germany's reach for territory plunged the world into ruin and disaster. At the same time, the necessity of putting limited resources to optimal use had a very positive dimension: it stimulated a spirit of discovery and often gave Germany a competitive edge. For this reason, Germany took a leading role in fields such as forestry and engineering.

The first half of the twentieth century, especially the National Socialist era, was marked by a curious mix of utilitarian exploitation and a reactionary, *volkish* regard for nature in Germany. For ideological purposes, the Nazi regime celebrated the image of Germans rooted in nature. As a matter of political practice, the Nazi Minister of Agriculture Richard Walther Darré endorsed the principle of compulsory conservation, rejecting the free market and the global economy as aspects of alleged "Jewish world domination." Traditional labor-intensive methods in agriculture served both Nazi ideology and the regime's efforts to secure full employment. That, however, was only one side of the story. To realize its "racial" and military goals, the Nazi regime had to exploit Germany's domestic resources more intensively, if not necessarily more efficiently, than ever before. Forced industrialization thus overshadowed the romance of traditional agriculture. Achieving economic self-sufficiency, rearming, and pursuing an aggressive foreign policy took precedence over protecting the environment in the years before 1939. During World War II, conservation and nature protection were abandoned. Germany thus found its own way to environmental wastefulness. In some respects, however, it did so by following the American pattern of development. For example, the tractor, which had been put to massive agricultural use in the United States in the years after World War I, found similar dissemination in Germany only after World War II. More generally, Germany became a consumer society later than the United States. Because this transition happened at a time when the culture of mass consumption had already lost some of its magic, Germans ended up choosing a more moderate path than that of the Americans.

On both sides of the Atlantic, modernity went hand in hand with the waste of energy and environmental degradation. Interestingly, however, in Germany, opposition to environmental challenges emerged early. In 1850, for instance, the city of Freiberg in Saxony witnessed a modern debate over air pollution because its iron foundry was contaminating the air and stunting the growth of trees in the region. Germany's environmental history has been shaped by an economic and demographic growth less dynamic than America's, by an early awareness of pollution and resource depletion, and by discontinuities in political history. In addition, Germany's dependence on coal has always been greater than that of the United States.

Nowhere was coal more important than in eastern Germany, especially during the era of the German Democratic Republic. The United States may be notorious for its profligate waste of oil, but the example of the GDR – where, unlike in America or West Germany, coal always remained the central fossil fuel – shows that a wasteful and environmentally destructive economy is possible in a society not based primarily on oil. The per capita use of energy was higher in socialist Germany than in any Western country. In the GDR, economic goals trumped nature's imperatives – not least because of East Germany's Cold War competition with the West. A mixture of industrial ambition and self-induced pressure to modernize led to dramatic levels of air pollution and to other devastating consequences. The scope of this degradation is astounding when one considers that mechanization happened more slowly in East than in West Germany and that the East German use of chemicals in agriculture reached prewar levels only in 1956–7. From the 1960s on, the GDR, trying to accelerate the pace of growth, massively expanded and intensified agricultural production, with serious consequences for the environment. The strict separation of crop cultivation and livestock production under the so-called Grüneberg Plan of 1977–8, named after the communist functionary Gerhard Grüneberg, was one example of the GDR's environmentally devastating policies. Generally, in East Germany, visible disaster areas predominated, whereas in the West, more indirect forms of damage to the environment prevailed.

FROM USING NATURE TO PROTECTING THE ENVIRONMENT

Even though the systematic exploitation and destruction of nature were powerful trends in American history, countertrends also existed since at least the early nineteenth century. Some of the most influential intellectual architects of the global environmental movement came from the United States. So have the sharpest challenges from environmentalists, the most subversive methods of grassroots organizing, and the most radical governmental protections. For example, Americans created the great nature parks that became a model used around the world, from the Bavarian forest to the Kruger National Park in South Africa.

The history of the environmental movement in America began with romantic and transcendentalist ideas, which followed from the desire of middle-class city dwellers to protect "unspoiled" and spectacular natural places from the interfering hand of agriculture, industry, and city. At first, Americans saw "wild nature" as unproductive or even threatening. In the course of the nineteenth century, however, the concept of *wilderness* began to acquire a positive meaning. In his 1864 book, *Man and Nature*, George Perkins Marsh noted the enormous destruction of nature in earlier centuries and tried to foster a rethinking of the relationship between humanity and nature. With the closing of the frontier in the 1890s, ever more Americans, particularly the well-to-do, sought out encounters with "pristine nature." In their wilderness excursions, the elite recapitulated the pioneers' "transformative" frontier experiences. Men like Theodore Roosevelt found a necessary counterbalance to industrial modernity in these experiences. For him and many like-minded Americans, environmental conservation entailed the maintenance of landscapes far from civilization – and of great game animals that could be hunted there.

Americans also started to prize their spectacular natural monuments and the beauties of a specifically "American nature." The "unspoiled" landscapes of the late nineteenth and early twentieth centuries seemed proof that the American nation represented a God-given unity. Monumental wonders of nature, like the Grand Canyon, acquired new meaning as they were transformed from places of local or regional significance to national symbols. In 1864, President Abraham Lincoln signed an act of Congress ceding Yosemite Valley to the state of California. Eight years later, Yellowstone National Park became the world's first national park. Other parks followed, each protecting spectacular or singular landscapes. Nature and nation were thus identified with one another. By the time of World War I, exploring the Rockies could be seen as an "American experience"; traveling in the Swiss Alps, in contrast, as an "unpatriotic activity." Indeed, the slogan "See America First" carried a political message throughout most of the twentieth century and particularly during the Cold War.

Politics and culture played a major role in nature conservation, but it was economic rationality that often provided the decisive motive to encourage environmental conservation. Railroad companies were at least as important in realizing the first national parks as nature writers or artists. The experience of nature would be the high point of each trip to a national park. In the course of the twentieth century, automobile tourism fostered the creation of a dense network of roads and motels that turned "wilderness" – discovered through a windshield – into a popular form of leisure for an increasingly urban and affluent America. Traveling through the parks would become a fabled pilgrimage to the American landscape, and the stream of visitors rose steadily. From 1914 to 1917, the number doubled from 240,000 to almost a half-million. In 1940, some 17 million people visited the American national parks, and by 2005 the figure had reached more than 380 million. For America's urban population, and for visitors from all over the world, America's national parks had become the place par excellence to relax and to explore.

The layout of the parks did not necessarily ensure the protection of nature, however. Park design was often tied to the production of an illusion. When the Blue Ridge Parkway was built in the 1930s, for example, many recently constructed houses were demolished and only three log cabins from the eighteenth century were left standing. The weathered Old Mabry Mill was spared only because, from a distance, it looked older than it actually was. Such staging reflected the notion of a nature park as a big open-air museum, which was supposed to seem pure and, at the same time, attract millions of visitors. The extent to which nature had been turned into a commodity was evident from the wild animal shows that were put on at national parks to entertain the tourists. Ironically, the tourist industry thus developed into the greatest environmental threat to these areas.

Compared to the efficient use of nature – for tourism, for mining, for forestry – the idea of the extensive protection of nature remained the preoccupation of a small minority. Apostles of environmentalism like John Muir, the founder of the Sierra Club, had very little influence, as was apparent in the conflict over the Hetch Hetchy Valley in the years before World War I. After many years of bitter struggle with the city government of San Francisco, Muir had to concede defeat, and the Hetch Hetchy Valley was turned into a reservoir for San Francisco. The wishes of a small group of elitist campers and self-indulgent "nature cranks," as the preservationists were called by their opponents, had little authority as long as San Francisco could represent the interests of its five hundred thousand residents, whose supply of drinking water would have been in danger without the reservoir. The preservationists who, unlike the less radical conservationists around Teddy Roosevelt, saw a contradiction between conservation and the use of natural resources, were deeply disappointed by their defeat at Hetch Hetchy Valley. For many of his contemporaries, however, John Muir's excessively metaphysical and romantic answers to the dilemmas of modernity were at fault, and his ideas would become popular only after his death. Today, the Sierra Clubs have a membership of about 1.3 million.

In the first decades of the twentieth century, the will to environmental protection, grounded in science, could point to certain partial successes. Not only dramatic landscapes like that in Yellowstone but also less spectacular areas like the Everglades were deemed worthy of protection, mainly because of their biodiversity. The Wilderness Society has engaged in far-reaching forms of preservation since 1935. Acknowledging the negative effects of automobile tourism, it argued that for ecological reasons, large tracts of land should be left to themselves. The Wilderness Society celebrated an important success, together with other groups, in 1940, when it was able to prevent the construction of a highway in a Californian nature park. During World War II, however, many such preservation endeavors were eclipsed by military-economic interests and utilitarian concerns.

With the passage of the Wilderness Act in 1964, larger natural areas, making up 3 percent of all U.S. territory, were to be kept free from all human uses. Since then, areas without roads have been designated within nature parks and in Alaska. In the reform-oriented atmosphere of the 1960s, environmental thinking won broad support. Paradoxically, it was the affluence derived from the destructive exploitation of the country's natural resources that made it possible to consider environmental problems that had previously been viewed as luxury concerns. A change in environmental perception made the wages of destruction apparent.

In addition to nature-park advocates, reformers of the early twentieth century, who had warned about the health effects of industrialization and of slums, were pivotal in fashioning an environmental consciousness in America. Women were more engaged in such reform in America than in Germany. For example, the physician Alice Hamilton played a key role in persuading the federal government to recognize occupational illnesses, as had already happened in Great Britain and Germany. The "Pittsburgh Survey" (1907–14) sponsored by the Russell Sage Foundation helped further public awareness of the link between pollution and illness. The survey offered data showing that 55,000 residents of Pittsburgh had come down with typhus between 1883 and 1908, with 7,500 of them dying from the disease. The mortality rate of this industrial city, its drinking water polluted with chemicals, was six times higher than in New York and thirty times higher than in Berlin.

Like the Pittsburgh Survey, Rachel Carson's book *Silent Spring* (1962) had a profound impact on public awareness of the health risks posed by contamination of the environment. It stood for thirty-one weeks on the *New York Times* best-seller list and sold more than one million copies in hardcover. Carson, a marine biologist, lamented the indiscriminate use of pesticides, above all, DDT. The Department of Agriculture contended that Carson's arguments were without scientific foundation, but that claim was refuted by an investigative commission convened by President John F. Kennedy. DDT, for which the Swiss scientist Paul Müller had received the Nobel Prize in 1938, was banned in 1972, though, cynically, the United States continued to export it to other parts of the world. Critical thinkers like Carson and Dennis L. Meadows, the author of the Club of Rome's highly influential report, *The Limits of Growth* (1972), brought new ideas into the debate: conservation was defended with more than just aesthetic or scientific arguments, as the worries of experts made it clear that manmade destruction could mean the end of humanity.

Such claims had wide social resonance. In 1970, between ten and twenty million Americans took to the streets on the first annual "Earth Day" to protest environmental destruction. In the 1970s, many laws were passed on the federal, state, and local levels to address environmental issues; President Richard Nixon established the Environmental Protection Agency; and courts became more receptive to the arguments and concerns of environmentalists.

The shift in American political orientation that had begun with Franklin D. Roosevelt's New Deal deepened in the 1970s. Conservationism had originally found its advocates on the right but, in the 1960s, environmental protection belonged more to the left, expanding out from the elite circle of scientists, government officials, and business grandees who had, for the most part, been the early conservationists. The power of environmental ideas in America later colored the presidential candidacies of Ralph Nader (of the Green Party) and of Democrats Al Gore and Barack Obama.

In Germany, the debate over nature conservation arose a bit later than in the United States. At the turn of the twentieth century, in the middle of an intense period of industrialization, discussions about protecting flora and fauna (particularly birds) and about establishing state parks grew into a broader public debate. An active and proud bourgeoisie thus discovered a new area of interest, and members of the working class were also involved. There has never been a German counterpart to the Sierra Club, a broad-based organization able to influence government policy through its lobbying efforts. The German movement for conservation and environmental protection has long been characterized by a continuously shifting array of organizations and initiatives.

The first organization to apply itself nationally to the conservation of nature and to offer criticism of the destruction that industrial capitalism had wrought was the Bund Heimatschutz, or German Homeland Conservation Club. Founded in Dresden in 1904, it constituted part of the conservative reform movement and operated almost exclusively within the educated middle class. Fewer figures from the business world became involved in the conservation movement in Germany than in the United States. The German movement also lacked the specialists in fields such as agriculture and forestry who were so important in bringing scientific expertise to American conservation efforts.

The name of the Bund Heimatschutz deserves special attention for it is a clue to German environmental thinking: protecting the "homeland" entailed conservation, but it also involved the conservation of monuments, customs, and mores. The Bund did not only combat the building of dams; it also gathered folk songs and folk customs. "Homeland" and nature implied a blending of nature and culture. At the center was not a wilderness such as the American West but a cultural landscape that had been cultivated over centuries. One of the first areas put under state protection in Germany, for example, was the Drachenfels, a mountain on the Rhine. Topped with the picturesque ruins of a castle, the Drachenfels evoked the landscape of medieval sagas, but it was certainly no wilderness. In 1837, the Prussian Crown purchased the ruins and surrounding area to stop it from being used as a source of stone for the construction of the Cologne cathedral.

It would be too simple merely to stigmatize the Bund and its members as reactionary. They were not seeking out an antimodern world but rather an alternative route to modernity. The first head of the Bund, the painter and architect Paul Schultze-Naumburg, saw human interference with nature and even industrialization as unavoidable; he felt that a more careful and considered way of living with nature had to be found. This ideology did not inhibit Schultze-Naumburg from joining the Nazi Party in 1930.

In addition to the Bund, numerous other organizations advocated conservation. The working-class Friends of Nature stood alongside regional groups like the Isar Valley Club and the Protectors of Birds. By international standards, the early environmental movement in Germany was not especially conservative or reactionary.

What was unusual, rather, was the strong current of cultural criticism that ran through its arguments.

Local and regional concerns and landscapes played a bigger role in the early environmental movement in Germany than in America. There is nothing like the *Schrebergarten* – mini-gardens often found on the periphery of German cities – in America, except perhaps the World War II–era "victory garden." The Sunday stroll through the outskirts of German cities – a middle-class tradition with attendant etiquette, forms of greeting, and styles of walking and dress – was a sign of social distinction; America, in contrast, with its egalitarianism and mobility, had few places or social reasons for such a stroll. As opposed to in America, nature embodied regional roots and long-lasting emotional ties to region and locality in Germany.

Early environmentalism in Germany was notable for its combination of civic initiatives and government work. This combination revealed both the success and the limits of environmental conservation, as German environmentalists preferred behind-the-scenes political jockeying to mass mobilization. Thus, the will to conservation could be tamed by the state in the first half of the twentieth century.

Where environmentalism was concerned, the Weimar Republic began with a bang. Article 150 of the Republic's constitution placed environmental conservation under the jurisdiction of the national government. However, the field of concrete action belonged to the states, whose measures were neither very coherent nor very effective. In a general atmosphere of crisis, the political horizon of environmental debates was increasingly confined to populist–racist ideas. Walter Schönichen, a prominent advocate of environmentalism, noted shortly after the Nazi takeover that because "the unrestrained encouragement of foreign, un-German folkways has now been eliminated," the purification of the landscape had to follow. Environmental protection legislation, finalized in June 1935, seemed to realize all the hopes that environmentalists had for the Nazi regime, insofar as this new legislation went beyond maintaining existing protected areas, imposed penalties for violations of the law, and organized nature protection on the national level. In practical terms, however, this legislation meant little, for the Nazi regime was not subject to its own laws. Another reason for the low status of environmental protection resided in the understanding many activists had of nature in the 1930s. They were primarily concerned with the museum-like conservation of quasi-religious, excessively stylized "original landscapes," not least forests, that they perceived as pristine nature. In the end, environmentalists were able to secure a shadow presence in the National Socialist regime, but they did little for the environment.

After 1945, environmental protection moved from the national level back to the state level. At the same time, it lost some of its legal power of assertion. Both in East and West Germany, reconstruction and economic growth, rather than protection and conservation, took priority. It was not until the late 1950s and early 1960s that American-style nature parks were set up in relatively large numbers.

Environmental questions became an important, politically controversial subject in Germany roughly one decade later than in the United States. Around 1970, the West German public started to accept environmental conservation as a central issue and as an important object of public discussion. Within a few years, there was enormous energy behind the cause of protection. At that point in time, ecological problems had become widely visible; for instance, when detergent powder generated twelve feet of foam on German rivers. Yet, these visible problems were not sufficient to promote environmentalism; a changed consciousness and an intensified public discussion were also necessary. Scientific experts had a role to play, as did popular television series like *Ein Platz für Tiere* (A Place for Animals), which was broadcast from 1956 to 1987. Furthermore, the crisis-ridden mood of the 1970s, exacerbated by the precipitous increase in the price of oil, contributed to the rise of environmental awareness. Suddenly, the environment had changed from a niche issue to a story for the wider public to discuss.

When the ecological dark side of the postwar economic boom became apparent, people all over the Western world tried to battle the problems, or at least those on their doorstep. NIMBY – Not In My Back Yard – became both a catchword and the name of a new movement. Dense population and a high degree of industrialization meant that in Germany, many people were confronted with potential environmental problems in their neighborhood: from contaminated food to nuclear power stations. Indeed, although the appetite for energy was increasing, tolerance of reactors close to home declined.

In West Germany, one of the countries most likely to be annihilated in the event of a third world war, the antinuclear and environmental movements reinforced one another and joined forces. This alliance scored a clear triumph in 1975 when it blocked the construction of a nuclear power plant in the southwestern town of Whyl. The campaign made Whyl a household name throughout the Federal Republic and beyond the country's borders of Germany, and stickers with a smiley face bearing the slogan "Nuclear power – no thanks" became ubiquitous.

West Germany was amenable to the discussion of environmental degradation and to assessing the costs of postwar economic growth, whereas the GDR regime tolerated no criticism. The East German parliament passed a "law for the planned organization of the socialist environment," but the irrelevance of this law soon became apparent: it entailed as few binding limitations as it did effective sanctions. In fact, the GDR was producing the highest per capita levels of sulfur dioxide emissions worldwide by the end of the 1980s. East Germany did not experience the "environmental revolution" that happened in the West in the 1970s. Instead, only small groups of dissidents were involved in environmental protest and action.

In West Germany, ecological thinking became increasingly political, scientific, and professional during the 1970s. That change was reflected in the emergence of the term *Umweltschutz* (environmental protection), which signaled a concern with establishing a sustainable relationship with nature rather than simply safeguarding select natural wonders. The debate about the destructive impact of air pollution on Germany's forests gave environmental protection a new urgency. The Green Party, founded in 1980, put the principle of sustainability at the center of its agenda. Although many environmental problems were less urgent or visible than in the decades before, the Greens quickly scored substantive political successes on both the local and federal levels. In contrast to the earlier conservation movement, the Green Party did not see itself as an elite organization that would work with the government but rather as a party eager to mobilize and enlighten the public. The party allied itself with movements of social reform, strengthening the progressive spirit that had swept through the 1960s and 1970s. Today, environmental issues stand at the center of political debate and discourse in Germany.

Although differences between developments in Germany and the United States have been significant, the two countries have also shared and exchanged important experiences in their environmental histories. Many modern manufacturing techniques and lifestyles are damaging to the environment, and these techniques and lifestyles have had the widest scope in America. In the 1920s, the assembly lines of Henry Ford and the industrial production innovations in River Rouge triggered a "Ford mania" in Germany that swept across the entire political spectrum. In the early years of the Federal Republic, the automobile came to symbolize Western or American freedom. Echoing this symbolism, shopping malls situated outside city centers make the "new eastern states," the former territory of the GDR, look more "American" than the rest of the Federal Republic. The attractive positive consequences of industrialization, suburbanization, and mass consumption have blinded some German observers to the accompanying environmental problems. In this respect, the American model encouraged Germany on the path to a wasteful use of space and resources.

At the same time, cultural imports from the United States have helped enliven Germany's will to protect the environment. In 1898, for example, Wilhelm Wetekamp, a teacher, alluded to the United States when he argued in the Prussian House of Deputies for establishing national parks in Germany. The first German park "for the protection of nature" opened in 1921 as a result of the discussion that Wetekamp had triggered. Transatlantic learning processes were later informed by the visit of West German officials to Pittsburgh and Los Angeles in the early 1950s. As a result, urban planners increasingly began to study the ecological consequences of industrialization in cities. The catalytic converter is another important environmental import from the United States. Adhering to strict regulations for keeping the air clean, Americans had put catalytic converters in their cars in the 1970s, long before the Germans. The very "invention" of German environmentalism in the 1970s drew on a transatlantic network of experts and on the help of UNESCO, the OECD, and even NATO.

American environmentalism has been salient not just for the governmental protection of nature but also for Germany's civic environmentalism. Rachel Carson's *Silent Spring* and Al Gore's *Earth in the Balance* were bestsellers in Germany. After the Oscar-winning film *An Inconvenient Truth* was released, the news weekly *Der Spiegel* labeled Gore an "eco-starlet" and "the hottest living political activist."

Conversely, Germany's culture of measurement and regulation has long interested Americans. For example, the principle of conservation in German forestry, based on traditional knowledge as well as on centuries of analysis, made a great impression on the American wilderness advocate Aldo Leopold. Leopold's trip to Germany, where he visited the world-famous forestry school at Tharandt, and his contact with the ornithologist, Arnold Freiherr von Vietinghoff-Riesch, inspired his experiments with "re-naturing" back in America. At the end of the nineteenth century, German-born Bernard Fernow directed the forestry division of the

U.S. Department of Agriculture, and Gifford Pinchot, the French and German-trained "father of American forestry," headed the newly established U.S. Forest Service. America's first zoning laws, enacted by New York City in the 1920s, were based on a German model. Characteristically, American zoning laws were not as strict as the German, which were intended in large measure to protect existing unbuilt spaces. Another significant line of influence running from Germany to America is evident in the domain of protest, as the dynamic German antinuclear-power movement inspired activists on the other side of the Atlantic.

Natural phenomena do not respect political borders. Since the 1970s, efforts have been made to fashion international agreements on ecological questions. The United Nations Environmental Programme, which was established in 1972, has played an important part in those efforts. The UN Conference on Environment and Development in Rio de Janeiro in 1992 was a key event in the development of international environmental cooperation, yielding agreement on measures for climate protection and the reduction of greenhouse gas emissions. At the follow-up conference in Kyoto in 1997, delegates from all over the world committed themselves to legally binding limits on carbon dioxide emissions. The United States and Germany differed emphatically in their attitude toward the Kyoto conference: whereas the United States, holding to its national autonomy, refused to sign the Kyoto Protocol and has only hesitantly take action to cut is greenhouse gas emissions, Germany quickly ratified the protocol and achieved notable emissions reductions. Ironically, the United States, which had done more than any other country to persuade Germany to abandon its *Sonderweg*, its "special path," after 1945, thereby opted for unilateralism and international isolation.

CONCLUSION: ENORMOUS EXPLOITATION AND SELECTIVE CONSERVATION

A comparative environmental history of Germany and the United States illuminates significant parallels. On their way to modernity, both countries practiced an exploitation of nature that was unprecedented. On both sides of the Atlantic, energy-intensive industrialization and urbanization led to the pollution of water, soil, and air. In both societies, industry and politics colluded in the exploitation of natural resources. Like the other Western industrialized nations, the United States and Germany have developed unsustainable relationships to nature and the environment. The best example of unsustainability is carbon dioxide emissions. With regard to other ecological questions, the distance between Germany and America is not so great, and even their differences should be kept in perspective. According to some calculations, for example, the combined economies of China and India will be responsible for up to 75 percent of global carbon dioxide emissions by 2020.

Despite many differences between Germany and America, their environmental journey toward modernity has points of intersection. For decades, the cultural approach to conservation had not incorporated nature as a whole but rather had limited itself to small enclaves – specific landscapes, species of animals, or forms of energy. These cultivated spaces were selected either for aesthetic or scientific reasons, thereby creating sites of memory that were reminiscent of the premodern era. In this context, the natural ideal of "wilderness," which is so beloved in the United States, is problematic: separating "untouched" areas of land from "developed" areas is prohibitive of a more holistic view of the environment. Likewise in Germany, today's focus on the preservation of a certain kind of premodern cultural landscape – with juniper heaths and orchards – is questionable, as these areas have long lost their social, cultural, and economic purpose. In both countries, the protection of specific areas has gone hand in hand with the radical exploitation of other landscapes and natural resources of all kinds. Taboos regarding the destruction of some landscapes and extreme forms of developmental utilitarianism coexist. This simultaneity of selective preservation and enormous exploitation might well be seen as one of modernity's central paradoxes.

Further Reading

Blackbourn, David. *The Conquest of Nature: Water, Landscape, and the Making of Modern Germany* (London, 2006).

Chaney, Sandra. *Nature of the Miracle Years: Conservation in West Germany, 1945–1975* (New York, 2008).

Cronon, William. *Changes in the Land: Indians, Colonists, and the Ecology of New England*, 2nd ed. (New York, 2003).

Dominick III, Raymond. *The Environmental Movement in Germany* (Bloomington, 1992).

Lekan, Thomas, and Thomas Zeller, eds. *Germany's Nature: Cultural Landscapes and Environmental History* (New Brunswick, 2005).

Mauch, Christof, ed. *Nature in German History* (New York, 2004).

Mauch, Christof, and Thomas Zeller, eds. *The World beyond the Windshield: Landscapes and Roads in the United States and Europe* (Athens, 2008).

Mauch, Christof, Nathan Stoltzfus, and Douglas Weiner, eds. *Shades of Green: Environmental Activism around the Globe* (Lanham, 2006).

McNeill, John R. *Something New under the Sun: An Environmental History of the Twentieth-Century World* (New York, 2000).

Merchant, Carolyn. *American Environmental History: An Introduction* (New York, 2007).

Opie, John. *Nature's Nation: An Environmental History of the United States* (Fort Worth, 1998).

Patel, Kiran Klaus. "Neuerfindung des Westens – Aufbruch nach Osten. Naturschutz und Landschaftsgestaltung in den Vereinigten Staaten von Amerika und in Deutschland, 1900–1945," *Archiv für Sozialgeschichte* 43 (2003): 191–223.

Radkau, Joachim. *Nature and Power: A Global History of the Environment* (New York, 2008).

Rollins, William H. *A Greener Vision of Home: Cultural Politics and Environmental Reform in the German Heimatschutz Movement, 1904–1918* (Ann Arbor, 1997).

Steinberg, Theodore. *Down to Earth: Nature's Role in American History* (Oxford, 2002).

Uekötter, Frank. *The Green and the Brown: A History of Conservation in Nazi Germany* (New York, 2006).

Uekötter, Frank. *The Age of Smoke: Environmental Policy in Germany and the United States, 1880–1970* (Pittsburgh, 2009).

White, Richard. *"It's Your Misfortune and None of my Own": A History of the American West* (Norman, 1991).

Williams, John A. *Turning to Nature in Germany: Hiking, Nudism, and Conservation, 1900–1940* (Stanford, 2007).

Worster, Donald. *Rivers of Empire: Water, Aridity, and the Growth of the American West* (Oxford, 1992).

Worster, Donald. *The Wealth of Nature: Environmental History and the Ecological Imagination* (Oxford, 1994).

Worster, Donald. *Nature's Economy: A History of Ecological Ideas* (Cambridge, 1998).

12

Film and Television

EDWARD DIMENDBERG AND ANTON KAES

On September 28, 1993, two of the most respected German and French newspapers, the *Frankfurter Allgemeine Zeitung* and *Le Monde*, published an unprecedented open letter condemning Hollywood for strangling the European film market and thereby endangering Western culture itself. Written by Wim Wenders and others, and signed by four thousand European film artists and intellectuals, the full-page ad responded to the 1993 General Agreement on Tariffs and Trade (GATT) negotiations between the United States and the European Union. GATT sought to foster free trade and thus end subventions and protective tariffs on a wide range of goods and services, including audiovisual media. The American delegates argued that movies are products like peanuts or automobiles and must not be subsidized in the global marketplace. They decried film subsidies and television quotas as unfair protectionism. The Europeans, by contrast, pleaded for the continued protection of their cinema. They countered that movies are not commodities but rather expressions of national identity, history, and tradition. For them, filmmaking in continental Europe was inconceivable without state funding. This clash over two concepts of culture threatened to derail the entire free-trade agreement. In the end, the Americans acquiesced, confident that even a subsidized European cinema would not pose a threat to Hollywood.

The basic claim made by European filmmakers is hard to dispute. Hollywood blockbusters have captured between 70 and 90 percent of the German market for the last three decades. Even prize-winning domestic productions never reach comparable audiences. Although the public attack on Hollywood in 1993 was sharper than usual, it only reinforced the old self-image of Germans as victims of a predatory American entertainment industry – a competition that dates to the 1920s, when a German film critic called Hollywood's influence more pernicious than Prussian militarism because it wins over hearts and minds. (In 1926, almost half of the films shown in Germany were American imports.) Over the years, the German film industry has turned to imitations, co-productions, and noncommercial art films to counter Hollywood's domination. Critics have asked: How could German filmmakers match the modernity of American cinema without abandoning their venerated ideals of high culture? Is film a universal language, as was claimed in its early years, or is it specific to a time and place? Discussions in Germany about cinema have always performed double duty as debates about German culture and national identity.

AN ART FOR THE MASSES?

When Oswald Spengler published *The Decline of the West* in 1918, conflating the collapse of the Kaiserreich with the fall of occidental culture, he denounced mass entertainment as a symptom of the demise of Western civilization. Along with other phenomena of modernity, which for him included Expressionism, boxing, and poker, Spengler disparaged cinema as a sign of urban decay and inhuman mechanization. He was not alone in his contempt for the new technical medium that had rapidly gained popularity since the turn of the century. Most cultural critics in Germany considered movies a threat to the standards of German high *Kultur*. Requiring neither education nor literary taste, film entertainment appealed to the masses and seemed patently egalitarian and democratic. This low art emerged from, and betrayed affinities to, the fairground, the amusement park, and the variety show. The young United States, with its immigrant population, more easily assimilated the robust plebeian energy of the new medium. Germany, by contrast, had long compensated for its lack of political unity by emphasizing the unifying power of culture. Moving pictures, by nature mechanical and technical, were aggressively modern, and the German cultural elite thought them the perfect expression of America itself: superficial, immature, and vulgar.

Public showings of moving pictures to a paying audience took place in Berlin, Paris, and New York within a few months of each other in 1895–6. On November 1, 1895, Max and Emil Skladanowski displayed several six-second films – acrobatic circus acts and slapstick routines – as part of a variety show at the Wintergarten in Berlin. It was the first public film screening (even two months before the Lumière brothers' unveiling of their Cinématographe at the Grand Café in Paris), but Skladanowski's Bioskop was soon superseded by more advanced projection technologies in Paris and New York. As camera and projection equipment quickly improved, a film-specific aesthetic emerged that used close-ups, editing, and quick crosscutting between different locations to convey dramatic tension. In Germany, the new medium soon came into conflict with the established arts, especially literature and theater. What novelist Alfred Döblin dismissed in his 1909 essay "The Theater of the Little People" as shockingly crude but nonetheless fascinating entertainment for the working classes portended an all-out assault on German culture. The masses had discovered the easy pleasures of the cinema, and no admonishment from bourgeois intellectuals could reverse the process.

The German crusade against cinema as the source and symbol of everything wrong with modernity continued nonetheless. A sizeable movement, known as *Kinoreformbewegung*, began in 1912, uniting priests, pedagogues, and cultural activists in their condemnation of cinema as a scourge on public morality. Their disdain for moving pictures went to such extremes that they welcomed the out-break of war in 1914 as an opportunity to defend German culture against foreign civilization. In 1918, Wilhelm Stapel held the unsteady, easily distracted "homo cinematicus" responsible for the outcome of the war. Although similar voices decrying the deleterious influence of the nickelodeons and the "cheap theaters" could be heard in the United States, in Germany these fierce polemics sug-gested that movies threatened not just morality but also the nation itself. The very institution of cinema catalyzed fear within the educated middle classes about modernity – the mechanization of culture, the triumph of mass entertainment over education, the destabilization of traditional values, and the focus on frivolous consumption; in short, the "Americanization" of Germany.

From the start, American cinema differed from German cinema in the size and makeup of its audience. The rise of cinema as a mass medium coincided with mass immigration to the United States. During the first decades of the twentieth century, more than twenty million migrants from Eastern and Southern Europe flocked to the urban centers on the East Coast and formed an enormous multiethnic audience. Movies catered to and entertained immigrant audiences. Films did not require knowledge of English, and they were cheap and communal. And, moreover, they taught survival skills: they translated the anxieties and fears of immigrant life into farce and slapstick, acted out the troubles that arose from misunderstanding the American way of life, and often expressed frustration with slum landlords, judges, and cops, all of whom were outwitted by simple immigrants in early movies. Mack Sennett's Keystone Cops and Charlie Chaplin's slapstick introduced the irreverent and often subversive spirit of vaudeville comedy to early cinema. American film thus aided in the assimilation of large masses of immigrant workers. German films did not have such large urban immigrant audiences, nor did they possess the anarchic energy of early American slapstick.

Hollywood subsequently sought to attract the more prosperous middle classes and convince them of the respectability of the medium. By 1911, D. W. Griffith and others began to promote film as an instrument for moral and political education. Artistic questions became increasingly significant. Hollywood began to produce mass spectacles like Griffith's *Birth of a Nation* (1911) and *Intolerance* (1916) and Thomas Ince's *Civilization* (1916). In Germany, famous literary authors such as Hugo von Hofmannsthal and Gerhart Hauptmann began to show interest in writing screenplays. The so-called *Autorenfilm* (films by authors) sought to transform purportedly uncultured entertainment into literary art. Ironically, this move toward culture proved controversial, not merely among its custodians. In 1913, German film-theater owners publicly worried that literary high culture would deter a mass audience. That same year, Kurt Pinthus edited the first anthology of literary screenplays, which engaged with the rich tradition of dream and fantasy in German Romanticism (and the self-reflexivity of the medium itself). The first masterwork of German cinema, *Der Student von Prag* (The Student of Prague) by the Danish director Stellan Rye, also appeared that year. It employed the *Doppelgänger* motif from German Romantic literature to explore the unprecedented power of the new medium to mirror and double reality. To this day, German cinema remains known for its adaptations of literary works, for the deployment of theatrical *mise-en-scene* (a legacy of the stagecraft by Max Reinhardt and Leopold Jessner), and for developing a counter-cinema in the name of high art.

Such emphatically artistic, even literary, cinema, although extolled by film critics and film historians, represented a relatively small portion of the overall production of mass entertainment. Neither Griffith nor German "film authors" could compete with the rapid output in both countries of mostly formulaic genre movies, roughly divided into comedies, melodramas, and detective films. Westerns emerged early as the quintessential American film genre. A mythically inflected look back to the nation's pioneers, their conquest of nature, and their battles against Native Americans, the Western genre film became a vehicle for the emergence of a uniquely American film style defined by breathtaking panoramas and violent action scenes; rugged individuals and outlaws; fast-moving horses and trains; holdups, shootouts, and showdowns. Exploration of the frontier and the process of its inhabitation (dating back to nineteenth-century literature and today continued in science fiction movies about travels to outer space) became the source of endless fascination also in Germany, which developed its own tradition of Westerns with Karl May's *Winnetou* and *Old Shatterhand*. So-called Isar or Neckar Western serials, mass produced in Southern Germany, boasted titles like *Bull Arizona: Der Wüstenadler* (Bull Arizona: The Desert Eagle, 1919) and featured Germans playing cowboys and Indians. They imitated the kineticism of American Westerns and substituted character psychology for action and expansive landscapes.

Titles of early German cinema reveal the influence of Anglo-American popular culture. German detective film serials were populated by such characters as Sherlock Holmes, Nick Carter, and Stuart Webbs. Detective and adventure films crossed borders and established conventions and standards still in force today. This global reach of early genre cinema rendered national distinctions unimportant for film audiences indifferent to whether a film was produced in Paris, Hollywood, or Berlin.

The outbreak of World War I on August 1, 1914, changed the universalism of silent film overnight. In Germany, films from France, Great Britain, and, after 1917, the United States were identified as products from enemy countries and banned. Suddenly, the origin of a film became an issue, and the concept of a "national cinema" was born. Given Germany's conflicted relationship to mass culture, the call for domestic film production came as a surprise. Some Germans thought the war was being fought to defeat the forces of Western modernity, including the mass entertainment of film. In 1914, only 12 percent of the films shown in Germany were produced domestically, clearly not enough to meet growing audience demand. A ban on foreign movies stimulated German production and the establishment of a state-financed production company, Universum Film AG (Ufa), in December 1917. Belatedly, the Military High Command wanted to enlist cinema for propaganda, just as Great Britain and the United States had done.

Privatized after the war, the Ufa studio soon became the largest and most ambitious German film production company, a magnet for creative talent from theater and the other arts. Hyperinflation during the postwar years made film production extremely cheap in Germany (even Griffith came to Berlin to shoot *Isn't Life Wonderful?* in 1923) and gave rise to an unprecedented level of innovation. Radical aesthetic experiments such as Fritz Lang's *Der müde Tod* (Destiny, 1920), Robert Wiene's *Das Cabinet des Dr. Caligari* (The Cabinet of Dr. Caligari, 1920), and F. W. Murnau's *Nosferatu* (1922) contributed to the worldwide development of a new film language that did not merely depict the world but also created it anew for the medium. Inventive manipulation of light and shadow and the subtle filming of body language and gestures enabled film to suggest psychological states, even without sound, whose absence was understood as an opportunity to tell a story through purely visual means. Germany pursued a market strategy during the 1920s that separated a small number of artistic films from the mass production of commercial serials and melodramas.

Yearly production totaled more than five hundred films in 1920. *Monumentalfilme* ("monumental" in sets and production costs) and consciously modernist films in the mold of Expressionist art sought to capture foreign markets. Why else would the protagonists in *The Cabinet of Dr. Caligari* be given non-German names like Jane, Alan, and Cesare? Robert Wiene's experimental film was promoted with great fanfare as a film "from Europe" in New York in 1921 and led American film critics to champion it as the epitome of the "art film." Its critical success on the heels of Ernst Lubitsch's *Madame Dubarry* (Passion, 1919) caused Hollywood to panic briefly about competition from Germany. Suddenly, German cinema had become a serious rival. The *New York Times* came to the rescue of the native film industry by denigrating German cinema as overly artistic, somber, and unpalatable to American tastes – clichés that haunt American views of German movies to this day.

Even some German critics in the Weimar period bemoaned the literary and artistic bent of their cinema that valorized acting, atmosphere, and character development over "modern" unliterary action. They praised and envied modern American movies and their fast editing, which they saw as more filmic and true to urban life. Yet, to identify German movies with high culture is to disregard the country's vast popular cinema and to uncritically accept the self-promoting rhetoric of the art film. In 1926, Fritz Lang claimed that Hollywood, although technically unparalleled, could not have made a film like *Metropolis* because Americans lacked the *Geist* (spirit) that animated his use of light and camera. As if to prove his point, *Metropolis* staged the revolt of a German "Expressionist" son against his "Americanist" industrialist father – an allegory of how unbridled Fordist technology and instrumental rationality (shown in unforgettable images of labor chained to the machine) need the mediating counterforce of the heart. The film used the latest technology to criticize technology, a contradiction that epitomized the deeply felt German ambivalence toward American technological modernity. Ironically, Lang's overly expensive critique of Americanism nearly bankrupted Ufa, making it necessary for two American film companies – Paramount and Metro Goldwyn Mayer – to distribute the film.

Hollywood studios were no strangers to Weimar Germany. As soon as the ban on foreign films was lifted at the end of World War I, American movies arrived along with jazz, the Charleston, and the marketing of a new modern lifestyle – a wave that swept Germany and filled the vacuum left by the discredited Wilhelmine culture. Young Berlin avant-garde circles around Bertolt Brecht and George Grosz adopted Americanism with enthusiasm because it repudiated Germany's semi-feudal tradition and the classical–humanist culture that had not prevented the brutality of the world war. German audiences discovered the films of Charlie Chaplin, Harold Lloyd, and Buster Keaton and became enthralled by their kineticism and break from literary and theatrical conventions. For Germans, to love Chaplin and his universal language of gestures also meant to be part of a worldwide community – even Walter Benjamin, in his 1929 essay on Chaplin, noted the revolutionary power of laughter that knows no borders. Americanism mobilized Germany for a Western modernity that dictated fashion, manners, taste, sexual mores, and leisure. American movies celebrated the lifestyle of consumption and magnified promises of material abundance. They created images and fantasies about the New World that shaped the German encounter with modernity.

By the middle of the 1920s, a new urban mass audience had developed in Germany consisting mainly of white-collar workers. In Berlin alone, 31 percent of the labor force were secretaries, clerks, and salesmen who had a regular income, fixed working hours, and leisure time at their disposal. This was the audience that preferred "modern" American fare; no fewer than two hundred American films played in Berlin in 1926, confirming the common perception of Berlin as the most American city in Europe. In the mid-1920s, Berlin boasted more than 350 movie theaters, several with more than one thousand seats. Sixty million movie tickets were sold in Berlin each year. Theaters and book publishing found themselves in a crisis. It was already feared in the mid-twenties that Hollywood was on the verge of conquering the world.

The German film industry was well aware of this asymmetrical power relationship and tried to address it through ineffective protectionist laws, which stipulated that American film imports could not exceed more than 50 percent of the films shown. Hollywood also flaunted its power by luring away German directors. In 1922, Mary Pickford invited Ernst Lubitsch to direct a film production of *Faust* in which she wanted to play Gretchen. Although this collaboration never materialized, Lubitsch remained in the United States. Fox Film Corporation hired Friedrich Wilhelm Murnau, the most "German" of German filmmakers, explicitly to raise the artistic level of its productions. Murnau's *Sunrise*, an art film based on a novel by Hermann Sudermann and a script by Carl Mayer, was given an Expressionist look by his German set designer Rochus Gliese, and today it ranks as one of the most accomplished films of the silent era. To make its film productions appear more sophisticated, Hollywood regularly hired famous German actors, including Conrad Veidt, who appeared in American productions in 1927 and 1928. Emil Jannings received the first-ever Oscar for Best Actor in 1929 for his roles in *The Way of All Flesh* and *The Last Command*, although he returned to Berlin shortly thereafter when the sound film betrayed his German accent.

This transatlantic traffic occasionally moved in the other direction. For instance, Georg Wilhelm Pabst selected the American actress Louise Brooks to play Lulu in his film *Die Büchse der Pandora* (Pandora's Box) in 1928. Ufa also engaged Josef von Sternberg, an experienced Hollywood director (who was born in Vienna but grew up in New York), to direct its first sound film, *Der Blaue Engel* (The Blue Angel) in 1930. Von Sternberg transformed the novel by Heinrich Mann into a sly allegory of the conflict between two concepts of culture: one embodied by the classically educated, if conceited, professor and the other personified by the seductive and pragmatically cynical nightclub singer who comes to town to provide commercial entertainment. His film was relentless in ridiculing the German professor's outmoded notions of classical culture, propriety, and dignity as he falls for the modern vamp — a perfect staging of the precarious status and ultimate downfall of traditional high art, gendered as feminine, in the age of cinema. Well into the 1960s, Theodor W. Adorno, Herbert Marcuse, and other critical theorists attacked the veneration of American mass culture.

THE TRAUMA OF POLITICS

Political crises of the twentieth century affected both the American and German cinemas. *The Birth of a Nation* (D. W. Griffith, 1915), a notoriously racist account of the American Civil War, inaugurated the tradition of big-budget extravaganzas about decisive turning points in American history. Spectacle, melodrama, and action-filled tableaux quickly found favor in Hollywood; with few exceptions, defining military or historical moments were translated into films so as to promote national myths.

From the settlement of the frontier explored by the Western to the world wars, American cinema repeatedly turned to issues of national and territorial identity. If the negotiation of such traumatic episodes by Hollywood inevitably stressed entertainment over explanation and heroic exploits over collective dynamics, the continuous production of films rooted in some element of American history counts as one of the most abiding features of its national film culture. Revisiting its past continually in its movies, America is the first nation whose ascent as a super-power was registered by its cinema. Every event of significance in its history – wars, assassinations, or the attacks of September 11, 2001 – has become subject matter for film.

German cinema tended to avoid historical dramas in favor of more literary and allegorical genres, epitomized by Fritz Lang's two-part *Nibelungen* saga (1924), whose critique of violence did not provide a clear political conclusion. This tendency changed with the onset of National Socialism. Centralizing all aspects of film production and distribution, Joseph Goebbels put film under his command to capitalize on its potential for propaganda. Leni Riefenstahl, actress and director of so-called mountain films (*Bergfilme*) in the 1920s, produced *Triumph des Willens* (Triumph of the Will, 1935) and *Olympia* (1938), two of the most famous propaganda films in the history of cinema.

Meticulously filmed and constructed through montages of close-ups and long shots, *Triumph des Willens*, depicting the 1934 Nuremberg Nazi party rally, and *Olympia*, on the 1936 Berlin Olympics, seamlessly fused aesthetics and politics. Their deification of Hitler, depiction of joyful community among Nazi rank and file, and idealization of the athlete as a living embodiment of classical ideals proved more compelling and persuasive than any other Nazi cinematic effort. As epic as any Western and as kinetic as a Busby Berkeley musical of the same period, Riefenstahl's films introduced a new style of filming the body, separated from its individuality and subordinated to a political "mass ornament" (Siegfried Kracauer). No filmmaker before or since has filmed crowds more effectively and demonstrated their value to the process of ideological mobilization. Here, at last, German cinema had apparently generated a narrative of national integration and rejuvenation. Synthesizing modernism and fascism, Riefenstahl discovered the means by which film could produce a social unification far more effective than previous German art films or genre cinema, even as it led to war and eventual self-destruction.

Radio also played a significant role during the Third Reich as a medium for the dissemination of both propaganda and popular-culture entertainment programs. The appearance in 1933 of the "Volksempfänger 301," a mass-produced radio named after the day that the Nazis took power (January 30, 1933), brought the medium into 65 percent of all German households by 1941. Formerly, a radio cost as much as four hundred Reichsmark. Bowing to intense government pressure, the domestic radio industry cut costs and, by 1938, the "Deutsche Kleinempfänger" could be purchased for only thirty-five Reichsmark. Millions of radios were acquired during the 1930s and, by 1939, more than half of German households were listening to war coverage and light entertainment programs.

Unlike in Germany, where the state monopolized film production, the American federal government resisted the establishment of a national film office during the New Deal. This decision may explain why documentary films produced under government auspices were ideologically heterodox. Film production was never nationalized and centralized in America during the prewar years, and such ideological pluralism continued during the war, as demonstrated by the overt leftism of a film such as *Native Land* (Leo Hurwitz and Paul Strand, 1942).

The response among Hollywood filmmakers to the growing Nazi threat was surprisingly tepid, a consequence of both American isolationism during the Great Depression and an explicit ban on anti-Nazi propaganda enacted in 1934 by the Production Code Administration, a voluntary self-censorship organization formed by the studios to circumvent government film censorship. Among the few outspoken critics of these policies were Jack and Harry Warner, who founded Warner Brothers Studio. In 1933, the studio decided against a possible acquisition of Ufa and instead released the animated *Bosko's Picture Show*, which portrayed Hitler as foolishly inept. The following year, Warner Brothers stopped conducting business in Germany.

It was a Warner Brothers production, *Confessions of a Nazi Spy* (Anatole Litvak, 1939), that transformed the trickle of anti-Nazi films into a flood after America entered the war. Based on a true story, the film was among the first to portray the Nazis as enemies of the United States and provide an intimation of what the proliferation of their spy rings in America might portend. The film met with sharp criticism not only in Washington but also in Hollywood, where other studios were reluctant to jeopardize the German market for American films. The ban against anti-Nazi content was lifted in 1941, but not before Charlie Chaplin released the most famous of all films attacking Hitler, *The Great Dictator* (1940). Financed entirely by the director and authorized by no less than President Franklin Delano Roosevelt, the film played on the often-noted physical resemblance between the comedian and the German leader. Commencing with an intertitle that read "This is the story of the period between two world wars – an interim during which insanity cut loose, liberty took a nose dive, and humanity was kicked around somewhat," the film presented Chaplin as the dictator Hynkel, a megalomaniacal bully bent on world domination. In the film's famous concluding scene, Chaplin directly addressed the camera and implored his spectators to oppose nationalism, militarism, greed, and social injustice. Attacked as inflammatory by isolationists, the film was also criticized as communist or Stalinist despite the fact that Chaplin contemplated including a parody of Stalin as well. Yet, the most strident critique came from the filmmaker himself, who confessed that he never would have directed the film had he known about German concentration camps. Only after the Japanese attack on Pearl Harbor in December 1941 and the American entry into the war did close cooperation between Washington and Hollywood commence. A flood of anti-Nazi films in all genres (even animated cartoons) followed and did not abate until after 1945.

Even before the start of the war, Fritz Lang, himself an émigré and recent arrival in America, alerted Americans to the dangers of abandoning the rule of law. *Fury* (1936), a hard-hitting account of mob violence inspired by real-life lynchings, presaged the social and political critique articulated by film noir. An innocent man seeking no more than to marry and lead a banal middle-class life is accused of a crime on the basis of circumstantial evidence. A crowd mobilized by the sensationalist mass media sets fire to the jail in which he is imprisoned. Fate irrevocably disrupts his life and reveals to him the irrational aggression that underlies American society. A happy ending tacked on by MGM fails to dispel the German exile's ambivalent view of the supposed American immunity to fascism.

Fury infused Hollywood cinema of the late 1930s with a rare philosophical clarity and social critical depth. It suggested that Americans must reject the xenophobia and violence that recently had seized Germany. Lang's didactic moralism recalled the similar defense of legal authority at the end of *M* (1931) but acquired a new meaning by its transposition into American cinema. All modern societies, not just Germany, must remain eternally vigilant and protect their democratic institutions. Having witnessed the destruction of Weimar Germany's democracy, Lang had unexpectedly been transformed into a prophet in his newly adopted homeland. Although praised by reviewers as a work of social criticism, *Fury* was a box-office flop.

No fewer than 1,500 film directors, actors, and technicians fled the Third Reich Germany between 1933 and 1941. Most found work in Hollywood, thus enriching an industry that they often understood to be antithetical to serious film art. They became part of an exile community of writers, directors, actors, composers, set designers, cinematographers, and technicians dubbed "Weimar on the Pacific." Directors such as Fritz Lang and Billy Wilder learned how to negotiate the business of studio filmmaking and enjoyed considerable success in Hollywood. Lang, for instance, made more than forty films in America. By contrast, Robert Siodmak, who had fled first to France and later the United States, returned to Germany in the 1950s. He was the exception that proved the rule, for most German political emigrants remained in America after 1945.

Many American industries flourished during World War II, but few experienced stronger growth than Hollywood. In exchange for collaborating more closely than usual with censors, lending creative and technical support to the production of wartime documentaries, and avoiding downbeat or controversial subject matter, the American film industry operated in a deregulated business environment that it would rarely enjoy again. Skillfully produced series such as *Why We Fight* (Frank Capra) presented the cause of the Allies in weekly newsreels. As the wartime film audience, now largely female and relatively prosperous thanks to the war economy, flocked to the cinema to view newsreels and uplifting dramas, box-office receipts reached an all-time high that lent the period from the late 1930s through the mid-1940s the characteristics of a golden age.

America had won the war and emerged as the most powerful economy in the world, but at what price? Thanks in large measure to the efforts of émigré filmmakers such as Lang, Billy Wilder, William Dieterle, Edgar G. Ulmer, Robert Siodmak, and Fred Zinnemann, film noir injected the American cinema with a psychologically acute vocabulary for exploring the trauma of recent history beyond the framework of the action film. Film noir added a strong and dark, often cynical sensibility that had rarely been seen in Hollywood productions. Unable to adjust to the rhythms of postwar life and trapped in deadening urban routines, its stock characters – the hapless loser, the displaced veteran, and the treacherous femme fatale – represented what many postwar Americans feared they might become. Try as they might, many Americans were unable to quell the restlessness that surfaced in other cultural forms such as Abstract Expressionist painting and psychoanalysis, which had recently come into fashion. Film noir appeared to more than a few postwar critics as Weimar cinema redux, crafted in some cases by the same directors and technicians who had found refuge in Hollywood.

Writing in 1946, Kracauer noted the brutality and antidemocratic tendencies in recent cinema. Atrocities and sadism had reached the homefront in what he called "Hollywood's Terror Films." Weimar cinema and the "German-style" penchant for allegorical narratives proved well suited to this new social environment. More than a few noir films suggested wide-ranging critiques of twentieth-century modernity, rumblings of subterranean discontent and latent violence, which was all the more jarring when contrasted with the sunny optimism of nearly every other form of postwar mass culture. No single trauma generated the film noir genre. Film historians alternately have proposed shifting relations between the sexes, urbanization, and political repression to explain its appearance. There can be little doubt, however, that the war acclimated American spectators to an unprecedented degree of onscreen violence, epitomized by the newsreels of concentration-camp footage shown in theaters toward its conclusion. That such brutal images refused to disappear with the cessation of hostilities, as Kracauer observed, suggests that one function of postwar American cinema was the psychic fortification of spectators through a prophylactic dose of violence. Whether in the mythic landscape of the American West, the battlefield, or the conflict-laden domestic milieu of melodramas such as *Rebel without a Cause* (Nicholas Ray, 1955), violence in the postwar American cinema was seldom far from view.

With their country occupied by the Allies, their principal cities in ruins, and most families devastated, postwar Germans found signs of the war all around them. Compulsory visits to concentration camps and screenings of documentary films administered by the occupation authorities rendered the comparatively banal violence in noir films tame by comparison. German cinema faced the task of making sense of the catastrophe, attributing guilt, and establishing a moral compass for both individuals and the state. Decimated by forced emigration and ideological collaboration during the Third Reich, the postwar German film industry enlisted Weimar-era industry professionals such as producer Erich Pommer, who returned from Hollywood exile to oversee its reorganization.

Commentators have attributed the demise of American film noir at the end of the 1950s to the decline of the B movie (a consequence of the landmark Paramount Decree of 1949 forcing studios to sell their movie theaters), competition from television, and the changing (increasingly suburban) American landscape itself. In truth, however, noir did not disappear so much as travel upmarket and provide the frame of reference for self-conscious and socially critical art films such as *Point Blank* (John Boorman, 1967) and *The Conversation* (Francis Coppola, 1974). The same was true in West Germany, where filmmakers of the New German Cinema such as Rainer Werner Fassbinder and Wim Wenders cited film noir in works such as *The American Soldier* (1964) and *The American Friend* (1977). These films betrayed an anxiety of influence in their very titles as German directors sought to develop an authentic national cinema.

Urban movie palaces – architecturally lavish structures in art deco, Egyptian, or modernist style – had been the preferred space of film consumption in both Germany and the United States from the 1920s through World War II. Although the death of the local movie house was mourned on both sides of the Atlantic in films such as *The Last Picture Show* (Peter Bogdanovich, 1971) and *Im Lauf der Zeit* (Kings of the Road; Wim Wenders, 1977), suburban cineplexes located in shopping malls became the dominant space of film consumption in the United States in the post-1945 period. Cinema uncoupled itself from its urban origins more quickly in America than in Germany, where even today most film viewing still takes place in cities.

Television entered into competition with cinema relatively late in Germany, unlike in the United States, where it competed with Hollywood starting in the 1940s. Live broadcasts of the soccer World Cup in 1954 (when West Germany surprisingly won the title) brought television to the attention of the masses, but it was not until the mid-1960s that middle-class households sported a television set. West German viewers had a choice of two networks (ARD and ZDF), both of which were financed through license fees rather than advertisements. The privately owned commercial cable channels RTL and Sat 1 were not added until the mid-1980s. Publicly funded German television networks (with programs like the *Kleines Fernsehspiel* on ZDF, the educational so-called Third Program, or the German-French culture channel ARTE) have become major sponsors of German cinema and favorite sites for showcasing films with little commercial appeal. They often co-produce and show alternative documentaries, experimental work, and hybrid forms that are shot in 35 mm but presented as television mini-series, including such ambitious works as Rainer Werner Fassbinder's nearly 16-hour adaptation of Alfred Döblin's novel *Berlin Alexanderplatz* (1980) and Reitz's monumental eleven-part mini-series *Heimat* (1984), which was followed by a thirteen-part sequel in 1992 and a third installment, in six parts, in 2004. German television's own entertainment production includes long-running popular serials, such as *Tatort*, a crime serial, and *Lindenstrasse*, a soap opera. Their audience easily eclipses that of even the most successful German films.

STRICTLY BUSINESS

At the same time that Weimar cinema developed a unique formal language for representing the German experience of modernity, it also adopted a marketing strategy to differentiate its product from Hollywood on the world market and establish a brand identity. There is good reason to consider the film industry the first truly global enterprise, for shortly after its commercialization at the end of the nineteenth century, silent films crossed national borders in all directions to reach a world market. Thanks to its large domestic audience, rapid implementation of labor-saving production techniques, and the devastating effects of World War I on its European competitors, the United States emerged as the most economically significant film-producing nation in the 1920s. From that point on, German cinema inevitably developed in competition with and in reaction to its American counterpart.

Despite proclamations by Joseph Goebbels about realizing a conspicuous national profile for German cinema, American films, especially Walt Disney productions, remained popular in Germany up to the onset of World War II. In 1936, Paul Martin's *Glückskinder* (Lucky Kids), a German screwball comedy (and remake of *It Happened One Night*), was praised for beating the Americans at their own game. Such escapist fare comprised the bulk of Nazi film production, leading to a golden age of the German film business, a rare moment when the lucre of commerce trumped the luster of high art. Never again would so many movie tickets be sold, from approximately 250 million in 1934 to more than a billion in 1944. Annexations of territory only partially explain this boom. German moviegoers were offered a broad palette of genre films including melodramas, literary adaptations, historical epics, musicals, and comedies, all of which generally steered clear of swastikas. These films insulated wartime audiences from the devastation around them. Except for some anti-Semitic propaganda films like Veit Harlan's *Jud Süss* (1940), overt political manipulation was relegated to newsreels, the production of which increased dramatically after 1939.

One of the first measures of the U.S. Office of War Information (OWI) in occupied Germany was to break up the Nazi-controlled Ufa by separating its production, distribution, and exhibition departments, thereby destroying its once effective vertical integration and establishing an infrastructure that guaranteed a continued American presence. German cinema would never recover from the loss of a commercial film studio culture. By 1949, Hollywood films accounted for 70 percent of the films shown in the American sector. But German production also increased, going from 9 feature films in 1947 to 111 in 1957. In that year, 800 million movie tickets were sold in the Federal Republic of Germany and 316 million in the German Democratic Republic. (In a reunited Germany in 2005, only 127 million tickets were sold.) West German cinema churned out unabashedly commercial fare, ranging from Bavarian sex comedies, melodramas, and Westerns to the most German genre of all, the *Heimat* film, which addressed issues of community and regional belonging. *Schwarzwaldmädel* (Black Forest Girl, Robert Sander, 1950), the first example of a *Heimat* film and also the first color film in Germany, attracted sixteen million viewers.

East German cinema productions included politically incisive engagements with the recent Nazi past and feature films that served as reminders of socialist values. Founded in 1946, the Deutsche Film-Aktiengesellschaft (DEFA) made use of the old Ufa production facilities, which were located in the Soviet-occupation zone and built up its own state-controlled film studio. Wolfgang Staudte's *Die Mörder sind unter uns* (The Murderers Are among Us, 1946), the first postwar German film, addressed the nexus of war trauma, guilt, and revenge by following a German soldier and former physician who returns home from the front. Under the influence of a woman who had survived a concentration camp, he refrains from killing his former commanding officer, who had been responsible for the death of innocent women and children. To dramatize these stark moral decisions and to break with the conventions of Nazi cinema, the film adopted the silent film language of harsh shadows and extreme camera angles. In its moral seriousness and visual expressiveness, *Die Mörder sind unter uns* stands as one of the few German noir films.

Between 1945 and 1989, DEFA produced no fewer than 900 feature films in all genres (including science fiction films and Westerns made from the perspective of Native Americans), in addition to thousands of documentaries, educational films, and didactic cartoons for children. The ruling Socialist Unity Party (Sozialistische Einheitspartei Deutschlands, or SED) banned films that questioned or critiqued socialist progress. For instance, Frank Beyer's *Spur der Steine* (The Trace of Stones, 1966) was released only after the fall of the Berlin Wall. Despite or possibly because of censorship pressures, DEFA produced a number of memorable films that, while addressing antifascist and anticapitalist themes, slyly criticized the new socialist order: notable examples include Konrad Wolf's *Der geteilte Himmel* (The Divided Heaven, 1964), Frank Beyer's *Jakob der Lügner* (Jacob the Liar, 1973), and Heiner Carow's *Solo Sunny* (1980).

As the West German postwar generation came of age in the early 1960s, the lack of an indigenous film culture became rapidly apparent, especially in comparison to the French New Wave, the East European cinema, and the American independent cinema. Twenty-six aspiring filmmakers, among them Alexander Kluge and Edgar Reitz, published a widely quoted manifesto in the context of the 1962 short film festival at Oberhausen. One of their demands was that the state provide substantial subsidies for the development of a new German feature film. The Federal Republic complied and began investing large sums of money in films that they hoped would yield prestige for Germany abroad. This was the beginning of an ever more complicated system of financing on the federal, state, and local levels that remains in place to this day. Once again, culturally ambitious productions and popular genre films went their separate ways.

Only rarely, as in the case of Volker Schlöndorff's *Die Blechtrommel* (The Tin Drum, 1979) and Rainer Werner Fassbinder's *Die Ehe der Maria Braun* (The Marriage of Maria Braun, 1979), did the New German Cinema truly capture a larger global audience. Most films depended on the film-festival circuit and institutions such as the New York Film Festival, the Museum of Modern Art, Berkeley's Pacific Film Archive, and Francis Ford Coppola's (now defunct) Zoetrope Studios. Above all, the Goethe Institute did much to help the young German filmmakers succeed abroad. New German Cinema was often held up as an alternative to Hollywood because it broached taboo subject matter, explored different narrative forms, and experimented with a film language influenced by opera (Werner Schroeter and Hans Jürgen Syberberg), theater (Rainer Werner Fassbinder), or literature (Alexander Kluge and Volker Schlöndorff). Ironically, the movement was not acknowledged in West Germany until it had found a limited but vociferous fan base in art cinema and academic circles in the United States and France.

At its deepest points, the chasm between the subsidized mode of production in Germany and the Hollywood industry model suggests little evidence of similarities. Whereas studios or corporate investors fund Hollywood films in exchange for a percentage of future revenues, German films produced within the system of state subsidies are largely amortized by the time they reach the film screen and need not turn a profit. Removed from the pressures of the free market, German filmmakers are able to take risks, sometimes at the cost of alienating or entirely losing their audience by making overly rarified and intellectual films.

Although the German system of government subsidy helped realize some distinguished films, it also spawned many mediocre efforts and downright failures. By the 1980s, it appeared ineffective to more than a few observers. American films continued to dominate the German box office, and the market share of domestic productions seldom rose above 15 percent. Domestic production was based on complex funding structures consisting of federal, state, and local subsidies, television rights, and co-production monies from European and American film companies.

Several recent German films such as *Lola rennt* (Run Lola Run; Tom Tykwer, 1998), *Good-bye Lenin* (Wolfgang Becker, 2003), and *Gegen die Wand* (Head-On; Fatih Akin, 2004) have found sizeable national and international audiences. Increasingly, contemporary German cinema strives to balance artistic ambition with genuine mass popularity, formal innovation with concessions to genre conventions. Satirical spoofs like Michael Herbig's *Der Schuh des Manitu* (2001) and *(T)Raumschiff Surprise* (2004) went for all-out entertainment by self-consciously parodying German appropriations of American genre films. *Der Untergang* (Downfall; Oliver Hirschbiegel, 2004), an account of Hitler's final days, is but the latest in a string of German films about the National Socialist past that enjoyed critical success and even modest business at the box office in the United States. It was nominated for an Oscar for Best Foreign Language Film in 2005. More recently, the Oscar-winning *Das Leben der Anderen* (The Lives of Others, Florian Henckel von Donnersmarck, 2006) appropriated the language of Hollywood to investigate the political repression of the East German cultural elite. Foreign films released in the United States are more likely to be noticed if they address their national histories and play on the authenticity of their local settings. A survey of German movies distributed in the United States in the last thirty years reveals the Nazi period and the Holocaust as the predominant subject matter. Can it be that Hollywood alone possesses the ability to produce genre films that easily move across national boundaries and captivate a global audience?

Already in the 1960s, Hollywood had demonstrated its ability to capture the demographically significant youth market. *Easy Rider* (Dennis Hopper, 1968), a low-budget motorcycle film featuring sex, drugs, and rock music, convinced Hollywood just how lucrative such films could be. Many of the most prominent directors of the postwar American cinema, including Robert Altman, Peter Bogdanovich, Francis Ford Coppola, George Lucas, Martin Scorsese, and Steven Spielberg, began their careers making similar low-budget genre films for the drive-in movie circuit, while still remaining true to their own personal and aesthetic concerns. They demonstrated that it was possible to make ambitious films with minimal studio interference and no subsidies.

With the possible exception of Robert Altman, all of these figures eventually reverted to making films whose dependence on established stars, spectacular action, and generic narrative suggested acquiescence to the dominant Hollywood paradigm. In the 1990s, young directors such as Todd Haynes, Gus Van Sant, and Todd Solondz revived the idea of a quirky independent narrative cinema, formally accomplished yet idiosyncratic and drawn to losers, social misfits, and provocative explorations of marginality. It remains to be seen whether they, too, will be absorbed into the mainstream of the industry.

By the twenty-first century, a curious paradox was evident in American cinema. Although Hollywood's domination of the world market had never been greater, the possibilities for producing and distributing offbeat films through such institutions as the Sundance Film Festival, the Independent Film Channel on cable television, and DVD sales gave film audiences an unprecedented opportunity to view a wider range of fare than ever before. Today, anyone with a digital video recorder can make films, and digitalization has radically democratized their reception and production. Distribution, rather than production, has become the challenge for most filmmakers concerned with making work outside of the mainstream. With a population almost four times that of Germany, America enjoys a large domestic audience that can support numerous local film cultures as well as $200 million mega-productions. *Spider Man 3*, released in 2007, cost more than $250 million and opened in 4,200 cinemas in the United States and Canada, 522 in England, and within a week in several hundred additional movie houses in Brazil, Italy, Japan, the Philippines, Russia, South Korea, Germany, and elsewhere. Although panned by critics, it earned just short of a billion dollars.

Capitalizing on its position of strength, Hollywood remains adroit at recruiting collaborators from abroad, including German directors such as Wolfgang Petersen, Wim Wenders, and Werner Herzog. A patriotic film such as *Independence Day* (Roland Emmerich, 1996), which grossed more than $800 million worldwide, illustrates the ease with which a German avant-garde filmmaker can flourish within the American system. Depending on a global and ever younger demographic, Hollywood cinema has evolved a new aesthetic. Dialogue in blockbuster films is replaced by physical violence and special effects. Stories (often sequels) are predictable, images are conventional, and politically controversial viewpoints are avoided.

With an increasingly international audience, the American cinema is today engaged less in a process of national integration than in disseminating lifestyles and values around the world. Scholars of contemporary globalization fiercely debate whether these ideologies actually represent American interests and ideals or merely contribute to a modern capitalist culture whose connection to the United States decreases as it grows more ubiquitous. Growing foreign investment and offshore ownership in the contemporary global entertainment industry further complicate the definition of national film cultures in the twenty-first century. When a studio that is located in one country and is supported by banks and investors in other countries co-produces a film that has a multinational cast and crew, what is the nationality of the final product? Such cases have become common and suggest the need to address film authorship and content within the web of global capitalism itself.

Improbably, the most significant transformation in American entertainment at the end of the 1990s developed in a medium that for years many had already pronounced lifeless and moribund: television. This new burst of creative energy circumvented the major networks – ABC, NBC, CBS, and Fox – and flourished on cable, thanks to the innovative series of the Home Box Office (HBO) channel. Spurning advertising-driven programming and theatrical film distribution, HBO developed a new business model organized around subscriptions and DVD sales. An audience of educated and often affluent viewers, typically older than the teenage demographic targeted by Hollywood blockbuster films, and the very group whose alleged disappearance the studios had blamed for the move toward special-effects–driven mega-productions, flocked to HBO programs.

In series such as *The Sopranos, Six Feet Under*, and *The Wire*, sex and violence served up in frequently startling forms commanded the attention of even the most jaded spectators. Yet, if their sensational content provided an initial hook, these series also contained excellent writing and unforgettable characters, qualities that had been sorely lacking in American cinema since the 1970s. Treating the Italian American mafia, the inner workings of a family-run mortuary, or the power struggles within police bureaucracies and drug dealer cartels, they presented conflicted and psychologically compartmentalized individuals with a narrative intricacy evocative of the nineteenth-century novel.

Film auteurs such as Peter Bogdanovich and Agnieszka Holland directed individual episodes of these series. Ethnicity, gender, and the family, long staples of American cinema, had rarely appeared so compelling on the small screen. Developing over the course of four or five seasons and often stretching to as long as forty hours, the new cable programs were equally nimble at analyzing legal and political institutions. Even when they emphasized entertainment and titillation, as in *Sex and the City*, the results broke new ground for the depiction of previously taboo subject matter. German media, whether subsidized or driven by the profit motive, broadcast on television, or shown in movie houses, have yet to rise to the standard attained by the best of these productions.

Conventional network television, both in Germany and the United States, is struggling to retain young viewers, who have turned to the Internet for information and entertainment. With the American conversion to digital television in June 2009, radio remained the sole analog medium. Yet, podcasting and Internet access have allowed it to survive, indeed to thrive as a searchable audio database. All entertainment today has some Internet presence, from official Web sites to fan sites, to YouTube, to downloading music. The once powerful music industry today faces an uncertain future. Satellite television allows for the reception of thousands of channels of international programming.

Every sound and image, it appears, becomes part of an expanding archive. Yet, whether this archive will remain accessible and preserved in the face of constantly evolving broadcast standards, hardware, and software remains a widely debated question. Although the first phonograph records, motion pictures, and magnetic tapes are still playable, contemporary digital media may fare less well. Today, as revenue from the retail sale of DVDs and cable and satellite broadcast rights far exceeds that of ticket sales at the box office, film industries the world over have become providers of digital content. Concerns about intellectual property laws, copyright enforcement, and piracy are shared by film producers everywhere and could well bring the American and German media industries closer in the coming years.

The widening gap between blockbuster films such as *Avatar* (James Cameron, 2009), conceived as a franchise for branding, and those limited to distribution in theaters or on DVD underscores this tendency toward global marketing, whose origin may be located in the commercial success of *Jaws* (Steven Spielberg, 1974). Emblazoned on toys and t-shirts, spun off into books, and transformed in video games, contemporary mega-productions increasingly present themselves as vehicles for creative marketing and "commodity tie-ins." They circulate through the culture in a manner quite unlike previous films. Facilitated by new technologies for viewing a movie in a home-entertainment environment, on a laptop computer, or even on a cell phone, twenty-first–century cinema is in key respects fundamentally different from the spools of celluloid publicly exhibited during the last hundred years.

It remains to be seen whether the vastly lower costs of producing and distributing films digitally will realize the promise of avant-garde and independent cinemas and differentiate the mass audience or simply promote cultural standardization on an even vaster scale. If digitalization inaugurates a new mode of cinematic production, it may well mark the end of one cultural form and the beginning of another, both in the United States and in Germany.

Further Reading

Allan, Sean, and John Sandford, eds. *DEFA: East German Cinema, 1946–1992* (New York, 1999).

Birdwell, Michael E. *Celluloid Soldiers: The Warner Bros. Campaign against Nazis* (New York, 1999).

Burgoyne, Robert. *The Hollywood Historical Film* (Boston, 2008).

Dimendberg, Edward. *Film Noir and the Spaces of Modernity* (Cambridge, 2004).

Eisner, Lotte. *The Haunted Screen: Expressionism in the German Cinema and the Influence of Max Reinhardt.* Transl. by Roger Greaves (Berkeley, 1969).

Elsaesser, Thomas. *Weimar Cinema and After: Germany's Historical Imaginary* (London, 2000).

Fehrenbach, Heidi. *Cinema in Democratizing Germany: Reconstructing National Identity after Hitler* (Chapel Hill, 1995).

Gemünden, Gerd. *Framed Visions: Popular Culture, Americanization, and the German and Austrian Imagination* (Ann Arbor, 1999).

Halle, Randall. *German Film after Germany: Toward a Transnational Aesthetic* (Carbondale, 2008).

Hansen, Miriam. *Babel and Babylon: Spectatorship in American Silent Film* (Cambridge, 1991).

Kaes, Anton. *From Hitler to Heimat: The Return of History as Film* (Cambridge, 1989).

Keil, Charlie. *Early American Cinema in Transition: Story, Style and Filmmaking 1907–1913* (Madison, 2001).

Kracauer, Siegfried. *From Caligari to Hitler: A Psychological History of the German Film* (Princeton, 1947/2004).

Monaco, Paul. *The Sixties: 1960–69* (Berkeley, 2003).

Musser, Charles. *The Emergence of Cinema: The American Screen to 1907* (Berkeley, 1994).

Prince, Stephen. *A New Pot of Gold: Hollywood under the Electronic Rainbow, 1980–89* (Berkeley, 2002).

Rentschler, Eric. *The Ministry of Illusion: Nazi Cinema and Its Afterlife* (Cambridge, 1996).

Saunders, Thomas J. *Hollywood in Berlin: American Cinema and Weimar Germany* (Berkeley, 1994).

Thompson, Kristin. *Herr Lubitsch Goes to Hollywood: German and American Film after World War I* (Amsterdam, 2006).

Von Moltke, Johannes. *No Place like Home: Locations of Heimat in German Cinema* (Berkeley, 2005).

13

Education: Universities and Research

KATHRYN M. OLESKO AND CHRISTOPH STRUPP

At the beginning of the twenty-first century, the United States is the world's undisputed leader in higher education and scientific research. Universities such as Harvard, Yale, and Stanford are synonymous with academic excellence. Students and researchers from all over the world flock to American universities. In the natural and social sciences, English is the lingua franca of scholarly discourse, and when the Swedish Nobel Prize committee makes its yearly announcements, the question is not if but how many Americans will be among the winners.

A century ago, however, American higher education was widely viewed as inferior to its European and, most notably, its German counterparts. Research opportunities were limited, and original American contributions to science and scholarship were rare. Over the course of the nineteenth century, about ten thousand American students spent time at German universities with academics who were the leaders in their fields.

At the same time, reform initiatives in the United States, were transforming small colleges established in the colonial period, improving state universities in the Midwest and West, and supplementing the system with private research universities. American reformers of higher education looked to Germany for inspiration – or at least referred to Berlin, Göttingen, and Heidelberg as role models to advance their own ideas. Yet, by the beginning of the twenty-first century, the tide had turned. In a reversal of roles, German academics, politicians, and the media looked to America for models of reform in the hope of creating a "German Harvard."

Even more so than higher education in general, science is, by its very nature, characterized by a transnational exchange of questions, ideas, and people, but there has always been a special dimension to the German–American scientific relationship. Over the course of a century, that relationship was marked by mutual admiration, cooperation, rivalry, and, finally, voluntary and forced exchange.

Nevertheless, there are distinct national characteristics of science and education in both countries, deeply embedded in their social, political, and intellectual traditions. The organization of universities and research institutes, the selection of students, academic career paths, the level of state and private funding, the overall image of science and technology, and many other features remain different in Germany and the United States.

Over the course of the twentieth century, the United States was one of the greatest promoters of science and rationality as the route to modernity, whereas German scholars and parts of the German public were often their greatest critics. On both sides of the Atlantic, the optimism of the Enlightenment – which identified science unequivocally with reason, emancipation, and progress – was increasingly replaced by skepticism concerning the extreme rationalization of life, loss of traditional values and securities, and the ethical challenges posed by technical and scientific advances. Two world wars, the moral nihilism of the Third Reich, the possibility of human self-annihilation through atomic warfare, and double-edged breakthroughs in biochemistry and genetics accentuated the unintended consequences of science and technology and intensified concerns about their roles in daily life. At the same time, the dramatic advancement of knowledge and of science-based technological triumphs in areas as diverse as transportation, communication, and medicine emphasized the potential of science and education for the betterment of humankind.

The institutionally based cultivation of science and technology has been identified with "modernity" since the seventeenth century. What that identification has meant, though, has not always been clear. This chapter looks at how two large-scale structural changes – the rise of the mass university and the emergence of R&D (research and development) – and locally contingent external pressures, political and ethical, transformed the relationship between knowledge production and modernity in Germany and America during the twentieth century.

THE MASS UNIVERSITY

German and American memoirs from the late nineteenth century often described the atmosphere at universities as a close companionship of teachers and students within almost family-like structures. A century later, complaints about the "anonymity" of modern "learning mills" prevailed. Within the span of less than a half-century, universities on both sides of the Atlantic turned into "mass universities" and faced the challenge of educating tens of thousands of students.

Despite the rising demand for higher education at the end of the nineteenth century, university instruction in both Germany and the United States remained the privilege of the elite. Stories of the Rockefellers, Vanderbilts, and other millionaire entrepreneurs suggested that there were other routes to economic success than going to college. Nevertheless, professions requiring university degrees grew, and the idea advanced rapidly that the scientifically trained expert was superior to other types of individuals in industry and bureaucracy. Scientific progress, technological breakthroughs, bureaucratic expansion, and the growing complexity of the business world all contributed to processes that both motivated more young people to pursue higher education and created more jobs for college and university graduates.

In Germany, the number of students rose from thirty-five thousand in 1890 to almost two million in 2000. In the United States, enrollment went up from fifteen thousand to sixteen million in that period. The growth in demand repeatedly led to pessimistic prognoses about the role of the university in society and to complaints about the devaluation of the ideal of disinterested intellectual and personal development (*Bildung*) in the interest of a marketable education. It also regularly stimulated heated debates about how to reform and adapt higher education to demographic and economic realities.

Germany and the United States both responded to the challenge of the rising demand for higher education first by enlarging existing institutions. In 1901, Berlin, with 6,700 students, was Germany's largest university. A century later, the largest German university, the University of Cologne, enrolled sixty thousand students, and in America the larger state universities reached student populations of twenty to thirty thousand.

A second response to accommodating more students was the creation of new institutions. In Germany, the establishment of universities in Frankfurt, Hamburg, and Cologne between 1910 and 1920 was followed by the founding of several new institutions in East Germany in the 1950s and a wave of new universities in West Germany in the 1960s, when recognition of the economic necessity of an educated workforce and generous budget policies paved the way for an expansion of tertiary education. Additional universities were created in the early 1990s after German unification as the East German system adapted to West German role models. In America, which was spared the shock waves of repeated political regime change, growth was more gradual but nonetheless transformative. The expansion of state university systems by building new campuses continued into the twenty-first century: in 2005, for example, the University of California founded its tenth research university at Merced.

Finally, in both countries, the range of institutions diversified with the introduction of *Fachhochschulen* – specialized colleges and professional schools – in Germany and the exponential growth of two-year community colleges in America after World War II. Both types of institutions served a clientele that was more interested in receiving a marketable education than in research training. By the end of the twentieth century, a second wave of diversification occurred with the establishment of small private universities in Germany and academic for-profit and online institutions in America.

The variety of choices at the tertiary level, however, preserved crucial structural differences between the two countries. From the outset, the American tertiary system of higher education encompassed state as well as private universities and special institutions such as women's colleges and the so-called historically black colleges for African Americans. In Germany, by contrast, universities were state institutions with largely homogeneous characters.

In America, the success of private universities, with their industrialist benefactors and their business-oriented boards of trustees, established a solid link between higher education and the business world. This linkage strengthened in the 1910s and 1920s with large-scale donations from philanthropic foundations. This relationship had fundamental consequences for the evolution of higher education in America because it led to a highly competitive and hierarchically structured system. Through tuition fees and selective entrance testing examinations, the American system fostered academic elites. This process accelerated in the 1920s when Harvard, Yale, MIT, Chicago, Columbia, and a few others with research-oriented graduate programs overshadowed institutions that focused only on undergraduate education.

The German university, by contrast, was shaped throughout the nineteenth and twentieth centuries by its strong link to the state rather than to private benefactors. Academics and politicians alike maintained an ideal of parity and equality in higher education, with very few competitive elements built into the system. Students could not be rejected and did not have to pass entrance exams. Universities' budgets, academic appointments, and course structures were subject to state approval. Only beginning in the late 1990s did German universities gradually gain greater organizational independence. Nonetheless, 92 percent of university budgets still came from public funds in the year 2000, compared to just 34 percent in the United States. Not until the beginning of the twenty-first century, in 2006–7, was the foundational principle of relative parity and equality among the German universities altered with the elevation of nine universities to "centers of excellence." Even though financed by public funds, this program explicitly abandoned the ideal of equality by distributing funding not according to social or political criteria but rather with the goal of preparing the best German institutions for global academic competition.

The differences between the quasi-private nature of the American system and the public nature of the German system had serious consequences for the relationship between universities and students. In America, universities competed for the best students and students, in turn, competed for entrance to high-ranking institutions (and were willing to pay for it). In Germany, there was little incentive for universities to modernize curricula or create new educational fields that would attract more or better students, and there was no incentive – and hardly a way – for students to compare universities and select an institution based on the quality of its programs.

A final organizational difference that shaped reactions to the mass university in both countries was the internal structure of tertiary education. In the United States, more egalitarian and professionally managed university departments, which were in place even before 1900, proved to be accommodating to new generations of scholars and scientists – and one can also think here of the hundreds of German academic refugees who entered American universities in the 1930s and 1940s – and more flexible in integrating new or interdisciplinary topics than the German model of separate chairs and small research institutes. Whereas the ratio of students and teachers between 1900 and 2000 remained relatively stable in America as a result of large-scale employment of professors, by the end of the twentieth century in Germany, that ratio had deteriorated substantially because of the very limited growth in number of professorships. In contrast with the budgets of the largest state universities in Germany, which often do not exceed four hundred million euros, America's Ivy League flagship university, Harvard, has an annual budget in excess of two billion dollars. Although the quality of higher education in Germany thus suffered as a result of budgetary constraints, a well-developed system of research institutes outside the universities offers additional opportunities and a safe haven for top-quality research.

What were the social consequences of this development? Despite the massive expansion of higher education and the constantly rising number of university students, the ideal of equal opportunities in education for everyone intellectually qualified remained unrealized in both countries. Whereas an ideology of *Bildung* as a selective privilege persisted until well after World War II in West Germany and in East Germany (there as a reward for political loyalty), in the United States the progressive concept of education as a democratic instrument of personal advancement, embedded in the system even before 1900, could not be realized everywhere because of economic and social barriers to higher education.

Nonetheless, the social base of the student body broadened considerably in both countries. Scholarships and student-aid programs, such as the American GI Bill of 1944 and the federally funded Pell Grants, the East German "Workers and Peasants Faculties" (*Arbeiter-und Bauernfakultäten*), and the West German student aid program introduced in the 1970s, the so-called *Bafög* (from *Bundesausbildungsförderungsgesetz*, or Federal Education Support Law), indicated that there was active interest on both sides of the Atlantic in encouraging the pursuit of higher education and creating the conditions for building a more highly qualified workforce. None of these programs, however, could fully overcome the inherent class bias of tertiary education. New types of students were not easily accepted into the established routines and rituals of the university. In Germany, this was true, for example, of the *Werkstudent* who had to support himself instead of collecting a monthly check from home. In the United States, Harvard, Yale, and Princeton in the 1920s and 1930s devised systems to limit the number of freshmen without roots in the WASP elite, in particular, Jewish students.

Both systems did slightly better in integrating women. A few American universities first opened their doors to female students in the 1870s; in Germany, the full-fledged official entry of women took another thirty years. Even though women quickly took advantage of the new educational opportunities – by 2000, women constituted slightly more than half of the student body in each country – there remained a gender bias in terms of the subjects they studied and the careers they chose. A similar uneven picture has characterized the ethnic diversification of the student body.

The changed social composition of the student body played an important part in altering the role of the university as a social and political institution. Whereas German and American universities and their students in the first decades of the twentieth century were characterized by and large as conservative pillars of the social and political order, the "student revolution" of the 1960s was a highly visible expression of the changed politics of the student body and of a new relationship between the universities and society. After the events of the 1960s, the public image of students as clean-cut fraternity men (and women) was supplemented by that of students as long-haired hippies with revolutionary attitudes. Universities and professors could be either institutions of the establishment or motors of (sometimes unwanted) social change – or even both.

By the early twenty-first century, American research universities led in the global competition for academic talent and in the ability to provide educational services in diverse ways for the public, suggesting that the United States managed the challenge of the mass university better than Germany and that the disrupted political and economic history of Germany in the twentieth century may have made the difference. The fact that reform debates and calls for broad changes took place regularly in both countries throughout the twentieth century indicates, however, that the adaptation of higher education to the needs and demands of society was, for both nations, an open-ended project.

RESEARCH AND DEVELOPMENT (R&D)

A second structural change in science and education that occurred simultaneously with the growth of the mass university in the twentieth century was the rise of R&D on the assumption that research in science and technology was a necessary precondition for economic growth.

The concept of R&D changed the way private businesses operated. In both Germany and the United States, companies in innovative new fields such as chemicals, electrical products, and pharmaceuticals started to build their own laboratories and employ scientists even before 1900. General Electric, Westinghouse, and AT&T in America and Siemens, BASF, and Bayer in Germany stood for a hitherto unknown direct link between science and industry. The many consequences of this link – institutional, financial, social, and political – came to fruition in the twentieth century. Public investments in science and higher education increased substantially. In the university, the natural sciences and technical fields gained prominence in the curriculum. Outside the university, state research institutions and industrial research laboratories became additional and, at times, competing sectors of scientific activity and knowledge production. The character of research itself changed. The Berlin theologian Adolf von Harnack, a power player in German academia, envisioned as early as 1908 a *Grossbetrieb der Wissenschaft* (large-scale scientific enterprise) with teams of researchers working on ever more complex and long-running projects that could no longer be carried out by individual professors or at individual universities.

Whereas the importance of R&D was recognized in Germany in the nineteenth century and in America only slightly later, the different configuration of the triangle of state, industry, and university in Germany and America accounted again for important differences in stimulating, organizing, and financing R&D. From the beginning, in Germany large-scale investments in equipment and personnel were financed mostly publicly. The Kaiser Wilhelm Gesellschaft zur Förderung der Wissenschaften (KWG) under the patronage of the German emperor was founded in 1911 and established a network of research institutes (Kaiser Wilhelm Institutes [KWIs]). The KWIs conducted basic research in chemistry, physics, and physiology as well as applied research on coal, aeronautics, and other areas.

From the 1920s on, additional public money was channeled into research through the Notgemeinschaft der deutschen Wissenschaft. Research in new subfields such as nuclear physics required investments that the regular budgets of the universities could no longer provide. During the Third Reich, financial support for science and research grew again considerably but was closely linked to the ideological, economic, and military goals of the Nazi regime.

Both post–World War II German states recognized the need for an active research policy to promote technological and economic progress but found it difficult to implement such a policy. In West Germany, the sovereignty of the *Länder* (states) in matters of science and higher education limited the options of the federal government. Nevertheless, within a few years, the structure of grantmaking institutions and research facilities outside the universities reached a new level of complexity. The Notgemeinschaft was reconstituted as the Deutsche Forschungsgemeinschaft (DFG), which supported research at West German universities with federal grants. At the end of the twentieth century, its budget totaled more than 1.3 billion euros. The number of KWIs, renamed as Max Planck Institutes after 1945, multiplied. The Fraunhofer Society, founded in Bavaria in 1949, cooperated with industry in applied research. It also carried out research for the Defense Ministry. The West German government always took pride, however, in the low percentage of its R&D spending that was defense related, and the military never gained as much access to West German universities and industry as the American military did after 1945. Several institutes for nuclear research came into being in West Germany after the end of Allied restrictions in 1955. Along with other institutes that focused on large-scale energy, health, and transportation research, they were organized under the umbrella of the Helmholtz Society by the late twentieth century.

The European Union (EU) laid the most recent cornerstone of public support for R&D in Germany. Beginning in the 1950s, West German nuclear research and other big science projects were carried out in cooperation with other Western European countries. A milestone in the implementation of a coordinated European science policy was the European Community's coordination program of 1971. In 1997, the EU reoriented its science policy to integrate, for the first time, pressing social issues – especially aging and unemployment – as focal points of R&D. In the early twenty-first century, the EU spent more than ten billion euros per year on scientific infrastructure and research programs in the member states.

The well-funded Max Planck and Fraunhofer Institutes, the institutes of the Helmholtz Society, and transnational research projects such as those supported by the EU constituted the foundation of basic research in many academic fields in Germany at the end of the twentieth century. The system helped keep politically and socially controversial research for the military, on nuclear energy, or, more recently, in the field of biotechnology out of the universities. However, it also contributed to the isolation of high-quality research and often prevented the development of innovative clusters of pure research, applied research, and science-oriented industry. The ideal of the unity of teaching and research as a basis of scientific excellence, expressed around 1800 by Wilhelm von Humboldt and Friedrich Schleiermacher in Berlin, seemed to have lost much of its appeal.

Public and political debates in Germany in the 1980s and 1990s revolved around how to improve the efficiency of the system and how to make sure that the country – with its limited natural resources and high labor costs – could maintain a position at the forefront of scientific and technological progress. Not until the late 1990s, after a series of devastating evaluation reports, did the government increase funding and initiate reforms that fundamentally changed the way universities, research institutes, and funding organizations operated. These reforms stressed academic independence from political influence, intellectual and organizational cooperation, and interdisciplinarity – in the interest of securing a broad fundament of excellent research for the German economy, stopping the "brain drain" of researchers to the United States, attracting new talent from outside, and improving the position of German science and research in Europe.

The complex landscape of research support in West Germany and the difficulties in implementing changes had much to do with the federal structure of the state. The centralized state of East Germany, which was at least as dependent on successful R&D as its neighbor to the west, created a system with a very different outlook that gave priority to the Academies of Sciences as the main centers of research. From their inception, however, their work was hampered by politicization, the interference of the planning bureaucracy, and a lack of resources and open intellectual exchange. East German researchers achieved minor successes in R&D but, overall, the results were disappointing and did little to help the country's economy. After German unification in 1990, the East German research infrastructure was dismantled, but remnants of its optical and microelectronic research lived on in Silicon Saxony, one of contemporary Germany's successful high-tech clusters centered in and around Dresden.

In the United States, the early phases of R&D were characterized by close cooperation among industry, philanthropic foundations, the National Research Council – a state-affiliated coordinating body that was founded in 1916 by leading natural scientists – and universities such as Massachusetts Institute of Technology (MIT), University of Chicago, and the California Institute of Technology. In the nineteenth century, the federal government had played a limited role in research areas such as geography, meteorology, and medicine. After 1900, this role expanded gradually with newly created institutions that served the growing scientific needs of industry and assisted in public oversight and regulatory functions. After World War I, however, federal engagement declined, and its earlier role was often assumed by major private foundations. In the 1920s and early 1930s, foundations financed and shaped large research projects in fields as diverse as physics, astronomy, and sociology, usually at Ivy League universities.

The breakthrough of publicly financed "big science" did not come until World War II with the Manhattan Project, which developed the atomic bomb. A scientific, technological, financial, and military challenge, the Manhattan Project encompassed at its peak a dozen research and production sites across the country and employed a quarter-million people.

The successful use of research in the war and a variety of political and economic factors – most comprehensively outlined in the landmark policy report, *Science: The Endless Frontier* (1945) by Vannevar Bush, the director of the Office of Scientific Research and Development – contributed to a national consensus on science policy that was followed by a massive allocation of public funds in the late 1940s and 1950s. The American government decided not to establish a broad system of independent federal laboratories but rather to create instead a system of financial remuneration ("grant overhead") for housing federally funded projects on research university campuses. This alliance of higher education and defense research that encompassed private universities such as Johns Hopkins University, as well as state institutions such as the University of California at Berkeley, was a key element of the American system after 1945 that had no counterpart in Germany.

The National Science Foundation (NSF), created in 1950, supported research projects on a grand scale throughout the country. Additional funding came from dozens of federal departments and "mission agencies," with the Department of Defense and other defense-related entities in the lead. In 1960, a few years after the detonation of the first Russian nuclear bomb and the "Sputnik shock" following the successful launch of a Russian satellite into space, 53 percent of all American R&D spending was defense-related. By 2000, after the Cold War had come to an end, the figure had fallen to 14 percent.

In 2000, the United States spent more than $280 billion or 2.6 percent of its GDP per year on R&D, with roughly one-third coming from public funds and two-thirds from industry. The percentage of GDP spent on R&D was only slightly higher in the United States than in Germany, and the division of funding sources was almost identical. Throughout the twentieth century, Germany certainly accepted the challenge of adjusting its science system to accommodate R&D, but different academic traditions and, again, outside factors such as political and financial obstacles limited its success.

In the twentieth century, American liberal capitalist democracy, with its intense cultivation of an entrepreneurial spirit, legitimated the participation of academic scientists in lucrative economic ventures that opened up with the expansion of the American economy after World War II. Known as "geographical areas of excellence," these sites of knowledge-based innovation combined academic science, education, and industry. Examples include the Route 128 corridor in Boston and Silicon Valley in California. Attempts to do the same in Germany's welfare state – where there is an aversion to risk-taking and where academic scientists are strapped by civil-service regulations – have produced mixed results. Among the late-twentieth-century successes are Measurement Valley in Lower Saxony (which included a university, a *Fachhochschule*, and more than a dozen industrial sites) and Silicon Saxony in Dresden (which included international companies such as Advanced Micro Devices [AMD] and venture capital firms). Elsewhere, venture capital and a cultivation of the entrepreneurial spirit were difficult to attain.

POLITICS AND KNOWLEDGE

By the 1890s, higher education had formed the foundation of achieving cherished Enlightenment promises: the promise of progress through the application of science and the promise of individual emancipation through the exercise of reason. Hence, late-nineteenth-century theorists of modernity, such as Max Weber, continued to regard science as objective and rational, outside the realms of politics and economics, and beyond the sphere of subjectivity.

Developments in the twentieth century challenged Weber's assessments. On both sides of the Atlantic, science and technology transformed World War I, contributed to the drive for the rationalization of health care and industry in the 1920s, undergirded the application of the biological and social sciences to the understanding of human subjects in the 1930s, and were crucial to the outcome of World War II. Yet, what had been blithely accepted before 1945 became the object of intense scrutiny after the revolt against modernity's rationalist foundations. Political pressures and ethical dilemmas transformed how science and education were integrated into daily, social, and national life. Despite some ups and downs, both countries were on similar counter-rationalist paths of converging modernities across the transatlantic divide by the end of the century.

The scientific empires of the twentieth century were not of land but of knowledge turned into instrumental means for controlling populations, resources, economies, domestic and foreign policy, and even international affairs. Whether the state was fascist, democratic, or communist made no difference. Although politically motivated ideological varieties of science were short-lived – "Aryan" science never took root permanently, for instance – political control over state resources in support of science meant that those areas of strategic interest to the state would receive the lion's share of public funding. This mixing of national priorities and scientific research on both sides of the Atlantic shifted scientific research in the direction of national interests. Highly politicized branches of science eroded – and, in some cases, destroyed – many of the fundamental values associated with academic research, including objectivity, academic freedom, openness, and professional disinterestedness.

For a good part of the century, the scientific cultures of Germany and the United States had shared much in common when it came to politics. At the end of the nineteenth century, the participation of scientifically trained experts in government became essential to the formulation of domestic and foreign policy. This process intensified in the twentieth century with the integration of social scientists into civil service, whether it was President Franklin D. Roosevelt's "brain trust" or the Third Reich's use of social scientists specializing in *Ostforschung* (Eastern European studies) in carrying out its plans to colonize Eastern Europe. In both countries, the deployment of experts in state agencies at all levels in the areas of uniform weights and measures, communications, health policy, industrial codes, and agricultural and food testing grew significantly during the first half of the century.

Military exigencies led to the most extreme cases of the politicization of science and higher education. In the United States, universities housed the Reserve Officer Training Corps during World War I, while university-based scientists worked on topics ranging from radio signaling and artillery range-finding to chemical weapons. In Germany, the early success of the KWIs in developing new chemical weapons, synthetic fuels, and other substitutes for natural resources led to a smooth integration of research agendas into national-defense initiatives in World War II, when KWI scientists contributed to aerodynamics, plant breeding, and weapons development, all in the name of national priorities. The continued militarization of science and technology in World War II marked the advent of a new era of "big science" symbolized by rocket research in Germany at Peenemünde (and, later, at Camp Dora in Nordhausen) and by the Manhattan Project in America.

The close relationship among academic scientists, industry, the military, and the state that had evolved during World War II became *the* defining feature of American science policy in the second half of the century. Senator J. William Fulbright, borrowing from President Dwight D. Eisenhower, gave it the moniker it has been known by since: the "military-industrial-academic complex." The policies of the Western Allies in what was to become West Germany effectively prevented a similar complex from emerging there. Consequently, for several decades after World War II, the relationship between science and politics diverged in West Germany and the United States even though similar issues of national defense and international affairs confronted both countries. What the two countries still shared in common, however, were the *terms* in which the relationship between science and politics was addressed: discussions took place along an axis defined by public welfare at one end and national defense at the other. Yet, although the parameters of debate were similar in West Germany and the United States, the scales tipped in favor of public welfare in West Germany, whereas Americans capitulated to national defense.

Nothing had a greater impact on science and academics in America after World War II than the inauguration of the "national security state": the state whose policies were designed for protection against foreign enemies, specifically from the atomic and hydrogen bomb-wielding Soviet Union. The national security state funneled resources into matters of national defense. Anthropologist Hugh Gusterson has aptly called that condition a "securityscape." A central feature of that landscape was laid during World War II when the Office of Scientific Research and Development (OSRD) commandeered civilian scientists from academia and industry to work in contract laboratories supported by federal funds for defense-related R&D. One example was the Radiation Laboratory at MIT, which employed four thousand scientists in 1945 and since its inception had been supported by OSRD to the tune of eighty million dollars. When the National Security Act of 1947 established the Department of Defense (DoD), funding for science immediately after that came directly or indirectly from the DoD.

The imperatives of the national security state literally defined the role of science in American life after World War II. Key areas that received support included nuclear science, high-energy particle physics, electromagnetic radiation at the microwave level, materials science, quantum electrodynamics, computer technologies, electronics, systems analysis, artificial intelligence, and game theory – the last four all essential for conducting the "art of war." Scientific training, especially of physicists, became a matter of national-security policy overseen by the NSF, which inaugurated one of the most prestigious graduate fellowship programs for science in American history. New institutes created or supported by DoD or Atomic Energy Commission (AEC) funding transformed universities into arms of the military: the Jet Propulsion Laboratory at the California Institute of Technology, the Applied Physics Laboratory at Johns Hopkins University, and Lawrence Livermore Weapons Laboratory at the University of California, Berkeley, to name a few. MIT on the East Coast and Stanford University on the West Coast were completely transformed by defense-related funding. In 1949–50, the federal government spent $1.5 billion on R&D; 90 percent of that came from the DoD and AEC, and nearly all went to support the physical sciences in academic settings.

Caught in the web of national-security-state initiatives, higher education in the United States metamorphosed. During the Cold War, those with defense-related funding wrote the textbooks in the physical sciences, which reflected the conceptual priorities of defense projects. University-based scientists became entrepreneurs, cashing in on the practical applications of defense-supported work by establishing spinoffs from university to industry. The MITRE Corporation (MIT Research), established in 1958 in Bedford, Massachusetts (to be near MIT) and McLean, Virginia (to be near the Pentagon), was one such example. Other firms, like the RAND Corporation (1948), the most influential think tank of the Cold War period, became known as universities without students for the high number of scientists employed to tackle national security issues.

The social sciences were similarly affected by national security interests. The field of area studies, for example, was expected to help American policymakers understand the decision-making practices of foreign governments. MIT's Center for International Studies was first and foremost an instrument of American policy. It created frameworks for institutionalizing development, generated profiles for police and counterinsurgency consulting, and studied sleep and sensory deprivation of prisoners and the effects of radiation on corpses. Over the course of the Cold War, *basic* research became a chimera: references to "pure science" reflected a false ideology of a time long gone by.

Believing that Cold War tensions would bring the worst, American academics engaged in actions antithetical to traditional scientific and scholarly values, including the right to publish and communicate ideas. Not until the social movements of the 1960s and 1970s were the innards of the military-industrial-academic complex exposed to public view. Before then, attempts to create an alternative set of priorities for science were few and far between. One notable challenge to the national security state was the attempt in 1950 by left-leaning members of the Federation of American Scientists (FAS) to orient the NSF toward social problems, to reconcile expert authority and public will, and to open science to public access and public opinion. Although the NSF in the end turned out to be outside the sphere of military directives, FAS arguments for democracy, freedom, social goals, and public welfare fell on deaf ears. Socially relevant research took another turn. Under President Lyndon B. Johnson, American social scientists were enlisted to fight the War on Poverty (1964–8), a war they eventually lost. At the time, though, the idea that the behavioral sciences could bring vision and order to public policy was viewed as a liberating force in public life in the transition from warfare to welfare.

The impact of politics on science in the two German states differed markedly. In East Germany, science policy was tied to communist social and economic goals, with little concern for outcome, efficacy, or public opinion. The rebuilding of science, technology, and industry in democratic West Germany after the war occurred under the aegis of the occupying Allied powers, who tried to impose their own priorities. These priorities included the all-important question of Western security in the shadow of the Iron Curtain. Moreover, the Allies viewed science as a democratizing force, as essential for political stability, and as best governed by a decentralized system of support in which the state and federal governments shared financial responsibility. Hence, in West Germany, too, security was a guiding principle in the promotion of scientific research but, unlike in America, military initiatives were not assigned priority.

Instead, West Germany played a dominant role in turning the postwar agenda for science and technology in the direction of public welfare. In addition to government agencies overseeing the development of research, West Germany established research institutes on public health, the economy, communications, and the environment. Its policy of active cooperation with the states and industry notwithstanding, the federal government provided (and still provides) the lion's share of funding for research. After 1969, the federal government paid for 90 percent of the operating costs of the country's major science institutions, and the states only 10 percent.

In contrast to the United States, where the national security state and federal funding priorities created top-down pressure to steer science in certain directions, in the Federal Republic, there was a bottom-up effect. The public played a strong role in influencing the direction of scientific and technological research, further reinforcing the orientation of West German science toward public welfare issues. The strong emphasis on public welfare originated in several postwar developments. First, Werner Heisenberg – who during the war had headed Germany's failed atomic bomb project – played a major role not only in mobilizing the public against NATOs plans to equip the West German army with battlefield nuclear weapons (a proposal that was defeated in 1958), he also considered it essential that science play a role in public affairs. Second, public protest, including student demonstrations, tempered science policy in the second half of the century. Third, West German intellectuals rallied public opinion around scientific and technological issues. Jürgen Habermas – whose ideas on the public sphere as the realm of critical reason described a reality he sought to create – was a lightning rod for galvanizing public opinion on issues concerning science and technology, especially in his influential essay on "Technology and Science as Ideology" (1968). Even West German sociologists contributed to the emphasis on public welfare in science policy. After the founding of the Federal Republic, they conducted a spirited public debate on whether expertise and democracy were compatible (the so-called technocracy debate). In the 1980s, sociologist Ulrich Beck popularized the idea of the "risk society," a society in which class struggles took place over which groups would assume the greatest life-threatening risks in society, such as living near a toxic waste dump. His ideas raised public awareness of the social consequences of unregulated scientific research and industrial development.

In the United States, the combination of science and politics during the Cold War challenged scientific values and placed in question the identity of the university as an educational institution. As early as 1948, Robert Oppenheimer caustically identified the University of California as "a great liberal university that is the only place in the world, as far as I know, that manufactures, under contract with the government, atomic bombs." Even President Eisenhower came to view the military-industrial-academic complex as a threat to freedom. So, during the same period in which Habermas and other German intellectuals were reclaiming the public sphere and reminding citizens of a moral commitment to exercise reason, American scientists and politicians wondered about the deleterious effects of secrecy and national security on academic freedom, open communication, scientific curiosity, and scientific thinking in general.

Events of the early twenty-first century altered German and American national science policy. Germany's dedication to public welfare was strengthened by the EU, whose science policy committees denied the "fact–value" distinction and affirmed the crucial role of a critical, well-educated citizenship in making decisions regarding science policy. That dedication to public welfare – specifically to the provision of adequate and safe energy supplies – was tested by Germany's 1998 decision to phase out the use of nuclear power plants and to increase reliance on alternative forms of energy. Meanwhile, in America, threats to academic freedom emerged in the wake of antiterrorism measures after September 11, 2001, especially the Patriot Act, which squelched the free expression of opinion and narrowed discussion in the marketplace of scientific and technological ideas.

ETHICAL DILEMMAS

The separation of fact and value that undergirded classical notions of modernity proved untenable in the wake of postwar developments, especially in the immediate aftermath of World War II. One of the most remarkable consequences of the Nuremberg Trials was the protracted development on both sides of the Atlantic of ethical standards for scientific research, especially in the biomedical sciences. The soul-searching formulation of appropriate ethical guidelines for scientific research, especially research on human subjects, tempered knowledge production in the second half of the twentieth century on both sides of the Atlantic.

The 1930s marked a massive ideological distortion of science in Germany and America in the area of eugenics, the attempt to eliminate biological forms of inferiority from the population in part to relieve pressure on the state's resources. In America, all but about a dozen of the contiguous forty-eight states had eugenic sterilization laws in 1935, but only a few, including California and Virginia, actually enforced them, resulting in the sterilization of about thirty thousand people overall. In Germany, between 1934, when enabling legislation was passed, and 1937, the Nazis sterilized almost a quarter-million people identified as carriers of hereditary diseases or as socially "undesirable." In both countries, political and medical terms were used interchangeably to articulate a health policy that had overtones of eugenic theory.

Developments during World War II accelerated the pace of ethical discussion. The dropping of atomic bombs on Hiroshima and Nagasaki raised ethical questions about the role of science and technology in the modern world, as did human experiments performed in Germany in the 1940s. The trials of Nazi doctors at Nuremberg after the war went well beyond examining the eugenic racial policies of the Third Reich to include purportedly scientific experiments on human subjects intended to help win the war: experiments on pressurization and submersion to help save pilots and sailors, experiments with reconstructive surgery to help those who returned maimed from the front, and experiments with epidemics and biochemical agents as weapons. All fell under the label *entgrenzte Wissenschaft*: science without moral boundaries. The enduring outcome of these trials – one that had no equal in transforming scientific and medical practices in the twentieth century – was the Nuremberg Medical Code of 1947. A model document of human rights, social good, humanitarian concern, and professional standards, the Nuremberg Code guided the formation of legal notions of informed consent, institutionally based reviews of experiments using human subjects, and even the ethics of scientific practice itself.

The reconstruction of science and higher education in West Germany was accompanied by considerable attention to the moral issues raised by science and technology – more attention than such issues often received in Cold War America. Policies included a constitutional ban on certain types of human and genetic research and the decision to confine a nuclear program to civilian peacetime uses. Horror over Nazi experiments on human subjects and the subsequent formulation of the Nuremberg Code by the Allies did not prevent "science without moral boundaries" in Cold War America. For example, American scientists conducted massive federally supported secret radiation experiments on human subjects not only at the sites of nuclear explosions in America and in the Pacific but also at otherwise benign and ordinary locations such as community hospitals.

After the discovery of the structure of DNA in 1953, molecular genetics replaced eugenics as a means of population control. After scientific breakthroughs in biotechnology and medicine during the 1980s and 1990s, ethical conflicts became even more pressing and were everywhere the subject of intense public discussion. In Germany, public suspicion of genetic manipulation was deep and widespread, especially within the environmentally conscious Green Party, which feared a "genetic Chernobyl." Attacks on laboratories were not uncommon, academic–industrial connections were avoided, and the best researchers often left for Great Britain or America. Not until the 1990s – when Germany had only about a dozen biotechnology companies and the United States had more than 1,500 – did Germany try to catch up in biotechnology by relaxing its biotechnology laws and establishing elite "Bioregio" clusters at Heidelberg, Munich, and Cologne. The ethical guidelines regulating biotech research in Germany were stricter than those in America. Nonetheless, the Nuremberg guidelines remained in force on both sides of the Atlantic at the end of the century. Fields ranging from stem-cell research to nanotechnology were subject to careful ethical review in Germany and the United States alike, albeit with variations in institutional procedures.

The union of science, education, and moral values at the end of the century thus reshaped what modernity was all about. Far from being a purely "objective" state of existence, late-twentieth-century modernity on both sides of the Atlantic was a kinder and gentler modernity that placed moral rectitude front and center. Knowledge was not so much separated from values and politics as values and politics were essential parts of it.

CONCLUSION: CONVERGING AND COMPETING MODERNITIES IN GERMANY AND THE UNITED STATES

The institutional history of science and higher education in Germany and the United States during the long twentieth century was thus characterized by an increasingly diversified landscape of universities, other institutions of higher learning, and state and industry research institutes. Despite their differences, America and Germany had converged – albeit to different degrees – around similar structural issues in science and education by the end of the century: the need to reform both, the bureaucratization of both, and the imposition of economic imperatives (R&D) on both. Most significantly, also by the end of the twentieth century, America and Germany challenged the separation of knowledge and values that had seemed so central to modernity by integrating ethics into academics and scientific practice. Transatlantic developments were thus similar enough to speak of converging modernities: modernities that abandoned the ideas that knowledge was autonomous and that education took place in the ivory tower for those that grounded knowledge, its application, and its transmission in political, economic, and ethical realities.

Contingent factors – such as different roles for national politics and the public sphere in the "policing" of science – led to different national solutions to similar dilemmas and problems presented by science and education, however. The most outstanding difference was that between America's national security state and Germany's welfare state. Here, we may speak not of converging but rather of competing modernities. Events at the end of the twentieth century magnified that competition: America's engagement in the "War on Terror" once again channeled resources into fields capable of fighting that war (and at many levels), whereas Germany's integration into the EU, where science policy was decidedly directed toward social issues and promoted a strong social awareness in considering issues of science and technology.

Consideration of the structural challenges of the mass university and R&D and of the impact of the external pressures levied by politics and ethics on knowledge production demonstrates the enormous effect of local differences in modifying how modernity was expressed, even in cases where there was a shared transatlantic culture.

Further Reading

Ash, Mitchell G., ed. *German Universities Past and Future: Crisis or Renewal?* (Providence, 1997).

Forman, Paul, ed. *National Military Establishments and the Advancement of Science and Technology* (Dordrecht, 1996).

Galison, Peter, and Bruce Hevly, eds. *Big Science: The Growth of Large-Scale Research* (Stanford, 1992).

Geiger, Roger L. *To Advance Knowledge: The Growth of American Research Universities, 1900–1940* (Oxford, 1986).

Geiger, Roger L. *Research and Relevant Knowledge: American Research Universities since World War II* (New York, 1993).

Gusterson, Hugh, *People of the Bomb: Portraits of America's Nuclear Complex* (Minneapolis, 2004).

Hager, Carol. *Technological Democracy: Bureaucracy and Citizenry in the German Energy Debate* (Ann Arbor, 1995).

Hart, David M. *Forged Consensus: Science, Technology, and Economic Policy in the United States, 1921–1953* (Princeton, 1998).

Heim, Susanne, Carola Sachse, and Mark Walker, eds. *The Kaiser Wilhelm Society under National Socialism* (Cambridge, 2009).

Jasanoff, Sheila. *Designs on Nature: Science and Democracy in Europe and the United States* (Princeton, 2005).

Kohler, Robert E. *Partners in Science: Foundations and Natural Scientists, 1900–1940* (Chicago, 1991).

Leslie, Stuart W. *The Cold War and American Science: The Military-Industrial-Academic Complex at M.I.T. and Stanford* (New York, 1993).

Ritter, Gerhard A. *Big Science in Germany: Past and Present* (London, 1994).

Schrecker, Ellen W. *No Ivory Tower: McCarthyism and the Universities* (New York, 1986).

Thelin, John R. *A History of American Higher Education* (Baltimore, 2004).

14

Media: Government versus Market

PHILIPP GASSERT AND CHRISTINA VON HODENBERG

Separated by the Atlantic Ocean, two entirely different media worlds developed in Germany and the United States. Or so it seemed when, during the Allied occupation of Germany, the two societies encountered each other, only later to disparage their respective media traditions. A report to the American sector's military government stressed that "the traditions of German newspapers . . . are unsuited to developing a democratic mentality or only to maintain such a mentality. . . . German newspapers . . . are usually written and presented in a very boring way . . . going, as it were, over the heads of many of their readers." German journalists saw things differently, reprimanding the American mass media for their "principle of being without principle" and their hunt for "sensation in every area": "dominated by 'sob stories' and society stories, [American] newspapers are produced for the 'man of the street'; this is done by eliminating the political and emphasizing the 'human side.'"

This snapshot from the era of occupation reflects durable prejudices on both sides that derive primarily from the stronger market orientation of the American media. What is at issue in this stereotype? Have the mass media in the United States always been more commercial in nature? What was the orientation of the German media if not toward the market? Have there not been more parallels than differences in the media histories of the two countries? Can a transatlantic comparison distinguish which media system was more compatible with a "democratic mentality" and which with dictatorship? To answer these questions, one must take a close look at both societies.

In the nineteenth century, a new type of mass media emerged on both sides of the Atlantic that was directed toward an anonymous, transregional, and diverse mass public. Emerging mass media promoted developments that were fundamentally similar in both countries. They brought about a steadily advancing "mediatization" of politics and society, meaning that political and social systems increasingly conformed to the conditions of a mass media environment. Everywhere it occurred, mediatization was a powerful spur to the formation of national identities because the mass media were increasingly able to serve as a dominant forum – ubiquitous in the public mind – molding the themes and the language of political debate within emerging nation-states. In public spheres shaped by the mass media, national images overtook regional and local ones.

The United States and Germany both experienced the rise of new kinds of mass media at the same time, with some minor differences. We can identify four stages of the development of the mass media. Each stage was characterized by the breakthrough of a new dominant medium: the era of mass newspaper journalism, which gave way to the era of radio and then, in turn, television, and, finally, the Internet. The rise of a new dominant medium did not result in the substitution and elimination of its predecessors but rather in an enlargement of the existing mass media ensemble and a reconfiguration of the media's internal hierarchy. As a rule, new media led to an expansion of media consumption – at the expense of other activities.

In its essential features, the history of modern media thus runs parallel on both sides of the Atlantic. But when the media's growing significance is related to the evolution of political modernity and to such phenomena as democratization, war, and dictatorship, fundamental differences between Germany and America come into view. The mass media are tools of mobilization: they can contribute to politicization and stimulate the participation of citizens, but they can also serve as instruments of disinformation, opinion control, and propaganda. The mass media's role in modernity thus should not be inscribed rashly onto the honor rolls of democracy and pluralism. Rather, its role is indicative of a general ambiguity in the nature of modernity. Therefore, the use of media in different political systems must be scrutinized in detail. Parallel processes of mediatization yielded entirely different consequences in democratic systems, like the United States and the Federal Republic of Germany, and in dictatorial systems, such as in Nazi Germany and in the German Democratic Republic. The governmental or the capitalist roots of particular media traditions also need to be factored in to arrive at the two most important questions underlying the transatlantic comparison: Were the German media especially susceptible to antidemocratic manipulation because of their historic ties to the state? And were the American media's ties to the market really so strong that in the long run, they damaged American democracy? Without aspiring to be comprehensive, the following comparison of the two countries concentrates on these two questions.

NEW MEDIA AND THEIR EFFECTS

Mass media markets emerged on both sides of the Atlantic about a half-century before World War I. The first mass medium was the mass-circulation press, which remained the shaping element of the media environment until the 1920s, when radio took its place. Although the rise of a mass press was broadly parallel in both countries, there were already basic differences in the cultural and political blueprint of the mass media ensemble at this stage.

In the United States, democracy preceded industrialization. American culture had been encouraging greater informality and democracy since the 1820s. The sharp contrast between elite and popular culture wore away as "penny papers" began to impinge on urban markets in the middle of the nineteenth century. In these easily affordable papers, one could enjoy human-interest stories, reports of crimes and sex scandals, and news of the wider world along with detailed accounts of local events and doings. Harshly criticized for their superficiality and sensationalism, these precursors to the yellow press expressed the ascendant democratic spirit in the age of Jackson.

Various factors precipitated the early emergence of a mass media market. America was ethnically heterogeneous; it cultivated an anti-elitist cultural ethos and was oriented toward consumption. The media sector remained relatively free from state interference, despite Victorian prudery and self-censorship; the media even enjoyed government subsidies through postal privileges. Moreover, new technologies were rapidly embraced. The introduction of the telegraph in the 1840s revolutionized transregional communication. From that point on, news was transmitted (almost) unhindered by space and time constraints. There arose a national public sphere: Washington, and not the governments of the states or counties, moved to the center of political attention.

This first modern media revolution of mass newspaper journalism illustrates the enormous growth rates characteristic of the developmental phase of new media in general. Whereas the U.S. population doubled between 1870 and 1900 and the number of those living in cities tripled, the number of English-language newspapers quadrupled, from 489 to 1,967. Circulation grew sixfold, from 2.6 million to 15 million. This rapid growth was predicated on widening literacy and rapid urbanization; it also rested on technical innovations like the Linotype typesetting machine. Daily newspapers realized their highest profits shortly before World War I, because paper became cheaper while advertising income increased markedly. After this period, the number of publications rose, and newspaper empires – like the Hearst and Scripps-Howard chains – began to amass ever greater power in the media world. The number of papers declined during the Depression and, by 1945, the number of English-language papers had decreased to 1,744, with a consequent loss of variety in the press.

In Germany, the rise of the mass press was broadly parallel, but it took place somewhat later, by the final third of the nineteenth century. As in America, Imperial Germany's mass newspapers reached an industrialized, urbanized, increasingly literate society, and they grounded their massive expansion in the same improvements in paper production and printing technology. From 1871 to 1914, the number of daily papers rose from 1,525 to 4,200, page numbers tripled, and big-city newspapers often came out in two or three editions a day. The new mass papers called themselves *Generalanzeiger* – "general informers" or "general advertisers" – because they no longer wanted to serve a narrow class of educated readers or some such limited milieu, as had earlier newspapers. These new papers emphasized not only their wider reach but also their greater attention to news, turning away from an affiliation with a political party. The success of these papers – such as the *Berliner Tageblatt* and the *Berliner Zeitung*, both founded in the 1870s – followed from their emphasis on local interests and entertainment as well as on their low prices and new marketing strategies. At the same time, illustrated weeklies began to boom. The most famous example was the *Berliner Illustrierte Zeitung* (Berlin Illustrated Newspaper), which sold for a penny in the 1890s. Its predecessors, big family papers like the *Gartenlaube* (Summer House) or *Daheim* (At Home), had been successful since the 1850s and had circulations of between two thousand and four hundred thousand in the 1870s.

In both countries, the rise of the mass press dovetailed with industrialization and led to greater centralization of the political public sphere and to the weakening of regional and local identities. The blue-collar and white-collar masses were discovered as customers, and the exclusive orientation toward the intellectual elite was upended. Here is where the parallels between Germany and America come to an end. To look at the interconnection between politics and media and at journalistic practices in both countries is to encounter a clear set of differences.

The American mass press achieved rapid success because of its nominal independence from political parties and anti-elitism. Because competition was so strong, new methods of reporting were born in the 1880s. The "new journalism" exploited sensation and social criticism alike. Urban tenement housing was denounced, police brutality exposed, and unbearable working conditions were brought to light. With the female reading public in mind, papers began to employ women as investigative reporters. In a city of immigrants like New York, illustrations – woodcuts originally – had the advantage of being understood by people with a modest knowledge of English. In 1884, Joseph Pulitzer, the newspaper king and self-appointed advocate of the "little man," supported the presidential candidacy of the Democratic candidate, Grover Cleveland. With the subsequent victory of Cleveland, the yellow press had made its debut as a first-order factor in the arena of political power.

The German mass press was far less self-confident. It was not a trendsetter for social reforms, nor was it conceived to be as politically powerful as its American counterpart. Imperial Germany's publications did indeed participate in the era's ultranationalism, in Germany's striving to become a world power, and in the anti-British naval propaganda. They also enabled the rise of large transregional associations and mass movements. The mass papers seized on many scandals, but they tended to concentrate on the ruling elite's private lives and sexual ethics rather than exposing its political transgressions. The mass press in the Wilhelmine Era was limited in its powers of political mobilization for two reasons: the long tradition of censorship and authoritarian press control and the ethic of the "journalism of conviction" (*Gesinnungsjournalismus*). In German newspapers, interviews were uncommon and investigative journalism was scorned. Editors could be prosecuted and were often sent to jail for giving offense or for disparagement of any kind (of people, authorities, or the government). Such censorship went hand in hand with restrictive information policies. Only handpicked reporters had access to political circles and to press conferences. Editors were best able to acquire information through personal contacts and proven loyalty. In this climate of governmental media control and journalistic loyalty, violating boundaries garnered the reproach of "Americanism" – as early as the turn of the century.

America's mass press was held up in Germany as both a fascinating model and a cautionary horror. Again and again, Germans denounced the lack of respect, the penchant for investigations, and, above all, the commercialism of embodied American journalism, with its reliance on sensationalism and shallow entertainment. Even the new "general advertisers" embraced commercialization only half-heartedly. These newspapers had given up their earlier identification with specific milieus, but they maintained their apolitical status and orientation toward news only for a short time. Soon they returned to the tradition of the journalism of conviction. This journalistic ethos construed open party affiliation as honorable and courageous, and defined the editor's main task as writing elegant commentary for an educated elite. This long-lived German tradition hemmed in the explosive energy of an anti-elite mass press.

At the start of World War I, the two countries' media landscapes were structurally similar but qualitatively quite different. State intervention and an elite mentality were more pronounced in Germany than in America, and the German media were less commercialized. In context, it is surprising that the immediate impact of the war on the media was so similar in the two countries. In both, the state intervened massively, using the media as an instrument for mobilizing civilian and military potential. Whereas the German government built on an existing propaganda apparatus after 1914 and revived traditional forms of censorship, the U.S. government created a propaganda agency, the Committee on Public Information, after it entered the war in 1917 and also restricted freedom of speech and freedom of the press. In Germany, the return of direct censorship and a centralized authority for control were supposed to commit the mass media to the "civil truce" (*Burgfrieden*) between the political parties on the left and the right. The American Committee on Public Information drew on the services of many progressive journalists to produce brochures calling Americans to unity and to serve as "Four Minute Men" to deliver brief public lectures on the war effort.

The results of wartime propaganda were mixed. In Germany, the longer the war lasted, the more clearly the propaganda campaigns failed. By the end of 1916, censorship and propaganda had lost their effectiveness. More and more readers mistrusted the press, giving force to the proliferation of rumors that peaked during the Revolution of 1918. In the United States, propaganda was able to win the population over to the Wilson administration's internationalism. This was accomplished, however, by the systematic vilification of the enemy, which contributed at least indirectly to discrimination against certain ethnic minorities. An anti-German hysteria intensified, and pressure to conform politically mounted during the "Red Scare" that followed in the wake of the Russian Revolution. Political and ethnic minorities and, above all, the unions were the victims of repressive disinformation campaigns.

The mass media in both countries were subjected to more state influence than ever before during World War I. In the United States, this was achieved mostly by means of corporate self-organization; the state could exercise its influence without requiring formal censorship or coercion. This misuse of the media triggered a lively debate about the media's role in American democracy. To limit the influence of the state and commercial interests on the media, writers like Walter Lippmann argued in the 1920s for greater professionalism among journalists. From then on, articles were signed by name, and commentary grew in significance as a way to contextualize reporting.

In the 1920s, with the arrival of radio as a new medium, long-established transatlantic differences grew more noticeable. Radio sharpened the contrast between Germany, with its media tied to the state, and America, with its media tied to the market. In the United States, the telegraph and telephone did not belong to the government's postal monopoly. The introduction of the radio, too, from the first transmission in November 1920, followed a capitalist trajectory. The state was present only in the indirect form of a regulatory agency, in which political and commercial interests were tightly interwoven. The Radio Act of 1927 and the Federal Communications Act of 1934 favored large commercial broadcasters. Radio developed into an oligopoly dominated initially by two major networks (NBC and CBS). Government regulation disadvantaged noncommercial producers or those that served only a part of the public sphere.

Free-market policies lent dynamism to the growth of radio in the United States. In 1927, four-fifths of all radios worldwide were in American households. By the mid-1930s, there were radios in more than nine-tenths of all urban households, with the average American listening to four hours of programming a day. Early on, proponents had praised radio as a medium of democratization and enlightenment that would advance education and cultural progress. But before long, radio programs were being produced by commercial sponsors and advertising agencies to market goods. (It was in this manner that the "soap operas" got their name.) Because radio was oriented toward the market, it developed as a medium of entertainment, not news, that met the expectations of the white middle class.

Already by the end of the 1920s, political parties, acknowledging radio's growing reach, were spending one-fifth of their campaign budgets on radio advertisements. Calvin Coolidge was the first president to speak regularly on the radio and, by 1928, radio had cast its spell on electoral campaigns. Franklin D. Roosevelt was the first president to take full advantage of radio's possibilities, addressing the audience informally during his "fireside chats," without having to take a detour through the press. Roosevelt valued the medium of radio against the reputed Republican domination of print journalism; hundreds of thousands of listeners wrote back to the president. Roosevelt's opponents, like the anti-Semitic "radio priest" Father Charles Coughlin, also put the new medium to use. Minorities, radical parties, and unions remained underrepresented on the radio.

The early expansion and use of radio in Germany followed a very similar pattern, but the role of politicians, consumers, and the state deviated notably from the American model. From its inception, the Weimar Republic kept radio on a governmental leash: the Imperial Postal Ministry maintained its control over the radio, successfully restraining private economic interests. Radio had been broadcast since 1923, but it only crossed the threshold of a mass medium at the start of the 1930s. In 1932, there was a radio in about one-quarter of all German households, and almost all regional stations broadcast all day. As in America, the intended audience was the middle class, and the working classes were neglected. Distance from politics and a party neutrality colored the programming, a policy officially prescribed by parliament in 1926 and enforced by "political surveillance committees" appointed by the federal and regional governments. Thus, the Weimar Republic, with its democratic system under attack from all sides, abstained from pro-republican, pro-democratic radio propaganda, but it did continue the tradition of authoritarian censorship.

Radio in Germany was therefore noncommercial and hemmed in by the state well before Hitler came to power. Consequently, it was easy for the National Socialists to incorporate radio into their dictatorship, to centralize it, and to staff it with their own people. The propaganda minister for the Third Reich, Joseph Goebbels, understood radio to be "the most important instrument of mass influence." Soon radio's capacity to integrate and to distract was in the foreground while its capacity for long-term political mobilization was limited. Already by March 1933, Goebbels had discovered that broadcasting numerous speeches, sandwiched by marches and the music of Richard Wagner, annoyed audiences. Therefore, he instructed radio directors "not to put too much core conviction on display" and, crucially, not to bore the public. National Socialist radio placed great value on entertainment, and the amount of light music continuously increased, especially during the war.

The National Socialist dictatorship did not bring about a break in the established relations among the mass media, state, and market in the German version of modernity. Rather, the Nazis took the status quo to an extreme. In addition to putting radio stations under state control and forcibly integrating cinema and newsreel production into the Ministry of Propaganda and its Film Board (Reichsfilmkammer), the government made considerable efforts to suppress private economic influence in the print media. The National Socialists' Eher Press acquired an overwhelming share of the media market through the direct and indirect purchase of newspapers. Press conferences were reduced to events at which the Propaganda Ministry gave out detailed instructions to editors. All journalists had to submit to censorship and opinion control because their livelihood depended on maintaining membership in the Press Association (*Reichspressekammer*).

Through these measures, the National Socialists built up an effective propaganda system that had its greatest success in the propagation of the *Führer* myth. Radio, newsreels, film, and photography were instrumentalized as never before. At the same time, there were limits to the Nazis' control of the media; opinion control was never total. All this political mobilization proved to be fleeting, as shown by the shrinking number of newspapers. Readers' interest waned with the *Gleichschaltung* – the "synchronization" with Nazi policies and principles – of the press. Modern, American-style dance music (jazz, swing) could never be banished from the radio. Despite years of proselytizing, the public was not in a mood of martial excitement when war began in 1939. The mass murder of Jews was never discussed in the mass media, for the Nazis knew the limits of their own propaganda apparatus. Toward the end of the war, when victory became ever less likely, the regime lost almost all influence over public opinion. Propaganda to keep fighting ran up against distrust and, despite being a punishable offense, listening to "enemy stations" could not be prevented.

In the United States, the mobilization of public opinion had started well before the country entered the war in 1941. Radio achieved its belated breakthrough into the domain of news with live reports and conference linkups during the Sudentenland crisis of 1938, when Germany annexed a part of Czechoslovakia. American radio reporters like Edward R. Murrow and William L. Shirer left a deep impression during the "Battle of Britain" with their descriptions of the German bombing of London night after night. After the shock of Pearl Harbor and the German declaration of war on the United States, the media voluntarily supported the war effort. But, with memories of the experience of World War I still in mind, state control of the media met with opposition. Formal censorship extended mostly to military announcements and was largely honored by the media. Journalists spontaneously came to the nation's defense, trying to outdo one another in their patriotism. The mobilization of the public demonstrated that the decentralized media landscape in America, set up to serve the market, was at least a match for the German propaganda apparatus, if not its superior.

The end of World War II marked a caesura for the mass media in western Germany. Even before television's breakthrough as the leading major mass medium, the Allied powers completely restructured the media landscape of their respective occupation zones. The British, Americans, and French expropriated the National Socialist press cartel, thereby returning the print media to a state of capitalist competition. The newly licensed newspapers successfully competed against the so-called old publishers. The Western Allies also dismantled the Nazi censorship and propaganda apparatus, which redefined the role of radio in Germany. From that point on, radio stations were largely detached from direct political interference; by constitutional mandate, they were regionalized and turned into public corporations. Because the reform of radio followed a British rather than an American model, the electronic mass media were less commercialized than in the United States. All told, the occupation years in western Germany marked a period of structural transformation. The most important milestones were the re-commercialization of print media and the removal of radio programming from both state and market interference.

On the other side of the Atlantic, mass media continued down an already established path. The illustrated magazines of the 1930s and 1940s had anticipated the visualization of political reporting. Henry R. Luce and his weekly magazines, *Time* and *Life*, pioneered this form of reporting, achieving a new level of visualization that seemed to render the news more authentic. (This development built in part on German models.) World War II had delayed the general breakthrough of television. Institutionally and in terms of its programming, TV developed directly from radio – as would later be the case in Germany. American television stations, which started to broadcast regularly in 1946, evolved from the existing radio networks; in other words, they were commercially organized and drew on radio for their personnel and structure. They were regulated by the Federal Communications Commission, which minimized the chance for outsiders to enter the market.

Television emerged in a similar fashion in Germany and the United States. It took less than a decade for television screens to supplant radios as the central medium once and for all in the United States. The number of American households with a television rapidly rose from 8 percent in 1950 to 90 percent in 1962, reaching a point of saturation. In West Germany, one-quarter of households were able to watch television some six years after transmission began in 1954; by the end of the 1960s, three-quarters of all households could do so. There were several stages in the ascendancy of television. In its infancy, television went through a communal phase: in both countries, people watched programs together at home or in public places like pubs or hotel bars. Then the media landscape underwent a division of labor: while the screen dominated the living room, serving as an evening entertainment, people listened to radio mostly during the daytime, in the car or in the kitchen. Radio served niche audiences such as minorities, housewives, and young people. Television quickly developed into a medium of the hegemonic culture. In America, this meant that television was *the* medium for the growing suburban middle class, whose social norms it helped propagate.

Because of its market penetration and its visual claim on the public, television quickly became a preeminent political factor. The first presidential campaign to be conducted on television was that of 1952, when the (victorious) Republican candidate, Dwight D. Eisenhower, let himself be marketed in political advertisements. His vice presidential candidate, Richard M. Nixon, effectively countered charges of corruption in his televised "Checkers" speech. At the same time, one-sided reporting on General Douglas MacArthur, who had been relieved of his command during the Korean War and forced to return to America, drew the public's attention to the dangers of this new medium. That television performances can be decisive in a presidential election has been a truism since John F. Kennedy's telegenic appearance in the 1960 presidential debate, which was watched by some seventy-one million viewers. Furthermore, network news broadcasts became an ever more important source of information. The networks discovered the entertaining side of news coverage in the 1960s, and they invested heavily in it. At the end of 1963, CBS and NBC extended their nightly news programs from fifteen to thirty minutes.

The Vietnam War further illustrated television's political power. For a long time, networks had passed along off-the-record statements from military and governmental officials uncritically. This changed instantaneously with the Tet Offensive of 1968, when images of battle, given greater scope by the networks, flickered across TV screens – including the shocking photo of a guerilla's public execution by a Saigon police chief. President Lyndon B. Johnson drew his own conclusions about the power of media: he decided not to run for reelection in 1968 in part because he thought he had lost the mainstream media's political backing. The mediatization of politics seemed to reach a new level with the antiwar movement, as television cameras captured police brutally beating demonstrators chanting "The world is watching" during the 1968 Democratic Convention in Chicago. The presence of television cameras influenced the actions of political protest movements; success meant getting oneself on television.

The expansion of television's political potential challenged the political elite – in Washington as in Bonn. Because of the more personalized nature of American politics and the greater openness of the political decision-making process, American politicians were forced to rely on the media to further their aims. With the exception of the Watergate scandal, media and politics have generally had a symbiotic rather than antagonistic relationship in America. Journalists can count on politicians as sources, and politicians need the media for strategic communication. Political actors devote ever more time to working with the media. Thus, the media become a central player in American political life without being a formal part of the political system.

Earlier than their German counterparts, American politicians were forced to accept this new reality of a media-driven political environment. This had in part to do with the fact that in America candidates are elected directly, whereas in Germany they are chosen by political parties. As American politicians were starting to embrace TV in the 1950s and 1960s, the German political elite was entangled in bitter fights with the media networks. Chancellor Konrad Adenauer, who during the 1950s had been able to build an extensive base of support with the mass media's cooperation, increasingly put his energy into creating a new broadcasting network that he hoped to keep on a short government leash. Categorizing the existing public stations as "left-wing," he embarked on the project of fashioning a pro-government private station. By 1961, this project had failed miserably.

Likewise, the federal Press Office's efforts to combat critical reporting were steadily less successful. The Press Office, which had been created by Adenauer, reported directly to him, an arrangement that recalled prewar traditions of author-itarian media control. With six hundred employees in 1965, it was bigger than the chancellor's office. Its budget – in the tens of millions – was impervious to parliamentary control until 1967. The Federal Press Office invested heavily in pro-paganda for the ruling parties, subsidized conservative newspapers, and courted journalists. Its television department carefully monitored programming, protested critical reporting, and tried to influence personnel decisions within television sta-tions. In the end, however, the West German government was unable to suppress the political power of television and of the illustrated weekly magazines.

The 1960s were a golden age for political television and for major illustrated weeklies like *Stern* and *Quick* in West Germany. A new generation of journalists became engaged in muckraking and social criticism, pioneering a political and opinion-forming journalism for the masses. Adenauer's government handed itself another spectacular failure in 1962, when it engaged in a police action against the news magazine, *Der Spiegel*, unleashing the "*Spiegel* Affair." When the gov-ernment's accusation of high treason against the magazine could not be upheld, a wide segment of the public was prompted, for the first time, to protest limitations on press freedom. The crisis served to strengthen the mass media. Adenauer's suc-cessor, Ludwig Erhard, garnered abundant ridicule with his unsuccessful attempt to present himself as the people's chancellor. The media did not want to play along with his antipluralistic concept of a "formed society" (*formierte Gesellschaft*).

The mediatization of politics had made notable progress in West Germany by the mid-1960s, as confirmed by endemic "affairs" and by politicians' complaints about the onset of a "democracy of illustrated weeklies." The chancellors of the late 1960s and 1970s learned a lesson from this situation. Kurt-Georg Kiesinger and Willy Brandt did not try to practice media control from above and were more careful in their dealings with the media, adapting themselves more to journalistic practice. Willy Brandt, a former journalist himself, is often seen as the Federal Republic's first successful "media chancellor": through personal contacts with journalists and a skillful politics of image, he was able to secure the long-term support of the most important mass media.

It would be a mistake to ascribe the mediatization of politics to television alone. The rise of television notwithstanding, the print media had increasing numbers of subscribers and profited from continuously expanding advertising income. In West Germany, the illustrated weeklies enjoyed impressive sales and politicized their reporting at the same time. The loss of many small local papers because of the concentration of print journalism was more than compensated for by the rise of big transregional dailies and the yellow press. The yellow papers engaged in political journalism – particularly *Bild*, which had a daily readership of four million by 1962. *Bild*, along with other highly successful papers such as *Welt*, *Bravo*, and *Hör zu!*, was owned by the conservative media tycoon Axel Springer who, by 1967, had managed to buy up roughly one-third of the West German print media. Springer was infamous for his political ambitions: he was one of the most vocal proponents of German reunification and a fierce critic of the student protest movement of the late 1960s. Growing opposition, in public and parliament, successfully put the brakes on Springer's publishing power. In 1967–8, he lost the battle for a private television channel and had to sell one-third of his publications.

In the United States, the print media briefly won back the leading role in the shaping of public opinion during the 1970s. This occurred even though suburbanization and the younger generation's declining willingness to read newspapers were undermining the print media's economic base. If television was following public opinion during the later years of the Vietnam War in only very gradually expressing reservations about the war, newspapers and magazines were ahead of the curve, echoing earlier traditions of investigative journalism. The revival of investigative journalism raised the status of journalism as a "fourth estate," with a monitoring role in politics, to its apex in the 1970s. One monument to this development was the publication of the Pentagon Papers – secret documents relating to the Vietnam War – by the *New York Times* in June 1971. Then came the *Washington Post*'s famous revelations about Watergate, which exposed the Nixon's administration's dirty tricks during the 1972 presidential campaign. Not even the "great communicator" Ronald Reagan could overcome the crisis of the presidency initiated in the early 1970s, as the "Iran-Contra Affair" of 1986 made clear. Later, Bill Clinton's scandals would underscore the political power of the media once again.

The culture of investigative journalism, often mythologized in America, could never develop fully in Germany. During the 1970s, though, the mass media of the Federal Republic, and the journalists working for them, became increasingly conscious of their power. Radio stations and the illustrated weeklies took it on themselves to "democratize" West German society and to publicize political conflicts. Editors fought (mostly in vain) for "inner freedom of the press" – in other words, for their independence from the publishers. Although awareness of being a fourth estate now spread more widely, generally the exercise of political power by journalists remained taboo.

In the United States, Ronald Reagan owed much of his political success in the 1980s to his television skills and the media work of his administration. But the idea of a unified public sphere, created by the evening news and authoritatively communicated by its anchormen, was already in decline at this time because of the rapid spread of cable channels, which were reaching 43 percent of the population by 1985, and the advent of video recorders. Potentially, the public gained more autonomy, while national programming lost out to local content; both the channels and the viewers grew more specialized. Thus, a modern media landscape directed to the anonymous "masses" and to the nation at large was losing its salience even before the introduction of the Internet. At the same time, the concentration of the press continued apace: since the 1980s, most large American cities have had only one daily paper. "Big media" like Rupert Murdoch's News Corporation, Time Warner, and Viacom came to control a wide range of media – from news magazines to radio stations to Hollywood studios. The deregulation of the 1980s further heightened their power. The investigative journalism that had forced Richard Nixon's resignation was losing influence.

After a long political battle in Germany, private radio and television stations were allowed to operate in the late 1980s. Conservatives saw this development as a means of breaking the "monopoly of opinion" fostered by public stations, alleged to be suffering under left-liberal domination. Liberals interpreted a multiplying number of stations as competition, from which the educative function of media could no longer be protected. Although it was often resisted and criticized as "Americanization," the commercialization of media was more restrained in Germany than in the United States. Despite the growth of cable television stations, which had resulted in a segmentation of the public since the 1970s, West Germany's news programs like *Tagesschau* (Daily Review) and *Heute* (Today) could still serve as national forums for political debate.

Developments in the German Democratic Republic stood in sharp contrast to the history of media in the United States and in West Germany. In East Germany, the authorities tried to neutralize the mediatization process through state control and de-commercialization. Their efforts misfired not least because of the considerable power of West Germany's media in the East. The ruling Socialist Unity Party (Sozialistische Einheitspartei Deutschlands, or SED) had latched on to German traditions of state media control. Although the SED recognized the appeal of Western popular music and blockbuster films, and worked them increasingly into its programming, pride of place was given to ideology. More than anything, television and radio were supposed to convey the party line; the entertainment quotient was noticeably smaller in the East than in the West. The GDR media thus struggled to beat the competition from the West despite the fact that West German broadcasts were accessible in almost all of East Germany. Everybody watched the TV series *Dallas*, and young people danced to popular music on West German radio – with the notable exception of those living in the "valley of the clueless" around Dresden, where West German signals were hard to receive.

After trying for several years to pull down west-facing antennas from East German roofs, the SED regime gave up its efforts to prevent its citizens from tuning into West German radio and television in the early 1960s. In 1973, East Germans were officially given permission to watch and listen to West German media. Western broadcasters broke through the isolation of GDR citizens and disrupted the regime's stranglehold on information. Images of a supposed consumers' paradise in West Germany undermined the reputation of the East German economy. Occasionally, West German broadcasters placed themselves directly into political events, as in the uprising in June 1953 and then in the last moments of the GDR. West German television stimulated the revolution of 1989 by showing footage of East Germans eager to flee the country filling the West German embassy in Prague and of the Leipzig "Monday demonstrations" against SED policies. The inability of East German politicians to keep pace with Western-style reporting was grossly obvious. Clumsy statements by Günter Schabowski, the Central Committee's Secretary for Information (i.e., the party's press spokesperson), during a live press conference led to the opening of the Berlin Wall on November 9, 1989. The GDR's attempt to construct modernity without mediatization had failed dramatically. The Party could rein in its own media, but it could not keep its citizens from turning to the Western media.

Have the media worlds in Germany and the United States grown more similar since the end of the Cold War? On the one hand, with the rise of transnational media conglomerates – like Rupert Murdoch's News Corporation and the

Bertelsmann publishing empire – globalization has brought economic concentration and limited available content. On average, Hollywood studios now earn more than half their profits outside American borders. CNN, which began broadcasting in June 1980, has a worldwide audience, and it has been a model for similar channels in Germany. For the big media companies at least, the vision of a "global village" has become reality. At the same time, the explosion of television and radio channels has encouraged segmented and local broadcasting, which has led to the scaling back of the political potential residing in a nationally oriented media.

With the rise of the Internet, will the media landscape designed for an anonymous mass public disintegrate? In fact, the Internet is further splitting the media into niche markets that are socially and ethnically distinct from one another as they are by gender and generation. In the United States, Internet bloggers have systematically weakened the decades-long dominance of the liberal "mainstream media," like the *New York Times* and above all the evening news on the "big three" networks. The average American has access to many more news sources than were available a few years earlier. The Internet has undoubtedly democratized the media landscape and has eased access to the public sphere. The presidential campaign of 2004 exposed the Internet's new importance in several ways: in the Democratic primaries, the outsider Howard Dean made himself into a serious candidate through his skillful Web strategy and, for the first time, fundraising and campaign volunteering were successfully coordinated online. In the last days of the campaign, Republicans also used the Internet to mobilize voters in critical constituencies. More recently, Barack Obama beat Hilary Clinton for the Democratic Party's presidential nomination relying on Internet-based fundraising and campaign organizing. His ability to mobilize support over the Internet and through Web-based content also gave him the edge over Republican candidate John McCain in the general election in November 2008.

It remains to be seen how politicians and journalists will react to the Internet's new possibilities. Newspapers have long supported the other media through their investment in reporting and fact-checking. At this point, the Internet does not provide quality journalism to the same extent that newspapers still do. With the crisis of print journalism, which has hit American newspapers harder than their German counterparts, the question has been asked: How will democratic control of the media be exercised? Web sites like Daily Kos allow thousands of citizens not only to write their comments on blogs but also to develop detailed legislative agendas and criticize the mainstream media, sometimes taking on high-ranking politicians. The Internet is a much more interactive medium than either radio or television. Yet, because of the dependence of influential and heavily trafficked Web sites on advertising, it remains questionable to what extent successful Internet sites can avoid the path to a commercialized mass medium.

BETWEEN THE STATE AND THE MARKET

At first glance, a comparative study of German and American mass media shows considerable commonalities, just as it sheds light on deep-seated differences. The essential parallel can be found in the very process of mediatization. The development of the modern media landscape was basically the same (with moderate chronological differences primarily caused by World War II). With each new medium, the media landscape grew in its capacity to penetrate and to mobilize societies. This growth demanded significant adaptations by political actors and also created new potential for manipulation. Yet, to a certain extent, the process of mediatization followed its own logic. Neither the Third Reich nor the GDR could keep the irrepressible power of audiovisual mass media at bay, nor could short-term crises block the rise of a new medium. Thus, radio gained in stature despite the Great Depression, and the triumph of television was only slightly delayed by World War II.

In both Germany and the United States, political systems reacted differently to advancing mediatization. For the most part, American politicians, accustomed to the give-and-take of a (mass) democracy, quickly adapted to changes in the media landscape, consciously promoting media expansion and distribution, starting with the nineteenth-century press and continuing with radio and the Internet. In the ethnically heterogeneous United States, where elections encouraged the personalization of politics, politicians saw new media as an advantage – as a new, more direct, and popular way of addressing the public. This is why, in America, media innovation was often accompanied by the rise of a particular kind of politician who had mastered a new means of communication: what Franklin D. Roosevelt achieved with radio, John F. Kennedy achieved with television. Ronald Reagan found similar success in a media environment that was shaped by cable television and video recorders. With the growing democratization of decision-making processes in Washington, political success was often directly tied to the ability to influence the "agenda setting" of the media.

In Germany, political success has not overlapped so directly with the ability of politicians to cultivate their media presence (with the exception of Hitler's successful media stylization in the Third Reich). Politics was less personalized and parliamentary caucuses (*Fraktionen*) played an important role. Political parties were bound to social milieus for a longer period of time, and the political culture generally hewed more strongly to community values. Nevertheless, West German politicians were forced to develop a certain expertise in the handling of the media. The first two postwar chancellors, Konrad Adenauer and Ludwig Erhard, had difficulties in accommodating themselves to a media-driven political environment and hoped to rein in the media. Only in the late 1960s did West German politicians join the age of medialized politics. In the GDR, the party elites were even less media savvy – indeed, they were inept – when it came to the mass media marketing of personality and politics.

It is not only the example of the GDR that justifies the following generalization: the political powers-that-be never were able to achieve full control of the mass media. Top-down manipulation was always limited by the media itself. Even in periods of extreme authoritarianism, the German government's grip on journalism and the media was never complete. In the 1920s and 1930s, many observers considered total control of the media possible because of (the largely overvalued) propaganda successes of World War I. Still, Nazi propaganda was in no way omnipotent, despite presenting itself as such and despite its reinforcement of racial and social prejudice.

American politicians, too, have repeatedly failed in their attempts to influence the institutional framework through which the media shapes political reality. In the 1920s and 1930s, Republicans had the bitter experience of observing that a radio oligopoly, which they had carefully organized around their own free-market ideas, would be mastered by the Democrat Roosevelt. Similarly, Lyndon Johnson's and Richard Nixon's efforts to halt critical reporting about Vietnam backfired. The Iraq War's embedded journalism, which had been promoted by the George W. Bush administration as a tool for generating public support, created an initial wave of patriotism only to help the public's shock over the war's consequences take root afterward. The all-encompassing "culture industry" of media manipulation that many thinkers feared was never realized.

Although media control is always limited, again and again the modern mass media have served as instruments of antidemocratic control. This is obvious in the case of the two German dictatorships. In a way, it was also true of the authoritarian media policies of Imperial Germany, of the Weimar Republic, and of the first few years of the Federal Republic, which felt itself to be under internal and external threat. An authoritarian manufacturing of social consensus, assisted by mass media, was also a favorite recipe in the United States at times of foreign policy crisis. Whether the mass media-fostered consensus was defined as anti-imperial as in World War I, antifascist as in World War II, anticommunist as in the Cold War, or antiterror, it was often employed against internal dissenters as well. These crises, with their accompanying roster of victims, have regularly led to disillusionment.

The most important difference between the American and the German developments concerns the mass media's long-lasting state connection in Germany and its equally long-lasting commercialism in America. On both sides of the Atlantic, the dramatic rise of a mass press was primarily generated by private initiative. However, in Germany, from the beginning, governmental intervention and authoritarian mentalities reined in the potential of the mass media as factors of political power. With the introduction of radio, the gap between mass media in Germany and the United States widened because German radio was in the hands of the state – or partially state-controlled public corporations – whereas in the United States, a market orientation dominated. World War II and the rise of television did not interfere with these traditions. The transatlantic gap did narrow somewhat during the Allied occupation period, then with the authorization of private broadcasting in West Germany during the 1980s, and at last with the collapse of the GDR in 1989–90.

Which, in the long run, presents the greater danger to the survival of democratic systems: the mass media's proximity to the state or their proximity to the market? The German and American example show that commercialization does not inevitably lead to pluralization and democratization. Similarly, the idea that commercialization in itself is detrimental to a democratic political culture does not hold true. Different media will follow different formulas for commercial success, at times fostering and at times obstructing pluralization and democratization. Whereas the American "new journalism" of the 1880s achieved success with investigative reporting and social criticism, American television in the 1950s stressed social cohesion and WASP middle-class values. In the 1960s, *Stern* and *Quick* competed with other West German weeklies through the provision of critical political journalism, yet private TV stations have, since the 1980s, wooed audiences by suppressing prime-time political content. In the present day, muckraking strategies have made the Internet into a salient source of news. Commercialization thus encourages the media to cater to audience interests, and audience interests can be, but do not have to be, a counterforce to democratization and pluralization.

At the same time, economic concentration of the media market has tended to limit the media's range. That many American cities have only one newspaper today may be the cause of uncritical local reporting. However, the image of a disappearing local media culture is exaggerated; newspapers today are only one of several sources of news. In Germany, too, processes of media concentration have not yet resulted in narrowing the diversity of opinion. The Axel Springer trust, whose market power has been heatedly debated in the Federal Republic since the 1960s, never even came close to amassing any direct political capital from its domination of certain niche media markets.

If the mass media's ties to economic power are to be evaluated on a case-by-case basis, a close alignment of media with the state clearly endangers democracy, as a look into German history amply demonstrates. In the Weimar Republic, state control of the media played into the hands of the Nazi dictatorship, and the Third Reich's tradition of media control was continued without interruption by the East German government. In the early Federal Republic, authoritarian efforts at media control might have become entrenched had the protective hand of the Allies not been there. This transatlantic comparison has shown that the state's encroachment on modern mass media was never total. It also shows how easy it can be for the state to corrupt a polity's democratic integrity.

Further Reading

Baughman, James L. *The Republic of Mass Culture: Journalism, Filmmaking, and Broadcasting in America since 1941* (Baltimore, 1992).

Bernhard, Nancy. *U.S. Television News and Cold War Propaganda, 1947–1960* (New York, 2003).

Bösch, Frank, and Norbert Frei, eds. *Medialisierung und Demokratie im 20. Jahrhundert* (Göttingen, 2006).

Butch, Richard. *The Making of American Audiences: From Stage to Television, 1750–1990* (New York, 2000).

Czitrom, Daniel J. *Media and the American Mind: From Morse to McLuhan* (Chapel Hill, 1982).

Daniel, Ute. "Die Politik der Propaganda: Zur Praxis gouvernementaler Selbstrepräsentation vom Kaiserreich bis zur Bundesrepublik," in Uta Daniel and Wolfram Siemann, eds., *Propaganda: Meinungskampf, Verführung und politische Sinnstiftung (1789–1989)* (Frankfurt, 1994): 44–82.

Davies, David R. *The Postwar Decline of American Newspapers, 1945–1965: The History of American Journalism* (Westport, 2006).

Douglas, Susan J., "Mass Media: From 1945 to Present," in Jean-Christophe Agnew and Roy Rosenzweig, eds., *A Companion to Post-1945 America* (Malden, 2002): 78–95.

Esser, Frank, and Barbara Pfetsch, eds. *Politische Kommunikation im internationalen Vergleich: Grundlagen, Anwendungen, Perspektiven* (Wiesbaden, 2003).

Gitlin, Todd. *The Whole World Is Watching: Mass Media in the Making and Unmaking of the New Left* (Berkeley, 1980).

Hickethier, Knut, and Peter Hoff. *Geschichte des deutschen Fernsehens* (Stuttgart, 1998).

Hodenberg, Christina von. *Konsens und Krise: Eine Geschichte der westdeutschen Medienöffentlichkeit* (Göttingen, 2006).

McChesney, Robert. *Telecommunications, Mass Media, and Democracy* (New York, 1993).

McPherson, James Brian. *Journalism at the End of the American Century, 1965–Present* (Westport, 2006).

Münkel, Daniela. *Willy Brandt und die "Vierte Gewalt": Politik und Massenmedien in den 50er bis 70er Jahren* (Frankfurt, 2005).

Requate, Jörg. *Journalismus als Beruf: Entstehung und Entwicklung des Journalistenberufs im 19. Jahrhundert. Deutschland im internationalen Vergleich* (Göttingen, 1995).

Ross, Corey. *Media and the Making of Modern Germany: Mass Communications, Society, and Politics from the Empire to the Third Reich* (Oxford, 2008).

Schildt, Axel. *Moderne Zeiten: Freizeit, Massenmedien und "Zeitgeist" in der Bundesrepublik der 50er Jahre* (Hamburg, 1995).

Schudson, Michael. *Discovering the News: A Social History of American Newspapers* (New York, 1978).

Starr, Paul. *The Creation of the Media: Political Origins of Modern Communication* (New York, 2004).

Wilke, Jürgen, ed. *Mediengeschichte der Bundesrepublik Deutschland* (Cologne, 1999).

Index